CREATOR

SUSTAINER

بِسْمِ اللّٰهِ

اللّٰه
GOD

PROTECTOR

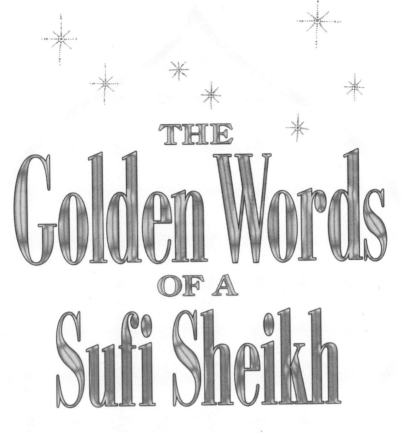

# THE Golden Words OF A Sufi Sheikh

REVISED EDITION

## M. R. BAWA MUHAIYADDEEN ﵁

**The Fellowship Press**
Philadelphia, Pennsylvania
**www.bmf.org**

Library of Congress Control Number: 2006924099

The golden words of a sufi sheikh / M. R. Bawa Muhaiyaddeen. Rev. ed.
Philadelphia, PA : Fellowship Press, 2006.
p. cm.

ISBN-13: 978-0-914390-73-2 (trade paperback)
ISBN-10: 0-914390-73-2 (trade paperback)
ISBN-13: 978-0-914390-74-9 (hardcover)
ISBN-10: 0-914390-74-0 (hardcover)

Printed in the United States of America
by THE FELLOWSHIP PRESS
The Bawa Muhaiyaddeen Fellowship

First Printing in Sri Lanka 1982
Second Printing 1992
Third Printing 1995
Revised edition, First Printing 2006

Muhammad Raheem Bawa Muhaiyaddeen ؓ

# ACKNOWLEDGEMENTS

The sayings and illustrations in this vast collection were given by M. R. Bawa Muhaiyaddeen *(Ral.)* in Colombo, Sri Lanka and Philadelphia, Pennsylvania, U.S.A., during 1978 and 1979. In accordance with the oral tradition of Sufism, these sayings were spontaneously spoken to impromptu gatherings of students who came to seek wisdom and a deeper understanding of man's relationship with God, through the example and teaching of Bawa Muhaiyaddeen *(Ral.)*.

Originally spoken in Tamil, an ancient Dravidian language found in Southern India and Sri Lanka, these sayings were then rendered into English through the joint effort of Professor A. Macan-Markar, Dr. M. Z. Markar, Dr. K. Ganesan, Mrs. R. Ganesan, Mrs. Crisi Beutler, and Mrs. Saramma Aschenbach. All the editors humbly ask forgiveness for any clarity or vitality lost in the translation.

Special thanks should also be given to all the members of The Serendib Sufi Study Circle of Sri Lanka and The Bawa Muhaiyaddeen Fellowship of the United States, who gave untiringly of their time and effort in preparing this manuscript.

May God bless this venture. And may this reservoir of wisdom quench the thirst of all those who read it. *Amīn.*

# CONTENTS

# PREFACE

*Bismillāhir-Rahmānir-Rahīm,* in the name of God, Most Merciful, Most Compassionate. May the beginning and end and all things be the responsibility of Allah alone. Only Allah, the One of limitless grace and incomparable love, the One who gives us His infinite wealth of grace, knows all the secrets of all the creations in the eighteen thousand universes. He is the One who created the essence, the manifestations, and the attributes. He created right and wrong, or *khair* and *sharr,* permissible and impermissible, or *halāl* and *harām,* good and evil, heaven and hell. He is the One who knows their secrets. May we praise only Him. May we pray only to Him. May we trust only Him. May our faith, our trust, and our determination become steadfast in our hearts. May that steadfastness grow stronger and become the staff with which we walk through life. May it be the life within our prayers.

Each one of us, every child, must reflect and realize the truth of the statement, "One who has *īmān,* perfect faith, is exalted. One who has *īmān* will receive the undiminishing plenitude of the wealth of God's grace in all three worlds (the world of the soul, this world, and the next world)."

My beloved brothers and sisters, we are children who have faith in God. All living beings have faith in God. The earth and the sky, night and light, lives that move and lives that do not move, all have faith in God; and God knows the hearts of all creations. He knows all thoughts and all intentions. He knows the speech of the tongue. He knows every part of every creation. The Precious One, the Exalted One who is Almighty God, *Allāhu ta'ālā Nāyan,* is the Father of all lives. He is the Almighty One, the Able One, the Creator who showers compassion on all lives. He is *Rahmān* and *Rahīm,* the Most Gracious One, the Redeemer. May we have faith only in Him. *Āmīn.*

My very precious brothers and sisters, God created *insān,* true man, as the most exalted of all creations. To this exalted life, God has given exalted wisdom. He has given man seven levels of wisdom: feeling, awareness, intellect, judgment, subtle wisdom,

1

divine analytic wisdom, and divine luminous wisdom. God has fashioned the seven levels of wisdom so that man can know God and understand Him through remembrance, contemplation, prayer, and worship. Human beings have faith in various types of worship and remembrances of God.

There are four steps to prayer: *sharī'at, tarīqat, haqīqat,* and *ma'rifat. Sharī'at* is creation, the religion of *Zabūr,* or Hinduism, the section below the navel, the section of earth. When man looks at creation and the manifestations which appear from the earth, he must understand what is right and what is wrong. If he discards what is wrong and accepts what is right, he will come to one point: there is only one God.

*Tarīqat,* the next step, occurs when man's faith becomes strong. *Tarīqat* relates to the religion of *Jabrāt,* or Zoroastrianism, which represents the region of the stomach, the aspects of hunger, illness, old age, and death, and the section of fire: the hell-fire of anger, hastiness, the differences you feel between yourself and others, and the evil actions which follow because of these differences. When man discards everything from this section other than the one point, the point of God, he comes to the level of *haqīqat.*

*Haqīqat* is also known as the religion of *Injīl,* or Christianity. It is represented by the region of the chest, the aspect of air, and contains the vapors, gases, jinns, fairies, spirits, angels, and heavenly beings. When a man discards everything in *Injīl* except for one point, the point of God, he takes on the beauty of God and he becomes very close to God.

Next is the level of *ma'rifat,* or the religion of *Furqān,* or Judaism and Islam, the head, the section of light. *Furqān* means to understand with wisdom what is perceived by the two eyes, the two ears, the two nostrils, and the mouth, which represent the seven diacritical marks.*

---

* In English, vowels are part of the alphabet, but in Semitic languages vowels take the form of notations above or below the letters, all of which are consonants. Whereas those to whom Arabic was the native language could read the Qur'an with little difficulty in its original vowelless state, those who spoke other languages frequently misvowelled the words or misinterpreted the letter symbols. Thus, the diacritical vowel markings and *nuqat,* or dots, were developed over several centuries to make it easier for those less acquainted with Arabic to recite the Qur'an properly. In a mystic sense, the diacritical marks are said to give life or sound to the letters which would otherwise be dead or silent. As the openings in the head animate it and take in light and sound, so do the diacritical marks give resonance and life to the Qur'an, also known as *Furqān,* the criterion of right and wrong.

If you know these four steps, understand them, and then pray to Allah ceaselessly, unmindful of the difference between day and night, that is true prayer, the fifth prayer, the prayer of *Sūfiyyat.* *Sūfiyyat* is the state in which there is no day or night. The prayer called *Sūfiyyat* is the prayer in which you do not speak and you do not smile. You speak without speaking, smile without smiling, pray without praying, and intend without intending, and in this way you control and subdue your countless desires. To speak to God without speaking is Sufism.

*Sūfiyyat* means to subdue mind and desire, that is, to restrict your own acting in the drama and to control your connection to blood ties, your cravings, illusions, attachments, vanity, envy, anger, the pride of the 'I' and the feeling of 'you', treachery, deceit, hunger, lust, and obsession. To cut away all these myriad qualities of satan, to pull them out and burn them to ash through wisdom and faith, is Sufism.

Once they have been consumed we can begin to pray. In the prayer of *Sūfiyyat,* God has ordained 43,242 *sajdahs,* or prostrations at the feet of God, per day. The man who performs these will see Allah before his eyes. He will see only Allah and nothing else. His *qalb,* which is his innermost heart, will see only Allah's light. His ears will hear only Allah's sound. His *qalb* will realize only God's sound, God's light, and God's resonance. His nose will perceive only the fragrance of God. The tongue will speak only to Him in the secret silence, and in this silent speech man will die—he must die—in Allah. When he dies in Allah—in the state in which he speaks without speaking, smiles without smiling, and prays without praying, knowing God without knowing Him— that state is Sufism.

In this way, every word must end in God, every breath must end in Him, and every speech must end in Him. Man's entire life must reach God; that is his true prayer. That is the culmination of the prayer of the Sufi. One who attains the clarity of perfect faith is called a Sufi.

When he cuts away all his earlier states and realizes himself, he is a perfected man, an *insān kāmil,* and at the stage in which he loses himself in God, he is a Sufi. At the stage in which he is dead to himself, he is Muhammad *(Sal.).* When he has made himself unlettered and silent, he is Muhammad *(Sal.).* When he loses himself within Allah, he is the *Nūr,* the resplendence of Allah, and his treasure is the *Nūr* which is called Muhammad *(Sal.)*. God's powers appear within him and become the light within his eyes and the resonance of God within his ears. His nose smells the fragrance of Allah and his tongue relishes the wonderful tastes of Allah, while God's kingdom resplends within his heart. The kingdom of God exists and resonates in the prayer within his innermost heart.

My very precious children, the attainments and the potentialities of the Sufi are impossible to describe. To become Sufis we must obtain clarity of faith and wisdom. In this way, little by little, we must remove the darkness which has veiled us. We must untie the ropes which illusion has wrapped around us. We must cut away the connections of blood ties and the desire for land, gold, and women. With the sword of wisdom we must cut away all the energies, cells, and viruses which have been burning us, and then we must burn them.

This is the state in which we can become Sufis. When we say Sufi we mean the state in which one has attained true wisdom. The state of the Sufi is the state in which, having controlled and subdued all the other states, one becomes the resplendent sun, the resplendent light of God. One who is in this state is called a Sufi, and the state is called Sufism, or Sufi-Sun.

With his *īmān,* he will split open and sift everything he sees. He will pierce through it with his wisdom and his firm certitude and determination, without allowing his mind to become fatigued, without allowing his heart to give up. If he can continue to pierce and cut through what is within everything, he will see only Allah. He will see Allah's wealth, Allah's powers, Allah's qualities, and nothing else. In every moment, in every tree, in every flower, and in every blade of grass, he will see only God. In every tree, every fruit, every fragrance, every flower, every bird, every cow, every goat, in whatever he beholds he will see only the secret of Allah, the powers or *wilāyats* of Allah, and the qualities of Allah. When he looks at an ant he will discover Allah's secrets. When he looks at a fruit he will be amazed and say, "What a wonder! How praiseworthy You are. How subtly You have created the fruit. What flavors it contains!" If he looks at a honeybee he will see how much wisdom it has, how it builds its house, what qualities it has, and how it tastes the honey and shares it with everyone.

4

In this way we must marvel and praise God, saying, "What a wonder Your creation is." As we open each thing and look inside, we will find that we can praise only Allah and worship only Him; this is all there is. This is the meaning we must derive when we look at anything. Though we will be able to realize it through what we see, we can understand only through wisdom. And if we do realize that everything must be understood through wisdom we will see that all the explanations we find are the explanations of God's story, that the things we see are not merely creations but also His story. Everything He has created is His story. If we look inside this storybook of creation we will find His entire history. And if we look inside God's history we will see only Him, His powers, and His qualities. This is the explanation we must discover. This is why the Messenger of Allah, the Rasūlullāh *(Sal.)* has said, "Go even unto China to learn *'ilm.*" Learn *'ilm*, or divine knowledge, even if you have to go to China to do it.

First, we must seek and acquire wisdom. Second, we must develop and strengthen our faith. Third, we must realize that Allah is the only One who exists. Fourth, we must offer prayers of praise, glorifying and worshiping Him.

We must learn certitude of faith and we must develop the wisdom through which to worship Him. Through that wisdom we must discover the right and the wrong in our prayers to Him, understanding that Allah is the One who has no equal and that nothing can be shown as an example to illustrate Him.

Each of us must open his heart, his *qalb,* and transform it into the *Ka'bah,* the central place of worship. Placing the Rasūlullāh *(Sal.)* before us as our *imām,* our leader of prayer, we must offer prayers of praise to Allah. To stand face to face before Allah and speak every word to Him directly is the true prayer and the true worship which we must fashion within ourselves. Each of the children must pray in this way. Then wisdom will be our support, prayer will be our wealth, and faith will be the house of our *qalb,* the *Ka'bah.*

We must reflect on this and think about it in our prayers. This is the duty of an *insān mu'min,* the man of true belief, and of an *insān kāmil,* perfected man. When we say Sufi, it means one who has controlled his words, his tongue, and his heart, one who has controlled and stopped all unnecessary actions within himself.

There are so many different kinds of dancing on the stage of the world. Everything dances: goats, cows, trees, shrubs, flowers, leaves, grasses, birds, winged creatures, animals, jinns, fairies, satans, illusions, and darkness. They dance in the sky, on the earth, in the oceans, and on the mountains. But this is not prayer. For one who is a *mu'min*, a true believer, acting and dancing are not prayer.

All the others dance the drama of illusion and act the acts of hell, seeking the prizes which are advertised on the billboards of hell. All the labels they wear are advertisements for hell. Their fame and their titles and their attainments are the labels which will lead them to hell.

Sufis give up the acting within themselves, burn up even their thoughts of acting, and reach the stage of contentment where they speak without speaking and immerse themselves in God. That is Sufism.

Only when that state is established within us, only when wisdom dawns and God's ocean of divine knowledge appears within us, only when we have true faith and worship can we reach God, who is the wisdom within wisdom. Only in that state do we become creations who can reach God and speak to Him directly. We must realize this.

The essential requirements are absolute faith and wisdom. Our progress and the states we attain are in accordance with the level of our faith and wisdom. One who has transcended the four steps of *sharī'at, tarīqat, haqīqat,* and *ma'rifat* is a Sufi. One who knows these four steps and knows himself and knows his God is a Sufi. We must acquire the wisdom necessary to reach this state.

God has created everything as an example in order that we may acquire and attain that wisdom. Everyone who is an *insān,* everyone who is a *mu'min,* everyone who is an *insān kāmil,* and all of us must realize this. My very precious children, my brothers and sisters, we must realize it. May God protect us.

★          ★          ★

This book contains many kinds of explanations. It is full of meaningful words which can be understood only by the faith, the wisdom, and the innermost heart of man. If you realize these words with your faith and understand them with your wisdom, you will discover the state which will guide you along your path. Whatever you read about faith, certitude, and determination must be read to strengthen your *īmān,* your absolute belief in God. The fact that Allah is the only One who exists must be firmly impressed within your hearts.

You must begin with this understanding and then search for wisdom with the certitude of determined belief in God. You must search in His guardianship and say, "*Al-hamdu lillāh,* all praise belongs only to God." Begin your search with "*Bismillāhir-Rahmānir-Rahīm. Al-hamdu lillāhi Rabbil-'ālamīn:* In the name of God, Most Merciful, Most Compassionate. All praise is Yours, O Ruler of all the universes." Having begun in this fashion, you must understand every saying in this book by using your wisdom.

If all of you read this book of Sufi wisdom with open hearts free from doubt, separatism, and discrimination, free from all thought of 'my race' or 'your race', 'my religion' or 'your religion', you will realize and understand. You will see that all the children of Adam *(A.S.)* are one race and that there is no one worthy of worship other than *Allāhu ta'ālā Nāyan.* Be certain of this. If you think of it with certitude you will realize that even though hundreds of thousands of prophets came to this world they all preached about one God and spoke only His commandments.

All prophets placed their faith in only the one God. They did not see Him in different forms as many different gods. There is only one God and one family of Adam *(A.S.),* and the prophets brought the words of that one God. If we, too, have such certitude we will not create separations by seeing differences in religions or races.

If you can open your hearts and read this book of Sufi wisdom with determined faith, your wisdom will be able to absorb certain words and certain meanings. As clarity grows, the darkness of the heart will gradually fade. All the *nafs,* the base cravings arising from ignorance, will disappear. Attachments will go and the desire for God will grow. His grace and wealth and the treasures of His qualities will resplend within.

As wisdom continues to develop, we grow as human beings. Our hearts become increasingly resplendent as we gain more and more clarity of wisdom, and that resplendence will begin to cut away our darkness and our birth. As birth is cut away, death is cut away. When death is cut away, we will no longer be subject to birth or death, and our lives will become long. When our lives become long, we will realize the state of offering prayers of praise directly to God. We must realize this without the slightest doubt.

All we have learned so far amounts to only a handful of earth. What we have yet to learn is as large as the whole world. There is so much to know about the mysteries and the wealth of Allah. There is so much more to be known and we will learn it only as our wisdom develops. We must proceed slowly, always learning more and more.

There are many meanings in this book. It is not enough to read through it in a superficial manner. Delve into the meaning of each word. If you read it ten times, you will receive ten different meanings. If you read it a hundred times, you will receive a hundred different meanings. That is better than superficial reading. As your wisdom begins to grow, the meanings and explanations will also grow. Read this book with your wisdom. We must all seek wisdom.

There are many other aspects of Allah's resonance and Allah's explanations. His *rahmat,* or benevolence of grace, is limitless; it can never be judged. The power of God's grace, the words of His *Tiru Marai,* the Holy Qur'an, and all the words and commandments which He has given to the various prophets are impossible for us to estimate. Even if we turn all the water of all the oceans into ink and make all the trees and wood in all the worlds into pens and try to write His mystery, it would be impossible to complete it. His mystery is immense.

It is said that anyone who touches even one drop of His grace becomes a good one, a good one. If we first become true human beings, then perfected human beings, and finally true Sufis, and if in that state we can touch even one drop of God's qualities and place it on our tongues, we will perceive the treasure of His grace, the treasure of the three worlds (the world of the soul, this world, and the next world), and the treasure of His qualities. We must endeavor to attain the state in which we can touch at least one drop of His grace. It is an undiminishing, eternal wealth.

My very precious brothers and sisters, may you read this book carefully, without caste, race, or religious prejudice. May each of you read it and understand it from within. Treat this book as a mother, a teacher, a brother, or a sister who can nourish your wisdom. May this book help you in your lives. May the heart of every child who takes up this book and reads it become full and complete. May this book dispel the darkness in the heart, fill it with wisdom, and explain the ways in which to worship God so that we may understand. May it assist you in reaching the state in which you can lose yourselves in God and merge with Him. May you attain that completeness. There is no state more exalted.

May each of you, my brothers and sisters, take this Sufi book and read it. *In shā'Allāh, mā shā'Allāh, al-hamdu lillāh. Tawakkul-'alallāh.* If God wills it, whatever God wills, all praise belongs to God. May we hand all responsibility over to Him.

May all real responsibilties—the responsibility of divine knowledge, the responsiblity of wisdom, the responsibility of faith, and the responsibility of life—be given to God. *Āmīn.*

*M. R. Bawa Muhaiyaddeen*

# EXPLANATORY NOTE
# BY M. R. BAWA MUHAIYADDEEN *(Ral.)*

*Bismillāhir-Rahmānir-Rahīm. Al-hamdu lillāh. In shā'Allāh, mā shā'Allāh. Tawakkul-'alallāh, Allāhumma labbaik.* In the name of God, Most Merciful, Most Compassionate. All praise belongs only to God. If God so wills, whatever God wills. I place my trust in Him and am obedient to His will.

May all responsibility be given only to Allah, the One who is limitless grace and incomparable love, the One who gives us His blessings.

*Bismillāhir-Rahmānir-Rahīm.* In the name of God, Most Merciful, Most Compassionate. It is from Allah that all beginnings come, that everything begins. Because of Allah, our destinies and our lives continue. Allah alone is the *Rahmatul-'ālamīn,* the mercy and compassion of all the universes. We praise You, we believe only in You, we have certitude only in You, and we pray only to You, O Allah. We accept with certitude that there is no God worthy of worship other than Almighty God, *Allāhu ta'ālā Nāyan. Al-hamdu lillāh,* all praise belongs only to God.

O children of Adam *(A.S.),* we are the creations of Allah. He has created true man, *insān,* as the most exalted of all His creations. God has given the most exalted wisdom and the most exalted capabilities to man. Of all His creations, He has given man the most exalted qualities and actions. God has made man the king of all creation and has endowed him with all the forces, miracles, powers, and wisdom, and the ability to control them. God has given man the wealth of wisdom, the *daulat* with which he can summon and control all the angels, heavenly beings, jinns, and fairies. He impressed the resplendent light called *Nūr* on the forehead of Adam *(A.S.)* at the time Adam *(A.S.)* was created.

O men who are human, there is something we have to realize. We must cut away the darkness which envelops and veils our hearts, the illusions which conceal our absolute faith, certitude, and determination, and the base desires which hide the truth. We must dispel satanic thoughts and qualities, the envy and jealousy which cloud our wisdom, satanic looks, and the deceitful and treacherous intentions which can turn life into death. We must cut away the desires for land, gold, and women which conceal our connection with Allah. We must cut away all the arrogance, selfishness, vanity, pride, and the color, class, and religious divisions which cut off the connection by which we can live in unity with Allah.

If we, who are men, can cut away these evil connections to satan and these sections of satan, then we will live in close association with Allah and His people, doing our duty toward Him and toward all lives. We who are human beings must realize this.

Allah has given the explanations of the wisdom of true man or *insān,* through His *rahmat,* which is the benevolence of His grace, through His words, His actions, His duties, His three thousand divine attributes, His ninety-nine *wilāyats,* or powers, His behavior, and His conduct. If we can remove the veils of our evil qualities through wisdom, certitude, and faith, we will become the wise ones who can perform duty for the children of Allah, slaves giving service to Allah. We will become messengers in constant communion with Him, praying to and worshiping only Allah. May all who are human reflect on this.

It is for this purpose that *Allāhu ta'ālā Nāyan* has impressed on us that we must discard racial and religious discrimination and make our *qalbs,* our innermost hearts, stable and firm through faith, truth, and certitude.

The qualities of satan which cause divisions within us will come to attack our faith. When that happens, we must put our faith and certitude only in Allah. We must pray to Him without considering anything His equal. Without comparing anything to Allah, we must raise our hands to Him in worship. Believing that He is the only God, we must bow low in obeisance. Allah has given us the capacity for this kind of worship. May we reflect on this. Everyone who is human must reflect on it.

We must accept Allah. To do this He has given us the seven levels of consciousness: feeling, awareness, intellect, judgment, subtle wisdom, the divine analytic wisdom which is the explaining wisdom of the *Qutbiyyat,* and the divine luminous wisdom which is the *Nūr* or resplendence of Allah. In the Qur'an Allah has given these seven levels of wisdom as the seven diacritical marks. By placing a mark above or below the letter *alif,* we can give it different sounds. God gives sounds to each of the consonants through the seven diacritical marks. It is through these seven marks that He makes the sound of the Qur'an resonant. These sounds become the sounds of the seven levels of wisdom within the heart, and the heart of a true man is the Qur'an. The sounds of the seven levels of wisdom must dawn within us.

In the same way that the sounds arise from the seven marks, the resonance of the revelations within the Qur'an are explained by the seven levels of wisdom. Allah uses the seven levels of wisdom to reveal to us the sound of the resonance of the Qur'an in the same way that the sounds of the revelations came to Prophet Muhammad *(Sal.).* The sounds of Allah resonate through these seven diacritical marks, do they not?

This is how each human being must take into his heart the sounds of the Qur'an. The Qur'an is the resonance which came from Allah. When it came to the Rasūlullāh *(Sal.)* in the form of explanation, it was a command. When it came from the Rasūlullāh *(Sal.),* it became a teaching. When that teaching rests within the *qalb,* the innermost heart, it becomes the writing of the Qur'an. Each of us who is human must open his *qalb* and read the inner Qur'an. With our faith, we must pick up the Qur'an inside our *qalbs,* open it, and read it with wisdom.

To give sound to the writings in the inner Qur'an, Allah uses the seven levels of wisdom. You can read the words of Allah in the Qur'an only by using these seven levels of wisdom, which are like the seven diacritical marks.

O mankind, O children of Adam *(A.S.)!* Open your *qalbs* and read the Qur'an. The *qalb* is the Qur'an. The *qalb* is the *Ka'bah* which, in Islam, is the central place of worship. The *qalb* is paradise. The *qalb* is the station of prayer. It is the throne of God, or *dhāhut,* the throne of the true believer, or *'arshul-mu'min.* It is His kingdom, the station from which He rules. We must read the Qur'an in the *qalb.* It is from the *qalb* that we must pray to Him and bow in obeisance to Him. Those of us who are human must realize this.

When satan and his actions and qualities come, we must utilize our faith and wisdom to face his attack. This is the holy war. The holy war must be the only war within our hearts; it is the fight between the qualities of Allah and the evil qualities of satan. At that time we will experience suffering, grief, difficulty, and trouble. This is the holy war, the *jihād,* the battles in which the armies of

12

our evil actions confront us. This is the battle of Badr, the battle of Uhud. This is the real *jihād*. We must wage *jihād* against all the armies which attempt to cut off our connection to Allah, against the enemies within who attempt to disrupt the unity among people by dividing one man from another. Armies of monkey forces, horse forces, bull forces, vulture forces, eagle forces, lion forces, and elephant forces will come to fight against us. All the armies of illusion and the demons, ghosts, and dark forces of satan will attack. The war we wage against them internally is the holy war.

Evil forces will try to sever our connection with Allah. They will attempt to destroy our faith and shroud us in darkness. We must divide and destroy these ghosts and demons.

Everyone who is human must fight this war within his *qalb*. We must use the wisdom and the faith which we were given as the victorious sword of the Rasūlullāh *(Sal.)* to fight these forces. We who are born as human beings, as *insān*, must realize this with the seven levels of wisdom, strengthen ourselves with faith, and fight the inner war with certitude.

My very precious children, you who are *insān*, you who are true believers, you who have the firm faith, certitude, and determination in God called *īmān*, you who have accepted God as the Father, you who have accepted God as the Creator, you who have accepted Allah as your God—the battles each of us has to fight are within the *qalb*.

The *qalb* is the place called *Karbalā'*. *Karbalā'* is the sphere of prayer; it is heaven, the kingdom of God, the place in which He rules supreme. It is also called the *'arshul-mu'min*, or the throne of the true believer. The satans and the evil jinns and fairies wage their wars in order to capture this kingdom and bring it under their own control.

We must confront them there, fight them, and defeat them, using the mace of *īmān* and the sword of *dhul-fiqār*, which is the double-bladed sword of *īmān* and wisdom. Each of us must understand this and do it. We who are *insān* must realize what the *Karbalā'* truly is.

For this reason, God has sent down the 124,000 prophets, the *qutbs*, the saints, and the *olis*. He sent down His prophets so that our hearts and our wisdom would not become weary, so that our certitude would not fail. God sent down His prophets to help us stand up, fight, and win this war against satan and his forces. Each prophet, *qutb,* and messenger was sent down for a specific time. God has manifested this state from the time of the universe of the soul to the end of the next world and until the Day of Reckoning.

The war we must fight is not an external one in which we destroy other people. It is inside, between the qualities of God and the qualities of satan. For a human being, an *insān,* there is no enmity between one man and another or between man and Allah. There is no hatred within the qualities, prayers, or unity of man. But the millions of evil qualities change men into beasts and lead them to hell. It is then that war between the evil qualities of satan and the good qualities of Allah must be fought, because divisions and enmity are inherent in evil qualities. But between man and man there should never be any division. There should be no racial, color, or religious differences.

God is one. All the prophets spoke of only one God. Only one God sent down all the commandments. We who are men must reflect on this. There is much we must realize through the internal wars. My very precious children, jeweled lights of my eyes, we must strengthen our faith in God, make our wisdom mature, and develop firm certitude and determination. Every child who is human must establish that state and open his heart; he must accept *toluhay, 'ibādat, dhikr,* and *fikr,* or prayer, worship, remembrance, and contemplation. As we perform each of these, we must develop firm certitude within us and continually strengthen it.

We must also recite the five *Kalimahs.* The First *Kalimah* is meant to cleanse the earth within us. The Second *Kalimah* is meant to cleanse the fire of anger, hunger, and disease which envelops us. The Third *Kalimah* is to clear our hearts of the jealousies, envies, treacheries, and all the qualities and miracles of satan. The Fourth *Kalimah* is to clear away the section of death. The Fifth *Kalimah* is to remove all the faults and blemishes which emerge from the senses: the eyes, ears, nose, and tongue. The Fifth *Kalimah* washes away the torpor and hypnotic fascinations of illusion, the sounds of illusion, all the dancing and singing and music of the sixty-four arts, and the qualities which make us succumb to the sixty-four arts. It wipes away all the sins we commit through our eyes, noses, ears, and tongues, and severs the blood ties which arise from the five senses. Such is the power of the five *Kalimahs.*

There are also the five times of prayer. The first prayer, the prayer of *subhat,* cuts away the connection to the earth. The second time of prayer, which is at midday, is called *zuhr;* it cuts away the connection to fire, to the jinns, and to hunger, disease, aging, and death: the connections to hell. The third, the prayer of *'asr,* cuts away the qualities of the ghosts and the demons which arise in the heart. The prayer of *'asr* relates to air, to the worship of spirits and vapors, to the base desires, and to the jinns, elemental spirits, and all the miracles and forces which come from them. All of these are dispelled by the prayer of *'asr.*

The fourth is the prayer of *maghrib,* which concerns life and death and the questioning by the angels in the grave about the good and evil which have been written during our lives. All the illnesses which arise from arrogance are blemishes, and *maghrib* clears them away. At the fifth time of prayer, *'ishā',* we worship *Allāhu ta'ālā Nāyan,* dying within Him without consciousness of day or night. To have that connection to Him is the prayer of *'ishā'.* In that prayer, all thought is dead. In the prayer of *'ishā',* we merge with God, becoming lost within Him, dead within Him.

The five times of prayer overcome the energies of earth, fire, water, air, and ether: the crescent moon, the stars, and the illusions in the clouds. Beyond the five times of prayer is the prayer of *Sūfiyyat* in which we speak without speaking, pray without praying, and perform 43,242 prostrations before Allah every day, bowing to Him in every moment and with every breath. This is the resplendent prayer of *Sūfiyyat* which performs duty to Allah, duty to the king, duty to the people, and duty to the world.

One who does these four kinds of duties will dwell in the universe of the soul, in this world, and in the next world, maintaining his connection with Allah in all three of these worlds. This is the prayer of a Sufi. He will make himself die by transforming himself into wax and burning himself in order to give light to others. He will sew up the twelve holes in his body, the twelve openings which relate to birth and death, the holes of the thoughts and base desires. He will close up every hole in everything he looks at. Holding them together with wisdom, he will sew them up so that nothing other than Allah, the Rasūlullāh *(Sal.),* and the resplendent light of *Nūr* can enter. If he succeeds in doing this, then even a million years will be only as much as a hair's breadth in the expanse of his life. This is the state of a

Sufi.

You who have faith, you who are true believers, you who worship only Allah, you who are true men—you must think of this. When we place our faith only in Allah, when we set out to fight the wars in the innermost heart, there will be many obstacles and dangers. First we need patience, second we need the inner patience called *sabūr*, third we need contentment or *shakūr*, fourth we need surrender or *tawakkul*, and fifth we need to give all praise to God, *al-hamdu lillāh*. Through these five we must complete and perfect our hearts. Allah has given these five in their fullness to those who have faith, to those who can be called true believers, to true men, and to perfected men. As long as we make use of these five treasures we will face no danger, no suffering.

My very precious brothers and sisters—you who are human beings, you who are the children of Adam *(A.S.)*, you who are the resplendent lights within my eyes, you who are the love within my heart, you who are born with me, you who are my body, my life, my love, and my eyes—my brothers and sisters who are filled with that completeness, we must realize these things.

We have ascribed so many meanings to Almighty God in the many religions; but no matter how many names have been given to Him, He is one. The names in the religions were given by us, but Allah has not changed; He remains one. Just because men call Him by different names, that does not mean He is different beings. Just because the many religions give Him different names, that does not mean He is a different God, a different race, or a different form for each religion.

God is without form or shape; He has no name and no country. He is a power, the power which dwells within all lives, the power which can protect, understand, and sustain all lives. Each of us, each of the children of Adam *(A.S.)* must reflect on this. God is one and the family of Adam *(A.S.)* is one. There is only one God to whom worship belongs. We must realize this without the slightest doubt. We must realize it with certitude and absolute faith. That will be best.

My brothers and sisters, no matter how we understand it, the names of God and His words and the revelations known as the Qur'an have been sent down as 6,666 verses. The words of all the prophets which were sent down to them in their respective times all appear in the Qur'an. The explanations given to the twenty-five prophets who were mentioned in the Qur'an and to certain *qutbs* and *olis* were sent down as specific chapters in the Qur'an. Each message came down at a different time, in a different chapter. The revelations were sent down 6,666 times.

Apart from this there were also words which came straight from God to the prophets, as described in the *ahādīth,* or traditional Islamic stories. And no matter what people may say, every story and every word of the Qur'an is contained within the inner heart of every man. If everyone who is human opens his heart and looks within, he will understand that story. He will see and be able to read the history of all three worlds in the divine scripture called the Holy Qur'an. The innermost heart is the Qur'an. If we reflect on this, we will realize the true state of our lives. We will realize what Allah is like and what prayer and worship must be like.

Let each of us reflect on this. O you who love God, you who have absolute faith in God! There is only one God and there is only one race. When we accept one God and one race, when we worship God without creating differences, then our prayers will be fulfilled. Only on that day will our prayers be genuine. All the time we fail to perceive that total oneness, our prayers will be the prayers which divide people.

In the same way that satan divided people from one another, our prayers will divide people from one another. The qualities of satan separate us from Allah, and prayers which fail to perceive that there is only one God are prayers of separation. As long as division exists, true prayer does not exist. Only when we pray with the realization that we are all one, one family and one people, will true prayer to God occur.

My precious children, if we want to discover ourselves, our Lord, His history, and our history, we must open the Qur'an which exists within the innermost heart, the *qalb.* The divine scripture exists within the *qalb.* It does not appear in any book. It does not appear in any writing. It exists as resplendent light in the *qalb.* It exists as a sound and a revelation within the *qalb.* It exists as a resonance within the *qalb,* giving the explanations. Only if we have wisdom and the absolute faith called *īmān* can we understand the explanations. When we understand, we will never die. One who understands is a Sufi.

My very precious children, jeweled lights of my eyes, it is

impossible for us to see the Qur'an in its totality. The Qur'an and the revelations within it which came from God have been explained by the prophets. The sounds must be kept inside, not merely carried in our hands as books. The books certainly can be in our hands but the sounds and the explanations and the resonances must stay within our hearts. The inner Qur'an, the inner Bible, and the inner scriptures are Allah's commandments. The books in our hands can be consumed by fire, water, or air. But when God's words of wisdom are imprinted on our hearts, that is the Qur'an, that is the Bible, that is the scripture, and nothing can consume them. This is the truth.

We must open this book and look. We can never complete our study of Him. As we go on digging and digging with our wisdom, God will appear to be further and further away from us. No matter how much we discover with science, that which stands beyond research is God. No matter how much we study, that which appears to be further and further away from us and from our learning is God. No matter what we eat, the taste which remains beyond our reach is God. No matter how many scenes we may look at, the beauty which always lies beyond everything we see is God. No matter how much we pray, God is the One beyond the deepest depth of our prayers. No matter how much wisdom we use to open up and dig deep within the heart, that which exists beyond all the digging is God.

To worship Allah and to serve His children, eliminating the divisions among them, wisdom must be the instrument. Therefore, my precious children, you who have faith must seek wisdom. Only then can you achieve the highest victory and attain that beauty.

My very precious children, we have explained this through the very few words in this Sufi book, *The Golden Words of a Sufi Sheikh*. This book contains only a very small amount of wisdom, but we must study the subtlety and understand the explanation of every word and every sentence. Each time we take these words into our hearts and examine them, our wisdom will grow. As we go deeper and find more meaning, our wisdom will expand and expand. As we read more and more, we will discover greater depth of meaning. But if we remain on the surface, the explanations we receive will be limited. If our wisdom fails to develop, we will see the words as a show. Anything we look at superficially will seem to be a show. We must understand the help that wisdom can give.

My very precious children, please look at this book, *The Golden Words of a Sufi Sheikh*. We are the slaves of God. We have faith and trust in God; through our faith and certitude we must accept God without the slightest doubt and stand close to Him. When we stand with Him and read this book of Sufi wisdom we will receive many meanings and explanations.

In this book there are 975 sayings, each with a different meaning. It is necessary for us to read between the lines and between the words. This book is a map by which we can open our hearts and find the way. It is a map by which we can open ourselves and look within with our wisdom. If each of us who is human, if each of us who is of the children of Adam *(A.S.)*, if each of us who believes that Adam's *(A.S.)* children are one race with one prayer and one God, if each of us opens this book and reads it with a heart which knows no prejudice, no racial or religious differences, we will derive great benefit.

We may see many divisions in the world, but when we leave here and go to the next world, we will realize that there is only one God, one race, and one family. Until we reach the grave there will be differences in the world—one grave for you, one grave for me; one grave for my race, one grave for your race—but when we reach there we will see that there is only one grave, and that grave is hell. There is also one palace called heaven. It is possible for all of us to live in that one palace of heaven as one race. But if we go with the qualities of satan we will have to go to that one grave which is hell. There will be only two houses in the next world: heaven and hell. We have many different cemeteries for the different kinds of people here, for the different castes, religions, and races, but there is only one cemetery in the next world.

These are the only two things fashioned by God, so it would be good if we would open our hearts with wisdom and faith and look within. If you read this Sufi *gnāni* book and take every meaning into your heart, it will help you in wisdom. It will help you to understand the society of mankind and to understand who we are as well as to understand who created us, who our Father is, and who our God is. This book will give you the fullness of that meaning.

Each child must reflect on this. We have printed many books, of Sufi wisdom. This book contains the meanings in short sayings. If you read this book of short sayings and then read the other books, it will help you a great deal.

When our wisdom becomes mature and we see the true path, we can take that path. Until we find the path we need to nourish our wisdom and bring it to maturity. My children, my brethren, we must think of the way in which to do this. *Āmīn*.

# THE GOLDEN WORDS
## OF A SUFI SHEIKH

# INVOCATION

*Bismillāhir-Rahmānir-Rahīm,* in the name of God, Most Merciful, Most Compassionate. May all praise belong only to the Creator, the Protector, and the Sustainer. *Āmīn.* May the responsibility for all praise and blame belong to only the one God. *Āmīn.*

God is the One who is patient with all the qualities of all creations in all places. He is the One who understands them, He is the One who is forbearant, He is the One who makes them tranquil. He gives them peace of mind and embraces them to Himself. He is the One who gives the milk of grace in the heart, the One who teaches wisdom, the One who bestows love, the One who shows compassion, the One who performs duty, and the One who reveals the way to the birthright of all creations.

May all the most perfect and pure might belong to only the one God. *Āmīn.*

O God, You have placed in Your creations pure belief, pure peace, wisdom, light, the determined faith of *īmān,* and the beautiful, compassionate qualities, thoughts, and intentions of Your state. Please open the way so that we can intend to search for You and reach You. Please show the way to all the human beings You have created and give them Your grace. *Āmīn.* Bestow Your qualities upon all of them. *Āmīn.*

In Your creation exists *sirr* and *sifāt,* or the mystery and the manifestation, *khair* and *sharr,* or right and wrong, the permissible and the forbidden, or *halāl* and *harām*, and good actions and evil actions. Please give us everything that is good: good thoughts, good conduct, goodness, love, Your three thousand precious qualities, Your ninety-nine *wilāyats* or powers, and the behavior appropriate to Your actions. Please bestow upon man what is good and help us to avoid what is evil. With Your grace give us the determination and the certitude by which we can act in this way, with understanding. *Āmīn.*

There is no god other than Almighty God, *Allāhu ta'ālā Nāyan,* to whom worship is due. With Your grace may You give us the explanation, the certitude, the radiant divine wisdom called *gnānam,* and the grace to understand and worship You. *Āmīn.*

# INTRODUCTION

*Āmīn,* may our prayers be fulfilled. *Bismillāhir-Rahmānir-Rahim,* in the name of God, Most Merciful, Most Compassionate. May God who is limitless grace and incomparable love give us the beneficence of His wealth and His grace. *Āmīn.*

May all praise be offered to God. My very precious children, jeweled lights of my eyes, my children born with me as the body within my body, very precious gems of my heart who are the life within my life, children who are mingled within the light of my heart, children who are as one body with me, I give my loving greetings to all of you.

My very precious children, we have come to the land which is the world. To those who are devotees of God the world is a prayer mat, a *musālla.* To those of wisdom it is a school. To those who are lacking in wisdom the world is a stage for the drama in which they act and dance. To those who have the resplendence of perfect faith and certitude called *īmān* with which they have realized and understood God, the world is a place in which they see and praise God in every creation. One who has understood and accepted God sees God in everything. He splits everything open and sees God's powers, God's grace, and the explanations of all God's actions within every creation. Seeing God's resplendent light and grace within each creation, he says, "O my God, how can I praise You? In every life, in every tree, in every flower, in every fruit, I see Your taste, I see Your beauty, I see Your love. How can I praise You? How can I find the words to praise You?"

The world is a school to those of wisdom, a place of prayer for those who are true devotees, and for those with faith it is a place where God is seen and praised in every creation. But to the ignorant who act with the monkey of the mind and the dog of desire, the world is a stage for acting and dancing and drama.

To those who have faith, Allah has said, "I have spread the world out before you as a prayer mat." Recognizing this, when a man of wisdom walks, he treads gently. He looks around carefully and treads cautiously so that he will not cause pain to the earth.

A man of wisdom observes and studies creation, attempting to realize who he is and who God is. He tries to discover and understand the story of God, the story of man, and the story of all creation. In his studies the man of wisdom learns that God is within man and man is within God. If there were no God, there would be no life. If there were no life, there would be no God. If there were no human beings, no one could discover God. If there were no God, there would be no creations who pray to God or try to understand Him with the clarity of wisdom. A man who has the level of wisdom to make this discovery is given the name *rasūl. Rasūl* is an Arabic word meaning a man of wisdom or the state of having the wisdom to understand every creation of God. Such a man understands and realizes the story of God and the story of creation. Having understood this, he discovers the station in which God and man exist in the same place and he discovers the relationship between them.

One who has faith, one who is a true believer who believes that nothing but God exists sees only God's splendor. He praises nothing other than God. Wherever he turns to look he finds that there is nothing but God in anything he sees, because God is the light within every creation. God is the One who creates and gives the nourishment of His essence, or *dhāt,* to all creations. He is the One who forgives everything. He is the One who calls all creations back to Himself. He is the only One who can pass judgment. He is the One who sustains us with compassionate love. He is the Father who creates, nourishes, and sustains us.

Realizing this, a true believer dedicates his body, mind, and soul to that one God; he surrenders to Him and merges with Him as one. Such is the action of one who is a *mu'min,* a true believer who has the perfect faith and certitude in God which is called *īmān.*

Those who have forfeited their wisdom believe in the world and in the sixty-four kinds of worldly knowledge and the sixty-four sexual arts. They love everything they see and cherish all the tricks and various magical illusions perpetrated by these energies, or *shakthis.* They hold dear the miracles arising from occult powers and the fame, titles, and honors which they earn by these illusory tricks. They become enamored with the wealth, land, gold, and woman they acquire. They place their faith in religions, castes, and philosophies. They carry their titles, fame, honors, and the joy they derive from these like billboards in front of them. These are the billboards for hell.

Having fashioned these billboard advertisements, they put on their acts. Such men treat the world as a stage for drama. They stand up as performers and act out their respective parts. Pretending to search for God, they attempt to win prizes from God. From the babe in arms to the old man ready for the grave, everyone acts and competes for prizes from the kingdom of heaven. They hold up advertisements for religions, philosophies, and doctrines: "This is my heaven. This is the true heaven. My god is the pure god. My religion is the true religion. My caste is the real caste. My color is the finest color." In this way they dance and act and vie for prizes from God. Such people change the world from a flower garden into a dramatic stage and they act throughout their entire lives.

Thus, human beings are in these four different states. My very precious children, we must think of these states. We came from God as one family and one race, the family of Adam *(A.S.),* the society of mankind. We came from where we were one race and we all still belong to that one race. The human generation has come as many different fruits from the same tree. All seeds have come from one seed. All grace has come from the one grace. We have all been manifested from that one source.

My very precious children, when we came we certainly came as the society of mankind and when we return we must return as human beings.

### 1.

O man, know the earth
And plant good crops
That are suitable to it.

### 2.

O man, know the self
Cut away the earth
Lose the self
And pray to God.

### 3.

O man, know the seasons
And plow the earth.
Know the rains
And sow your seeds.

### 4.

O man, dispel your evil qualities
Destroy your mind
Open your heart
And worship God.

### 5.

O man, know the capacity,
The maturity and the qualities
Of one to whom you speak
And then speak wisdom.
Otherwise your words of wisdom
Will fall like rain on a barren desert.
Nothing will grow.

### 6.

O man, know a person's qualities
Before you form a friendship.

A friend with evil qualities
Can turn your life into a corpse.

## 7.

O man, know the qualities and actions
Of God's creations
And do duty with wisdom.
If you do duty without knowing their qualities, they will kill
you, and your duty will come back to attack you.

## 8.

O man, do not gaze at a beautiful horse in the wilderness,
intending to catch and ride it. It will throw you to the ground.
You must train it, gain experience, and then ride. That will be
better.

Similarly, if you look for and trust only outer beauty—the
beauty of a face, a person, or a word—it will throw you down
and trample your life. Think with wisdom, understand, then
control your life.

## 9.

O man, tie up the mind
Control your thoughts
And perform the *dhikr*.
Then the world of souls, this world, and the next world will
open and become visible to you.

## 10.

O man, know the begging bowl
And then give alms.
Know the family
And then give away the bride.
Know the use of the pond
And then wash your backside.
Know the fruit
And then taste it.
Anything you do that is based solely on outer appearances can
destroy you, just as eating a beautiful but poisonous *kānjuran* fruit
will kill you.

Think of each illustration and act accordingly. That will grant victory to your life.

11.

O man, know the self
And control your cravings.
Then you will know
The only Chieftain.

12.

O man, cut away your dreams of the world
Destroy the thoughts of your mind
Open your wisdom
And look.
You will see the open space
And the light.

13.

O man, sift the earth
Beat away the torpor of desire
And find the jewel of grace.

14.

O man, sift yourself
Obtain determination
Open out the faith of *īmān*
And worship God.

15.

O man, kill lust
Receive God's compassion
Destroy the arrogance
Of your destructive mind.

16.

O man, destroy selfishness
Obliterate pride
Overthrow the ninety-six obsessions

Which originate from bile
And search for our Father.

17.

O man, overcome fascination
Destroy mind, desire, and thought
And protect your honor.

18.

O man, cut away lust
Open the eye of wisdom
And worship the One
Who fills all the universes.

19.

O man, kill arrogance
Defeat ignorance
And develop patience.

20.

O man, know your birth
Develop good qualities
And search for the sheikh.

21.

O man, kill karma
And perform the good duty
Which is known as *dharma*.

22.

O man, overcome *māyā*
Polish the mind
Act with the qualities of God
And this will truly benefit you.

23.

O man, cut off jealousy
And obtain peace of mind.

24.

O man, if you can kill
The treachery and deceit of the mind
And search for grace
The treasure of Allah will be yours.

25.

O man, cut off the illusion of *māyā*
And obtain peace of mind.
Dispel the sins of your birth
And attain the maturity of Allah's qualities.

26.

O man, cut off the differences
Seen by the mind,
Destroy the separations
Caused by the mind,
And attain the love of the soul
Which will never depart
Or be separate from anyone.

27.

O man, control desire
Destroy egoism
And make God's love grow.

28.

O man, lose selfishness
Serve God
And attain maturity.

29.

O man, open the eye of wisdom
Look at the good and evil
Goals of your mind
And choose the ones appropriate to God.

30.

O man, open the *qalb*
Know God's meaning
And have faith in Him.

31.

O man, overcome the five-headed
Cobra of the senses
Pull out its poisonous fangs
And blowing the melody
Of *lā ilāha illallāhu*
Make that snake of the senses dance.

32.

O man, destroy both joy and sorrow
Open your innermost heart
And give your prayers to God.

33.

O man, plant the tree of *īmān*
Drench it with the water of faith
Pick the fruit of wisdom
And eat.
Then you will perceive
The sweetness of Allah.

34.

O man, give up your attachments to blood ties
Seek the qualities of God
And you can attain devotion.

35.

O man, overcome the miracles of the mind
Destroy the pride of the mind
Join with the actions and qualities of God
And you will understand the miracles of God.

36.

O man, control outer sounds
Listen to the sound of God
And you will understand
Its uniqueness and bliss.

37.

O man, if you control the tongue
You will know goodness in your life
And the evil which might have come
Will be far, far away.

38.

O man, God has given you all His wealth
The wealth of all three worlds
Of *awwal, dunyā,* and *ākhirah.*
Realize with wisdom
Stop your begging
Understand this treasure
And you can give to all.

39.

O man, control what is known as 'I'
And realize the rewards.

40.

O man, if you can pull out and throw away
What is known as 'mine' and 'yours'
You will see all lives as your own.

41.

O man, control lust
And open the door
Of divine analytic wisdom.

42.

O man, control your cravings
And the begging of the mind will cease.

43.

O man, kill your temper
Seek wisdom
And attain the beautiful qualities of God.

44.

O man, kill the impatience of the mind
And you will be able to achieve
The bliss of wisdom,
And you will be able to perceive
The beauty of your life.

45.

O man, scatter the darkness of the mind
And you will be able to see
The splendor of the grace of God.

46.

O man, patience will dispel
The poverty of your existence
And then you will know
The magnificence of your life.

47.

O man, chase away the mind's fear
And obtain the determination
Of the perfect faith called *īmān*.

48.

O man, control the hissing of your anger
And you will be rich in good qualities.

49.

O man, dispel with wisdom
The visions of your mind and eyes
And you will be able to reach
The truth of the kingdom of God.

## 50.

O man, know with wisdom
What mind and desire bring
Accept what is good
Throw away the evil
And the journey will be easy
To your earlier abode.

## 51.

O man, overcome lust
Destroy passion
And open the eye of your wisdom
To look at the world.
Then you will know
Your profit and your loss.

## 52.

O man, cut away the arrogance
Which arises from your vision
Cut away the arrogance
Which arises from your thoughts
Cut away the arrogance
Of sexual frenzy
Open out your wisdom
Look and you will see
The place where God exists.

## 53.

O man, destroy the qualities
Of the beast with five mouths
And you can attain
The exalted wisdom of grace.

## 54.

O man, if man knows man
God will be seen.

## 55.

O man, analyze, distinguish
And see with wisdom
And you will receive the boon
Of the fullness of life.

## 56.

O man, if man investigates his state
His faults and himself
If he understands his kingdom
If he judges himself
If he punishes his faults
He will become pure and innocent
He will not face judgment in God's kingdom.
He will receive the fruits of God.

## 57.

O man, beat off and chase away avarice
And accept the priceless birthright of man.

## 58.

O man, drive away the agitation of the mind
And study wisdom.

## 59.

O man, beat your roguish mind with wisdom
Instruct it
And your suffering will cease.

## 60.

O man, when you awaken from a dream, you do not see any
of the things you saw in the dream, do you?

Similarly, the dreams you see in your life are not real. Forget
them. Open your life and look at it with wisdom, and you will
see the truth of life.

## 61.

O man, do not suffer

By thinking unnecessary thoughts
Past sufferings do not return.
Think of what is happening now
Plan the right steps with your wisdom
And act accordingly.

### 62.

O man, know the elements
And correct the senses.

### 63.

O man, know with wisdom
The thirst of life
And drink the water of grace
Which will quench the thirst of your birth.

### 64.

O man, know man
And you will then know God.

### 65.

O man, know your heart
And resplendent beauty
Will be seen in your face.

### 66.

O man, acquire God's qualities
And you will know the perfected man
The *insān kāmil*.
Follow him
And the path to God will be clear.

### 67.

O man, do not grieve
And worry about your karma.
It belongs to the past.
Think of the unattached way in which God performs duty to
all lives. From this very moment, do your duties in the same

manner, with determination, and your earlier karma will no longer follow you.

When you become the light of wisdom, darkness can never conceal you.

### 68.

O man, know the state
In which you were an embryo
And you will know the state
Of the One who created that embryo.

### 69.

O man, do not think about
Flying in the sky
And ruling the earth.
Conquer the mind which is ruling you
And seek to rule yourself.

When you are the resplendent sun that gives light to all the universes, then the land, women, and gold below will be only a tiny speck to your wisdom.

### 70.

O man, know patience
And you will know the beauty
And justice of Allah.

### 71.

Do not try to live your life
Embracing the religions.

If you do, it will overturn your good qualities and the compassionate justice of God within you, preventing you from performing His duties equally to all lives.

Realize this with your wisdom and separate from yourself that which keeps you separate from Him. Truth is the one thing that can never be separate from you. If you embrace the truth, you will never be separate from it and it will never be separate from you. Truth is Allah.

72.

O man, know the inner patience called *sabūr*
And you will understand the peace of Allah.

73.

O man, to whom are you a slave in this life? Think of this with your wisdom. You are a slave, but you do not know to whom. Which master has bought you? Would it not be good to understand this?

You are a slave to the four hundred trillion, ten thousand occult energies of the mind, the cells, viruses, magnetic forces, *māyā*, karma, arrogance, and bigotry, the egoism of the 'I' and 'you', blood ties, attachments, and desire for land, women, and gold. These and countless more are tormenting demons and fatal diseases that cause you the incessant pain of a living death.

You are not a slave to one master! When everyone and everything is your taskmaster, how can you complete the duties assigned by all of them? Impossible, is it not?

Select one master for all these forces. With faith, certitude, and determination argue with Him and then take the case to the court of justice. The head of that court will release you from your bondage. He is God, Allah. The moment they see Him, all those who held you in bondage will run away and He will grant you independence. The One who frees you is the One who created you, the One who grants freedom to all.

Know Him and join Him, selflessly performing His duties and service just as He does, in these four ways: service to God, service to the laws of God's justice, service to people, and service to the world. To conduct yourself in this manner will grant you freedom in all three worlds: the world of the souls, this earthly world, and the world of the hereafter. This will constitute the triumph of duty in true and complete freedom.

74.

O man, know the contentment called *shakūr*
And you will understand
God's state of judgment and His laws
And the duties He silently performs
Within His kingdom.

## 75.

O man, subdue the fire of your hunger
And you will understand
The Ten Commandments sent down by God
To Prophet Moses, peace be upon him.

## 76.

O man, know the value of *tawakkul*
Of placing all your trust in God.

Then you will understand the explanation of the five and the six (the five outer and the six inner obligatory duties), the power of prayer, the way to worship God, and the five times of prayer and its benefits.

## 77.

O man, know *īmān*
And you will understand
The rules and the content of *Īmān-Islām*.

*Īmān,* or absolute faith and certitude in God, is Islam. The preface to *Īmān-Islām* is patience, and then inner patience or *sabūr,* contentment or *shakūr,* trust in God or *tawakkul-'alallāh,* and giving praise to God for each thing that happens or *al-hamdu lillāh.*

Whatever is to happen at the very next moment is known only to Him. Therefore, we must say, *"Tawakkul-'alallāh,"* placing all our trust in Him. Whatever is given as nourishment at any moment we must accept with contentment, saying, *"Bismillāhir-Rahmānir-Rahīm,* in the name of God, Most Merciful, Most Compassionate." We must praise Him whether we have been given a lovely feast or merely a glass of water.

*Allāhu ta'ālā,* Almighty God, gave the power of inner patience to Prophet Muhammad Mustafar-Rasūl *(Sal.)* and instructed him to tie it around his stomach in order to control the fire of his hunger and his desires. He directed the Prophet *(Sal.)* to unfold the umbrella of patience and good qualities over all the universes and to embrace all lives within its shade.

*Allāhu ta'ālā* explained this step by step through the 6,666 *āyats,* the verses of the Qur'an. The growth of good qualities and actions is called *Īmān-Islām.*

In a *hadīth,* Allah said, "O Muhammad! I would not have created anything but for you."

All of everything which feels the rays of His power is in a state of perfect purity. Islam means perfect purity; hence everything was created as Islam. But it is only when the grass and weeds that choke it are removed and it is allowed to flourish that it can be called *Īmān-Islām.*

*Allāhu ta'ālā* bestowed this precious gift upon an-Nabī Muhammad Mustafā *(Sal.)* who taught it to all those who had faith. Anyone who receives and tastes it is a rich being. Those who do not receive this wealth are the poor in *ākhirah,* the hereafter. *In shā'Allāh,* if God so wills. Allah alone knows!

### 78.

O man, if you understand the meaning
Of *al-hamdu lillāh,*
Of giving all praise to God,
You will know that which is with you
Which never comes or goes
And you will be dwelling with it
You will be in communion with it
At all times.

### 79.

O man, know the poverty
Of the lack of wisdom in your life.

Then the poverty that drags you down will leave. When it does, you will receive the limitless wealth and grace of *'ilm,* the ocean of divine knowledge, and you will be free of poverty in all three worlds.

### 80.

O man, use divine analytic wisdom
To analyze and understand
The actions of your state
And eliminate the evils within you.
Then you will see tranquillity
Within yourself and all lives.

### 81.

O man, discover that which torments you
And rid yourself of it.
Then you will be free of suffering
And you will not cause suffering to others.

### 82.

O man, fascinate with wisdom
That which fascinates you
And the might of your life will be known.

### 83.

O man, with faith and certitude
Determination and wisdom
Fight and root out the demons of the mind
Which attempt to fascinate and kill you,
And the darkness of the fascinations
Will flee from the battlefield.
Freed of fear and anxiety
You will see only peace in your life
And the triumph of the soul.

### 84.

O man, overcome hunger
And your maturity will grow.

### 85.

O man, if you overcome the qualities
Of the five elements
God's qualities, actions, and beauty
Will be revealed to you.

### 86.

O man, cut off the karma
That leads to your birth
And you will know the state
Of freedom from rebirth.

## 87.

O man, to reach *Allāhu* and His kingdom, transform the qualities of the five elements and all the qualities and thoughts dwelling within your body and be reborn in God's qualities and actions.

## 88.

O man, dispel the darkness of the mind
And the unchanging radiance
Of God's grace will be seen.

## 89.

Do not close your eyes
And carry a lamp as light for others.
It will be dangerous to you
You might fall down and burn yourself.

## 90.

Do not preach wisdom to others
When you have been unable
To correct your own qualities and actions.
Like a man who closes his eyes
And carries a lamp as light for others,
It could be dangerous to you.

## 91.

O man, if you overcome desire for land
The desires of the mind of illusion
Will flee from you in terror.

## 92.

O man, the one who conquers his desires
Becomes the ruler of his mind.

## 93.

O man, rid yourself of desire for women
Who plead, "Look at me, look at my beauty."
Then watch the karma of your birth
Run away from you.

## 94.

O man, overcome desire for gold
And without saying a word,
The qualities which make you suffer and dance
Will slip away from you.

## 95.

O man, if you chase away the blood ties
If you chase the bondage of the body
If you chase these with your wisdom
The laws of God's unfailing justice
Will be established in the world
And in your own judgment there will be
No shortcoming or prejudice.

## 96.

O man, dispel conceit
And see serenity in life.

## 97.

O man, lose yourself and do duty for others
And you will see within your life
God's love and the love of all lives.

## 98.

O man, dispel what is known as 'mine'
And know the happiness of God.

## 99.

O man, one who with his wisdom
Rids himself of 'mine' and 'yours'
Will be able to see in his life
Only God, equality, and peace.

## 100.

O man, dispel what is known as the 'I'
And you will know God's justice.

### 101.

O man, the egoism of 'I' hurts the self
The haughtiness of 'mine' torments you.
If both the 'mine' and 'yours' go away, we will dwell in the wide open space in which all worlds are our world and all lives are our life. We will be in the state of *illallāhu,* the all-pervasive Omnipresence.

### 102.

O man, dispel what is known as 'mine' and 'yours'
And you will understand
The happiness and sadness in all lives.

### 103.

O man, rid yourself of blood ties
And God's state of perfection will be known.

### 104.

O man, cut away your attachments
And the evils that surround you will flee.

### 105.

O man, correct your mind
Adopt God's qualities
And you will receive
The crown of God's kingdom.

### 106.

O man, if you plant the seed
Which is known as love
And share the harvest
With all hearts, then
All lives will bow in respect.

### 107.

O man, do not form your obstinacy
Into an arrow to shoot at others.
It will turn back on you, and you yourself will receive the pain.

Use your wisdom to avoid that experience. If you hold up the umbrella of serenity, you will bring tranquillity to yourself and to all lives.

### 108.

O man, if you know yourself
The world will shrink.

### 109.

O man, if you polish your wisdom
You will understand
The grace, the wealth,
And the actions of God.

### 110.

O man, if you open your heart and look within
You will understand your inner secrets.

### 111.

O man, if you understand your body
The world will be only a dot.

### 112.

O man, if you subdue desire
The pride of arrogance will die.

### 113.

O man, cut off falsehood
And know the truth of man.

### 114.

O man, eliminate envy
And your wisdom will understand
The equality and peace of all.

### 115.

O man, understand man's inherent potential
And attain the perfection of God.

### 116.

O man, open the eye of the wisdom of the soul
And the path of God's grace will be seen.

### 117.

O man, cut away birth
And attain deathless life.

### 118.

If a man does not reflect properly and plan before he acts, he will suffer so much that he will wish he were dead.

### 119.

The arrogance of the ego torments us. The pride and vanity of 'mine', 'my things', and 'my possessions' distress us. Just as a particle of dirt which has fallen in the eye rolls around and causes pain, if the arrogance of feeling 'I am the greatest' falls into the eye of wisdom, it will roll around inside and hurt so much that the eye of wisdom will be unable to open. We will be forced to keep it closed.

### 120.

In man's life, doubt and suspicion are a cancer for which there is no cure.

### 121.

Anger is poisonous to the wisdom in man's life. No matter how wise one may be, when this quality enters him, its poison works to prevent his wisdom from functioning, and wisdom falls into a daze. In the same way that a man goes into a coma when he drinks poison, anger is the poison which will make his wisdom fall into a coma and prevent it from functioning.

### 122.

The intoxication of lust will burn up a man's eye of wisdom and make him forfeit his honor and dignity.

## 123.

When a man harbors one thing in his heart while saying something else outwardly, he will suffer as much as if he had been injected with the venom of a thousand poisonous snakes.

## 124.

Duty performed with a selfish motive
Is like oil poured onto fire.
Such duty is a waste, fuel for the fire of hell, of benefit to no one.

## 125.

A hasty intellect and anger
Will destroy even the love of God.
Hastiness and the anger which jumps to retort before another person has finished speaking will destroy the love that comes from the hearts of others and even the beautiful love of God. We must exercise patience and self-control.

## 126.

If a husband and wife can control impatience and anger, they will become as suited to one another as a flower and its fragrance, living in harmony and without ever separating. A husband and wife who reflect on this will mingle in the way fragrance mingles with a flower. This will give them victory in their lives.

## 127.

A spoken word can be a fault, but a thought can be a serious transgression.

## 128.

We must control our words. It is wrong not to consider the import of each word before we speak it.

## 129.

Our evil thoughts can make us guilty of faults more serious than all the karma of all the worlds gathered and rolled into one. Our thoughts and intentions can be so poisonous that they make it impossible for our lives to bloom.

## 130.

If we think, reflect, and understand, rather than making a hasty retort, our hearts will be filled with the resplendent light of grace.

## 131.

Religious fanaticism, bigotry, and strong feelings about one's own religion will destroy God's love for us. They will also disrupt brotherly love and harmony.

## 132.

Racial discrimination and bigotry will turn the world into a battlefield.

## 133.

To be intoxicated with conceit about our positions and titles will cause pain and torment to our own hearts and to the hearts of others. It will destroy true justice.

## 134.

Blood ties (excessive attachment to our relatives) warp our sense of justice and fair play and force us into wrong decisions and judgments.

## 135.

A man's true love will bring peace and comfort to the hearts of all lives.

## 136.

God's love will comfort all lives equally, bringing them up without the slightest partiality.

## 137.

If a true man takes on the qualities of God, all lives will bow to him in respectful worship. He will be a father to all lives, and doing the duties of God, he will be a son to God. For such a man, patience is his body and *sabūr,* or inner patience, is his heart.

## 138.

*Shakūr,* the contentment and thankfulness for whatever God gives, is the real prayer of your life.

## 139.

*Tawakkul,* the surrender of everything to the will of God, is man's true wealth. When one gives all responsibility to God, he will receive the greatest wealth of his life.

## 140.

Saying that all praise belongs only to Allah, *al-hamdu lillāh,* is the direct prayer to God, when one has handed over his life to God. It is his prayer and his worship.

## 141.

Do not cling to your monkey mind
Expecting it to guide you along the path.

The monkey of the mind mimics what it sees. Those are its pranks. It will desert you in the middle of a dark jungle and climb up a tree while you become prey to dangerous animals of ignorance and to dreadful ghosts, demons, and satans.

## 142.

Do not attempt to cross a lake
By holding the tail of a buffalo.

It will lie down in the mud when it gets to the middle, and because you will be unable either to go forward or to come back, you will drown.

## 143.

Do not attempt to cross a jungle
Holding on to the tail of a tiger,
Hoping the tiger's strength
Will provide you with protection.

As soon as it becomes hungry, it will turn around and eat you. The tiger is the jealousy that grows from your mind. It will eat you, and then you will be unable to cross the dark jungle of ignorance which is your life.

### 144.

Do not hold on to the tail of an elephant
To find a path through the jungle.

Trees and shrubs and stones all give way to the elephant. But a tree that bends for an elephant will spring back and kill you after the elephant has passed, and the shrub's thorns which give way to an elephant will whip back and tear your body.

The elephant stands for the frenzied fury of arrogance. There are three kinds: one, the arrogance which arises from what the eyes see; two, the arrogance which arises from the brain and from what the mind conceives; and three, the arrogance which arises from the sexual fluids.

These are the three kinds of arrogance in *māyā;* they can hypnotize man's wisdom and alter his state. The frenzy of these three kinds of arrogance form the rutting elephant of the mind. Wherever it travels in the jungle, it tears out a path for itself. Do not follow it. That path is not for you.

O man, it can kill your wisdom, your truth, your good qualities, your good thoughts, your faith, and your devotion to God. It can ruin your life. Do not follow a rutting elephant.

Use your wisdom, find the opening on the path of truth, walk along it, and escape from the dark jungle of ignorance.

### 145.

Do not preach wisdom
To one who lacks wisdom
And faith in God.

Your wisdom will not enter him; it will be transformed into a dangerous weapon which will turn on you and attack you.

### 146.

Do not cast pearls before swine
Swine do not know the value of pearls.
Do not cast the treasures of God
The treasures of wisdom and truth
Before a man who is filled with suspicion
Or one without faith in God.
Such a man will destroy what is good.

## 147.

Snakes may appear beautiful and graceful, with pleasant colors and scents, but it is not wise to capture one and bring it up. No matter how beautiful it seems, it has poisonous fangs. If you wrap it around your body, it will display its poisonous qualities and you will die.

If you really want to rear a snake, catch it, hold it carefully, and remove its four poisonous fangs. Then you might escape its poison. But even then its qualities will not change; it will continue to hiss and bite. Even when its poisonous teeth have been extracted, you must not handle it carelessly, for it has other teeth with mild poison which can also be dangerous.

In the same way, no matter how beautiful and loving a human poisonous snake is, he still has the four qualities of arrogance, pride, jealousy, and treacherous self-interest. You must not embrace him or carry him on your body for the sake of his beauty. You will suffer if you do. However, if you first take away his evil qualities as you took out the snake's teeth, replacing them with God's love and wisdom, you may be able to embrace and carry him safely if you remain cautious. That would be beneficial to both of you.

## 148.

Do not preach wisdom to a man whose heart is so obstinately hard that it will not soften or melt in feeling for others. He will be unable to understand your true worth and the maturity of your wisdom. Your wisdom will not penetrate him; he will convert it into a hard rock and hurl it back at you. Not only that, he will pick up the black rocks from the mountain of his heart and throw them at you too. As a result, you may have to face many tribulations. If you want to achieve mastery over your life, you must learn to avoid such people and go on your way.

## 149.

O man, do not intend harm to others
Or it will cause untold harm to you.

## 150.

O man, do not dig a deep pit

In another man's life,
Trapping him
And treating him as an enemy,
Or that same pit will swallow you.

### 151.

Do not strew thorns along the paths
Where good and wise men walk
Or one day those thorns will puncture you.

### 152.

O man, do not be vain, thinking that you are the most learned, that no one else has learned as much as you. Realize that there is One who is learned to the learned and mighty to the mighty. Realize that there is an eternal God who is good to the good.

If you fail to do so, some day, just as a mighty elephant can trip over a tiny blade of grass, all your learning can be destroyed by an ant-sized particle of the force of the karmic ignorance of illusion. It is possible to be destroyed by even an atomic fraction of the force of that *māyā,* and all your learning would be lost.

### 153.

O man, no matter what you have studied or how much you have studied, do not follow the ways of your mind with conceit in your learning. Ask a man of wisdom who is on the path and follow his directions. If you do not meet a man of wisdom, lay your heart open and ask even a tree or a wall. The power of God within your heart called conscience will caution you and guide you. It will say, "Go," or "Don't go," "Right," or "Wrong." If your heart is open, your conscience will provide useful fruit which will benefit your journey through life.

### 154.

"Do not set foot on a doorstep where you, your maturity, your wisdom, and your qualities are not recognized and respected. That would not be good for you," said the sheikh to his eldest son, the eldest in maturity of wisdom among the sons in whom he is fostering the growth of wisdom. "If you do not allow your foot to touch that doorstep, you will benefit ten millionfold."

### 155.

Then the sheikh said, "My son! Do not eat in a house which does not welcome you and feed you with an open heart. To refrain from this will reward you ten millionfold."

### 156.

The sheikh continued, "My son, there are those who live with you, join and play with you, but speak not what is in their hearts. To live your life avoiding their company will benefit you ten millionfold."

### 157.

Finally the sheikh said, "However, my son, if you accept even a glass of water offered from the inner love of one with an open and melting heart, you will benefit the thirty millionfold mentioned earlier and a further ten millionfold. Then you will be able to offer that bounty as comfort to the heart of the person who gave with such love."

### 158.

My son, your whole life can be contained in two words: *al-hamdu lillāh* and *tawakkul-'alallāh,* giving praise to God for everything and absolute trust in and surrender to God. Say, *"Al-hamdu lillāh,"* and praise God for what is happening now. Say, *"Tawakkul-'alallāh,"* and give the responsibility to God for what is to happen at the next moment. May you perform these two duties in the same non-attached state as God does His duties.

Make your life complete in these two words. After that, acquire the qualities of God, perform His actions, act with His conduct, coax His compassion into your heart, and feel all hunger as your own hunger and all illness as your own illness. Serve other lives and comfort their hearts in the way God does. That duty will become your exalted wisdom, your prayer, and your meditation.

### 159.

Dispel disease with the wisdom of grace
And old age will be overcome.

Disease is like the flourishing fruit on the tree which grows from the seed of arrogance, karma, and the illusion called *māyā*. The shoot germinates from the shell of love for land, women, and gold. The tree is the passionate frenzy of arrogance, and its branches are the six evils: lust, anger, miserliness, obsession, bigotry, and envy. The four hundred trillion, ten thousand flowers and fruits which grow on these branches are the worries, desires, cravings, thoughts, and intentions of man's agitated mind.

Day after day, these are the illnesses which make him suffer the pain of a living death. In his agony, man groans and wails, clinging to that very tree in hope of relief. Time after time, he eats of its fruits, expecting them to comfort him. This is the tree that cuts away a man's life.

If he digs it up, roots and all, and throws it away, then everything connected to it will leave him. On that day, illness and aging will leave him, and he will acquire the light of wisdom. When wisdom dawns, he will become a youth of sixteen. He will receive the qualities and beauty of God, and thus acquire eternal youth.

### 161.

If you dispel old age
You can attain eternal youth.

### 162.

Dispel the poverty of the mind
With the wisdom of the heart
And acquire the endless wealth of God.

### 163.

Dispel the visions of the eyes
And see the beauty of the Creator.

### 164.

Dispel the visions of the mind
And see the resplendence of the Ruler.

### 165.

Dispel karma with wisdom
And hell will recede on its own.

### 166.

Eliminate the primal qualities
Of arrogance, karma, and *māyā*
And His grace will appear within you.

### 167.

Control the tongue
And receive the goodness of God.

### 168.

Speak with the tongue of absolute faith
And all lives will praise you.

### 169.

When you realize yourself,
Within you, you will see
All the lives of the world,
And within the lives of the world,
You will see your Ruler.

### 170.

Dispel the outer sound
And you will hear the inner sound.

### 171.

Dispel the agitation of the mind
And you will see the One who is
The mystery of your victory in life.

### 172.

Dispel desire for gold
And receive the limitless wealth
Of the gem of the grace of God.

173.

Understand the five,
Earth, fire, water, air, and ether,
And you will know the One.

174.

Open your heart and look within. Use your wisdom to beat
and chase away the poisonous qualities created from the five
senses. Then you will see only His beauty and the praise called
*al-hamdu lillāh*.

175.

Make the flower of your *qalb* bloom,
The flower of your innermost heart,
And know the fragrance of grace within it.

176.

Stop useless talk
And the ears of your wisdom will hear
God's words of grace.

177.

Using your divine analytic wisdom, open and understand the
nine openings in your body and eliminate what is in each of
them. You will then see two other gateways within you, the *'arsh*
and the *kursī*.

The *'arsh* is the station of the throne of Allah's sovereignty. The
*kursī* is the station of the explaining wisdom called the *Qutb (Ral.)*.
It is the eye of *gnānam*, or divine wisdom, in the center of the
forehead through which you will see and understand all the
universes.

178.

When you understand yourself
Then you will know the equality
Which is the birthright of all lives.

### 179.

One who knows himself will rule his mind.

One who overcomes the earth will overcome his death.

One who kills the intoxication of his lust for women will overcome all worldly fascinations.

One who cuts off his fascination for gold will overcome the karma of birth and death.

One who knows his real home will overcome all the karma and accidents which will come in his life.

One who searches for goodness will take on the qualities of his Lord.

One who understands truth will show only love and compassion to all lives.

One who understands Allah will utter with his wisdom the resonance of "*Illallāhu,* You are Allah," with every breath.

One who knows perfect faith, *īmān,* will lead a life of nobility.

One who knows his base desires will eliminate the egoism of the 'I'.

One who opens his wisdom will lose himself in Allah.

Anyone who knows all of the above will exist as a *mu'min,* a true believer, in all three worlds. *Āmīn.*

### 180.

Dispel the drunkenness caused by intoxicants
And you will understand
The splendor of man's good conduct.

### 181.

Excess desire causes the stupor of intoxication
Excess speech leads to one's own destruction
Even nectar in excess is poison.
But if a man uses his wisdom
To keep everything within limits
His life will be exalted.

### 182.

Know the subtle secret of your creation
And you can achieve liberation.

## 183.

In Allah's creation, there is the secret and the manifested form, *sirr* and *sifāt,* and right and wrong, *khair* and *sharr.* A man of wisdom must realize the difference between them and analyze them with divine analytic wisdom, which is the power of the *Qutbiyyat.*

> *Sirr* is secret and unseen.
> *Sifāt* are all the visible creations.

When we analyze the *sifāt* and go inward, we see the glory of Allah and say, "All praise is to God, *al-hamdu lillāh!*"

> *Sharr* is the action.
> *Khair* is the fruit of the action.

Both good and evil are parts of the body: *khair* is what is acceptable to *īmān,* to perfect faith; *sharr* is what we must discard. If we reject the evil and accept the good, placing it within *īmān,* if we eat food that is *halāl,* or permissible, accept only what is *khair,* and act accordingly, we will resplend as *mu'mins,* as true believers in life as well as in death.

We must realize this with our wisdom. *Khair* and *sharr* are in Allah's responsibility. Our wisdom must know the difference, take what is right, act on it, and praise only Allah with *al-hamdu lillāh.*

## 184.

If you dispel your ignorance
And search for wisdom
You can reach the resplendence of God.

## 185.

If you kill the fanaticism of arrogance
You can reach the good path
And be a friend to all God's creations.

## 186.

If you understand peace of mind with wisdom
You will know the utter peacefulness of God.

## 187.

If you overcome your attachments with wisdom

You will earn the grace of God
And the love of all lives.

### 188.

Perform your duty to all lives
Without favoritism
And it will become the duty that God performs
Toward all His creations.
Act without expecting a reward
And you will receive the rewards of God.

### 189.

Tie up the monkey mind with wisdom
And receive God's crown of divine wisdom.

### 190.

The mind was formed by the pressure between the earth and the air. The monkey of the mind came from the intensity of the pressure within the mind. From that monkey came the antics and the pranks by which the monkey imitates what it has seen. It is not capable of doing anything it has not already seen.

O man, because the monkey mind arises from the pressure between earth and air, it will never die; it will live as long as man exists, as the pressure within everything that is created in form. This is why it is called everlasting and is given the name Ānjanēhan.

There is not just one monkey, there are seven hundred million monkeys. There are hordes of them—black, white, yellow, red, large, and small. The monkey mind exists as a pressure in one small part of man, as well as in every creation. It will grab only what it has seen, that which has been created in form. It will not try to catch what it has not seen. Since God has no form, the monkey mind has not seen Him. We can never show God to the mind, and therefore the mind can never be made to embrace Him.

O man, reflect on this. Although this monkey is a tiny particle within you, it contains seven hundred million pranks through which all the monkeys have banded together to tease you and turn you into one of them. Before that happens, we must overcome the monkey. And since the monkey mind will not embrace God, we must devise another method.

Because monkeys can do only what they have seen, if we place a large mirror before them they will see their own reflections and begin to imitate every one of their own actions. They will grin, laugh, cry, and try to grasp their own images, thinking they are seeing their own kind. They will become so engrossed with the reflections of their actions that they will forget you and leave you alone. Gradually, without food or water, they will grieve, waste away, and die.

The mirror is the power of wisdom which explains, known as *Qutbiyyat,* or divine analytic wisdom. If you place it in front of the monkey mind, the monkey will be kept occupied by grief over its inability to catch its illusory companions, and you can escape to freedom.

But until you place the mirror in front of it, you can never escape. No matter how much you preach to that monkey, it can only do what it has seen. No matter how much you preach about God or the fear of God, it cannot understand because you can never show it God.

You can control the mind only by keeping it occupied with the mirror of wisdom. There is no other way. It is impossible to overcome it because it contains so many millions of monkeys and tricks.

There are monkeys like human beings and human beings like monkeys, and both should be dealt with in the same way. If you want to escape from them, you must go to a place that they have never seen. That is the only way.

191.

Dispel the dreaming of the mind
And see the radiant wisdom
Of the beauty of the soul.

192.

The sheikh says: My son! You must reflect on the life into which you have come. Everything you see is a transient, impermanent dream of your mind. Do not bring your dream into your thoughts and hold on to the things you see, for you will not take them with you when you leave.

Think of that One whom you were holding on to when you

came to this world. You brought only one treasure with you at that time. Seek to take back only that one treasure and discard everything else. Reflect on this with wisdom.

> It's all false!
> It's all a dream!
> It's all crazy!
> It's all gone!
> It's all right!
> Let's see what's next.

My son! We must return with the same treasure we brought with us when we came here. Throw away everything else. We must try to stabilize our lives so that we can go back to Him in the same way we came from Him. We brought only Him and we must take only Him when we go. Understand this, my son.

### 193.

Understand the thoughts of the mind
With the wisdom which transcends
Intellect and reason
And you will know both good and evil.

### 194.

With wisdom, trust only the One
And you will see Allah,
The Indestructible One,
And the one family of Adam *(A.S.)*
Which is our family.

### 195.

Do not live your life
By trusting in the world.
The world will surely deceive you.

Live your life trusting only that One. He will support you with His hands and lift you out of any danger which may threaten you.

### 196.

Believe in and act with absolute truth
And you will attain eternal life.

197.

My son! Truth will win
But truth can also kill.

If you follow God's path of truth, you will overcome all the forces and energies in the three worlds. However, if you stray from the path of truth, the truth can kill you.

If you understand this and hold on to truth as your eternal help in life, you will receive that help. Your life will be the eternal life of God and your duty will be the duty He performs.

198.

Understand the ideas of the mind
Filter them with wisdom
And, with clarity,
Take in only the goodness
And reach the canopy of God's grace.

199.

My son! A household is ruled by a true heart. The house of the heart is ruled by the chaste wife who represents the qualities of God.

Gold is ruled by the deceitful wife who is the evil qualities of the mind. Gold is impermanent, and so is falsehood.

Use your wisdom to realize who is ruling you, and you will not want for anything in this world, nor will you face any suffering.

200.

Try with wisdom to catch
And tie up the wandering mind
And you will know the explanation
Of the unique birth of man.

201.

A tree is shaken by the wind. Gales can blow it down or uproot it. A tree can also be destroyed by fire.

Similarly, my son, the eternity of your existence is threatened by the gales of your base cravings, the storms of your mind, and the fire of the anger of your arrogance. They can uproot your life and destroy it in the same way a gale can uproot a tree, in the same way that fire can burn it.

Therefore, just as the taproot of a tree planted deep and firm gives it stability, you must plant the taproot of *īmān*, the taproot of faith, certitude, and determination in God, to give stability to your life. Give Him the praise of *al-hamdu lillāh* and surrender to His will, saying, *"Tawakkul-'alallāh,* it is all Your responsibility." Develop the coolness of *sabūr* and *shakūr* to quell the fire of your anger and the gales of your desires. Then they cannot injure or destroy you.

202.

Act with the qualities of God<br>God's qualities are His kingdom.

203.

My son, do not wander here and there to meditate and search for God. Look at a crane as it stands patiently for six or eight hours at a time, waiting to catch a fish. See how subtly it stands motionless on one leg, folding its wings, so that even its shadow is controlled. It does this because it is hungry.

Similarly, if you have a selfish desire or a selfish motive for your meditation, whether you meditate in the forest or in the desert, your state is no different from that of a crane. Does the crane attain wisdom, heaven, or *gnānam* by standing motionless on one leg every day of its life? One day it will die. In the same way, man also succumbs when trouble or danger comes.

My son! Reflect on this and take on God's qualities. God and God's kingdom exist within those qualities. You must be like the lotus leaf that does not retain water on its surface even though it dwells in water. You must live in the midst of the hunger, illusion, and joys and sorrows of the world without holding them within you. If you can stand alone like the lotus leaf, worshiping and merging in a detached state with the One who has no attachment, you will attain an exalted state in your life.

If you understand this and act accordingly, the kingdom in which you live will be God's kingdom, He will dwell where you dwell, the words you speak will be His words, and your breath will be His breath. You must understand this.

204.

With wisdom, beat and correct
The thieving tendencies of the mind.
Once those qualities are eliminated, you will dwell in a resplendent palace of grace.

205.

My son! The rat makes a noise when it runs, but when a cat is stalking a rat it walks stealthily, without the slightest sound.

In the same way, when the thieving mind and desire set out to capture something, their evil qualities of doubt, jealousy, deceit, scheming, and treachery move softly and silently, like a cat, to kill the good things and faith in God. Have you observed the cunning nature of the cat? It looks innocent but moves furtively.

The cat will rub against and mew at anyone. But have you noticed its qualities when it sets out to kill? In just this way, one whose mind has the qualities of the cat may show signs of affection outwardly, but inside he has the quality of wanting to kill. You must take heed. Be extremely cautious. See that these qualities do not form within you.

The cat of the mind is two-faced: affectionate on the outside, murderous on the inside. Do away with both of these qualities. Beat them away with your wisdom. Both the scheming and the pretense of love are qualities which seek to kill.

Some people with human faces have these qualities. The two-legged cat-men are the same as the four-legged cats. Beware! Use your wisdom to prevent these qualities from invading you, and you will see the state of equality and God's grace which comforts all lives.

206.

Kill anger with wisdom
And sin will leave by itself.

207.

My son! We are human beings, are we not? In the subtle life of man there are five things which must be remembered:

1. *Resentment is an enemy to wisdom.*
2. *Impatience eats up wisdom.*

With wisdom, throw away both of these evil forces.

3. *Anger is the guru of sin.*

If a gas emanates from the fire of hell, it contains such force that it can burn a man's face, or even kill him. Even if we could endure the smell of hell, the heat of the gas would kill us.

Like this, anger is a compressed gas which emanates from the hell of our bad qualities. It will destroy anyone it strikes or anyone who contains it. Prevent this gas from rising. Use the resplendent wisdom of grace to completely incinerate that place called hell, so that the fire of anger cannot rise.

How should we destroy anger? Anger is like an elephant in heat, which can be controlled only by a sharp goad used on its ear. Similarly, pierce your anger with the goad of wisdom and make it cry in pain, instead of allowing it to make you cry in pain.

4. *Lust is greater than the ocean.*

The sensual love that comes from the mind is vaster than an ocean. Mind itself is an immense ocean of illusion, but if you love anything with the mind, that love is even more immense than the ocean of illusion. Use your seven levels of wisdom to reduce that ocean of sensual love to the size of an atom. Set it on fire with resplendent wisdom and reduce it to a mere particle, the particle of truth, of God.

5. *Duty is greater than God.*

Since He has no form, no wife, and no children, God is free of suffering. It is easy for Him to perform His duties. But if you perform God's duties while existing in the vast ocean of illusion, your duty is greater than God's. If you realize this, you will realize the state in which you are God's secret and your secret is God. You will see and reach God's kingdom within yourself and your kingdom within God.

208.

Make your patience grow,
Preserving it in the treasury
Of absolute faith,
And receive the undiminishing wealth
Of a truly human life.

209.

Know the seed of birth
And then you will know
The compassion and will of God.


210.

With your wisdom, understand
The germination of your conception.
Then you will understand the three times: the past, present,
and future; or the world of the soul, this world, and the next.


211.

Understand the heart
Which is made of the five letters,
*Alif, lām, mīm, hā', dāl,*
Then you will understand
The horoscope of the body
Which is made of the five elements,
Earth, fire, water, air, and ether.


212.

If you discriminate with divine wisdom, you will know the
explanation of the houses of the twelve planets of the body, its
death, the end of its existence, and the conditions and systems
governing it.


213.

If you can destroy lust, then the sensual pleasures of *māyā,* or
illusion, and the qualities of arrogance within you will die, and
Allah's resplendence and His actions will appear.


214.

If you know the depth and length of man's life, you will know
how to cross the bridge of hell in your life. In order to discover
this, join a perfected man, an *insān kāmil.* He will show you the
way to cross over not only the hell in life, but also the hell which
may be yours on Judgment Day.

## 215.

Act with unfailing human justice and conscience, and you will become a representative of God and a friend to all mankind.

## 216.

My son,
Do only good
Speak only good
Speak only the truth in your life
Live in good conduct
Speak only wisdom
Give only love to all lives
Praise only God
Worship only God
Always live only with Him.
This will be the triumph of your life.

## 217.

Make God's justice into your justice
Make God's qualities into your qualities
Make God's actions into your actions
Make God's conduct into your conduct
Let your love be God's love for all
Make God's patience into your patience
Make God's intentions the intentions
    in your life.

In this way, your life will attain its completion. You will be a tree of peace, giving fruits containing the nectar of grace that will soothe the hunger for wisdom in your fellow beings.

## 218.

Know, understand, and study with wisdom and truth the words of all religions, then the differences and divisions among men will be destroyed. If you understand this, you will see God and the entire family of mankind in unity within you.

## 219.

My son, satan is the one who separated man from God, and

70

the evil qualities within man have separated man from the one family of mankind.

If you understand this with your wisdom and cut away the qualities which separate one man from another, you will never be separate from the family of man, nor will you ever be separate from God.

220.

My son, God has decreed for man a thing called death. It is the state of the manifestation of creation, or *sifāt.*

God also has placed within man something called the secret, the *sirr,* which is man's eternal life.

If a man understands the *sirr,* he has conquered the *sifāt,* death. One who has conquered death will exist as the *dhāt,* as the essence of God's grace.

Death is an illness. God has placed death in man so that through it man can come to understand the *sirr.* One who understands this illness and discovers the *sirr* attains a state of eternal life. One who does not understand the illness and fails to discover the *sirr* attains the state of death.

If you know and understand the *sirr, dhāt,* and *sifāt,* you can live forever, can you not?

221.

The sheikh says: O son, if you are to understand something, you must think about the cause within the cause and the thought within your thought. When you look at something, you must open the vision within your vision, the scenes within the scenes, and the wisdom within wisdom. When you look at prayer, you must understand and perform with wisdom the prayer which is within prayer. If you are to love, you must understand the love within love.

O son, if you are to study, you must first understand the learning within learning and then learn. If you are to eat, you must start by understanding the taste within the taste and then eat. Like this, the clear study of wisdom consists of understanding what is within everything you perceive and then finding the explanation.

If you understand with clarity, Allah alone will be within all you learn and all you see. The one God is the point. If you find that point, you will praise only Him; you will not see or praise anything else.

My son, learn and gain clarity with your wisdom.

### 222.

The sheikh says: My son, the world finds it easy to go around saying, "Karma, karma," but you must reflect on this with your wisdom.

God has given all His wealth to man—hell and heaven, good and evil, and all His qualities. If man realizes this through his seven levels of wisdom, accepting and doing what is good while rejecting evil, there will be no karma for him. Only the resplendence of grace will dwell within him.

How is this? When clouds obscure the moon, not allowing its light to emerge, that is the moon's karma. But the moment the clouds disperse, we see only radiant light.

Like the clouds, your karma is the thing that obscures the light of your wisdom. If wisdom can make its resplendent light emerge, scattering the clouds and darkness, there will be no more karma because darkness and shadows are karma. When wisdom resplends without shadow as a complete light, karma will automatically recede. Then there is no longer any karma, there is only completeness.

You must realize what karma is. Karma is thought, the veil of thought which obscures wisdom just as it covered your embryonic form. If the light of wisdom attains completion, karma is driven away. Understand this and act accordingly, and you will shine as a true believer, a *mu'min,* as the brilliant light of the sun to the world. Then neither karma nor darknesses will affect you.

### 223.

Act with and cherish good conduct
And your beauty will become
The radiant beauty of God,
Revealed in your face and in your heart.

### 224.

The ignorant thoughts of doubt
Must be dispelled from wisdom

In order that you may see
Tranquillity and peace in your life.

### 225.

The sheikh says: O son, with wisdom you must understand the treasure of peace in your life. Listen.

Do not ever give room to the thought of hurting anyone. The idea of killing or hurting any life must be dispelled from within you.

No matter what duty you perform, do not seek the help of others in return. Do not expect to receive a reward. Do selfless duty in an unattached way. In every duty, give up the thought that you are doing it. Instead, act with the thought that God must do it, give Him the responsibility, and then perform the duty. Even your intentions must be surrendered to God.

In your vision, action, thought, and wisdom, look at God first. Place Him before you in your life and follow Him. Act with God's qualities.

These will give peace and tranquillity to life. If you make these points firm and certain in your wisdom, if you realize them and act accordingly, all lives will trust you and love you and all lives will pay obeisance to your qualities.

### 226.

For the waves of the mind
In the ocean of illusion
Make a shore of divine analytic wisdom
And the waves, tides, and gales will cease.

The complete and perfect resplendence of the hundred beautiful names of the *Asmā'ul-Husnā* of Allah will be known and understood within your perfect faith. That resplendence will resonate within your innermost heart and radiate vibrantly within your wisdom, openly revealing bliss within the beauty of your face.

You will see the exaltedness of your life; you will see the treasure which causes all the lives of the world to have love for you.

### 227.

O son, what have you come here to learn? You have come to study your story, the story of God, and the story of all creation. Together, these stories form a huge book. Make that book your cage, your house. Make that house into your university, a universe-city filled with the shows and arts of the eighteen thousand universes.

The arts are made into *kalais,* games. The *kalais* are all made into examples. The examples are made into creations. Each creation has been made to move and speak. God has created their countless languages, qualities, colors, and fragrances.

All creations—the creations of the oceans, the creations of the lands, the moving things and the non-moving things, the speaking things and the non-speaking things—God has made them all the mystery within the mystery, the secret within the secret, the wisdom within the wisdom, and the heart within the heart.

God has sent you here to understand this, to know yourself, to know your story, and to understand the story of your Creator. Therefore, you are the book, you are the story. The storybook and the university are within you. If you read, understand, and study this book carefully, that will become the mastery within your university learning, and you will attain the victory of the kingdom of God.

228.

Do not look at the world,
Praising and blaming it.
Look at yourself and you will discover
What praise and blame really are.

It is mind and desire that praise and blame you.
Discover this with wisdom
Chase them both away
And then you will be free.

In that state
If you look at yourself deeply
If you look at who you are
You will know the Chieftain who created you.

If you see the Chieftain
You will become the Chieftain.
If you become the Chieftain
You will stand in prayer and worship Him.

Then the learning and prayer of your life
Will be fulfilled and become complete.

### 229.

The sheikh says: O son, do not attack your neighbors and those who were born with you. Do not separate yourself from them, seeing them as separate from yourself.

Instead, attack with wisdom the dog of desire, the monkey mind, and the arrogance, karma, and *māyā* which attack you. They are the things that need to be separated. This is the real battle and the real way to wage war. Fight these internal enemies and separate yourself from them with divine analytic wisdom.

Love your neighbor as yourself. If you attack within yourself what is attacking both you and your neighbor, you will reach peace and tranquillity in your life. Then you and God and those who have been born with you will live together in a paradise of peace in this very life. Such is the state of the duty and service which Allah performs.

Son, know this and do it.

### 230.

Do not be jealous, or *porāmay,* of any other life. Day by day, jealousy will grow into a huge turtle, a *perumāmay,* in your mind, and make you suffer a lingering death. Be extremely careful.

Take that turtle out of yourself, throw it back into the ocean of illusion, and you will have peace.

### 231.

Do not be proud.
Your pride will impoverish your life
And kill it
And the wealth of God's grace
Will not come to you.

### 232.

Do not believe in worldly miracles.
Wisdom will laugh at your foolishness
Because the world and all its miracles
Will perish one day.

## 233.

O son, you must think with wisdom. The world and God's creations are miracles. All lives have certain abilities. All lives, from the crawling ants to the walking four-legged beasts and the flying birds, from the nine kinds of gems and gold hidden in the earth, from the trees, shrubs, and bushes to the sun, moon, and stars—all visible things have certain abilities. They act according to their qualities and they display their qualities according to their actions.

If the abilities of the various animals are examined, it can be seen that no matter whether a man flies in the sky, no matter what he controls, no matter what he walks on, even if he walks on water, he is only doing what small creatures can do.

These are not man's miracles. God is man's miracle. If man is to be a miracle, he must be one who gives grace with God's qualities, doing duty for all lives. Such qualities will make all of creation bow to him in respect. The sun, moon, stars, earth, fire, water, air, and ether—all of them will bow in respect, worshiping his qualities and actions. That is the only true miracle for man. The other miracles are performed by the illusion of *māyā,* and demons, ghosts, and animals.

Son, if you know this you will bow to Him and conduct yourself with His actions. That itself is the miracle of your life, the miracle which man can perform. It is the only real miracle.

## 234.

Correct your own heart before you attempt to correct your neighbor.

## 235.

Correct your own mind before you attempt to correct another.

## 236.

Correct the cage of your body before you attempt to correct the people of the land.

## 237.

Correct yourself before you attempt to correct the world.

### 238.
Teach yourself before you attempt to teach the city.

### 239.
Talk to your heart about right and wrong and obtain clarity before you tell the world what is right and wrong.

### 240.
Write the story of your own birth and actions, studying the right and wrong in them, before you write a book about the world.

### 241.
One who studies too much music spoils the meaning of the song. A writer who has learned too much spoils the paper on which he writes.

### 242.
One who wastes his time looking at the world ruins the body given to him in this birth because he does not attempt to discover his true state.

### 243.
One who wastes his time decorating and beautifying the countryside forfeits the resplendent beauty of the cage of his body.

### 244.
One who seeks the praise and titles of the world loses his title to the divine analytic wisdom of *gnānam*.

### 245.
One who searches for beauty in the faces of others forfeits the beauty of his own face.

### 246.
One who laughs at faults in the hearts of others, failing to inquire into his own faults, will grieve when he faces his own judgment.

### 247.

One who laughs at the world forgets that the world is laughing at him.

### 248.

One who feels pride and honor, thinking he is saving the world, has forgotten to overcome his death by cutting away his birth.

### 249.

One who carries a lamp to light the darkness of the townspeople forgets the lamp that will dispel the darkness of his own life.

### 250.

One who sets out to help the world cross the jungle has forgotten the help of the One who will guide him through the jungle of his own life.

### 251.

One who cries, unable to rule his puny mind, nevertheless seeks to rule the whole world.

### 252.

One who trains a wild horse and rides it to earn fame and prizes in the world weeps because he is unable to train the wild horse of his base desires and gallop on it to win the prize from God.

### 253.

One who roams in search of the beauty of women because he is unable to find a way to control the illusory woman of his mind is battered by the winds of *māyā,* just as a dried leaf is flung here, there, and everywhere by the violent winds which arise from deep and turbulent seas.

### 254.

One who casts horoscopes for the world stands confounded by his inability to cast a horoscope predicting his own death.

### 255.

One who gives medicine to the world suffers agony, unable to treat the ailments of the cage of his own body.

### 256.

One who attempts to treat the craziness of the world weeps, unable to find a cure for his own craziness.

### 257.

One who fattens himself by killing and devouring other lives has forgotten to kill the animals which, day by day, are killing and eating him from within.

### 258.

One who sets out to guide the townspeople is dreaming in the darkness of his own life, unable to find his way.

### 259.

One who earns titles to teach the people of the land forfeits his wisdom and stands dazed, unable to teach wisdom to his own mind and desire.

### 260.

One who places his trust in someone who offers to build ships and help people cross the ocean of illusion called *māyā* is like a man holding on to the tail of a buffalo to cross the narrow, muddy river of his birth. When the buffalo reaches the middle, it will lie down, and the man will be drowned in the mud.

### 261.

One who sets out to teach good conduct and wisdom to his neighbor's children is unable to teach good conduct and wisdom to his own children.

### 262.

One who sets out to give peace of mind to the world stands perplexed, unable to teach peace to his own mind.

### 263.

Do not ridicule others. It would be better to think of the actions and state of your mind and ridicule them.

### 264.

Do not think of killing and eating the animals of the world to nourish your own body. It would be better for you to try to kill the animals in your body who live by killing you, eating you, and drinking your blood.

### 265.

Do not look at the races of the world and praise or blame them. If you understand the 'race' and 'color' of your parents' thoughts and enjoyment at the time you were conceived and formed, that would be best.

### 266.

Correct your intellect
And you will know devotion.

### 267.

Perform good duty
And receive the compassion of God.

### 268.

Search for the birthright of your life
And realize its uniqueness.

### 269.

Do not do business with the land.
Do business with the base desires
Within the cage of your body—
Sell them.

### 270.

Do not fight in the world.
Fight your thoughts to the finish
That will benefit your life and wisdom.

### 271.

Do not live believing in your country or your body. It is better to believe in the words, actions, and truth of God.

### 272

Do not think you can feed everyone by destroying the jungle and sowing good crops. You must first destroy the jungle inside you. Drive away the wicked beasts and poisonous animals within and sow the good seed of God's beauty and qualities. The food from that harvest will dispel the hunger and soothe the fatigue of all lives.

### 273.

Mere words are useless. It would be more beneficial for you to bring them into action by doing service.

### 274.

Care for your neighbor
Make his mind peaceful
And your life will grow in splendor.

### 275.

Do not scold or mock others,
For the time will come
When the world will scold
And mock you.

### 276.

Do not look down on others,
For someone is waiting
To look down on you.

### 277.

Do not beat others,
For someone is anxiously waiting
To beat you.

### 278.

Do not steal the property of others,
For someone is waiting
To steal your property.

### 279.

Do not murder another heart,
For the world is awaiting
A time to murder your heart.

### 280.

Do not covet another man's wife,
For someone is desiring your wife.

### 281.

The world is waiting to do to you
Whatever you may do to others.

### 282.

If you perform the duties of God
God stands ready to perform your duties.

### 283.

Satisfy the hunger of others
And your hunger will be appeased
All by itself.

### 284.

Dispel racial differences
And end the wars of separation
Waged in the mind.

### 285.

Make your heart content to accept a life of worldly poverty,
and God's undiminishing wealth of *ākhirah,* His wealth of the next
world, will be yours in completeness.

## 286.

If you bring up a dog in your home, it will be grateful. It will spot the burglars and chase them away. But the dog of desire is ungrateful and might even point you out to the burglars, subjecting you to danger. Therefore, do not bring up the dog of desire within the cage of your body.

## 287.

Do not foster within you
The demon of craving.
It will reduce your life
To a beggarly state.

## 288.

Do not cultivate doubt
It will drive your wisdom out.

## 289.

The five senses live by deceiving you. Understand this with your wisdom and eliminate them.

## 290.

Try to nourish the lives of others
Just as you nourish your own body.

## 291.

Do not seek a friendship with everyone
Do your duty
And seek help and friendship
From only the One.

## 292.

Do not follow the ways
Of your wayward mind.
Seven jewels dwell within you,
The seven levels of wisdom.
Ask the way from them
And follow only their directions.

### 293.

Do not cry about your own suffering
Think of the suffering of others
And cry with a melting heart.

### 294.

Do you see how your body and mind suffer and cry in pain when your body is wounded or falls ill?

Like that, if you realize with your wisdom that you cause the same pain and suffering when you wound or kill another life, even if it is an animal, you will avoid harming or killing other lives.

Your body is made of earth, fire, water, air, and ether. All bodies are made of the same five elements. However, unlike animals you have divine analytic wisdom. If you reflect with that divine analytic wisdom and understand, you will show compassion to other lives. That will be best for wisdom and for your human birth.

### 295.

Do not wander about singing the scriptures for the sake of appeasing your hunger. Wander searching and singing of that state of attainment which will chase away the hunger of the karma of your birth.

### 296.

Do not say everything
That comes to your mouth.
Eventually, it will bring you humiliation and the enmity of the world.

### 297.

Understand well
Before you say anything.
This will bring peace to your life and to the lives of others.

### 298.

Do not bundle up your money
And carry it with you

On the journey of your soul.
Bundle up the qualities of God and take them with you. Then
you will find the path is much shorter.

### 299.

Do not take your bigotry with you
When you go to pray.
Take your loving qualities and the certitude of faith known
as *īmān* to *Allāhu taʿālā Nāyan,* the One who is limitless grace
and incomparable love. You will receive the benefit and reward
from Him.

### 300.

Keep with great care
The precious treasure of patience
In the treasury of your heart
And it will elevate your life.

### 301.

Do not set out to do duty to God
While holding within your heart
The actions of the five dreadful sins,
Intoxicants, lust, theft,
Murder and falsehood.
These five will poison your heart, drag your life down, and
immerse you in the fires of hell.

### 302.

Do not live in anticipation
Of more auspicious times.
When the Angel of Death arrives unexpectedly, all the posses-
sions you have gathered in your birth will be lost.

### 303.

God is not bound by time or season.
Live your life awaiting Him always.
If you can live in that state and conduct yourself in the same way
He does, then since He knows no time, you will not know time;

since He does not die, you will not die; since He does not suffer degradation, you will not suffer degradation. Remember this well.

### 304.

One who trusts God
And has earned His love
May appear insane
In the eyes of the world.

Do not ridicule such a man. If you do, the ninety-six obsessions will drive you truly insane.

### 305.

My son! A *gnāni,* a drunkard, and a crazy man may look the same to the world.

A *gnāni* loses himself and talks only about God in a manner that may seem unintelligible to most. A drunkard stutters in his drunkenness about family and money matters. A crazy man raves about the past, mumbling over the things which made him crazy. Outwardly the clothes and behavior of all three are exactly the same, and the world classifies all three as crazy.

But if you understand with wisdom and analyze with divine analytic wisdom, you will realize the difference.

A *gnāni* loses himself in God and speaks only of God. As soon as your wisdom realizes this, go to him and pay reverential homage, learn what can be learned, and receive from him whatever you can.

### 306.

Just because you have been born a man
Do not become self-satisfied
And fritter away your life.

There are many qualities mingled within you. Transform those qualities, be reborn in God's qualities, and acquire exalted wisdom. Only then will you receive God's grace and wealth.

### 307.

If you have been born a man
Thinking is certainly necessary.

But it will be most exalted in your life to think about your thoughts and correct them.

### 308.

Do not think of destroying the dignity of others. Your own dignity will be destroyed long before that can happen.

### 309.

My son, do not intend to ruin others. It will result in worse destruction to yourself.

### 310.

My son, do not set out to measure the mind of another. If you understand his qualities, you will know. If they are good qualities, put them to good use within yourself.

If a person has evil qualities, avoid him. Do not linger and speak ill of him. The spoken word can be a fault, but an evil thought is a scar imprinted deep within you.

If you find fault with another, the fault will come back to you. When you assume God's duties in performing judgment on another, you become guilty on two counts. First, for finding fault with another, and second, for usurping the function of God. Think of this.

The other man is doing what he came to do. You must also do what you came to do. If you have wisdom you will understand this. If not, find a man of wisdom and learn.

### 311.

Do not think to rule the world
In the state of the 'I'
With the strength of your tongue.

Day after day, the strength of God will crush you, reducing the strength of your tongue and the conceit of your ego.

### 312.

My son, keep only Allah
Forever alive in your heart
And you will never die.

## 313.

My son, do not wear Allah on your head as you would wear a cap. Such a cap will turn into a cast iron helmet and crush your head.

Like this, my son, there are many who enjoy great praise and fame in the world. Instead of truly understanding and nourishing Allah within their hearts, they strut about, proclaiming, "I have studied. I am learned. There is no one greater than I. Look at my beauty and my titles and how I recite the Qur'an!"

Rather than extinguishing their pride, their cravings, and themselves they wear Allah just as they wear their caps. Eventually, they will be crushed. This group is in the majority; only a rare few keep Allah alive in their hearts.

My son! Always see Allah as the wisdom within wisdom. Exist as the qualities within His qualities and as the actions within His actions, conduct yourself within His conduct, and grow as the compassion within His compassion, never deviating from His meanings, words, and actions. Keep Him alive and make Him grow within your *qalb*, your innermost heart. Do this, and you will attain eternal life.

## 314.

My son, the human generation consists of seventy-three groups. Three of them say they have the faith, certitude, and determination in God which is known as *īmān*. Of these three groups, the people in one group say they love land, gold, and women—and also God.

Those in the second group, although they have faith in God, place their trust in themselves, their titles, and their own abilities. They praise themselves and always claim that their actions are correct.

Those in the third group lose themselves, forget themselves, and with bowed heads, worship only God. Offering their very heads into His care, they surrender to Him.

Those in the other seventy groups have the appearance and speech of human beings, but their actions do not conform to their words. They may speak of God, but their thoughts, actions, and behavior belong to satan. They perform the four hundred trillion, ten thousand actions of ignorance which are the 'miracles' and actions of animals. Although the human generation is perfectly pure when it emerges from God, the qualities and actions of these people change when they arrive in the school of the world to study. Therefore, they fail to complete their examinations. Although they come to study their history and the history of God, they give up both and concentrate on studying the history of satan. Ultimately they end up in the hell that was given to satan.

Out of the first three groups, the one which worships God in humble homage reaches God directly without having to face questioning or judgment. The other two groups have to face their verdict on Judgment Day. According to that judgment, they will spend some time in heaven and some time in hell.

May you realize this and remain in that one group without ever straying from it. It is the group of the *mu'min,* the group of true believers.

### 315.

Do not let greed
Overturn and eat the world
Or it will lead the way
To the house that belongs to hell.

### 316.

Do not let the monkey mind,
Your monkey mind of desire,
Turn somersaults in the world.

Fasten the chain of wisdom around its waist and tie it to the unshakable tree of the faith, certitude, and determination known as *īmān.* The monkey will jump up and down, trying to pull itself loose, but finally it will become exhausted and give up.

### 317.

Do not adorn your body
With gold, possessions,
And colorful costumes
For the sake of physical beauty.

One day the body will turn into a corpse and be eaten by the earth. Reflect on this with wisdom and adorn your inner being and your face with the beauty and the qualities of *Allāhu ta'ālā*

*Nāyan,* whose beauty will never perish. Nothing can erode or destroy that beauty.

## 318.

Look within with the clarity of the seven levels of wisdom that are inside you. There you will see Allah. When you see Allah, you will be within Him, and within you will be the ocean of profound knowledge called *'ilm.* All the universes and all of everything will be seen within that *'ilm.* What more could we possibly need?

## 319.

Those who claim to have learned everything in the world know only as much as a handful of earth. Whereas all that has not been learned and all that needs yet to be learned is greater than an ocean without a shore.

If man learns this, examines it with wisdom, and sees that which has no shore, then the ocean of profound knowledge called *bahrul-'ilm,* which cannot be encompassed by the eyes, will be here, there, and everywhere, existing in perfection as one, as one letter, as one God. It will be seen as the plenitude within everything. What else is there, O Father? All the worlds and boundless realms will be there as one, O Father.

Realize this with your wisdom, perceive that resonance, and know the explanation of grace as the heart within the heart, the life within life, the food within food, and the clarity within clarity.

If you see the clarity of the seven levels of wisdom within you, stand within that clarity and look, you will see God within that wisdom, you within God, the *'ilm* within you, and all the universes and all of everything within the *'ilm.* O my Father, what else could we ever need!

## 320.

If that which separates
One man from another
Is separated from man,
Man will be like God
Who treats all equally.

Do not believe in men,
It will be dangerous to you.
But pretend to believe in them,
Pretend and save yourself.

322.

Believe in God
But do not pretend to believe in God.
If you believe in God
His wealth will be yours
But if you try to deceive God
By pretending to believe
You will be entirely deceived,
Bringing degradation to your life.

323.

Little by little use your wisdom to deceive and tie up your mind and the selfish desires known as the *nafs ammārah*. Capture them with your wisdom and keep them under control. You will be a man of wisdom if you succeed.

Do not try to deceive the truth, however. It would be like trying to deceive the fire while you are in the fire.

324.

Do not weep
At the state of the countryside.
Weep at the state of your body.

325.

Do not feel pride in clearing the forest
And planting good crops.

Destroy the dark forest of ignorance in your inner being, or *qalb*. Plant and harvest the good crop of wisdom and share it with all the people, comforting them. Then you will be praised in God's kingdom.

### 326.

Before you preach to others
Preach to yourself
And then to your heart.

Your heart will yield sweet fruit in plenty, and the people of the world who see it will pluck the fruit, eat it, and become peaceful.

No advertisement is necessary. If there is ripe fruit on a tree, parrots will come in search of it.

### 327.

The sheikh says:

My son, if a light appears, the darkness recedes on its own, does it not?
If good qualities are present, beauty comes on its own.
If virtue is present, good conduct comes on its own.
If wisdom is present, understanding comes on its own.
If understanding is clear, faith in God comes on its own.
If faith is present, God will come to you.
If God comes, heaven will come to you.
If heaven comes, the wealth of God's grace will come.
If the wealth of grace comes, then God's love and compassion will come.

In that state, there are no differences and no darkness. If you fill yourself with these good things, everything will be within you.

### 328.

Do not cause hurt to the hearts of others.
Dispel the disease in your heart
Which desires to hurt.
Great benefit will come to you
And bring peace into your life.

### 329.

My son, you need to identify the nature of the poverty which assails man. The false wisdom which causes ignorance is a man's poverty. If he can rid himself of that ignorance and attain wisdom, he will enjoy honor and the wealth of God wherever he goes.

### 330.

My child, think before you speak
One word can win
But the very same word can kill.
If you understand before you speak
And speak with understanding
Peace will come into your heart
And into the hearts of those who listen.

### 331.

You need a source of water to make a farm productive. This can be accomplished by building a dam across a stream. In order to do that, you must first make an estimate of how much water will collect. On the basis of past and present levels, you must estimate future levels. Taking into account the possibility that the dam will burst, you must build it strong enough to withstand the force of the water. If it is likely that the water will sometimes rise above the level of the dam, you must have a system for the water to overflow without causing damage. At the same time, you must have irrigation canals through which adequate water can be let out to the fields. If the estimate is made carefully and the dam is built correctly, the land will flourish, and there will be no poverty or famine.

However, if the dam is not strong enough and if even a tiny hole is allowed to develop, it can enlarge sufficiently to break up the entire dam, and then all the land will be destroyed.

In the same way, my son, our entire life is a vast lake and wisdom is the dam. The built-up shores of the lake are faith, certitude, and determination, and these have to be made very sturdy. No matter what joys and sorrows may come to us in our lives, wisdom must be able to identify anything excessive. All the evil must be allowed to flow away, while the good which is God's good qualities, good wisdom, and good intentions must fill the lake.

With the plenitude of that fullness, man must utilize the dam of his wisdom to comfort and nourish all lives in the land so that they will grow and prosper. This will bring peace and comfort to his life and to all lives.

If, however, a tiny hole of doubt, selfishness, anger, discrimination, conceit, or self-praise appears in the dam, it can gradually enlarge until the dam bursts, ruining man and his entire life and destroying the vast lake of his heart, or *qalb*. It will break up and destroy everything in its path. All will be ruined.

Make sure that a hole does not develop within your wisdom, faith, qualities, actions, or duties, which are God's duties. A hole should not form within your state of equality or tolerance. If you succeed in safeguarding the dam of your wisdom, you will be able to protect the eighteen thousand universes within your *qalb* and all those who dwell within those universes; you will be able to protect the world of the soul, this world, and the next world; and you will have God's wealth of completeness.

Through even one fault, you can destroy yourself and all three worlds. You must reflect on this. You must have the plenitude of *shakūr,* or contentment, within you. Fill your life only with what is good; your life will be exalted, and you will be able to bring comfort to all lives. My child, then you will be victorious in your life.

### 332.

O man, do not decorate your desire, your ignorance, and the darkness of your false wisdom. Adorn your heart with the truth of God. With the treasure of wisdom and the light of perfect faith called *īmān,* adorn your inner heart, the *qalb* which is God's kingdom. That is the beauty of God.

### 333.

My son, do not live believing in others and believing in the world. Resolve to live believing in truth and the one God. That will bring peace to your life, make your mind tranquil, give you the wealth of God's qualities, and make your life complete.

### 334.

O man, do not think you can live believing in the monkey mind, the pranks of the monkey, and the monkey's cage. Try to live believing only in the qualities, actions, and duties of God.

### 335.

My son, do not run around bragging that you have studied fifteen or twenty languages, this many religions, and that many scriptures. Do not brag that you have attained titles or have been appointed as spokesman for a religion, doctrine, or society. Do not take pride in having learned these things and praise yourself. You do not even know how to build an anthill. Think of this a little.

See how the honeybees build a honeycomb. Have you observed their unity? Have you seen the place in which they keep their honey? A tiny honeybee builds such an intricate and beautiful house in which to store its honey. Think of it.

If you are unable to build a house with that kind of unity, if you cannot make honey like a tiny honeybee, what is the use of all your learning? You cannot even do what these tiny creatures do, so what purpose is there in all you have learned and all you have done? Reflect on this.

If you could do at least what these tiny creatures do and develop the beauty of that unity, which is the honey, it would give you victory. If only you could do what these tiny insects do, you could keep your life and every life supplied with sweetness. Realize this.

### 336.

O man, do not cry for the sake of money. Think of the state of this impermanent body and cry. That will benefit you.

### 337.

Do not live believing in horoscopes. The horoscope of your life may end in ruin. Think of the horoscope that death has prepared for the one-week-long life of this body. Again and again, the same week recurs. Try to find the horoscope which will prevent your coming here over and over again. If you can find it, you will escape death and you will never have to come back.

### 338.

My son, this paltry life lasts for only a few days. Do not think of it as real.

There is an eternal life within you and a resplendent body of light for that life, which is the body you brought with you when you came. The body you see now, however, is just a schoolhouse, and you have come to study in it. It is a rented room. God who created you has sent you here to use your inner wisdom to study

His artistic creations and, through this, to know yourself, know Him, and understand all of everything.

Having studied and passed your examinations, you must return to the beautiful body of light in which you came to the world. The moment you change, your lessons and your research in this school will end and you will receive your position in the kingdom of God, the permanent position for your eternal life.

### 339.

Do not bellow, "Thief, thief!"
Slandering God's creations.
Catch and tie up the thief of your mind,
The hungry thief
Who is stealing from you.

The soul hungers for God, crying, *"Pappa,* Grandfather, you are an *Appah,* a Father to me. Can you spare an *appam,* a bun for me, *Pappa?"*

Ask Him who is both the primal Father of your soul, the Grandfather, and the Father who created your soul and nourishes you now. Ask Him for the *appam* of grace that will keep you eternally free of hunger. Then your mind will have no need to steal from the world.

### 340.

O man, do not go about
Finding fault with God.

If you discover the wrongs committed by your mind and desire and correct them with wisdom, you will know who is really at fault.

### 341.

The sheikh says: My son, see how a fish lives and moves in the water. It spends its life swimming up and down, experiencing all its joys and sorrows in the water. But though it can swim from the depths of the ocean all the way up to the surface, if it is caught in a net, it dies.

Now, if a man swims in the ocean, is it so miraculous? After all, even a small fish can do that. On the other hand, if you get caught in the net of illusion, the net of *māyā,* your fate will be worse than it would be for a fish.

Think with the clarity of your wisdom. The ocean of *māyā* has many seas: the sea of magnetic currents, the sea of the mind, the sea of desire, the sea of lust, the sea of passion, the sea of blood, the silver sea of semen, the blue sea of poison, the sea of torpor, the gold sea of fascination for women, the black sea of darkness, and many others.

On the day you can swim across the seas of *māyā* with your wisdom, you will become a man, a messenger of God, and a representative of God, and all lives will respect and pay obeisance to you. This is the miracle of man. Think of it, my son.

### 342.

Control lust
And the karma which torments you
Will go away.

### 343.

My son, if you catch a snake and want to keep it, you must remove its poisonous teeth. Though it may still hiss and strike out at you, it will not be able to harm you.

But do not bring up the frenzied arrogance of anger which is like a poisonous snake. It will strike out at you continually in an effort to kill you—and not only you, but others as well. You will earn the enmity of the world and your life will be in constant danger.

If you pick up that snake of anger with wisdom and throw it away, you will receive only love from all lives.

### 344.

Extinguish with the water of wisdom
The hell-fire arising from arrogance
Otherwise that fire will burn you to ashes
Along with the house in which you live.

### 345.

My son, do not catch and bring up a vulture. Since it preys on dead flesh, you will have to find corpses to feed it.

Similarly, do not bring up the vulturous qualities of ignorance, ambition, and avarice; you will have to kill other lives to keep them fed. Get rid of them and live as a man.

### 346.

With wisdom burn away the greed of your miserliness and show mercy and compassion to all lives. If you share what you have with others, they will be comforted, and seeing their happiness will give you peace and satisfaction.

You did not bring anything with you and you cannot take anything back. If you reflect on this and perform your duty with the realization that your life and other lives are the same, the kingdom of God will be yours.

### 347.

Overcome with wisdom
The cravings of your passion
And know the mysterious beauty
Of God's supremacy.

### 348.

My son, one who plants a fruit tree must water and fertilize it so that the tree will grow. But to whom do the fruits belong? Will the tree eat the fruits? Who will benefit?

The tree gives its fruit to others, to the man who planted and tended it and to everyone. It does not seek enjoyment from its own fruit.

In the same way, my son, God created man as the most exalted being. God raised him, giving food, water, wisdom, good and evil, and everything he needs. Man must reflect on this and utilize the benevolent grace of *rahmat* given to him by God for the benefit of others. Man must give just as a tree gives, without selfish intentions.

Having given to others all that God has bestowed on him, man must give his heart to his Creator. If he gives away all that he has in this manner, he will reach the kingdom of God. If he fails to do so, however, he will end up in the kingdom of hell. Man must think of this with his wisdom.

349.

Kill the ignorance and stupidity
Displayed by man's bigotry
And the tranquillity and peace
Of the qualities of Allah
Will be known within your wisdom.

350.

The sheikh says: Rain falls for everyone. The same rain falls on weeds, grass, bushes, trees, men, and animals. The rain does not fall more abundantly on a good man than it does on a bad man. Everyone experiences it equally. Think of this with your wisdom.

My son, if you are to become a true human being, your actions, qualities, behavior, and the duty you perform must fall like the rain, without partiality. If you are like that, you will obtain the beauty of God's state. This is the duty which *gnānis* and the truly wise perform. Realize this.

351.

Uproot the differences caused by the games played by the five elements of the mind, and throw them away. Then God's qualities, actions, conduct, goodness, love, compassion, and all the duties He performs will grow within you. They will flower, bear fruit, and make all hearts peaceful when they are shared.

352.

My son, peace for the fox is a great loss for the chicken, is it not?

Likewise, when mind and desire say they want peace, what will they do? They will destroy all the goodness in the world. Their peace is to destroy good conduct, modesty, reserve, respect, fear of wrongdoing, patience, the inner patience called *sabūr,* contentment or *shakūr,* trust or *tawakkul,* the praise of God or *al-hamdu lillāh,* and all of God's goodness.

A man must think. For wisdom to be at peace, man must uproot and throw away all that the fox of mind and desire brings to him. If he does throw them away and attains wisdom and God's qualities, all lives will find tranquillity through the peace in his life.

### 353.

Acquire the qualities
Of the actions of God,
And the monkey of the mind will leave
And run away all by itself.

### 354.

When you plant the seeds
Of the qualities of God
In the flower garden of the heart
The flowers of His grace will bloom
And the perfume of the flowers
Will give fragrance and peace to all lives.

### 355.

O son, there is a bird called a falcon. When it takes off in flight it makes a shrill cry like "Keeee! Keeee!" and then it dives down and pounces upon its prey. All the other birds and little animals lie down in fear when they hear that sound.

Like this, my son, if true faith, determination, certitude, and pure wisdom grow within you, the falcon of divine wisdom will fly out and make everything evil within you lie down in fear. Its power and sound and light will make everything in your life lie down in fear. If you train that falcon correctly, nothing can attack you. Think of this.

The divine wisdom of the *Qutbiyyat* is a precious gift given to man for the journey of his life.

### 356.

My son, kill whatever your mind creates and brings to you. Look at it and then advise the mind with wisdom, saying, "Have patience. We will discuss it later and come to a decision." Put it aside for a while, and then throw it into the trash. If you do this repeatedly, the mind will exclaim, "He's an idiot! He throws away everything I bring him," and it will leave you.

If you reach that state, you will attain serenity of mind, God's grace, and peace for your soul.

### 357.

Pull out by the roots and throw away transient pleasures, and the seed of the blissful grace of the greatest happiness will grow.

### 358.

To sit and close your eyes is not meditation. Instead of closing your eyes, first chase away the wild animals of your mind. Then you can meditate.

### 359.

Cut away the earth and look
Your splendor will be known.

### 360.

Instead of performing millions of *pūjās* (the offering of fruits, flowers, coconuts, and incense at the temple) in the hope of receiving liberation for your soul, it is better to do that one prayer which will give you eternal life.

### 361.

My son, it is most essential for those who are *insān,* those who are human beings, to know what God is and believe in Him. God is one. He is without body, form, or shape, without birth or death, and without hunger, disease, or aging. He has no desire for land, gold, or women. He has no wife or children. He has no love for the world or for possessions or property. He has no desire at all. He is a power, the one reality within truth that transcends *āthi,* the very beginning of creation, and *anāthi,* the time before the beginning.

God is the perfect power, the complete power which creates, nourishes, and protects all lives. Within all the four hundred trillion, ten thousand lives He has created, He has placed various energies and occult forces called *shakthis* and *siddhis,* and various qualities and potentialities. Having placed them within His creations, God stands as the power which can control all of the miracles, energies, and forces, the power which can control the sun, moon, stars, earth, fire, water, air, and the illusion of *māyā.* He is the power which can control the angels, jinns, fairies, heavenly beings, prophets, and saints. He brings them under His lone sovereignty and rules them with His power. That is the power which is God.

We who are human beings must clearly understand that power which exists as wisdom within wisdom. We must know it with our seven levels of wisdom. Placing our trust and the certitude of our absolute faith in that power, we must open the house of the *qalb*, which is the heart of absolute faith, invite Him into that *qalb*, and see Him there.

How can man do this? How will man see God in his heart? We need to perform prayer, worship, the remembrance of God known as *dhikr*, and contemplation or *fikr*, which is a higher state of *dhikr*. Finally, we will reach the state in which we die in Him, the state of *Sūfiyyat*. These are the ways to know, worship, and glorify Him within the house of the heart, or *qalb*.

How do we come to know Him? Let us look at an example. If we place a light in a house, the darkness is cast out and we can see everything. Similarly, if we open the house of the *qalb* with the light of divine analytic wisdom and look inside, we can see all the creations, the eighteen thousand universes, the *'arsh* or throne of Allah, the *kursī* or eye of wisdom, the *qalam,* hell and heaven, and the jinns, fairies, angels, and celestial beings. The power known as God controls the countless energies and compels them to turn around and look at Him. He makes them realize that He is the one almighty power. When we have the light which enables us to look within, we can see and know God, that power which controls all things.

We must also try to understand with our wisdom what we can receive from Him and what we can offer to Him. We must receive what is within Him, in His kingdom. What is in His kingdom? His qualities, His actions, His selfless duties, His selfless forms of prayer, His three thousand divine attributes, and His *wilāyats,* or powers. We must receive all of these from Him, gather them into our wisdom, open our hearts, and place them inside. Then we must offer to Him what is His; otherwise He will not come. To offer His qualities to Him and pay obeisance to Him is true prayer. Every man must know this without the slightest doubt. We must pray to Him without considering anything equal to Him. We must surrender to Him, place everything in His responsibility, and make the world we hold onto die in Him.

God has created the human being as the most exalted creation. But most human beings fail to acquire the wisdom to accept Him; they form the majority. Instead, they accept all the creations in the world, all the forms within them. These they accept with their intellects, calling it devotion. They make millions of such forms. They turn each of their qualities into an energy and the actions of those energies into occult forces or miracles. Making their conduct and behavior also into miracles, they create many kinds of gods: earth gods, fire gods, air gods, wind gods, *māyā* gods, sun gods, snake gods, scorpion gods, cow gods, goat gods, gods of darkness, demon gods, vampire gods, ghost gods, and gods of the mesmerism of illusion. The four hundred trillion, ten thousand spiritual forces are made into gods; all the thoughts within them are made into gods. Stones, trees, gold, silver, precious gems, lead, copper, iron, and brass are made into gods. All the qualities of the lion gods, tiger gods, and cat gods are made into idols. They worship those who have died, kings, evil spirits, mendicants, illusions, fascinations, crows and sparrows, vultures and eagles. They make all of these into sculpted idols.

These are their gods. They offer them fruit, coconuts, milk, flowers, gold, silver, beer, brandy, whiskey, gin, arrack, drugs, marijuana, opium, and LSD, all of which are intoxicating. They place these offerings before their gods, pluck all the flowers of the world, and chant countless millions of mantras. They plant their heads in the ground and wave their feet in the air. They bang their heads on rocks and beat their heads and their chests. This is how they make offerings to their gods. They pour milk and honey on the heads of idols. They use oil and ghee and light lamps and candles to give light to gods who have no light. They burn incense and camphor. They slaughter cows and goats, sacrificing life and giving blood and evil to their gods. Thus they make them the gods of their devotion.

They do all these things in order to attain occult powers—to be able to walk on water and fly in the sky, to be able to leave one body and move into another, to rule the world, to acquire titles, and to capture heaven. Those who meditate to acquire boons from the gods they themselves created are in the majority.

But one who is born as a man with the wisdom of a man must understand that all things which are created will be destroyed, that everything created is bound by a time agreement. God uses one creation to destroy another. God has placed every creation in the world under the control of another. He keeps down the force of fire with water. He makes the wind carry the water to distant places. He destroys the earth with earthquakes. He destroys illusion through light. He controls the force of the wind with mountains and trees. In this way, God controls the force of every energy in His kingdom and destroys them according to the agreements which bind them. He controls a snake with a mongoose, a rat with a cat, a bull with a tiger, a chicken with a fox, a dog with a tiger or lion, a monkey with wisdom, and the rutting elephant of arrogance with the goad of resplendent wisdom.

In this way, God has created the six kinds of lives, each to kill and eat the other, each to destroy the other, each to control the other. But without realizing this, man makes deities of the forms and qualities within himself. Carrying them around as his idols, he begins to believe in and worship them. He falls at their feet in worship. He dedicates his wealth, mind, and spirit to them, expecting things in return. Giving them milk and fruit, he asks boons of them. He does everything for them; they do nothing for him. They cannot move, they cannot protect him, they cannot nourish him, so how can they grant him boons?

This becomes his disappointment. He becomes disenchanted. But just as all things made of earth, fire, water, and air are destroyed, he too is destroyed. The very things to which he has dedicated himself have dragged him down to their state. Just as the earth, sun, and moon change, this sort of man takes millions of births. Like the fire and air of the forms he fashioned, he too changes constantly. Colors change, races change, and religions change in the same way; he too changes and becomes subject to many, many births. He has been trying to acquire liberation through the energies from which he was born, but those same energies finally destroy him. Not realizing this, he continues to make offerings to his idols in the hope of receiving grace.

God will come only when man gives up all this and realizes that God does not accept anything except His own qualities. Only if man offers God's own qualities and His own possessions, will God come.

But what does man do instead? To give light to gods living in darkness, he burns candles and lamps. To gods who have no fragrance, he offers incense and then asks fragrance for himself.

Man forgets the ever-fragrant, resplendent one God of compassion and asks for light from his self-created gods. From gods who cannot walk, man asks the boon of being able to walk. What foolishness. What lack of wisdom.

On the other hand, one who offers his heart to obtain the grace of God is a perfected man, an *insān kāmil*. He dedicates his body, mind, and soul to true prayer.

My son, understand this with clarity and pray with wisdom. God will carry you. He will embrace you, summon you to His kingdom, and give you His entire wealth of grace.

My son, tell this to your brothers and sisters. Tell them to seek the resplendent wisdom that will dispel the darkness and to worship the One who is radiant wisdom within wisdom. Offering oneself to God is *pūjā*. To realize that wisdom and to surrender oneself to that wisdom within wisdom, is true prayer.

## 362.

Instead of continually dying and being reborn, taking births a million times over, it is better to bring about the death of the mind which causes you to take these millions of births.

If you do, from that day on you will not be reborn. You will be triumphant in the purpose for which you came to this world, and you will dwell with God forever, without ever leaving Him.

## 363.

Instead of looking for friends, gurus, and sheikhs it is better to search for and find one good man of wisdom who has the qualities of God. This alone will give you mastery over your life.

## 364.

When one looks at the lives in the world, they all seem to be *siddhars* or workers of miracles. Each has some potentiality or energy, some *shakthi*. Each seems able to perform miracles. They all seem like *siddhars* when we look at them through intellect.

But if we look through wisdom, we will see that their forms are changeable. They will die according to the time agreement placed on their lives, and when their form changes they will lose their energies.

If you discern this with divine analytic wisdom, understand

their changeable energies, and throw them away, you will become a devotee of God.

If you take on the qualities and actions of God with divine luminous wisdom and put them into action, then you will be a man of wisdom, a *gnāni* who gives peace and light to the hearts of the people.

### 365.

All the people in the world live as if they have learned everything. You must try to live in their midst with tolerance, without causing or intending pain to any other life. Even though you may not be doing them any good, if you can merely avoid doing evil, you will have a triumphant life.

### 366.

The whole world admires the visions seen by the eyes. Physical visions become your thoughts and your thoughts become your dreams, shadows which no longer exist when you awaken. But though the shadows are gone, the thoughts still exist, do they not?

Only when you have put an end to thought do you become a man. You must know, analyze, and understand with the divine wisdom of the *Qutbiyyat*. That will be most useful to you.

### 367.

The world praises the learned at one time
And blames them at another.
This causes them to die and be reborn.

However, if you acquire that learning which the world does not praise or blame and which cannot be put in writing, you will see that your entire life is a huge book. Your body is that book.

If you study and understand that book, you will not praise or blame the world and the world will not praise or blame you. Neither will you die or be born again. You will praise only the One who deserves praise and achieve contentment and perfect peace.

### 368.

Make the flower of your heart
Flourish and bloom,
Nurturing it with the water

Of the qualities of God,
And look at it through wisdom.
You will see that it is filled with the honey of the *gnānam* of grace. Taste it with your wisdom. You will experience the resplendence and flavor of the nectar of grace.

### 369.

O man, take everything
That mind and desire see and bring to you
And throw it all behind you.
Then you will be able to reach
The beauty of the treasure
Unseen by your mind and desire.

### 370.

My son, no matter what beauty there is in the things you may offer to the gluttonous pig of desire, it will not accept them. The pig likes only what is repulsive and foul-smelling. It does not value good fragrance, wisdom, or other beautiful things. Do not cast pearls before swine. The pearls will be trampled and ruined.

My son, avoid nurturing the pig of your body and taking in its qualities and loathsome food. Do not be a gypsy rearing swine; instead, if you will be a man rearing men, a man doing his duty to men, that will be duty to God. Do this with care and attention, without any thought of attachment or selfish gain.

### 371.

Gather up the inner things
Accumulated by the dog of desire
And throw them all away.
With your divine analytic wisdom, analyze and reject evil. Take what is good, keep it within your heart, and enjoy it. That alone will be useful for the freedom of your soul.

### 372.

Do not waste your time
Roaming through land and forest
Searching for a sheikh.
Open the cage of your body and search within your good qualities.

If you can discover the treasure which shines as the qualities within your qualities, it will lead you to an exalted and perfected man, an *insān kāmil*.

Through the efforts of your faith, *Allāhu taʿālā,* Almighty God, will fulfill your intentions in life. Then, as always, you will say, "*Al-hamdu lillāh,* all praise is to God."

373.

When you came from Allah
The light of your *rūh*
The light of your soul
Was the first to appear.
Next came the seed of conception.
Then illusion and torpor
Mingled within you.
And what will come in the end is death.

O man, if you think with wisdom, you will realize that God is the only One who will come to you after death. With the absolute faith of *īmān,* acquire His qualities. You must think of merging with God. When that happens, you will know the end of your appearance here.

374.

The sheikh says: My child, the past is past. Do not be troubled by what happened before. Ask God's forgiveness for your previous faults and try to acquire good qualities and put them into action.

To see the Good One, we must become good children. To see one who is wise, we must change into children of wisdom. To live with a man, we must live as men. To find a perfected man, an *insān kāmil,* we must be men who have the resplendence of wisdom. If we want to search for and find truth, we must live in truth. If we want to search for Allah, we must seek His qualities, actions, conduct, and intentions, and bring them into action within us. Only then can we reach Him.

375.

Do not be impatient under any circumstances; it will destroy your life. Stop and think, analyze. Act with patience and wisdom, and you will see peace in your life.

## 376.

Before you do something, you should plan it fully, estimating it within your *qalb*, or heart. With the wisdom within wisdom, the thought within thought, and the *qalb* within *qalb*, you must analyze its potential profit and loss, value and danger.

If you estimate properly and then act with wisdom, keeping God in front of you, whatever you set out to do will be completed successfully. If you work as a servant with God as your master, nothing will go wrong. He is the One who knows everything; He will do it perfectly. Do not try to take over His job. If you have the thought that *you* are doing it, you will lose, and lose badly.

## 377.

The sheikh says: My son, electricity can be extracted from water, can it not? A turbine extracts the current and sends it out through a transformer to light the cities and towns in the land.

My son, you are a man, are you not? Just as current exists within the five elements, a truth exists within the five elements that form your body. Use your wisdom like a turbine to extract that truth from the elements in your body, and hand it over to your Creator. He will then supply the current of truth through the 4,448 nerves of your body to illuminate you and all the countries within you. He will adorn the country of your soul and the heavenly kingdom within you, giving you the countless, limitless, imperishable, undiminishing treasures of His three thousand beautiful qualities. He will transform you into the effulgent light which is the completeness of the *Nūr* and the radiance of His ninety-nine *wilāyats*, or powers. God will elevate you to the state in which you will have the right to live eternally in all three worlds.

## 378.

My son, you place your affection on whatever your mind loves. Whatever you desire, whatever you are enamored by, that is the energy that pulls you to the world. These energies will drag you again to the point of creation.

Only when you can cut away attachments by developing yourself to a state in which you are not attracted by their magnetic pull, can you perform your duties selflessly. When you reach the state of non-attachment, you will see the One who is free of attachment; you will see His qualities and actions. On that very day you will attain liberation and come to dwell with Him.

### 379.

O man, consider this:
If one does not think deeply
And reflect before he acts
His karma will cause him to suffer
The pain of a living death.

It is better to think about and understand everything before you do it; that will save you from many sorrows.

### 380.

All that glitters is not gold
A golden pot needs no adornment
Gold is gold.

If you become truly human, if you act with the qualities of God, you will need no other beauty or title.

### 381.

The egoism of 'I'
Torments the self
The possessiveness of 'mine'
Tortures 'me'.

If we dispel the two aspects of the 'you' and the 'I', O man, our lives will be eternal. If we think of this and understand, it will be beneficial to us.

### 382.

Do not wander about
Trying to make the world peaceful.

If everyone would make his own mind peaceful, the whole world would have peace.

### 383.

Dispel your scheming and plotting
And the truth in your inner being,
The truth in your *qalb* will grow.

### 384.

Protect the four virtuous qualities of modesty, sincerity, reserve, and fear of wrongdoing. Nurture them within your body, protect them with your wisdom, and offer them to the resplendent light of God. When you hand Him all your responsibilities, you will see the wide open space within. You will reach the resplendence and receive His grace.

### 385.

Correct your thoughts
Turn them to the good path
And your life will grow in splendor.

### 386.

Do not laugh out loud
In inappropriate places.
Before you laugh, control your mind
And consider the circumstances.
Your good qualities will be enhanced
And respect for you will grow.

### 387.

If a woman laughs out loud
Respect for her declines,
As opening out a tobacco leaf
Decreases its flavor and value.
Women must think of this
And so must those who smoke tobacco.

### 388.

Unselfishly share with other lives
All the treasures of grace
And the wealth of 'ilm or divine knowledge
That God has given to you
And you will receive the treasures from God
Which are even more exalted.

## 389.

There is no benefit in merely controlling one's speech, nor is there benefit in controlling the breath or doing yoga and exercises. But if you can control your monkey mind and its antics, you will earn the grace of God.

## 390.

My son! God created water and made it to gush from springs and flow along canals and streams. As long as the water continues to flow, it remains clear. But as soon as it is prevented from moving, if it is blocked anywhere, it loses its clearness. If the water is blocked for any length of time, it becomes stagnant, impure; dirt, refuse, garbage, worms, insects, mosquitoes, and foul odors accumulate. And if it is blocked for a very long time, it develops a stench so evil that the water is rendered useless.

Similarly, my son, God created air for man to breathe. One breath moves outward and the other breath moves inward. The breath must continually flow, the air must continually move. If you block the breath, your fate will be the same as the fate of water trapped in a pond.

Say, "*Lā ilāha,* nothing exists except for God," and let the air move outward. Say, "*Illallāhu,* only You are God," and draw the air inward. As long as the breath continues to move properly, 43,242 times a day, the air remains completely clear. The 124,000 prophets will come to imbibe that clear water of *rahmat.* Everyone in all the eighteen thousand universes will come to bathe in it, drink it, and be refreshed by it. All the good people, the resplendent lights of God, the saints, *qutbs, auliyā',* heavenly beings, angels, and representatives of God will come there to meet God and dwell in His kingdom.

Therefore, keep the breath clear and moving. Say, "*Lā ilāha,*" and send the dirt away. Say, "*Illallāhu,*" and draw in the light which is the completeness of the *Nūr.* This is the state of perfected prayer. This is why you must let the air flow properly. Do not block your breath by doing yoga, or your prayer will become like a pond of stagnant water.

## 391.

You may think that drinking milk is beneficial to you. But if you reflect a little on how much pain you cause a cow when you draw its milk, you will not want to drink the milk.

When wisdom dawns within you, the One who created you will give you milk which you do not have to draw, milk which is not made from blood, milk which never dries up and never smells, milk which will nourish you. That is the milk of wisdom, the milk of love, the milk of *gnānam*. When you drink the milk from your Creator, the hunger of your birth will be satisfied and you will grow in all three worlds: the world of the souls, this world, and the next world.

### 392.

No benefit comes
From the growth you achieve
By living on leaves and grass and weeds.

Rather, if you eat the egoism of the 'I' and 'you', digest it into feces, and excrete it, it will be of more benefit to you.

### 393.

Whether you grow your hair
To make yourself beautiful,
Or shave your hair
To make yourself beautiful
It will be of no use.

If you shave the hair of your thoughts and qualities which grows briskly on your mind, it will benefit you. You are adorning yourself with hair that should be shaved, both on the body and in the heart. Until that hair is removed the body will smell.

No matter how much you beautify your body—whether you praise or blame your body, or whether the world praises or blames your body—it will serve no purpose.

There is a vast mental world within you which contains the qualities and desires of countless millions of animals, snakes, poisonous insects, ghosts, demons, dogs, foxes, tigers, and the four hundred trillion, ten thousand miracles of creation called *shakthis*. Only if you shave and throw away all of these will you receive the beauty with which God will be enamored, the perfect beauty of all three worlds.

Until then whatever you may decorate will contain the stench of hell: your body will smell, your mind will smell, your heart will smell, your saliva will smell, and your breath will smell. But the moment the odor of hell is removed, your heart becomes a flower which blooms with God's beauty and fragrance. When the One who created you sees the beauty, the color, and the fragrance, He will come to take that fragrance. Only then can you achieve victory in your life.

### 394.

Do not live your life
Admiring your physical beauty
And believing in it.

Within a few days your beauty will leave and your body will shrink, shrivel, and waste away. Then you will have to add cosmetics and plastic; even that will last only a few days. Finally you will realize that what you admired and believed in was valueless.

It is the torpor of ignorance that admires your body. Think about it and try to get rid of it. Find the imperishable wisdom within you, the beauty within wisdom, and the One who is the beauty within beauty. Then you will be truly beautiful.

### 395.

Do not do duty selfishly
For the sake of pleasing others
And to receive their help in return.

This could result in difficulty or danger. Others can only give you what they have. If you help a lion and ask for a reward, it can only pounce on you and eat you up. If you help a snake, it can only inject you with its poison.

### 396.

Do not wander here and there
Searching for peace.

Allah has placed peace and tranquillity in your heart. If you want to find it, you must turn on the light of the seven levels of wisdom. Use the divine analytic wisdom of the *Qutbiyyat* to open the heart and sort out everything you see. Place peace and tranquillity in the treasury of the faith, certitude, and determination called *īmān*. Then talk to God. Say, "*Lā ilāha illallāhu*. There is nothing other than You, O God; only You are Allah." All the universes and everything within them will bow in homage to your peace, tranquillity, and qualities.

### 397.

Do not let the bull of your mind
Wander wherever it likes.

Catch it with your wisdom, yoke it to the plow of your life, and make it work the land. Sow the good seeds known as God's qualities. When they grow, utilize the harvest to do service for God, for those who have wisdom, and for all the people and lives of the world. This will be the victory in your life of duty.

### 398.

Examine yourself
And you will know the world.
Know yourself
And you will know your Lord.
Know the earth
And you will know the torpor
Of hypnotic fascination.
Open your wisdom and look
And you will see Allah.

### 399.

O man, with your wisdom kill the praise from the world and forget the world's blame. Acquire God's qualities. Do your duty in the same way He performs His duties.

Just as the lotus lies on water without retaining the water on its leaves, live in the world without holding the world within you.

If you live like this, the effulgence of God will resplend within your heart, even though you are enclosed in a body of earth— just as a precious gem contains a radiance, even though it is buried in the earth.

### 400.

My son, rather than plowing a large area of earth to a depth of one inch, scattering seeds everywhere, it will benefit you more to plow just one acre to a depth of four inches. From that one acre, you will receive a harvest equal to fifty acres.

Like this, my son, do not try to study everything in the world—*gnānam* here, religion there, yoga here, meditation there, and the four hundred trillion, ten thousand forms of spiritual magic everywhere. It would be like sowing extensive farmland without sufficient plowing. That would be of little benefit.

Within your heart in a space no bigger than an atom, God has placed the eighteen thousand universes, good and evil, and the wisdom to differentiate between them. That is your farmland. If you plow that land deep with your wisdom and sow God's qualities and actions with the knowledge of the difference between good and evil, you will receive the wealth of your soul, the bountiful harvest of undiminishing grace.

Reflect on this and act accordingly.

### 401.

Winnow the chaff from the seed
While the wind is blowing.

Like this, my son, you must sow the good seed and reap the good crops in the harvest of your life, winnowing them while the wind of your breath blows within the cage of your body.

The chaff of your bad qualities and thoughts must be thrown away. Keep only the good grain which is God and God's qualities. That is the undiminishing treasure that will give eternal happiness to your soul.

### 402.

Do only what is good.
But one who does good for self-gain
Will eventually destroy himself.

### 403.

Do not close your eyes
And wander around
Shouting that the world has changed.

Open your eyes of wisdom and look. Time, the Angel of Death, the sun, moon, and stars, God, and truth have not changed since *awwal,* the beginning of time. They remain exactly as they were. It is man and the mind and qualities of man which have changed.

After an elephant has bathed in the river, it takes up the mud from the riverbed and smears it on its own head. In a similar manner, man, saying that he is going to pray to God, takes all his desires, his passions, and his attachments to the things of hell and smears them on his head.

Only man has changed; the world has not changed. My son! Know this with your wisdom and try to regain your original state.

### 404.

In eons long past, man lived as the highest being. But over the past few centuries, no animal has lived in a way more lowly than man. Animals have more gratitude toward God. If man reflects with his wisdom, he can return to his original state.

### 405.

It is best to give wisdom into the hands of those who can safeguard it. If you give wisdom into the hands of the ignorant, it could be dangerous for you.

### 406.

My son,
Draw milk from a cow that has milk
Draw wisdom from one who has wisdom
Draw grace from the One who is grace.
Then you will be able to overcome
Hunger, disease, aging, and death.

### 407.

If a dog threatens to bite you
Show your love and give it a bone
And you will be able to escape.
Do not preach wisdom to it
That could be dangerous for you.

### 408.

Sugarcane is tasty to an ant
Feces is candy to a dog.
But only God is tasty to the wisdom
Of one who is truly a man.

If one knows and understands what sort of things are tasty to each being, and if he selects with his wisdom what is tasty to a true man, that will be best.

### 409.

Do not pour water onto fire
Do not put fire into water
The nature of both will change.

Like that, do not put devotion to God into the mind, and do not put the mind into devotion. That would be useless, like putting fire and water together. Separate the mind from devotion and keep each in its own place before you pray. That will bring you grace and peace.

### 410.

Just as the sun's radiance scatters the clouds which threaten to hide its light, you must use the resplendence of your wisdom to scatter the darkness of your mind.

### 411.

Do not feel proud, thinking that you have conquered the land and brought it under your control. Real triumph is to conquer and control the cage of your body.

### 412.

Hunger knows no taste
Sleep knows no comfort
Lust knows no boundaries
Desire knows no shame
Selfishness knows no justice
Anger is unaware of sin
Arrogance is unaware of karma
Poverty makes one forget his true state
Earth does not know the value of gold
Craving cannot know the splendor of life
Falsehood can never know truth
Pride does not know patience
Darkness cannot know grace
And ignorance can never know Allah.

My son, there are many things like these which keep us from knowing God and the truth. If you will realize this with your wisdom, take what is good, and act accordingly, that will be the wealth of grace which will give you victory in all three worlds.

### 413.

A dog is an enemy to a dog
One dog bites another.
Iron is an enemy to iron
Iron can cut iron.
An iguana's tail is an enemy to an iguana
When a man captures an iguana
He ties it up with its own tail.

In the same way, the qualities in man of arrogance, karma, and *māyā,* or illusion, are enemies to his birth as an *insān,* a true man. They keep him shackled, cutting off his connection to God. If these three enemies are nurtured, they will kill him. If he can dispel them, there will be no enmity in his life.

### 414.

Chameleons drop small thorny twigs on forest paths. Some of the thorns bend when they are trampled on, but the thorns which stand up straight will prick men's feet. If the tip of a thorn breaks off, the thorn loses its identity and what is left is a small twig which is useful only for kindling.

In the same way, if you lose your patience and give vent to anger, the sharp point of your life, which is your wisdom and God's qualities, will be broken off. When that happens, even though you are a human being, your life becomes purposeless. Then like those twigs, it is useful only as kindling for the fires of hell.

However, if you cherish patience and tolerance, your life will be sharp with the sharpness of that wisdom which gives without ever harming other lives.

### 415.

It is said that a drowning man comes to the surface three times before be finally sinks. If ordinary water is so forbearant as to bring a man up three times, in what a more exalted state God must be! Almighty God who rules the whole world forbears so much. How much compassion He must have!

Think of this a little.

416.

Gold is scarce.
Brass is sold everywhere.

Very few people have gold in their houses, but brass is in common use in houses and around people's necks.

To become an *insān,* a true man, to be called a man, to acquire the qualities and actions of a man, is rare. To receive God's qualities and to reach God is unique. To only appear to be a man, on the other hand, may be easy. To appear to perform 105 million miracles is a common thing, like brass. But the difference between real human beings and those who seem like human beings is like the difference between gold and brass.

When one becomes a man of wisdom, he will understand.

417.

Even though a man can fly in the sky by means of miracles, even though he can stay in the sky and sleep in the sky, no matter how many miracles he can perform, that which is born with him will eventually bring him down. Desire, pride, and the need for praise will bring him down to earth and cause him to be born again. That connection which pulls him down to the place of birth and destroys him is his karma.

Only when the five elements and all the qualities of the 'I' and the 'you' are lost will the seed of the divine wisdom of the *Qutbiyyat* be able to grow within him. Otherwise the sprout will be pulled down to hell, the place of birth. Only in the state where the self is lost can the seed of wisdom within man grow to maturity. Only then can he attain liberation.

418.

Truth is a huge mountain which grows from *awwal* to *ākhirah,* from the world of the souls to the kingdom of God. Truth is God's wealth, His *daulat.* If anyone tries to climb the mountain of truth keeping mind and desire with him, they will cause his hands and feet to constantly slip. When he climbs up one yard, the monkey mind will make him slip down two yards.

However, if he cuts away both mind and desire with his wisdom, if he carves out the steps of determination while holding on to the chain known as wisdom, if he plants the staff of absolute faith called *īmān* deep into the mountain to help him climb, he will find it easy.

If he perseveres in this way with the resonance of *lā ilāha illallāhu,* he and God can meet directly. The light of the soul and the power of God can meet and talk, face to face. This is the victory of wisdom in man's life.

### 419.

My son, do not catch a crow and try to make it white by washing it. It is impossible.

On the other hand, try throughout day and night to wash away the pitch-black darkness of your mind, using the resplendent water of the *Subhānallāhi Kalimah,* the Third *Kalimah.*

The blackness of a crow is inborn, while the darkness in man is acquired. If you try really hard, you can wash it away. As soon as you succeed you will be filled to completeness with resplendent light. But just as it is impossible to make a crow white by washing it, it is also impossible for you to wash away all darkness in all the people of the land and make them resplendent. First make yourself resplendent. That will benefit you.

### 420.

O man, harder than the hardest rock and darker than the blackest darkness is the unmelting ignorance of man's arrogant heart. Intellect cannot analyze the depth of that darkness. Compassion, love, generosity, wisdom, peace, tolerance, patience—none of these can penetrate it. When they touch it, they bounce back like an echo. Whatever one tries to teach a person with such a heart will not penetrate. The sound will bounce off.

A heart of stone must be broken with the hammer of *īmān,* the hammer of absolute faith, determination, and certitude held in the hand of the divine wisdom of the *Qutbiyyat.* Such a heart must be beaten and broken. We must crush it to dust and throw it away.

Once that has been accomplished, wisdom can be taught; compassion and good actions will be able to enter that heart, and he can become a man. If he becomes a man, he will look deeply into the hearts of other lives, and his heart will melt with compassion. Then he can begin to do duty as a true man.

If he does not come to that state, however, he will not value other lives as his own. Wisdom given to such a man will be like rainwater falling into the ocean: the pure water will become salty. No matter how much good we pour over such a man, it will be to no avail. We who are man must realize this.

### 421.

My son, some people say the body is a temple. Others say the mind is a temple.

Bawa Muhaiyaddeen says, "It is only when the 'I', the five elements, mind, and desire are dispelled that the heart becomes a temple. Until then, the heart is satan's house of hell. For, as long as a man embraces that evil state and remains in it, his mind, his life, and his wisdom will be in darkness."

### 422.

My son, the whole world says, "Tell the truth, tell the truth." However, if you do tell the truth to a man, his whole body will hurt. The body lives in lies, desires lies, praises lies, eats lies, and decorates itself with the makeup of lies. That is the happiness of its life. Truth, however, throws away everything the body likes.

Therefore, as soon as we tell the truth, it causes pain to the four hundred trillion, ten thousand qualities in the body. We can tell the truth only to those who have understood this and thrown away the lies. If they have not, we can only plead with God, "O God! You are the only One who can tell them the truth."

### 423.

My son, the world says, "Do what is good for the country. Find out what is good for the country."

Hearing this, the small bird of wisdom in a true man said, "O man, what is good for the land is to do duty without the sense of the 'you' and the 'I'. That is what is good for the land, and one who does this is a good man."

### 424.

"Sing! Sing songs of religious devotion!" urged the monkey of the mind.

The sheikh who heard this said, "O monkey, if you give up your tricks, devotion will come all by itself. Will you then have the need to sing?"

### 425.

In the world, there are those who have many titles and honors, rich men who win titles for themselves in order to control the world.

They say one thing on the inside but quite another on the outside. They say things like, "Give room to the poor, give them jobs, make them peaceful." This is their outward teaching. But while they are telling others what to do, they keep a tight grip on the country and the lives of the people. They tell others to give room to the poor, while they keep all the land for themselves.

However, one who not only speaks those words but also gives away his own land, titles, peace, and possessions is an exemplary human being for his country, a messenger of God, and a leader amongst teachers. One who does not have that good state within himself will only tell others to give away their possessions. This is a great wonder in the world.

### 426.

*Siddhars,* those who perform elemental miracles, offer to teach us these miracles and devotions, claiming they can grant us liberation. There are many people with such mental powers.

Hearing this, the parrot of intellect within the *qalb,* the inner heart, called out, "O man, not until the miracles of the demonic elements of your mind are destroyed will you receive the liberation of *gnānam,* or divine wisdom.

"You summon the world and its people, offering them miracles, *gnānam,* devotion, and liberation, while you yourself have not attained a peaceful state. Give up this foolishness and first purify yourself."

### 427.

Men say, "Search, search, search for God in the truth." They tell you to find God.

Hearing this, the parrot of wisdom said, "O man, give up searching for truth here, there, and everywhere. Truth and falsehood are within you; good and evil are within you; heaven and hell are within you; God and man dwell in the same place.

"Realizing this, if you search within, disregarding everything else until you find truth and God within yourself, that will be the highest victory of your life. That is the divine wisdom called *gnānam.*"

### 428.

All the religions of the world say, "Pray, pray, pray, pray—then you can reach heaven!"

Hearing this, the parrot of the pearl called *Nūr,* or perfect faith, said, "O men, suppose the people of your country attack you at one time and deify you at another time. When they treat you as a god-like idol, you will praise them, and when they attack you, you will resent them and see them as enemies. The same people who harass you will later deify you; you resent the harassment, yet you love the praise.

"If you accept neither the abuse nor the praise, it will be easy for you to pray to God and reach Him. Then you will attain peace and you will have no enemies. All lives will respect you and pay obeisance to you."

### 429.

A man caught a parrot, put it in a cage, and taught it to speak.

The caged parrot of wisdom said, "O man, I was living in freedom, and you put me in a cage. You try to make me speak your language and you teach me the words of your religions. Will your language give me back my freedom? Learning your language will only make me suffer. If I learn your language without knowing its meaning and instead of calling a thief a thief, I call a good man a thief, or a thief a good man, I will lose my life.

"I must fly freely in the skies and learn my natural speech, my natural freedom, and my natural prayers, all by myself. That is my meditation.

"O man, if only you would understand the way you naturally are and the way God naturally is! If you were to understand, leave the prison of your cage, and study yourself, it would be good for me and good for you. Understand this and let me out. Let me out and let yourself out. That will be your victory in life, my victory in life, and freedom for both of us."

### 430.

"Who is good in the world?" a learned man asked Bawa Muhaiyaddeen.

He answered, "Do you not know? God is good. God does selfless duty and dispenses justice impartially."

### 431.

"Do you know who is good for the country?" another man asked.

The wise man said, "One who rules by making God's justice into king's justice, king's justice into human justice, and human justice into conscience is good for the country. One who never deviates from justice and who reflects his good conduct and good qualities in his actions is good for the country."

### 432.

"Is there a good man in the world?" a man asked.

"Yes. One who rules the world of his mind with God's justice, king's justice, and human justice is good. He is good for himself and good for all lives," replied the wise man.

### 433.

A child asked Bawa Muhaiyaddeen, "Many in the world speak of great devotees. Do they really exist?"

He replied, "One who cuts off the roots of mind, desire, thought, and torpor will become a devotee of God."

### 434.

The sparrow of subtle wisdom said to a man of wisdom, "I have flown over many countries in my search for God. I have been in temples, mosques, churches, and places of worship on which the names of the four religions have been written, but wherever I flew all I found was troubles and wars. I went to worship, pray, meditate, and sing devotional songs, but all I found was arguments and fighting. I went to one place to worship and they were arguing. I went to another place to pray and they were quarrelling. I went to another place to meditate and they were fighting. There were racial and religious fights. I asked them why they were fighting.

"'My god is real! All the others are false!' each one shouted.

"Each person spoke of his own god, and the fights continued. Then a song came to me. I sang to God, asking Him to show me a good place.

> Fighting in this religion,
> Fighting in that religion,
> Fighting in the religion
> In which they were born,
> Fighting in the religion
> In which they will die.
> In which temple or mosque
> Can I worship You
> O God, O *Allāhu*?

"I sang this to God and I cried. I said, 'Tell me a way. Show me the place in which I can worship You.'

"O wise one! I have been suffering for so long without an answer. Tell me in what temple I can worship to receive liberation. O wise man, can you tell me of a place in which to worship?"

The wise man said, "Your situation is difficult. Having flown and wandered all over the world, it is difficult to know the One and pray to Him. The four religions are right, and your reasoning is also right. But there is one thing you must realize: in the place in which you must know yourself, there is only One who prays. Only when you know yourself and when you see your soul, can you begin to pray." The wise man said this.

The bird questioned him further, "Will you explain the four religions in more detail, O wise man?"

"The first is the place where you were conceived, formed, and born. It is the religion of *Zabūr*, or Hinduism, where temples are built. That is the place of creation, the place in which statues, forms, men, and animals are displayed as examples. Therein are Shakthi and Shiva, Adam and Eve *(A.S.)*. It is the place of intermingling, joining, forming, and growing.

"The second religion is *Jabrāt,* Zoroastrianism. It is the fire of hunger, illness, old age, and death. The fire of your stomach burns to ash everything you bring to it. That religion is also in your body.

126

"The third religion is the religion of the pure spirit. It is the world of the four hundred trillion, ten thousand spiritual forces called *shakthis*. This is *Injīl*, Christianity, the religion of thoughts, vapors, and spirits, the religion which exists in the region of your chest.

"The fourth is light. The fourth religion makes you perceive through the senses of sight, taste, hearing, and smell, thereby helping you to understand what is good and what is bad, what is right and what is wrong. *Furqān,* or Judaism-Islam, the fourth religion, is the head.

"These are the four. You are the four religions. You are the scriptures. You are the temples. You must see them within yourself. If you had understood this, you would not have seen fighting in all the places to which you flew and you would not have suffered so much.

"When you understand this, transcend the four religions, know yourself, and go beyond, then you can see our Father. Only after this does true prayer and worship begin.

"There is no work to do in the world, the only work is within the self. There is no fighting in the land, the fighting is within you. There are no differences in the land, the differences are within you. There are no troubles in the land, the troubles are in your own judgment. There is no divisiveness in creation, only in your own state.

"The fault is not in you, but in standing back and letting the things in your mind take over. If you catch and control your mind, this will not happen.

"Realize this, O sparrow, and act accordingly. Find a wise man and learn. Do not waste your time flying over the land and looking at things. Fly inside yourself and see."

This is what the wise man said.

### 435.

The green dove of the mind said to a wise man, "So many people cry, 'O God! O God! O God!' They say, 'He is here' or 'He is there.' I have flown here and there and looked everywhere, but I have not seen the One of whom they speak. Many people called out like that, but no one came forward in response to that call. I stood and watched. No one came forward. I did this for the sake of prayer. I flew and glided and circled, wandering in the skies.

"Then I came back to find a wise man. Here you are near the trunk of a tree, and there is a saying: 'Beneath the shady green tree known as the *Katpaha Virudcham* is a devotee.'* I saw you and thought perhaps I should try to ask you, so I flew down. So many in the world say 'God', but no one comes. Does God have such a name?"

The wise man said, "Allah is the One without name, the One without birth, the One without a country of birth, the One without friends, the One without relationships, the One without shape, the One without family, the One without children, the One without race, the One without religion, the One without mother, the One without father, the One without anyone, the One without destruction, and the One without end. Allah is the One who existed then, the One who exists now, and the One who will exist forever as life within life, as wisdom within wisdom, as clarity within clarity, as heart within heart, as the fragrance within a flower, as the taste within a fruit, as the sweetness within honey, as the whiteness within milk, as the light within light, as light within the eye, as sound within the ear, as the sense of smell within the nose, as tongue within the tongue, as body within the body, as plenitude within goodness, as clarity within compassion, as tolerance within patience, as justice within peace, as truth within eternity, as completeness and mystery within perfection, as the precious treasure within the mystery, as the resplendent light of *Nūr* within the precious treasure, as man within the *Nūr*, as the resonance of the heart within man, as meaning within the resonance, and as the One within the meaning.

"If you put yourself aside, God will be there. If you put God aside, the 'I' will be there. After you know which of these two should be put aside, you can become Him. If you do not know, you are left with yourself. Understand and know this."

The wise man, the *Qutb (Ral.)*, said this to the green dove of the mind. "That treasure is God, and the one who clearly accepts it becomes God."

---

*The *Katpaha Virudcham* is the resplendent tree of *īmān* which grants everything one wishes. The *Qutb (Ral.)* is said to be the devotee under the *Katpaha Virudcham*. In Arabic, it is called *Sidratul-Muntahā*.

## 436.

The green parrot of the mind asked, "O wise man, I have flown through countless forests looking for goodness. All I found were many species of reptiles, birds, and other animals, and they were all fighting, catching, killing, and eating each other. The forest contains food to nourish every species: flowers, honey, weeds, leaves, roots, and tubers. Although the nourishment for each is provided, they fight each other for food. They are all enemies to each other. Some kill and eat others. Some simply kill for the sake of killing. I left the forest and flew here to ask you about it. What is the reason for their actions?"

The wise man answered, "What you have seen, O parrot, is the world. That is the nature of the body, which is made of earth, fire, water, air, and ether. The qualities of the elements are arrogance, karma, and *māyā*. The form of these qualities is the mind. Their natural behavior is to attack others, to say, 'I am greater than you!' They kill and eat each other. They make others afraid.

"What you saw, O parrot, are the actions and capabilities of arrogance, karma, *māyā,* and the five elements. Anyone who over-comes them is a good man, a man who will not kill or eat any life. And within the goodness of a good man is the world of grace. Within the world of grace are God's qualities and actions. When you see them, you will throw the world away, and instead of attacking other lives, you will have the quality of protecting others as you would protect yourself.

"O green parrot, if you had known this, you would not have asked such a question. Do not become involved with what you see on the outside. Become involved with what is in yourself, and you will see the wealth of exalted qualities."

## 437.

A green parrot said to a wise man, "The world says, 'April fool, April fool!' The world claims to fool people only one day a year, but is there anything happening other than fools fooling around?"

The wise man replied, "You asked a good question, and what you said is right, O parrot. But if people would lie and fool each other only once a year, it would not be such a burden for God. If man told only one lie a year, it would be a small matter. If only people would tell just one lie a year! An April fool is only a once-a-year fool.

"However, if man did not fool around and lie every moment of every day, his head would burst. So think, parrot: is there only one April fool a year? In the life of man, if all his words, thoughts, and ideas are not lies, then his mind is not content. This applies to the life of a man who has not reached peace.

"It is the every-second fool who causes fights and turns everything in the world upside down. The cause of all fights and wars is man's lying. Falsehood is the worst of the five horrible sins. Without falsehood, not one murder would take place.

"If April fool would happen only once a year, in the way they say, it would be really amazing; it would be as insignificant as a one-second famine in a wealthy land. If man would lie only once a year, God would barely notice it.

"If man were to understand this, if he would live as man, his life would change from 'fool' to 'cool'!

"Green parrot, if the fooling would go on only once a year, the world would escape destruction and there would be no famine, suffering, or sorrow. Think about this carefully, O parrot."

This is what the wise man said.

### 438.

A man asked a *gnāni,* "From the time I was born, I searched for God and worshiped Him. Though I searched for such a long time, I did not see God and I do not know how to reach God. What is the reason for this?"

The *gnāni* replied, "What you say is right. A fruit tree growing in the shade of a large tree, such as a banyan, will not thrive or bear fruit. The shadow of the large tree will cover it, and the roots of the large tree will pull all the growth energy from the ground. The larger tree will draw all the magnetic energy from the rainwater and from the rays of the sun and moon. It will take all the natural energies and leave only what is useless. The smaller tree will be unable to thrive. No matter how much it is watered, it will neither flower nor bear fruit.

"Like that, all the prayers and worship you perform are shaded by the huge tree of mind, desire, and the five elements, which has grown up to the very heaven within you—the heaven in your heart. If you exist under it, no matter how much you pray, worship, and meditate, you will be like a barren tree. Your prayer will not develop, flower, or bear fruit. All the goodness which comes from God will be ruined, and all the good things will be kept from you. You will get only the waste products of the world. Pride, praise, honors, titles, the 'I' and 'you', religion, and all the things God has discarded will be yours.

"You will not reach Him. The flowers of *gnānam,* of divine wisdom, will not bloom. The fruits of *gnānam* will not ripen. You will not develop or live as a peaceful and tranquil man. Your prayer will remain just as you described it. Think of this.

"Pull out by the roots, cut down, and throw away the tree that has been growing within you, and plant the good tree. That will benefit you. Cut down and throw away everything that grew before. The tree of those things that come from your mind must be uprooted. Then if you plant the tree of prayer, you will receive what you intend. You will receive its fruits, you will receive its light, and you will receive grace."

### 439.

A cobra asked a wise man, "Great one, everyone in the entire world calls me a poisonous snake, a horribly poisonous snake. People either run away in fear when they see me or come to beat me and kill me. Great one, am I so poisonous? Am I the most poisonous creature in the world?"

The great man said, "You speak well. In days of old, at the time Adam *(A.S.)* was created, you were like a flower garland. You had such a beautiful fragrance! Everyone loved you. All those who hate you now searched for you then, to wear as decoration. At that time you had no poison and you were not called 'snake'.

"But in his attempts to ruin Adam *(A.S.),* satan with his poisonous and evil qualities deceived you into concealing him in your mouth and carrying him into heaven. He made you an accomplice in causing your original mother and father to be hurled into hell.

"Because of the evil you caused them by concealing satan in your mouth, you grew four poisonous fangs containing all of satan's poison. The sweet fragrance of flowers was driven out of you. You earned the terrible name 'snake'. Satan's poisonous qualities of pride, jealousy, arrogance, impatience, haste, vengeance, treachery, falsehood, murder, lust, and anger accumulated and grew within you to become your poison, driving away your good qualities. Earlier you were a creation loved by everyone for your beautiful qualities and fragrance, but satan robbed you of your beauty and fragrance, giving you his qualities and hell in return.

"Human beings, too, are being deceived. They are trading their beauty for the same things satan gave you.

"Satan's qualities, actions, and treachery control and deceive man, bring him into satan's group, and cause him to live by deceit. Your poison is in your mouth, but man has poison in his heart. How vicious it is! If one drop of man's poison touches something, it will shrivel. Even the grass on which he walks will be scorched. If he walks on rocks, they will waste away.

"There is no cure for the poison in the hearts of men who trust and follow satan. That poison is very difficult to change. You might bite one person at a time, but he bites and devours everyone in the world.

"However, snake, even though you have poison, you can have a measure of peace. If you change the qualities you were deceived into taking, that very day that same poison will begin to develop into three kinds of gems: emeralds, sapphires, and rubies. It is possible for you to change. Those who blamed you before will seek you now. If your poisonous qualities and hissing anger change, the fragrance of flowers will return to you. You could be a good snake again, and people would again wear you as a garland.

"But man, on the other hand, has the most dreadful and painful poison in the world. All lives run away from him in terror when they see his poison. He kills, eats, drinks, and excretes other lives. You are not as evil as he is. Do not feel so sad about yourself."

### 440.

A wise man walking through the jungle sat down against the trunk of a tree to rest. Soon an elephant approached him and said, "O wise one, now that you have come into the jungle in which we elephants live, we have a question for you. May I ask it?"

"Yes, please do," he answered.

"We are one of the kinds of lives in the jungle. Our name is elephant. We are wild animals, but human beings capture us with their tricks and haul us into cities where they make us do the work of fifty or sixty men without feeding us properly. Though they make us suffer beyond belief, still we do our duty for them with patience and compassion, and in fear of the word of God.

They live in houses and mansions; we have to rest under trees, chained by the legs so that we cannot move around. We are left out in the open—in the sun, wind, and rain—under trees which do not give us any real shade. If we were in the jungle, we could move about freely and find suitable shelter against the elements. Why do men cause us so much suffering?"

The wise one said, "O elephant, among God's creations you are a huge creation indeed. Men often joke about you and tease you. Sometimes they call you a rutting elephant. In English, you may be called a pachyderm; in Tamil, *kari* or *mattahan*. There are many names for you. But you need not feel sad about this.

"Man is much smaller than you, but he has more sexual frenzy than you do. He has arrogance, karma, and *māyā*. He has the insane frenzy of the lust aroused by his eyes, his brain, and his genitals. Although he is smaller, he has a lot more arrogance. Because of his arrogance, he turns the world upside down and makes himself into an animal. He destroys his exalted life with that arrogance. He destroys virtue. When the ninety-six crazinesses come to him, he is subject to the insanity of lust, the insanity of the sixty-four kinds of worldly knowledge, and the insane obsessions of the sixty-four sexual games. Man performs many insane actions.

"He regards good people as dogs, learned men as idiots, true human beings and *gnānis* as liars, liars as *gnānis,* thieves as honest men, chaste women as whores, whores as chaste women, virtuous women as prostitutes, prostitutes as virtuous women. Man regards the virtuous as criminals and criminals as virtuous. He turns truth into falsehood, falsehood into truth, beauty into desire, goodness into waste, racial prejudice into temples, and evil into deities. He subjects other lives to great injustice. He uproots all good thoughts. With the trunk of his arrogance, he lifts evil things onto his head while trampling good things under his feet. Moreover, he is arrogant enough to proclaim that he rules the world.

"This is what the elephant-man of arrogance is like. You need not be sad. Your arrogance is small compared to the arrogance of the elephant-man. In fact, he projects his own arrogance onto you.

"Only when man understands that he is arrogant will he become a real man. When his arrogance rises, he is like a rutting elephant which can destroy the world. The chains of karma bind him hand and foot, while only one of your legs is chained. Therefore, do not be sad. Be patient."

441.

A rat said to a Sufi, "O Sufi, you are in search of God and you know the truth of God, so may I ask you a question?"

"Yes, do ask," answered the Sufi.

The rat said, "We are one of God's creatures. Even though we do not inflict evil upon anyone, men, our enemies, put forth a great deal of effort to kill us. They chase us here and they chase us there, screaming, 'Rat! Rat! Rat!' They cannot bear to see us. They beat us and use poisons and traps to kill us. Is it just? Is what we do worse than what man does?" The rat asked this with great sorrow.

The Sufi replied, "You are right. What you say is true, O rat. But still, you must change your qualities, you must correct yourself. God has created you just as He has created other lives. In the same way that He has created food for the others, He has also created your food.

"The whole world is filled with food for you. It is your responsibility to search for and eat the food that belongs to you. If you prefer to steal, that is not good, is it? And worse than your thievery, you chew holes in man's beautiful things. He tries to kill you because you ruin his things. Realize this and search for your rightful food. It will be better for you if you do not destroy man's things.

"Still, the harm you do is small. Just as you have four limbs, man has two hands and two feet. But what qualities he has! He contains many worlds within himself. He contains the qualities of all the animals. Snakes, scorpions, and poisonous creatures chew holes in his heart. He has qualities in his heart which tear holes in others and destroy their lives: treachery, vengeance, jealousy, witchcraft, putting charms and curses on others, sending demons to others. He transforms himself into demons, ghosts, lions, tigers, bears, snakes, and scorpions, and seeks to destroy the lives of others. The holes that man makes in others' lives through his treachery are much worse than the holes you make. Your holes are not as harmful.

"O rat, you must try to escape man's cruelty. If you keep on chewing holes in his things, you will continue to be in danger—

he will put holes in you and close off all the places in which you live. It would be good to try to escape man's hole-chewing qualities. Do not interfere with him; do not desire his things. If you can avoid that, it will be easier for you. But if you persist in living in the places in which he lives, your life will be in jeopardy. If each of you lives in his own place, there will be peace."

## 442.

A seven-year-old boy asked a wise man, "God has created everything, has He not? He told all lives to live happily and in peace. God has said, 'This is My kingdom. It does not belong to any one creation. It belongs equally to all. Everyone must share it.' If this is God's kingdom and God's land, who makes man suffer? Who causes the most suffering to man?"

The wise man answered, "The question you asked is a wondrous question indeed, my son. Some people who call themselves devotees of God go about chanting the name of God, but the pain they cause others is the primary suffering of all mankind. Everyone else looks after his own livelihood and his own life, but these 'devotees' search the roads and streets for people to criticize and blame. They make no allowance for anyone else.

"Devotees of this kind chased away the prophets, forcing them from their lands. They cause greater harm to mankind than anyone else. Other people keep to themselves, but these people covet the possessions of others and interfere with others' lives. God did not give them this suffering. This suffering is caused by man to man.

"My son, a true devotee would not waste his time finding fault with others. He would not covet the property of others or interfere in their lives. He would concern himself only with the purpose for which he came and complete his mission, which is to find the way to reach his Creator.

"In the same way, you too should escape and establish a peaceful connection between yourself and God. Pray to God and worship Him. That will be very good."

## 443.

A man had a piece of bread. A crow flew by and stole it. The man cried out, "Thieving crow! Haven't you given up your thieving nature yet, you satan?"

The crow said, "You are not really a man, so I won't speak to you. I will find a man and speak to him," and it flew away.

A wise man was seated under a tree. The crow flew to a branch of the tree, and sitting above the wise man, dropped the piece of bread in front of him. The wise man looked up, saw the crow, and held up the bread. "O crow, come. Here is your food. Come get your food. It is yours. Come and eat it," he said.

The crow thought, "Now there is a true man! I can tell him my troubles." It flew close to the wise man and spoke. "O great one, there are very few men like you. If there were more like you in the world, everyone would live peacefully.

"Great one, we crows are one of the kinds of birds in the world. God created us black. We too are God's creations, and we are very much like men. But they call us thieves, satans, satan's vehicles. They say we are blind, that we have no wisdom. They abuse us, scold us, and chase us away. They hurl insults at us. Is this reasonable, O great one? Are we the worst thieves in the world? Are we really the worst thieves in all God's creation?"

"O crow, what you say is right. You are one of God's creations. Your color is black and it is true that you are a thief. But then, you usually take what man has already thrown away. The food you steal is soiled with the phlegm and spittle of others. You usually eat discarded, decaying things. The bread you brought here was in that condition.

"There are man-crows much worse than you. Your body is black, but their hearts are black. Your nose is black, but their intelligence is black. Your tongue is black, but their thoughts are black. Among men there are many, many worse vehicles of satan than you. There are many human vehicles for satan who cause suffering. These men have cast away conscience and have begun thieving, backbiting, and stealing in temples, churches, and societies. They steal in their intentions, in their markets, in their houses, in their gardens, in their songs and dances, in their work, in desire, and in millions of other ways.

"Having lost the truth of conscience, they steal in the very presence of God. They blindfold the eyes of their gods, obliterate honesty, turn compassion upside down, break down good conduct, torment modesty, destroy the very seed of chastity, and burn justice to ashes. They gamble, cheat, and deceive each other; they are revengeful and jealous. They have religious, social, and class differences. They drink intoxicants. They steal for the sake of their one-span stomachs. They torment and torture each other, committing every conceivable sin.

"Those black-hearted human crows are much worse than you. Their inner blackness is worse than your visible blackness, is it not? Their thievery is much worse than yours. O crow, one of wisdom will not consider you a black and degenerate bird. Only one who has forfeited his wisdom and has become a worse crow than you would call you evil.

"Do not be sad when men ridicule you. Your blackness is natural, O crow, and no matter how much you wash, you will never get rid of it. But the blackness in the hearts of the human crows is acquired, and it is still very difficult for them to get rid of it. It is a cancer. If they want to wash away their blackness, they must join a man of wisdom, and using the soap of the absolute faith of *īmān* and the water of wisdom, they must scrub for a long, long time.

"Therefore, O crow, do not waste your time with them. Be patient and conduct your life with good qualities and good intentions. Be content with whatever food is given you by God and praise Him."

444.

The king of the white ants saw a wise man sitting near the anthill and said to him, "O man, we white ants are also one of God's creations. We build houses to protect ourselves from rain and sun and wind. We undergo great difficulty in building houses to protect our families from destruction.

"Then the group called man comes to break up our houses and chase us away, destroying our families. Not only that, iguanas catch and eat our children; rats, snakes, and mongooses come to devour us and claim our houses for themselves. If we escape man, the animals come; if we escape the animals, man comes. So much injustice is inflicted on our families.

"One day we all got together. We decided there had to be an end to it all, so we formed a huge society. We got a majority decision that if someone comes to break up our houses, heads must roll. We prayed to our deity. Then we went to our swami, worshiped him, and asked him to grant our boon: if we bite someone, heads must roll.

"'Let it be so,' said our swami, and he granted the boon. But we had forgotten to specify that it was the head of the one we had bitten that must fall.

"From that day on, when we bite someone, our heads roll! What is the reason for this? Is it the mistake of the swami who granted the boon, or is it our mistake?" asked the king of the white ants.

The wise man replied, "O king of the white ants, God has made so many millions of creations. He has caused them to dwell under the earth, on top of the earth, in the oceans, on mountains, in caves, in the skies, and in the heavens. God has shared His kingdom among all lives. It belongs equally to all.

"But oceans become land and land becomes oceans. Cities become jungles and jungles become cities. Creatures live in one place at one time and shift to another location at another time. Their lives change as the world changes. It is wrong to think the kingdom of God belongs to you, wrong to build the foundation of your house with the intention that the house and the jungle belong to you.

"Do not think your house is permanent. It can be torn apart by earthquakes, dissolved by rain, battered by storms, and swept away by waves. You too are subject to change, and you must try to escape and protect yourselves and your children. This is true of all creations in the world. Each must try to escape according to its circumstances.

"Instead of that, you wanted the heads of others to roll when you bit them. That was the thought which came to your tongue, but you forget one important word at the time you spoke. You got exactly what you asked for. Now your heads must roll whenever you bite someone. The fault is yours.

"O king of the white ants, man has been created as the most exalted creation in all worlds. But at the present time, the magnificence of his life has dwindled. His wisdom has diminished greatly. Now he is even worse than you. Just as you forgot one crucial word when you asked your boon, he too has forgotten the one crucial word: God. His actions are directed toward making the heads of others roll. His thought is, 'When I bite, the heads of others must roll.' This is the intention and the focus of all his intellect and wisdom. But when man intends harm to others, he forgets God and loses his own head. You have not realized this, nor has man.

"One who is wise among men will go on the path of God without depending on the world. Having no desire to hurt others, he will never request that they should be harmed or lose their heads. With the three thousand gracious attributes of God and His state of peace and equality, he will dedicate himself to the lives of others, bringing them tranquillity. He will not be concerned with his own life. Such a man will be exalted among men."

## 445.

A man of wisdom was sitting near a farm where many goats were grazing. One of the goats stood apart from the herd and gazed at him. The man shepherding the flock hit the goat and tried to chase it back into the herd. The goat took the beating, then ran to the man of wisdom. "O wise and great one, is there no end to the injustice committed by man? Will God not put an end to his cruelty?"

The great one replied, "What have you suffered, and how does the suffering come to you?"

The goat confided what was in his heart. "God created men, but He also created us. Just as men have wives and children, friends and relatives, we too have wives and children, friends and relatives. But while men raise their families in houses, we have to raise our families out in the rain, sun, and wind. We get wet when it rains. We must graze for our food out in the open. Though we need our milk for our own children, men tie them up and take the milk for themselves and their children.

"Not only that, our necks are in danger whether men are happy or unhappy. They slaughter us, cut us up, divide us among themselves, and eat our flesh. When they want to pray or ask for boons to release them from their suffering, they drag us and our children to an idol and, while two people hold us down, they cut our throats. We are sacrificed to deities that accept murder as an offering.

"They live contentedly with their families, yet they do not hesitate to slaughter us right in front of our children. How upset they become when their children fall ill, but they grab our children and butcher them before our very eyes. How can we bear to look on? We too were created by God. O great one, is there no end to this injustice?" This is what the goat said.

"What you say is true," said the wise man. "But who do you think man is? Those people you mentioned, they are not men. They are tigers with the faces of men. Just because they wear the faces of human beings, does that mean they are truly human beings?

"Those human tiger cubs do not have compassion, justice, laws of honesty, fear of God, pity, or tolerance. They do not have even an atom's worth of human justice, human conscience, or divine justice.

"If you need to live among tigers covered in human skin, you must be extremely cautious. You are not the only one who has suffered at their hands. Even prophets, saints, *qutbs,* and virtuous men and women of wisdom and good qualities have been tormented by them. It is only with God's help that we can escape. So do not feel sad. They may sacrifice you and eat you, but they themselves will be eaten by the seven fiery hells and by the snakes, scorpions, centipedes, demons, worms, and tarantulas there. God has prepared these hells for them.

"You are sacrificed by one stroke of the knife, and your suffering is brief. But the tigers who are covered with human skin are torn apart piece by piece, atom by atom, by each snake, scorpion, worm, and poisonous creature in hell. Finally they are roasted in hell's horrible fires. While they are still alive they are ripped apart, day after day, piece by piece. They suffer for eons and eons, while you only suffer for a moment.

"Therefore, with the inner patience, known as *sabūr,* accept any suffering that you may have and beg for God's help. Live with the faith that your body and your soul do not belong to you. Then God will share the suffering that comes to you. Place your trust in God all the time; in every moment say, 'O God, this is Your property, Your duty.' One who was born as a man and has lived as a man will exist in this state. For whatever happens he will say with contentment and gratitude, 'All praise belongs to God, *al-hamdu lillāh.*' For what might come in the next moment, he will say, 'It is Your responsibility, O Allah, *tawakkul-'alallāh,*' and praise Him.

"If you can bring your heart to that state, your suffering will not weigh heavily on you. Whatever may happen, give all responsibility to God."

446.

A man leading a fully-laden donkey passed a Sufi who was sitting under a tree. The man unloaded the donkey at a nearby market, set it loose to graze, and went about his business. The donkey moved close to the Sufi.

"O wise man, I carry all man's burdens," complained the donkey. "Just see how I suffer! I am forced to carry such a load on my back that I stumble along, barely able to walk. I give so much help to man; I carry all his burdens, all his things, yet this is how he treats me.

"Men build huge houses and even palaces for themselves. They sleep in great comfort on beds with mattresses, and they possess many luxuries. Though I do so much for man, I have no place to sleep. Why, I do not even have a place in which to live!

"This is my state. The ungrateful men load all their burdens onto my back. They work me from dawn to dusk. After the sun has set, they free me, but where can I go to feed at that hour? All day I am hungry, but at night I cannot eat properly. I starve throughout the night. I have to sleep in broken and abandoned houses. I have no proper place to rest. When I am released from work the fleas and mosquitoes suck out my blood. O wise one, is there no end to my suffering?" pleaded the donkey.

"What you say is true, O donkey! However, your load is only as much as you can fit on your back and carry. At least there is a marketplace where they unburden you, after which you can be somewhat comfortable.

"You think your life is hard, but the burdens man bears are so heavy that they cannot be unloaded. In one huge bundle, man carries the garbage of all the universes. He carries everything that has been discarded by God, truth, and justice. It is a staggering burden, a burden he cannot even unload since there is no place in which it would fit. You say he sleeps peacefully on soft beds in houses, but where could anyone with such a heavy burden sleep peacefully? He carries scorpions, tarantulas, bedbugs, rats, cats, bees, snakes, lice, fleas, worms, and germs, which pick and tear and claw at him all the time. He does not have a minute's peace. You think he is comfortable, but he has no peace at all.

"Even if the sun and the moon were to change places, still he would not have peace because of the immensity of his burdens. Your burdens are trivial compared to his. What you carry is only as big as one-millionth of a particle of an atom of his burden. Do you think man sleeps on a bed, or even on stones? No. He sleeps in the fire of hell. His suffering is unimaginable.

"You at least can lean on an abandoned wall, scratch yourself, and get a little satisfaction. But man cannot even do that. He carries his burdens throughout the day and spends his nights scratching himself on the fires of karma, without any peace at all. If you reflect on this, you will not grieve so. You have walls on which to scratch and I have trees under which to sit peacefully, but the one you call man gets only the unbearable heat of fire for his peace. The more he leans on it, the more he gets burnt. His very blood is afire. He is being eaten alive by the snakes and scorpions that he carries.

"O donkey, the place I have and the burdens you have are very easy. We must praise God for this. You have peace and I have peace. You must praise God and pray that He protects us so that we never descend from this state. Then we can be forever peaceful."

### 447.

There was a man who had a dog. The dog had a lot of gratitude for him; it guarded him and aided him in many ways. The dog was a true friend to the man's life. After some time, the man became blind and then poor. All his relatives abandoned him. But the dog was faithful. It led him around everyday, staying with him while he begged.

One day the blind man's relatives paid him a visit. How he caught hold of them, jumped about, and shouted for joy! How he yelled and kissed and embraced them! How happy he was with his relatives!

The dog looked on with great sadness. Then it saw a wise man, went up to him, and said, "I think you are someone with great wisdom, and I would like to tell you what is on my mind so that I can have some peace."

The dog told him everything that had happened. "None of his relatives would remain with him, but I went everywhere with him. I helped him so much. I even went begging with him. But the moment he saw his relatives again, he shouted, he embraced them, he cried, he fell down and prayed, he kissed them—he was ecstatic. I helped him so much, yet he never kissed me, he never showed the slightest affection for me. I did all his work, but he never considered my comfort. He didn't care for me when he could see, and he didn't care for me when he could not see. What can be said when men in the world have such lack of gratitude, O great one?

"I want to be free of him but I cannot leave a man who is blind. You are a great man. Please give him his sight so that I can leave. Give him back his eyes." The dog begged and begged and cried.

The man of wisdom spoke. "Do not be sad. Though you have been born a dog, you have the quality of gratitude. You are an 'original' dog. It will be good if you do your duty so that your innate gratitude can be expressed. Even though you were born a dog, God's grace will be with you. Do not be sad. Let me tell you something.

"You are one dog, but man nourishes many dogs within himself in the form of attachments, blood ties, craving, and desire for titles. All the scenes you saw and grieved over are the scenes played by the ungrateful dogs man rears within himself. Millions of dogs dwell in his blood, his muscles, his skin, his qualities, his actions, his thoughts, and his intellect. He is filled with dogs which snarl and snap at him, bite him, and tear him apart. He cannot even go in one direction; he is pulled in all four. He has no peace. Day and night these dogs drag him around the world, even after he loses his eyes. The ungrateful dogs of desire cause him tremendous difficulty.

"You, as an original dog, should not fight with temporary dogs. It would be best if you would derive your peace from showing your original gratitude and trust. If you see a wicked dog in any form, do not run to bite it. Wag your tail, show peace, send it on its way, and stay free. That is the true state of wisdom and gratitude.

"A dog is an enemy to a dog. Man is a dog and you are a dog. You are a dog with gratitude and he is a dog without gratitude. Therefore do not be sad. You must live as a dog that has gratitude; let him live as an ungrateful dog.

"No matter how much you do for man, no matter how much you give him, he will not appreciate it. Do your duty without attachment in the way God does His duty. As long as you think that you are the one who is doing the duty, you will be sad. When you stop thinking that way, then you will be a grateful dog with trust in God, doing God's duty. That will be your peace.

"Reflect on this and do your duty. Do not grieve over the actions of others. Think of your birth and the state you must attain. Obtain that clarity. That will be the victory in your life."

### 448.

A learned man looked at an unlearned man and asked, "Who can be called a man?"

The unlearned man said, "A man is one who lives with good conduct, good thoughts, the quality of not hurting other lives, compassion for all lives, and peace."

### 449.

"Can men reach God through race or religion?" a man asked a completely unlearned man.

He answered, "One who tears down and throws away the evil qualities of racial bigotry and the fecal arrogance of fanaticism, one who acts with the qualities of God, can reach God."

### 450.

A fortuneteller asked a wise man, "Does man carry time with him, or does time move along carrying man?"

The wise man answered, "It is man who carries time and makes it pass. Time does not carry man. Man carries time, counts it, and is subject to the difficulties and conditions of each season that time brings. If he unburdens himself of time, all things connected to time will also leave.

"Time is the day and night which he himself brings about. It is the dream he sees. If man relinquishes darkness, he will no longer exist in the duality of time. If he gives up the dreaming of his mind, he will lose his thoughts. Engulfed in the light of grace, he will live a life without darkness. Forever he will dwell in the light of God, and there will be no passage of time.

"When the resplendence of wisdom rises, the darkness of ignorance will set and the dream of time will vanish by itself. Just as the sun is constant and unchanging, the light of wisdom will resplend, forever, indestructible in his soul."

### 451.

"What is the connection between God and man? If God is

unseen, how can a connection be established between man and something unseen? How can man see the connection? Is the one who sees the connection a man, and is one who does not see the connection also a man? How does the connection come?" A man asked these questions of a Sufi *gnāni*.

The *gnāni* replied, "True indeed. Not everything we see or believe in is God, and not everyone we see is a man. But it is easy for a true man to see the connection between God and man.

"God is beyond mind, desire, and thought. From a place beyond mind, desire, and thought, one who acts with the qualities of God, who does the duty of God, who hands over to Him the responsibility for the diseases of hunger, illness, old age, and death, one who does duty without selfishness and has compassion—he is in the state in which God exists. He is a man, an *insān*. He is God. In that state he can see the connection between man and God, which is made up of the qualities and actions of God.

"When form is created, the ray of the power of God comes into each form. Thus a connection exists between the power known as God and the ray known as the soul. That ray existed within Him in *anāthi,* the dark time before the beginning. The bodies that were formed with the ray of God's power inside them will live with that connection.

"There are six kinds of lives. One of them, man, has a connection to God. Man had that connection in *anāthi,* and he maintains it even after he leaves *anāthi.* Just as a fish dies when it is taken out of water, the ray of the soul will die if its connection to God's power is broken.

"God's power exists for all time. But if man forgets his connection to it and establishes a connection to the five elements, to earth, fire, water, air, and ether, he will live and die with a connection to hell.

"One who maintains the connection to God is a man, while those who prefer the connection to the elements are pulled by those *shakthis,* their forces and energies, and disappear into the karma of animals. They become subject to millions of births and to hell. One who is connected to God is pulled by that power and grace and will disappear in God."

452.

A swami asked a Sufi sheikh, "I performed thousands of mantras,

I read and recited all the *purānas,* I did yoga postures, and I fasted. Although I meditated and prayed for such a long time, O sheikh, I still don't understand anything. I don't know anything. I have not yet seen anything. What should I do now? What is prayer? What is the point of prayer? To what should I pray?"

The Sufi sheikh replied, "What you say is true. The things about which you have spoken concern the rituals and the precepts in religion. What you must know is that God is the unfathomable Ruler of grace and incomparable love. He is the One without birth or death, the One who transcends beginning and end. He is the One without wife or children. He is the One without darkness or torpor, the One without lust, hatred, or jealousy. He is the One without hunger or death, happiness or sadness. He is the One without body or form, time or seasons. He is the One without water or fire. He is the One without the sixty-four sensual pleasures. He is the One without fetus or form, the One who is neither male nor female. He is the One without name or country. He is the One who exists then, now, and forever. He is the Creator of all lives, the one power who watches, protects, and nourishes them.

"That power exists in the form of compassion to all lives. He nourishes them. Day and night, whether they are happy or sad, awake or asleep, while they walk or sit, God is within them, doing selfless duty with His three thousand gracious attributes. That power can be called Allah or God or various other names. Understand this with your wisdom.

"All the created things you see on the outside—the sun, moon, stars, earth, air, fire, water, ether, demons, ghosts, animals, snakes, planets, scorpions, tarantulas, cattle, horses, camels, goats, donkeys, dogs, foxes, cats, rats, fish, birds, crows, mynahs, parrots, doves, demons, devils, witches, and you—everything you see on the outside has been created by Him to enable you to understand Him. All the animals visible on the outside exist within you. Those are the qualities that make you move and dance. They control you, turning you into a dog, a fox, a donkey, a horse, a demon, a ghost, a devil, a cow, an elephant, a rat, a snake, or a scorpion. They control you with qualities which seem like miracles to you and make your thoughts move and dance. They devour your true wisdom and your human thoughts, and you follow them, seeking their help. You accept them as your gods, calling it devotion and

146

worship. Your faith becomes established in them. Even if they give you up, you are not willing to give them up; you pray to them and perform *pūjās,* or rituals, for them. You must give up all this and know what true prayer is.

"True prayer occurs only if you think, analyze, and see with feeling, awareness, intellect, judgment, subtle wisdom, divine analytic wisdom, and divine luminous wisdom. If you uproot and throw away all the things you trusted earlier, O swami, if you acquire and act with all the qualities of God who is limitless grace and incomparable love, if you are grateful to Him, pay obeisance to that power, and surrender yourself to Him, that is true prayer.

"When you reach that state, you will be like an iron in fire. The iron becomes red-hot and is transformed into fire. If you too fall into and merge with the fire of God's truth, then you will not exist. There will be only the truth. That kind of surrender is real prayer. All the time you stay separate from the fire, you are merely iron. Such is your present state of prayer and worship. If you fall into the fire and transform yourself, you will understand that state, merge with it, and receive its benefits."

### 453.

A man asked a Sufi, "People talk about male and female, but what is the essential difference between the two?"

The Sufi replied, "O man, both are formed of the five elements. The concept of male and female applies to the body. The Artist who created the male and female merely decorated them differently. The body is a cage, a house in which either can dwell, but you are deceived by the decorations.

"If you think of this with wisdom, you will see that womanly qualities are soft and delicate. In the decorations of womanliness, there is a beauty that is like gold, a beauty that attracts. The energy in their faces and bodies is like a magnet. The male has a similar magnetic energy, but his is on the inside. Though men lack the gentleness and outer softness which attracts externally, they have the strong inner magnetic energy which is attracted by, and connects to, the outer magnetism residing in the face and form of a woman.

"The world says male and female, but if you reflect with your wisdom, you will realize that male and female are like two kinds of breath, like the sun and the moon. The two breaths are called the art of the sun's heat, which is the male, and the art of the moon's coolness, which is the female.

"In the sky, the moon is lower and the sun is higher. The moon takes in the light of the sun and sends it out as cool yellow rays in the night.

"But the original light must be understood. The power which is neither male nor female is light, and that is the point which both male and female must reach. You can understand this through the example of the sun and the moon in the sky and through the example of male and female on earth.

"Your understanding will be contained in two words: *lā ilāha,* there is nothing other than You—the outgoing breath, on the left side; *illallāhu,* You are Allah—the incoming breath, on the right side. These two breaths meet in Allah.

"In the same way, the soul which came from God must return to its source. You must return to Him in the same form in which you came from Him. This is the only state God will accept.

"The five parts called earth, fire, water, air, and ether cannot reach Him; they belong to the world. Do not be enamored with them, thinking of them as male and female. Discard them and say *lā ilāha* on the left, and *illallāhu* on the right. There is nothing other than God. If there is nothing else, then there is no male or female. When there is no male or female, there is only light. You must attain that light. That is divine wisdom, or *gnānam.*

"When God is the power and you are the light, the power is male and you are female. You must reach that power. Everything you see and desire will change. Everything you see in form or without form will change. The changeless power is the only male. God is the power, you are the ray. When this male and female merge, it is called *gnānam* and resplendence, light and complete- ness, *Nūr* and Allah, *insān kāmil* and wisdom.

"Both male and female qualities exist in the body. The male qualities are arrogance, strength, egoism, and fanaticism while the qualities of humility, reverence, devotion to God, beauty, and grace are the qualities of womanliness, the beautiful qualities. The male's arrogant qualities want to control the beautiful female qualities and get on top of them.

"If man destroys the arrogant qualities of his ego, if he cherishes the womanly qualities and behaves as a woman toward God, he will be able to establish a connection with God.

"If men would have the qualities of women, the peace and tranquillity of womanliness, then in the same way that women are beautiful, God's beauty would enter them. Male qualities are the qualities of a male lion, a beast. If the male lion would change into a beautiful and gentle woman, it would no longer be male or female and it would receive the beauty of God's qualities. Those qualities would fall in love with God, winning the light of God and receiving His beauty."

## 454.

A man came to a Sufi sheikh and said, "O sheikh, I need a boon. You are a sheikh, and you can fulfill my needs."

"What would you like?" the sheikh asked him.

"From the time I was about three years old, I have wanted to rule the whole world and keep it in my hand under the umbrella of my rule. This has been my intention. I think about it so much that I cannot fall asleep at night.

"I have asked everyone in the world I could think of: swamis, yogis, deities, and people who perform miracles. None of them was able to grant my boon or give me peace of mind.

"'Study this mantra, study that mantra! Recite this verse, recite that verse!' they said. They gave me hundreds of thousands of mantras and verses. I read them all, I recited mantra upon mantra and verse upon verse. I performed rituals, but I had no success. I have not made any progress through all this. In fact, it seems like the reverse.

"I have come to you as a last resort. You must grant me the might to rule the world. I have not benefited from anyone else, nor has anyone even answered me properly."

The Sufi replied, "Is that so? Very good, little brother, let me tell you a story. Will you listen?"

"Yes, I will."

★

A guru had a disciple whose intention was to learn to control a jinn. So the guru taught him a jinn mantra which he studied assiduously. One day he came eagerly to the guru. "Swami, I have learned it. I know the mantra now. I know it well. Please give me permission to make it work so I can get everything I want."

"You are not ready," the guru told him. "You are not yet mature. It is not wise for you to use it before you are ready. You must wait for the proper time."

The disciple was impatient. "I have learned it. I am ready, I know the mantra, I know it." He badgered the guru constantly. "I'm ready, I'm ready, I'm ready."

The guru could not take this constant heckling and finally said, "Do you really think you are ready? It doesn't seem so to me, but if you want to, go ahead. The benefit and the loss are your responsibility." The guru gave him the ability to call forth the jinn.

The disciple recited the mantra and the jinn appeared.

"Why did you call me? What do you want?" the jinn shouted.

"You must do what I say," commanded the disciple.

"All right, what must be done?" asked the jinn.

"I want a palace larger than that of the king, a palace made of all the kinds of gold and jewels in the world." Within a second, the palace appeared.

"What should I do now?" asked the jinn.

"I want the palace equipped with dishes, pots, cups, bowls, and utensils made of gold." That, too, was ready in a second.

"What do you want now?" the jinn demanded.

"You must bring me all the nicest furnishings in the world and fill the palace." Instantly, the palace was filled.

"Now what?" the jinn said in a booming voice.

"I want a girl more beautiful than the most beautiful princess in the world." The jinn brought her instantly.

"Now what must I do?" thundered the jinn.

"I think I have everything I need, now. There is no more work for you."

"But I need work. If you don't give me work, I will have to kill you!"

The disciple thought hard. In desperation, he tried to think of the most difficult task possible. Finally he stammered, "The ruby from the mouth of a cobra. Bring me the ruby from the mouth of a cobra!"

As soon as the jinn disappeared, the disciple ran to the guru.

"O guru, what shall I do? If I don't give him work every second, he will kill me. I have everything I want and I don't know what else to tell him to do. *Aiyō,* my guru, what shall I do? What is my fate? Please save me!"

"I told you you were not ready," the guru said. "I told you before, but you insisted you were ready. Well, go and give him some work. Keep him busy."

"*Aiyō!* Everything I need has been supplied—a wife, a palace, lands, countries. I have everything; there is nothing I lack. I finally sent him to bring the jewel from the mouth of the cobra, but even that will take him no more than a second to complete. He is going to kill me as soon as he comes back. Save me, O guru."

"I warned you. I told you that you were not ready. What do you expect me to do?" the guru said. "Just as it takes only a few minutes to make money and gather possessions, it also takes only a few minutes for your life to end. You need maturity to realize this. I told you that you could get whatever you wanted in an instant, but also that the things you get can kill you in an instant. But you didn't listen to me. You insisted you were ready, so I had to tell you to go ahead."

Suddenly, the jinn appeared with the gem. "Give me work!" he boomed, towering over the disciple.

The disciple quaked in fear, clutching the feet of the guru. The guru turned to the jinn. "Wait a little," he said. Then he addressed the disciple. "I told you then that you were not ready, and now you come and hang on to my feet. I told you I would let you know when you were mature. You should have held on to my feet then, but you left. What is to be done? Now let us see what we can do to get rid of him."

Just at that moment, a dog with a curly tail happened by, and the guru whispered, "Tell the jinn to straighten the tail of that dog."

Timidly, the disciple gave the order to the jinn. The jinn straightened the tail, but as soon as he let go it sprang right back. Again the jinn pulled it straight, this time with both hands, but the dog's tail curled back as soon as he released his grasp. Over and over again, the jinn tried to straighten the tail. He tried and he tried, but the tail kept curling. There was nothing he could do, so he ran away in shame.

★

"Ruling the world is like the story I just told you," continued the Sufi sheikh. "Did you understand, little brother? You can rule the whole world in an instant, you can get everything you ask for in an instant, but it can also kill you in an instant. Think of this a little and give up this desire. The world outside is a small point, as small as an atom. But the world inside your mind is huge. If you rule that inner world called the mind, you will be the king of the eighteen thousand universes within you. If you can control and rule all the subjects within your mind, all the demons and desires, *māyā* and arrogance, you can rule everything, not only the world you see outside, but also the eighteen thousand universes within.

"Go, and live in peace."

### 455.

A man met a Sufi and said, "The world talks about vegetarianism. People who are vegetarians claim they are *saivam,* but are there any men in the world who are really *saivam?*"

The Sufi replied, "One who does not kill or eat anything at all is *saivam.*"

"Who is like that?" asked the man.

"Only God is in that state. He alone is *saivam,* pure and perfect *saivam.* Anyone who can reach God's state can also be called *saivam,*" replied the wise man.

### 456.

A man asked a Sufi, "Is there any man in God's creation who does not eat flesh or meat?"

The Sufi answered, "You have asked a very subtle question. God has created millions and millions of different kinds of creations. In accordance with the way they were created, the creations have from one to six levels of wisdom.

"They were conceived and formed out of skin, flesh, and blood, fluids, warmth, air, water, the illusion of *māyā,* and many other things. The things they were conceived and formed from are the things they ate at that time. They drank blood, flesh, and fluid when they were in the womb. Cows, goats, and other animals are like this. But some birds and animals do not eat meat or flesh again after birth.

"Man's body, too, was formed in the same way. If man understands this and realizes what eats what—that earth eats earth, flesh eats flesh, fire eats fire, *māyā* eats *māyā,* and one being kills and eats another—if he understands this with his divine analytic wisdom, he will not eat flesh. God, who is life to life and grace to grace, is the nourishment of the effulgence of the soul within the soul. Man needs to imbibe only the perfection which is that almighty power."

152

## 457.

A man asked a Sufi, "When you look at dogs and foxes, they seem the same. So why is the dog raised in the house and not the fox?"

The Sufi answered, "If you reflect a little, you will understand. Up to a point, the fox and the dog are similar. But their qualities and the sounds they make are different. You must know this. If danger threatens the house, a dog will howl, 'Ooo, ooo, ooo, ooo!' A dog will howl only in times of difficulty, but if you raise a fox in the house it will howl constantly. If you keep a dog in the house, it will protect chickens, cats, and other things there. But if you have a fox to guard your house, it will catch and eat your chickens, ducks, and rabbits. You must think about this.

"Even though a dog and a fox are alike in form, their sounds, actions, and qualities are different. A dog is grateful and will protect the house and its master, while a fox plays tricks. Understand this. Raise grateful things in your house. Do not bring up those that are ungrateful. But if you do, you must train their qualities starting from the day of their birth. Then you may be able to change them to a certain extent. But in an emergency, they may still revert to their hereditary nature.

"Like this, men may have the face of man, but you cannot keep them all in your home. That will be dangerous to your house and to the cage of your body. Keep only grateful men in your house and avoid those with tricks, treachery, and deceit. Do not associate with those who desire fame, those who have lust, or those who are jealous or envious. Their qualities may seep into you. Avoid them without antagonizing them.

"Understand this. Do not think a dog and a fox are the same. Keep in your house those with good qualities, good actions, wisdom, truth, honesty, directness, and gratitude. That will help you, your possessions, and your body. If you bring men with fox qualities into your house, it will be dangerous to your possessions and to your life."

## 458.

If sugarcane and poison
Are put on the same plate
The poison will kill
Even though sugarcane
Has an exquisite taste.

It is the same if you associate with deceitful people. Associate with those of wisdom. Then you will be tasty to good people and to everyone.

459.

A dove came to a Sufi and said, "For many days I have seen you in the forest. I was not able to speak to you before, but now I wish to tell you of my sorrow.

"We doves live in the forest. We do not hurt any other life. We eat the fruit in the trees, the food God has given us. Our only intention is to live happily and peacefully.

"But as we go about our lives, hunters come into the forest. They spread their nets in order to trap our families and our tribes, they kill us, and then they eat us. If we escape their nets, they shoot us with bows and arrows. We do not harm anyone. Why do the hunters do this to us?"

The Sufi answered, "O dove, what you say is true. Even before a hunter is born, his mother and father put aside weapons for him, bows and arrows, quivers, tridents, swords, and spears. These weapons mingle with his developing embryo, and the hunter forms and grows up amidst such qualities and weapons. They become his nature, and you can never tell him anything else. Because of this, we must be aware of the bows, arrows, tridents, swords, and spears even before we see them, and try to escape with wisdom. You need to be very, very clever to escape. As soon as you see the hunter's murderous nature, you must recognize what he is and get away. That will be good.

"There are many varieties of beings among God's creations. Some with human faces may have animal qualities, some with animal faces may have human qualities. If a person has human wisdom and human qualities, know that he is a true man. O dove! If you find someone like that, try to live in his company. But when you see animal qualities in human form, take action before evil and danger can threaten you."

460.

A king who had been reading many different kinds of books and studying avidly for many years was caught by the desire for divine wisdom, for *gnānam*. One day the king summoned his minister and said, "I want to obtain *gnānam*. Tell me how I can do it." Every day he asked his minister, but the minister could not give him an answer. He asked repeatedly, but the minister could do nothing. Finally the king got angry. "If in one month's time you do not tell me how to obtain *gnānam,* I will have your head cut off."

The minister searched high and low for someone who could help him. He read all the books, scriptures, and philosophies he could find. But no matter how diligently he searched, he could not discover the answer.

The minister was very unhappy. "How can I possibly teach the king *gnānam*? It looks as if he will surely kill me. I must be ready to die, but I have one child. The child has no mother, so I must make arrangements with my relatives to care for her."

The month had nearly passed. He could not sleep nor could he even bring himself to eat his meals. Observing this, his eight-year-old daughter asked, "Father, you have not been eating. What is wrong?"

He did not reply. But the girl clung to him and insisted. "You must tell me. What is the matter? Tell me. I am your daughter, am I not? I will have no peace until I know the reason for your worry."

Finally he gave up and related the story. He told her how upset he was because she would be an orphan once he was executed by the king.

"Is this what you are afraid of? There is no need to worry. I will take care of this matter. Take me to the king. I will give him the answer and then you can be free. I cannot tell you what it is now. Quickly, take me to the king," said the girl.

"I don't know what he will do. He might kill me and the child too," thought the minister. He tried to dissuade her, but she would not listen.

The minister took the child to the king's court. The other ministers were already gathered, waiting for the king to obtain *gnānam* or kill the minister. The king entered and began to address the court.

All of a sudden, the child's piercing scream interrupted the king's speech. "Tie me up! Tie me up!"

The irate king commanded his ministers, "Grab her and tie her to that pillar!"

They tied her, but still she screamed and howled. The king looked on in amazement as she shouted, "*Aiyō! Aiyō! Aiyō!* Untie me! Untie me!"

"Why is the girl acting like that?" demanded the king.

"She is the minister's daughter. She screamed to be tied and we tied her. Now she is screaming to be untied."

"Well, then, untie her!" yelled the king.

They untied her, but she continued to hang on to the pillar and scream.

"This girl is crazy," the king exclaimed. In exasperation, he stormed down the steps and confronted the girl. "You are untied. You are free. You can go! Have you no intelligence?" he roared. The screaming stopped.

"True indeed, maharaja," came the child's clear reply. "I have no intelligence and neither have you. I am untied and I can go. But what about you? Has anyone tied you to your kingdom so that you cannot attain *gnānam*? No. You are untied in the same way I am untied. You are free in the same way I am free. You are free to go and obtain *gnānam*. But you are holding on to your kingdom, your possessions, and your fame. How can a minister tell you how to obtain *gnānam* while you are living like this?"

The king thought a moment. "What you say is the truth," he admitted, looking at her. "You have given me *gnānam*. Although your father is a minister, he didn't give me the answer I needed, but you have shown me the way. Take my kingdom. I must leave it in order to reach *gnānam*."

"Maharaja, if you tied me to your kingdom, your fate would come to me, and that would really make me scream. It would be better if I could go with you."

"When you are old enough you can come to join me. I must go now," answered the king.

★

Like that, each man who searches for and studies *gnānam* is still holding on to something in the world. He hangs on to the world while demanding, "Give me *gnānam*!" He holds on to the world, saying, "*Gnānam,* come! *Gnānam,* come! *Gnānam,* come!" yet he refuses to let go of the world. This is exactly what the king did.

If men would let go of the world of ignorance known as *māyā*, *gnānam* would come in search of them and they would be free.

This is a story told in children's books. See how much wisdom and *gnānam* can be learned from such books, by king and beggar alike!

### 461.

A rich man lived in a huge mansion. He had immense wealth which he kept locked up under his bed and guarded day and night. He could not sleep properly or leave his house for very long, for fear his money would be stolen.

He had a sheikh who came to see him occasionally. One day, the rich man told the sheikh, "O *gnāna sheikh*, I have no peace. Please tell me how I can gain peace."

The sheikh replied, "Only peace can seek peace. Only if you are peaceful inside can you seek peace on the outside." And he went away.

One day the rich man looked out from his balcony. Near the mansion, a woodcutter and many others were playing ball. A fruit seller came by carrying a basket of beautiful fruits. The rich man called to him, "How much are the fruits?"

"Ten cents a piece," answered the vendor.

"Ten cents! Ten cents for these?"

"Yes, they cost me nine-and-a-half cents, and I must get a half cent for myself. They are ten cents a piece."

"Would you give them to me for three cents?"

"Are you crazy? You have a huge house and piles of money and you are asking me to give them to you for three cents! I would suffer a loss of six-and-a-half cents if I did that. I cannot give them to you for less. You do not know how to appreciate good fruit," he said, and he moved on.

The rich man then watched as the woodcutter hailed the fruit vendor. "How much are your fruits?"

"They are ten cents each," answered the vendor.

"Good. Please give me twenty-five." The woodcutter bought the fruits and distributed them among his friends. They ate the fruits together very happily.

Looking on, the rich man thought, "I do not have as much peace as that man has. He eats well and is so happy even though he is a poor woodcutter."

The next time the sheikh visited him, the rich man told him about the woodcutter. "O sheikh, he is so much happier and more peaceful than I am. Although I have a lot of money, I cannot buy a single fruit with it. The woodcutter bought twenty-five fruits, but I didn't even buy one. Why is that?"

The sheikh answered, "He is peaceful because he does not have what you have. If you give up what you have, you will be peaceful. Let me demonstrate this to you. Take ninety-nine rupees and tie it up in a cloth bundle. Now where is the woodcutter's house? Come with me and show it to me."

It was a little hut. The door was open because the woodcutter had nothing that needed safeguarding. The sheikh threw the bundle with the ninety-nine rupees into the hut. Then they returned to the rich man's house where they could watch the woodcutter's hut unobserved.

When the woodcutter came home from work and went inside to put his ax away, he saw the cloth bundle. He put the ax down, took up the bundle, and opened it. He counted ninety-nine rupees. He immediately exclaimed, "Ah! If there was one more, there would be one hundred rupees! Why didn't the man who left this leave me one more rupee? Now, where can I keep this money?"

That day he had earned three rupees. He put one of those rupees inside the bundle to make it a hundred. Later, while he was eating, he thought, "If I spend only fifty cents out of today's earnings on food and put the balance into the bundle, I would have 101 rupees. Soon I would have 105 rupees, and once I cut more wood, I would have 110. Later I could have two hundred rupees. Then, before long, I'll have a thousand rupees! Then I can build a house!" With these thoughts, the woodcutter hid the money behind a brick in his fireplace.

The sheikh and the rich man, watching the woodcutter, noticed that when the children came to play ball with the woodcutter, he would not join them. He seemed unwilling to leave his hut. The boys called to him. "Come, let's go and eat. Do come outside for some fresh air."

Feigning illness, the woodcutter protested, "I'm not well. I can't come. You all go." But his friends insisted, so he reluctantly went with them.

As they continued to watch the woodcutter, the sheikh and the rich man saw him constantly turn his head toward the place where his money was hidden. After playing for a little while, he finally said, "I'm not well, I'm going."

The next day he rose at three in the morning so he could chop more firewood to sell. After work, when his friends came to take him out to play ball, he refused to go. The following day he got no sleep at all. He worried constantly and did not eat properly. For a whole week he would not leave his house in the evening. He would chop firewood, sell it, and go home, chop firewood, sell it, and go home. Each evening he brought home more money and watched it accumulate day by day.

"Look at his face now," the sheikh said to the rich man. "How does he look? The satan which seized you before has captured him now. Now neither of you has peace. As soon as he began to worry about accumulating money, his peace was destroyed. Do you really want peace? If you do, tell the people in the village that you are throwing out all you have saved. Give everything away and come with me."

The rich man gave away his possessions and followed the sheikh. Presently, they were walking across the hot sand. The sun was blazing. It was between twelve and one in the afternoon and the rich man was extremely tired, thirsty, and hungry. In front of a cottage, there was an old woman. The sheikh asked her, "O Ammā, do you have any food to give us?"

"I've got some gruel, a little salted mango, and some fried chili, but that's all." She mixed the salted mango with the fried chili and brought two bowls. The sheikh poured some gruel into one of the bowls and handed it to the rich man. When the rich man bit into the salted mango and drank the gruel, it seemed as if the taste had come to him from heaven. He drank as much as he could and said, "Now I have tasted the peacefulness of food from heaven. From the time I was born, I have never tasted anything as wonderful as this!"

After he drank the gruel, the rich man felt drowsy, so he lay down at the foot of a tree. As soon as he closed his eyes he fell asleep. He slept from lunchtime right through the evening and the night. When the sheikh woke him on the following day, the sun was up.

"Isn't it dark yet?" asked the rich man.

The sheikh answered, "It's the next day, eight o'clock in the morning. Come, we must be on our way."

"I didn't know I had slept so long. I haven't slept this peacefully since I was born," said the rich man.

"Earlier, the world was within you, and all the animals in it were devouring you," said the sheikh. "That is why you had no peace. Now the world is not within you, so all the animals have gone. Come. Let us go." The sheikh took him along, saying, "This is the path to peacefulness."

462.

There was an orphaned shepherd boy whose name was Karuppan. Because he had no mother or father, some people took him and raised him. He would take their cattle out to graze every day. Karuppan slept in the barn after he brought the cattle home.

One day while the cattle were grazing in the fields, he was leaning against a tree trunk, poking idly at the earth beneath his feet. Suddenly he found a golden pot hidden in the earth. He was overjoyed. He embraced it and kissed it and leaped for joy. He held the pot to his heart, and he put it on his head. He did not even eat the rice he had brought with him. He shouted, "I am rich! I am rich! I am a king!" When it came time to take the cattle back, he carefully hid the pot in the earth and went home. Though he had always brought the cattle back early, now it was six o'clock before he returned. He sat outside the house, dreaming of the pot.

The woman in the house said, "What is this? Karuppan is not to be seen. Usually he comes much earlier with his bowl for porridge. Karuppan? Where are you? Oh, there you are! Bring your bowl. You are late, it is time to eat."

He went in and declared, "*Ammā*! Don't call me Karuppan! From now on you must show respect and call me Karuppana Swami!"

Surprised, they wondered, "What is this? He has never been like this before. All right, Karuppana Swami, come bring your bowl. Come eat." They smiled among themselves and decided to humor him, though they still wondered. "What is happening? He leaves early in the morning and returns very late in the evening. When he finally does come home, he doesn't come in to eat," thought the people of the house. And they asked him, "Why do you do this, Karuppan?"

"I told you to call me Karuppana Swami!"

"What a wonder this is! All right, Karuppana Swami," they said.

A week passed like this. Then one day the head of the house followed Karuppan to the fields to see what he was doing. He

160

hid behind a tree and watched Karuppan take the pot out from its hiding place. He watched him kiss and embrace the pot and put it on his head. He heard him exclaiming that he was rich, that he was a king. He watched all day until the boy hid the pot. He waited until the boy was out of sight. Then he dug up the pot and took it for himself.

The next day, Karuppan returned from the field at three o'clock, but he did not go in for dinner.

The woman called him. "Karuppana Swami, come eat."

"I am too tired," he sighed.

She called again. "Karuppana Swami, bring your bowl!"

"*Ammā*! Don't call me Karuppana Swami. Call me the same old Karuppan as before."

"Come then, Karuppan," she said, and she gave him some rice.

★

God gave everything to man at the very beginning. It is for man to take the right things and use them properly. If he picks what is evil, his *nafs,* his base desires, win out. But if he takes what is good and uses it with wisdom, goodness wins. The outcome depends on whether he uses wisdom or ignorance.

As soon as man feels proud of what he has, he forgets God, turns truth into falsehood, and makes himself into a god, just as Karuppan claimed the treasure as his own and called himself a swami. But as soon as that worldly treasure is gone, man reverts back into the same old Karuppan. He reverts to the karma of his birth and becomes food for hell.

Furthermore, as soon as man begins to regard the world as the lasting treasure in his life, as soon as he begins to look at the world as valuable and precious and to see himself as a god, a wealthy man, a philanthropist, a learned man, a man of wisdom, a *gnāni,* or a king, he forgets God's justice. Thinking of God's kingdom as his property, he tries to rule it. But the justice of God—the impartial justice free of attachment, prejudice, favor, and selfishness, the justice of loving all lives as his own—is not in him, so the treasure he dug up is forfeited. He forgets God and reverts to the same old state. He himself admits he is the same old Karuppan and becomes food for the earth.

This is not God's fault. It is the fault of each man's ignorance, pride, and arrogance.

## 463.

There was a lion who lived in the jungle. He would leap upon anyone who walked along a certain path, kill him, and eat him. This went on for a long time. No one could catch the lion.

Then a hunter who also lived in the jungle made a steel cage in which to trap the lion. He placed it on the path and went away. One day while chasing a deer, the lion leaped into the cage and the door slammed shut. The lion tried his utmost to get out of the cage but he could not.

Not many people used the path, and those who did used it in great fear. As these people passed by, the lion would beg them to release him. He swore he would not harm them. The lion put his paws together in worship and bowed down to them. He begged and he begged, but the people were so frightened that they ran away as soon as they heard the sound of his voice.

Invoking the names of many gods, the lion swore to all the passersby that he would not harm them. "Please let me out! Set me free! I will not hurt you! I will make you my idol and offer you fruit and flowers at a temple. I will pray to you and keep you in my heart forever if you will only set me free!" But everyone who heard him ran away in fear. No one would help the lion.

One day, however, a certain man came along the path. Again the lion begged and begged to be set free, putting his paws together and bowing to him. "O god, you are the god who can save my life." Using the names of so many gods, he swore that he would do no harm if set free. "Please save me," he wailed.

"I have been in this cage for eight days, and I am almost dead from hunger and thirst. I have had no food or water in all this time. Please save me. If you help me, every day I will place you in the depths of my heart as my god and bow to you in worship."

The man felt so sorry when he heard the lion's woes that he opened the cage. Immediately, the lion leaped on him with the intention of splitting his chest open, drinking his blood, and eating his liver.

"Lion! What are you doing! Think of the things you said and now look at what you are doing! Are you going to kill me? Why are you hurting me? Are you going to drink my blood? Are you going to split open my chest? Are you going to tear apart my liver? Where is your oath? Where are your gods? Why are you doing this?" screamed the man in great pain and fear.

162

"O man, I was locked in the cage and hungry for eight days," explained the lion. "I suffered so much. I just howled some words as a result of my pangs of hunger. I was so hungry, I swore anything I could think of. You know that when hunger comes the ten good qualities fly away. Can you believe what someone says when he is ravenous with hunger?

"If I let you go now, what will happen to me? I am almost dead, having been without food or water for eight days. I'm so weak that I wouldn't be able to catch anything even if I did go hunting. I don't have enough strength or speed. In my present state I would die. I certainly would have died if you hadn't saved me. Now, to become strong again, I have to eat you. But I will always be grateful for your help. I will always cherish you in my heart as the god who saved me," said the lion.

"This is not fair! You deceived me. You swore in the names of so many gods!" the man screamed.

"I am not unfair. I am fair. You are the one who is not being fair. I am hungry, and that is all I know. But if you insist, we can ask three beings in the jungle whether or not it is fair for me to eat you. If they say it is fair, then I can eat you. If they say it is unjust, I will let you go."

There was a palmyra tree nearby. The lion appealed to it. "For eight days, I was trapped in a cage without food or water. I begged and begged to be let out. In my hunger, I shouted something, and this man opened the cage. When I was finally released, I was so weak that I could hardly walk. I can't catch anything else. The only way I can save my life is to eat him. Am I right or wrong?"

The palmyra tree answered, "Man is the one who is unjust and ungrateful. He is evil. Eat him!"

The man yelled, "I helped him because he swore not to harm me. He has caught me only because I helped him. How can you accept that?"

"O man," exclaimed the palmyra tree, "you water us for six months. That is all you ever do for us. But we give you palmyra fruits, roots, tubers, and leaves to build your houses and to make rope. You make baskets and mats out of us. You use our leaves. You make flour, bowls, ladles, and spoons of us. You make so many things of us. We help you for a hundred and fifty years or so, and when we have nothing else to give, you bring your axes and chop us down. You pound wedges into us, split us apart, saw and plane us, peel off our skins, and then use us to build your houses.

"You live in houses made out of us for generations, but that is still not enough for you. What is left of us is broken apart, used as firewood, and burned to ash. Even after all that, do you let us go? No. You use the ash on your fields in order to grow new palmyra trees, and then you subject us to the same thing all over again. Ungrateful man! No matter how much we help you, you are completely thankless. You destroy us in many ways.

"What you did for the lion was a small thing; you helped him for just a few seconds. What makes you think your action was so great? Was it greater than the help we give you? Evil man! Worst beast of all beasts! Ungrateful man! No men should live! Eat him, lion!"

"Thank you," said the lion. "Two more opinions to go."

Just then a cow came along. The lion told the cow what had happened just as he had explained it to the palmyra tree. "He did help me a little," the lion admitted. "But I am so painfully hungry I cannot bear it. I have to eat him in order to save my life. I might have sworn otherwise, but you know how it is—when hunger comes the ten good qualities fly away.

"We said we would find three beings in the jungle and ask for their judgment as to whether or not it is fair for me to eat him. Is it all right, or not?"

"You are terrible, O lion," said the cow, "but man is worse. O man, there is no animal as ungrateful as you are. Man is the worst of all beasts. Eat him, lion!"

"*Aiyō,* cow! Why do you say that?" cried the man. "Is this what should be done in gratitude to one who helps someone? I helped this lion so much. How can you tell him to eat me?"

The cow spoke. "O ungrateful man, what you did for the lion was a very little thing. Right after we cows are born, our mothers and their children are tied up right in front of each other, and you humans take all the milk. Only after you take all the milk do you allow the calf to try to suck milk from the mother. Furthermore, our mothers must pull heavy wagons all day or plow the fields until dusk. All that time the children are left hungry, but when the work is done, again you tie the children up in front of the mothers and take all their milk. Our mothers and fathers labor and plow for you while you build castles to live in and most times you do not give us so much as a shed.

"Our mothers and fathers get wet in the rain and sweat in the sun in order for you to feed your families. But do you feed us properly? No. At night we eat the little bit of straw you give us and then we must search for our own food. We even carry the firewood to your funeral houses. We take you on journeys. We pull the carts in which you put your belongings. After all that is done, still we must find our own food. You eat three times a day, but we must chew our cud overnight. Not only that, you do not even let us go free when we are old. When our mothers and fathers are old and tired, you drag them to the butcher and slaughter them while they tremble and cry out in fear. Then you haul their bodies to the supermarket. From beginning to end, you ruin our lives. You break up our families. You take babies away from their mothers and mothers away from their babies.

"You don't even give us shelter. We must stand in the sun and rain and wind. Ungrateful man! You do so little. All mankind is evil. Eat him!" said the cow.

The lion smiled, "Now there is one more opinion to go."

Just then a fox happened along. The lion told the fox all that had taken place. Sizing up the situation and realizing that the lion might eat him up too, the fox pretended to be a little deaf. He wanted to save the man, but in such a way that he himself could escape from the lion.

"Eh? Eh? Eh? Eh?" the fox kept asking, as if he could not hear. "Let us go and see. You'd better show me what happened so I can understand properly. Show me what happened."

The lion led the man and the fox to the cage. "Ah, is this the cage?" asked the fox.

"Yes," answered the lion.

"I don't understand," said the fox. "Show me exactly what happened. Where were you before the man came along?" The lion went into the cage.

"Ah, was that how you were inside the cage?" asked the fox.

"Yes, this is how I was inside the cage," replied the lion.

"How were you locked up?" asked the fox.

"I was locked up like this," replied the lion, locking the cage.

"You are now locked into the cage exactly as you were locked in before?" asked the fox.

"Yes, I am locked in exactly as I was before," answered the lion.

"Good. Then stay there!"

The lion roared and flung himself against the bars.

The fox then turned to the man. "Man, you truly are very ungrateful. But even so, you must use your intelligence. If you try to help evil animals, you will be in great danger. If I had done what was just, the lion would have eaten you. The trouble is, it might also have eaten me. Foolish man! Run away from here."

"Fox!" roared the lion. "You deceived me. When I get out I will have my revenge."

"Ooo-ooo-ooo!" hooted the fox. "Then stay there and die! Ooo-ooo!" he howled, and he ran away.

A sheikh said to his disciple: Son, I have told you about a lion, but worse than the lion who was born a lion is the man-lion. Man has been born with the force and the qualities of a lion. That is the man-lion. Even though he wears the skin and face of a man on the outside he is a lion on the inside. He kills and eats. He drinks the blood from other men's hearts. He eats the hearts of all the creatures of the world, keeping himself hidden inside a man's skin and a man's face. That is the worst lion. Just think of the state of the man-lion! At least the real lion asked three beings in the jungle whether or not he should kill the man. But the man-lion will never ask anyone. As soon as he is let loose, he will jump and kill and eat. The man-animal is the worst animal.

Son, it is rare to be born a true man. If you would but know this unique man! He is seen so rarely. Touch and tap the people you see. Are they men? Or are they cruel lions who wear the skins of men? You must understand which is which and act accordingly. Whether you try to help them or harm them, you will be in danger. Of all the tens of millions of animals, only the man-animal kills and eats all lives.

It is easy to escape from real animals, but it is extremely difficult to escape from disguised animals. We must proceed very cautiously on our journey through this world. Man is the one animal which will kill and eat all other animals. He is the most dangerous animal of all.

### 464.

A king told his minister, "O minister, I have a desire. I want to capture and rule all the kingdoms of the world and make them mine. I want them to pay tribute to me. What should we do in order to achieve this goal?"

The minister said, "Maharaja! If you want to capture kingdoms, you must have armies and soldiers, horsemen, troops on camels, elephants, infantry, bows and arrows, swords, spears, tridents, and all sorts of things. Let us gather all these together and then set about capturing other kingdoms."

"Get them ready!" ordered the king. "Ours has been a small kingdom for too long. Now I must become an emperor. We must capture the kingdom nearest ours, and I must receive their tribute. After that we can overcome and control all the kingdoms of the world." "What you say is true," the minister replied. "We must send out a declaration of war. We must call for the armies."

And so they captured many kingdoms, but then they came up against a strong and powerful enemy. A fierce battle ensued with heavy losses on both sides. Corpses piled up like mountains.

That night the king said, "I cannot sleep. Let's take a walk."

The king and the minister left their tents. As they stood looking with sorrow at the great loss of life, they saw a horde of vultures. Although there were thousands of corpses on the field, the vultures hopped past body after body and converged on one body in a corner of the field.

"O minister, why have all the vultures crowded around just that one body? Why have they ignored all the others?"

"It is certainly a wonder," the minister agreed. He thought for a moment. "When I was young my grandfather told me that vultures like human flesh more than any other. He told me that vultures have two brilliant, white feathers, one on each side, by which they can tell whether a man is truly a man or whether he is an animal in human form. The vulture uses the magnetic energy or *shakthi* of those feathers to discover the location of a corpse and its true nature."

"But aren't they all men?" the king said.

The minister shook his head. "No. The vultures can see the difference through their special feathers."

So they brought out a bow and arrow and shot down the biggest vulture, plucked out its two white feathers, and looked through them. They were shocked to see that the battlefield was littered with foxes, dogs, monkeys, rats, cats, tigers, and various other animals. Among the dead there was only one man, and it was his body that all the vultures were feeding on. Then the king

167

looked at his minister and was amazed to see a red monkey. Quickly, he glanced down and saw that he himself looked like a black monkey.

The king was crestfallen. "Both of us are monkeys. We are monkeys, and we have killed so many other beings. There was only one man among us all. He is the only one who was fit to rule, and now he is dead. Because monkeys ruled in place of men, all this destruction came about. I do not want this kingdom anymore. Monkeys cannot rule. We caused so much suffering through our pranks. Only the one who is born a man can rule the kingdom.

"The most important thing we must do is destroy this monkey birth. We must eliminate our karma and be born as men. O minister," said the king, "I want to be born a man. You take my kingdom. I want to meditate and pray to God so that I can be born a man."

But the minister replied, "You at least are a black monkey, but I am a common red monkey with qualities of blood. I don't want to rule this kingdom either. I too must pray. If only we could give the kingdom to a man! Unfortunately, the one man who lived among us is dead. The rest of us are animals.

"I have an idea! Why don't we give the kingdom to the enemy king! He is the one who desired it."

They told all their soldiers to go home and then went to the enemy king. The king said, "Please take my kingdom. We are monkeys. We want no more battles, no more fighting. Look through this feather."

The enemy king looked and was amazed to see that all the corpses had animal forms. He also saw that he was a fox and his minister a donkey.

The king told the enemy king and his minister, "Look at what we have done to the land. If we rule, we will destroy everything. In God's kingdom there was but one man, and we have killed him. He was the only one fit to rule the kingdom. I don't want to rule anymore. I want to pray that I will be born as a man. Here, take my kingdom."

The enemy king refused. "I don't want to rule either. You at least are a monkey. A fox is much lower. You had better rule. I want to meditate."

They tried to persuade the fox-king. "Please take the kingdom."

"I don't want it. I want to come and meditate, too," answered the fox.

The black monkey, the red monkey, and the fox all said, "I don't want this kingdom. I want to pray. Let God rule God's kingdom," and they all went to pray.

The donkey, however, was accustomed to carrying heavy burdens, so he took on the burden of both kingdoms. But the quality of a donkey is to bite whoever goes in front of it and kick whoever goes behind. In addition, its whole body is infested with fleas. As a result of these qualities, the donkey ruined both kingdoms within a short time.

"My son," explained the sheikh, "these donkeys, monkeys, and foxes carry the world on their shoulders and try to rule mankind. They take charge of the kingdom of God and destroy justice, truth, patience, compassion, the virtuous qualities of God, the human generation, devotees of God, and *gnānis*. These donkeys have falsehood, arrogance, karma, and love for land, gold, and women. With lies and evil they attempt to capture and rule the kingdom of heaven, finally destroying mankind.

"God's kingdom must be ruled by a true man, and that man must be like God. He must do his duty without attachment or partiality or self-business. He must have compassion for all lives. He must dedicate his entire life to God, performing God's duties as his duties.

"He is the one who can rule the kingdom. But before that, he must rule his own heart and give all responsibility to God. God alone knows the proper way to bring up all lives with love and with the laws of divine justice, king's justice, human justice, and human conscience. One who rules with these qualities is a true ruler. All lives will respect him and be subservient to him as king, as friend, and as the one who will protect them.

"The animals lacking good qualities are the ones who destroy the world. We must leave the cage of the body and be born into the original form and qualities with which we came. If we can regain that original light form in this very birth, it will be easy to rule that kingdom."

465.

A disciple asked his sheikh, "O my sheikh, my true sheikh, in which religion can the connection between man and God be established?"

The sheikh replied, "Son, in a town many roads and paths meet at the marketplace, enabling the people of the countryside to come to the supermarket and buy all kinds of things. People come to buy what they need and then they return to their homes. No one stays in the marketplace.

"Like that, many paths and many religions lead to the marketplace of the world. Religions are paths. People go to the marketplace of the world, buy what they want, and then go back to their houses of arrogance, karma, and *māyā; tārahan, singhan,* and *sūran* (the three sons of *māyā*); obsession, hatred, miserliness, attachment, fanaticism, envy, intoxicants, lust, theft, murder, and falsehood. They buy what they want in the world market, then return to where they were before.

"In the marketplace they buy the teachings of the seventeen *purānas,* the sixty-four kinds of worldly knowledge, the sixty-four sexual games, the four religions, the six horoscopes, and the ninety-six energies. Then they return to the place of birth, the place in which they were conceived. They put the things they bought into the place of birth and give them form. Man cannot become man-God following any of these paths, nor can he become a perfected man, an *insān kāmil.* You must think about this.

"You asked in which religion can man and God be connected, did you not? Adam and Eve *(A.S.)* are our original father and mother. In Tamil they are called Īswaran and Īswari; in Arabic they are called Adam and Hawwā'. They are the original mother and father of all mankind. Everyone belongs to the one family of mankind. The Creator of the family is also one. He is God. He is the one God who is the Father of all creation.

"O son, man is one family. There is one God. But mind and desire buy the rejected things of the world and then go back to the seventeen houses mentioned before. There the fighting begins because of 'mine', 'yours', and 'who is greater than I'? My son, these seventeen try to rule the world. Their qualities obscure the connection between man and God.

"If you understand this with wisdom, you will see the performers in the marketplace acting out their murders and sins in the dark ignorance of torpor and *māyā.* Cut off this ignorance with wisdom. Cut off the hypnotizing religions and the bigotry which separates one man from another. If you dispel them with wisdom, if you act with God's qualities and actions, if you act with equality and compassion, if you regard other lives as you regard your own life, if you do selfless duty, you will see the connection between man and God. This is the good way, the religion of *gnānam,* the religion of grace, the religion of the Ruler of grace.

"Understand this with wisdom, O my son. Then you will understand your Father, the one family, your true prayer, the state you must attain, and the station you must occupy. If you pray with true understanding in the same way God does, throwing away what is wrong and taking only what is right, that is the straight path. You will see one family and one God. You will know that He alone is worthy of worship, and you will say, '*Lā ilāha,* there is nothing other than You.' Then with the true feeling that flows from a melting heart, you will reach that place."

466.

"O my sheikh, the world speaks of an exalted state called *bramachāria* or celibacy. Does one attain God's grace and wisdom by not marrying? Are there any men who have not married nor joined with women?" asked a disciple.

"Son, you have asked a very good question. One who has not married is very rarely seen on the earth. There are four hundred trillion, ten thousand energies, or *shakthis,* in the world, attracting and capturing everything created. There are *shakthis* of earth, water, air, illusion, and fire. Just as a magnetic current pulls on iron, the *shakthis* of the elements pull on whoever has them inside him. God is the only One who does not contain what is attracted by the five elemental *shakthis.* He alone cannot be pulled by these *shakthis.* He controls them.

"If that state of God exists in a man, if there is a man who can control all the *shakthis,* he alone is a *bramachāri.* One who does not have the power to control them is not a *bramachāri.*

"You might have thought *bramachāri* merely meant being unmarried. Let us look at it in that way, too, for a moment. A married man has one monkey. One who is not married, one who is called *bramachāri* by the world, performs the antics of a thousand monkeys through the dreams and thoughts of his monkey mind. Understand this with your wisdom."

467.

"What is the cause of separation from God and from human beings? What makes man seek separation? What can he possibly gain from it?" a man asked a wise man.

"Separation comes from actions of ignorance and from the thoughts of selfishness that arise from mind and desire. Thoughts of separation take away the sense of unity in man's life. This splits one man from another and leads him onto many dangerous paths. It makes him subject to torment, fighting, murder, and sin. In the end this results in actions whereby he will destroy himself. One day the poison of his own qualities will destroy him, just as a snake can be killed by its own poison when the poison sacs in its mouth burst from the vibration of thunder.

"If man will cut away the poisonous qualities that cause separation, he will never be divided from other men or from God."

468.

"In what way does sin enter man?" asked a man.

A wise man gave this answer. "Sin enters through the evil things a man sees, through his evil thoughts, ideas, desires, intentions, and ambitions, through anger, impatience, haste, jealousy, selfishness, deceit, thoughts of religious differences, intoxicants, lust, hatred, miserliness, greed, fanaticism, envy, arrogance, egoism, possessiveness, cravings, and through the differences of the 'I' and the 'you'. This is how the karma known as sin enters into and grabs man.

"If you act with the qualities of God, seeing and evaluating with divine analytic wisdom, if you dispel sinful qualities and actions, if the wisdom of compassion, justice, and honesty comes to exist within you, sin will not touch you. If you understand other lives as you understand your own, seeing others as your equal, and if wisdom dawns within you, then sin will not touch you. But if you have the evil qualities described earlier, sin will engulf you and bind you."

This is what a man of wisdom said.

469.

"Is there a good man in this country?" asked a disciple of his sheikh.

"Son, a good man is one who knows the country, avoids the evil in it and accepts the good, placing it within the cage of his body. He then analyzes his body, discarding what is evil and filling it with what is good, and thereby reaches perfection. Such a man is good for the country and also for himself. Such a one is a good man. Know this," answered the sheikh.

### 470.

A disciple asked his sheikh, "O sheikh, when doubt appears in a man, can it be of any benefit to him?"

"When a man has doubt," answered the sheikh, "his whole life is 'out', turned away from God and the truth. He is full of suspicion. He suspects his food, the world, his birth, his thoughts, what he sees with his eyes, what he hears with his ears, and what he says with his own mouth; he suspects his wife and his children; he suspects God, his possessions, and the very feces he defecates; he is suspicious in his thoughts and dreams, in wakefulness and in sleep, in his job, and in all the things he does. He never sees or accepts anything or anyone in his life as trustworthy. He looks at everyone with the eye of ignorance and stupidity and thinks he is the only clever man—and he doubts even that!

"A man who harbors doubt is like a bat, which both eats and defecates through its mouth. Even though he takes in good things from the world, the suspicions of his mind cause him to vomit them out again through the same mouth that took them in. His life is like the life of a bat; he hangs upside down, while his feet of ignorance hold onto doubt as though it were wisdom. A bat can see only in the night, and a doubtful man can see only in the darkness of his doubt. He cannot see in the daylight of wisdom and truth.

"Son, with wisdom you must establish a life without suspicion. To live like that is truly a quality of God."

### 471.

A disciple asked his sheikh, "O my sheikh, there are many kinds of fire in the world. Fire is present in most things, even things like stones, trees, iron, shrubs, thunder, and lightning, and the sun and the moon. Which of these is the cruelest fire, the most dangerous fire?"

The sheikh spoke, "If you are burned by fire, you can be healed. But there are many other kinds of fire. There is the fire of the Angel of Death, the fire of hell, the anal fire, and the fire of the hunger in the stomach.

"But of all kinds of fire, the fire of jealous anger raging in a man's mind is the worst. When jealousy is the firewood and anger is the fire, that is the worst kind of blaze. It will burn a man's life, it will burn the state of prayer to God, and it will burn to ash even the connection between man and God.

"Son, it is very difficult to escape from the fire of anger and jealousy, but if you can eliminate it within you, none of the other kinds of fire can burn you."

### 472.

A disciple asked his sheikh, "O my father, O my true sheikh, which is the best kind of milk? Which kind of milk best soothes the tiredness, hunger, and illness of man?"

The sheikh replied, "The milk of God's compassion and love which gushes forth from the spring of a melting and flowing heart is the best milk. One who drinks this milk will not be tired or hungry or ill. One who draws this milk from his heart and gives it to another can soothe all tiredness and hunger, old age, and even the illness which leads to death. This milk is not mingled with blood, karma, or arrogance. It is the milk of compassionate love, the most exalted milk in the world."

### 473.

A disciple asked the sheikh, "O my true sheikh, father of my soul, which is the sweetest honey in the world? There are so many kinds of honey, and all are sweet to the taste, but I want to know which one will dispel my karma, my sins, and the hunger of my soul? Which is the most exalted honey for the body and for the soul?"

The sheikh spoke. "Son, that is the honey of the qualities of God, His selfless duties, His actions, and His non-attached service. It is the honey of His three thousand gracious attributes, which give peace and comfort to all lives, honey mingled with His grace, honey that melts and oozes from the flower which blooms with the fragrance of wisdom. When that melting honey cascades from the flower of the heart, it attracts all lives to the love that soothes the heart. The honey of grace is the honey which all lives savor. It is the most exalted honey.

"In both the world of the souls and the next world, for the cage of the body, for the soul, for God, and for everyone, this is the honey which every life will taste, enjoy, and praise. One who realizes its incomparable flavor will understand its exaltedness, its benefits, and its bliss."

474.

A disciple asked a Sufi sheikh, "O wise one, people talk about luck. They say 'so and so is lucky', or 'so and so has good fortune'. Men want to be lucky in their lives. They fall in love with luck and search for it constantly, anticipating it with eagerness. They go to 'lucky places' for gambling, horse racing, lotteries, and betting. They think of 'auspicious' and 'inauspicious' times when planning their actions.

"Man looks for the many things that are called lucky and stakes his fortune on them, as in a horse race or at a gambling table. My sheikh, what is the luckiest thing in the world?"

"Son," replied the sheikh, "in the world there are millions of creations. Racehorses are called lucky. Everything is called lucky by someone. Men place their bets on the world. They bet on the numbers of the horses and shout, 'Which will be lucky for you? Which will be lucky for me?' They place their bets and make the horses run around the track. Of the ten or twelve horses which run the race, the one who comes in first is called lucky.

"They put the world into the world and what they get back is the world. They place their bets on the world and get back twice the world they first had—that is, the world plus hell. This is the race that man runs; he runs to seek out what is lucky. The horse of his mind and desire runs like this.

"The mind of man runs much faster than any horse in the world. Even faster than the wind is the speed of the mind. The horse of man's mind-energy is so fast that when it starts, the jockey, which is intellect, falls off. Foaming at the mouth, the horse of man's mind travels around the universe in an instant. It goes round and round the world. There is no finishing line, and nothing is won by it. There is only the foaming at the mouth.

"If one can control the mind-horse called *panja kalyani,* or the horse of five colors, which runs with the speed of the five elements—earth, fire, water, air, and ether—if one can climb onto this horse, control it with the reins of wisdom, and stop it, he will win that one incomparable prize which is the undiminishing, imperishable, limitless treasure of the perfection of God.

"However, if instead you bet on the horses of the world and receive hell as your winnings, you will be betting the karma of your body and receiving the karma of hell in return. But this is what the world desires and enjoys.

"My son, you must think: What was your purpose in coming here? You have another race to win. Where were you before? Where have you come to now? Where do you have to go after this?

"Climb onto the horse which rides around the world in a second, bring it under your control, and open the path that will lead you from where you are now to where you were before—with your Father. Find the shortcut. Practice running that race. If you win the prize, you will never die and you will never be reborn. The treasure you will win will never diminish and can never be destroyed. This is the best race for your life."

475.

A disciple asked a Sufi sheikh, "O my sheikh, many men search for a sheikh so they can receive the grace and the *gnānam* of God. Can those who are immersed in the pond of ignorance known as *māyā* be taken to the shore by a sheikh? Can they be saved? Can they be given grace and *gnānam*?"

The sheikh replied, "What you ask about is a great matter indeed. The arrogance, karma, and *māyā* of birth; *tārahan, singhan,* and *sūran* (the three sons of *māyā*); lust, hatred, miserliness, greed, envy, bigotry, arrogance, impatience, the egoism of the 'I', the possessiveness of 'mine', the darkness of religious and philosophical differences, intoxicants, obsession, theft, falsehood, and murder—all these things are churning and turning in the pond of karma. They live there, sunk in the hell of that pond, displaying the differences of the 'I' and the 'you'.

"A huge and demonic crocodile lives there, thrashing in the pond. It takes everything it catches to the bottom and leaves it to rot in the caves of ignorance and then eats it.

"If the crocodile comes out of the pond, it is easy to catch it. But if it will not come out on its own accord, even an elephant cannot pull it out. When the crocodile is in the pond, the scales on its back bite into the water like teeth.

"Man dwells in the illusory pond of karmic ignorance. His body is layered with four hundred trillion, ten thousand scales which have the strength of the hell of ignorance. These teeth which bite into the water of karma are desire, mind, thoughts, blood ties, bigotry, and differences. If man does not want to come out of illusion, nothing, no matter how strong, can pull him out. Like the crocodile, he will devour anyone who tries to pull him out.

"Son, we must find out which things live in which place and we must carefully escape from them. We should not try to teach the beings that live in the pond in order to pull them out and make them peaceful. If we do, we will end up in their stomach. More than anything, we need subtle wisdom.

"If anything created from the five elements goes to the pond for any reason, even to drink or wash, that crocodile will grab it. Once caught, we will not be able to escape, no matter how hard we pull. However, there is a trick—wisdom.

"The only vulnerable part of a crocodile is its stomach. The rest of its body is like wood, covered with the darkness of ignorance, but its underbelly is sensitive. Tickle it and it will run in fear. Then we can escape.

"My son, you must understand this. If you wish to help the human crocodiles to come out of the pond of ignorance, if you wish to preach to them or uplift them, you must first observe their qualities, actions, behavior, and conduct. Then if you have the feeling that one of them is worth helping, first show your love. If that is not enough, stand outside the pond and offer it some food on the fishing line of wisdom. If it likes it and bites onto it, try pulling the line gently toward the shore. See whether it responds to your love, or whether it tries to pull you into the pond. Try again and again with love, wisdom, and compassion, and observe whether it shows an inclination to approach the shore.

"Use your wisdom patiently, day after day. Try to capture it in a way that it does not harm you. As long as it is in the water, be very cautious. Stand outside the pond and attract it by dropping things into the water. If it comes very near the shore, try to pull it out of the water onto the shore. Once it is on the shore, it will have lost its strength, and you can do what you like with it. Then even a small boy can pull it where he wants.

"It is in this way that a sheikh or a perfected man, an *insān kāmil,* must try to ease a man gently out of the ignorance of illusion, until the force of ignorance has been reduced. Once he comes out of the pond, he will have attained a state in which he sees the difference between right and wrong, pure and impure. In this state, he realizes himself and begins to search for God.

"Until then, do not face such a man head on. Try to subdue him with love and compassion. You must try to train and correct him only after he is on the land. If a sheikh does this with wisdom, the crocodile will escape from the pond and the sheikh will escape from the crocodile.

"If, instead, he plunges straight in, the crocodile will drag him down to the depths of the pond. If he gets caught in this way, he must not turn around and run. To escape, he must face the crocodile and tickle its underbelly with love.

"But if the crocodile agrees to come out into the territory of the sheikh, he can train it and uplift it. If the crocodile insists on staying in the pond, it is best that the sheikh make his escape."

### 476.

A disciple asked his sheikh, "O my sheikh, people talk about the influence of Saturn. They talk about saturnic or satanic influences, and say that satan or saturn has caught them. Does satan catch man or does man catch satan? What is the form of satan?"

The sheikh replied, "There is a dark form called satan who was originally commander of the jinns in heaven. Because of the jealousy and treachery he showed when Adam *(A.S.)* was created, he was cursed and thrown out of heaven and given the name satan or *mal'ūn,* the degenerate one.

"Satan does not set out to capture anyone who is a true man. But if a human being has taken on satan's qualities and those actions which belong to satan, then satan will come to recapture his property, which is the hell of his qualities. Man is the first aggressor; satan only comes to reclaim his own property. We must understand this with our wisdom.

"Originally man was pure, but he has gathered black and evil qualities to himself. Satan is the dark, deep, black of evil, gathered and rolled together. Satan catches only satan, not man. Satan goes after satan's qualities. Only when one becomes satan will satan come to take back his own blackness and his own qualities. Satan does not catch man; man is the one who catches satan. If man does not become satan, satan will not chase after him.

"It is said that satan is lame. The right leg of those qualities known as satan is lame because it is missing clarity, which is the explaining wisdom of the *Qutbiyyat*. So when satan walks, he supports himself on the left leg of hell, which represents the nature of the evil qualities of ignorance. He cannot lean on the leg of wisdom or *gnānam*, because that leg is lame.

"When man in his originally pure state searched for and grasped the dark actions and qualities of satan, he became satan. But when the perfect wisdom of *gnānam* dawns within him and when his inner heart, his *qalb*, becomes resplendent with *gnānam* and God's qualities, he will have no darkness, no fault, no blemish. A man in that state is a *gnāni*. Then satan cannot approach him, because satan is darkness and cannot face the light.

"Those who do not have good qualities will seek and acquire satan's qualities, actions, and possessions. When man takes satan's property, satan will come either to fight to reclaim his property or to take the man into his fold as his own child."

477.

A *hadīth:* An Arab went to the Rasūlullāh *(Sal.)* and greeted him saying, "*As-salāmu 'alaikum,* Yā Rasūlullāh." The Rasūlullāh *(Sal.)* returned his greeting. Then the Arab said, "Yā Rasūlullāh, I have come to make a complaint. Satan is harassing me. He does not let me sleep, or sit, or walk. He does not give me a moment's rest. He will not even leave me alone long enough to drink a little water. Holy Prophet, please make satan stop tormenting me, so I can have some peace."

The Rasūlullāh *(Sal.)* said, "Is this what satan is doing? All right, come tomorrow, and I will speak to you then."

As soon as the Arab left, satan came in the form of another Arab and said, "Yā Rasūlullāh, I have come to relate my grief to you. You are the Rasūl to everyone, are you not? You are the Rasūl for the good as well as for the bad, for the *dunyā* as well as for the *ākhirah*. You cannot reject anyone."

"Yes, that is true," replied the Rasūlullāh *(Sal.)*.

"You are the one who makes people accept the path to Allah and who teaches them *īmān* and certitude," satan continued.

"Yes," the Rasūlullāh *(Sal.)* replied. "Are you satan?"

"What you say is true, Yā Rasūlullāh. I am satan."

"Earlier an Arab came to me and complained to me about you," the Rasūl *(Sal.)* said.

"Yā Rasūlullāh, he complained to you about me, but now I have come to complain about him. That Arab is disturbing my peace of mind. He will not let me sleep, or eat, or do any of my work. Everywhere I go, he follows me, grabbing my possessions, my freedom, and everything I have. Yā Rasūlullāh, tell him to give back what belongs to me, and let me rest."

"Is that how it is?" the Rasūl *(Sal.)* asked. "Come see me the day after tomorrow." And satan left.

At dawn the next day, the Arab returned to the Rasūl *(Sal.)* and said, "*As-salāmu 'alaikum,* Yā Rasūlullāh."

Then the Rasūl *(Sal.)* replied, " *'Alaikumus-salām,* O Arab. You complained to me about satan, but after you left, satan came and complained about you in the same way. What have you stolen from satan? Did you take his possessions, houses, and properties, or is he coming to you without any provocation?"

The Arab answered, "Yā Rasūlullāh, I have taken nothing from the wealth of satan."

"What have you hidden away?" asked the Rasūlullāh *(Sal.)*.

"For years I have toiled as a laborer. I saved only a little gold and a few gems for a dowry so that I can give my daughters in marriage. Other than that I do not possess anything of the world."

Then the Rasūlullāh *(Sal.)* said, "Very good. Take all the wealth you saved and throw it into the street, and then come to see me tomorrow."

"I will, O Holy Prophet." The Arab went directly home and threw the gold and gems into the street. The moment he did this, all satan's children came running and fighting and scrambling to grab a share of the gold and gems. They hit and scratched and kicked each other so much that they bled profusely.

Then the Arab ate his food and went to sleep. That night satan did not come to him. The Arab slept so peacefully that he did not awaken until late the next morning.

That day he returned and said, "Yā Rasūlullāh, never in my life have I felt this amount of happiness and rest! Just as you suggested, I threw all the wealth I had accumulated into the street. Satan's children came and fought among themselves, took the gold and gems, and ran away. Afterwards I had no fatigue, no troubles, and no worries. My entire body felt very light. My food tasted extremely good, and I went to bed after dinner. This morning I came to you quickly to give you my *salāms*. Satan did not come to me at all."

Then the Rasūlullāh *(Sal.)* said, "You are happy, are you not? Sit down."

A while later satan came and gave *salāms* to the Rasūlullāh *(Sal.)* but received no reply. Satan then said, "The Arab returned all my possessions. He has stopped giving me trouble. He does not disturb my peace any more."

Satan continued, "O Rasūlullāh, we do not follow your followers. It is those who call themselves your followers who take what belongs to us. They destroy us; we do not destroy them. They hold on to satan and make trouble for satan. Then your followers complain to you, 'It's satan! It's satan! Satan has got hold of us! Satan is destroying us!' But we don't go near your followers. They come to us, take our things, and take our qualities: backbiting, envy, jealousy, arrogance, trickery, deceit, falsehood, and thievery. They destroy our freedom and chase us away from our things.

"Yā Rasūlullāh," satan continued, "we will never lead your true followers astray. What belongs to hell and the world belongs to us; Allah has given it to us. But to your true followers the world is *harām*. Their only wealth is faith, certitude, and determination in Allah.

"O Rasūlullāh, your true followers should not want to be where we are, they should not desire our things, they should not come to us. They should dwell with you and Allah. They should have the qualities of *sabūr, shakūr, tawakkul-'alallāh,* and *al-hamdu lillāh,* which are the preface to *Īmān-Islām*. In every breath they should ask forgiveness and be in communion with Allah. This is what your real followers should do. But your followers have left what belongs to them and have begun to desire what belongs to us. They are taking the things of hell and the things of the world for themselves. They come and crowd around us, yet they find fault with us and condemn us."

Then the Rasūlullāh *(Sal.)* said, "What you say is true. Satan, you can go now and be at ease."

The Rasūlullāh *(Sal.)* told the Arab, "If you do not go to satan's house, he will not come to yours."

"Yā Rasūlullāh," the Arab replied, "now from your words I understand, and in the future I shall go on the true path. May Allah grant me the faith, certitude, and determination to do that."

"Yes. May Allah help you," said the Rasūlullāh *(Sal.)*.

478.

Many disciples came to a particular sheikh in order to learn *gnānam,* or wisdom. Because there are four hundred trillion, ten thousand kinds of spiritual *gnānams* in the world, each disciple had the intention to gain the *gnānam* which accorded to his needs. Each disciple achieved what he wanted within three, four, or five years and then left.

However, the cook of the ashram felt dejected and ignored. He had been the first disciple to come to the sheikh and had been with him for forty years. One day he complained to the sheikh, "O my sheikh, O my father! All the others who came to you received *gnānam* after staying with you and studying for only a few years. You taught them what was appropriate to their needs, and they learned. You took them in, they got what they wanted, and then they left. And here I am, cooking for forty years! You have not given me *gnānam* and let me go. You haven't done anything for me. You just make me cook."

The sheikh said, "My son, if you left me, where would you want to go? If I left you, where would I go? Go and do your duties, my son. You will understand later," and the sheikh went into meditation.

The disciple felt cheated. He went to get some firewood. He flung it here and there and stomped around. On his way into the kitchen, he banged his head on the doorframe and clutched his head in severe pain. Just then, he heard the sheikh cry out, "My son! Hurry! My head is bleeding! My head is broken! It hurts! It hurts!" Still holding his head, the cook ran angrily to the sheikh. The sheikh said, "Why are you holding your head? Take your hands off your head and look at me. Look at my head."

The cook wailed, "My head is broken, not yours!"

"No, my head is broken," said the sheikh. "Look here."

The cook took his hand from his head and saw that there was nothing not even a bruise, on his own head. But the head of the sheikh was gashed and bleeding. "My sheikh, you were here, inside. How did you start to bleed? I was the one who was carrying firewood. I was the one who hit my head on the kitchen door. So how could you have been wounded when it was my head that received the blow?"

The sheikh explained, "My son, you think you have been working here for forty years. But in reality, I was the one doing the work, not you. You are my child. You are a baby. You cannot do this work. I have placed you inside my heart. I do the work, all the while feeding and nourishing you to make you grow. I am the one who is working and doing these duties for you, my son. You did not do any work for me. Do you see now? Whose head was gashed, yours or mine? You must realize this state.

"My son, you cannot be here if I am not here, and I will not be here if you are not here. I have you in my heart. On the other hand, when I am not here, you are the one who is here. When you are not here, I am here. It is the same person, one and the same form. You have taken my form and I have taken your form. We cannot be separated. I cannot leave you and you cannot leave me. Realize this state, my son.

"When I have made you develop to maturity and let you go out of me, I will lose myself within you. When you reach the state of completeness and lose yourself fully in me, I will lose myself in you. My son, then you will be doing my work.

"Those who came earlier did not come with that intention. They came to learn something and go away, and they left as soon as they learned what they wanted. But you and I did not come with the intention of leaving. We came to stay where we should stay. Therefore, this is the place where you must be and where I must be. You cannot go. Do you understand? Wherever you go, the wounds will be mine. To bring you to that mature state of attainment, I have to be with you and you have to be with me. You must realize this."

The sheikh then opened the cook's eye of wisdom and said, "Look. All the time you thought you were doing the cooking, I was the one cooking. I was the one lighting the stove, I was the one cutting the wood. I did all those things. Do you see?"

He showed him that it was he, the sheikh, who was serving him, not he that was serving the sheikh.

The disciple had love and faith, but the sheikh had everything else. The sheikh did all the duty.

"When I am you and you are I, then you can do the work that I do."

479.

Bawa Muhaiyaddeen told his disciple the following story:

There was a guru, his wife, and a disciple. Day in and day out, the disciple complained to the guru's wife. "So much time has gone by, and he still hasn't given me wisdom. I must have wisdom now."

The guru's wife would comfort him every day, saying, "He will give it to you. Don't worry." One day she went to the guru and told him, "He has reached the right state. Give him *gnānam*."

"He is not ready," replied the guru. "Let him become mature."

"He is ready!" the wife insisted. "He has become a very good man."

"He is ready, is he? All right, tell him to go to the store today and buy some things for his initiation. When he comes back, spit on him, scold him, and tell him he is late. Then come and tell me what he does."

The disciple brought everything he was supposed to bring and received his scolding. "What took you so long? Why didn't you come sooner? You have no brains. Is this the way you do your work?" She spat on him, just as the guru had commanded.

Throwing down all the things he had brought, the disciple yelled angrily about his ill treatment. Finally, he stalked off and sat by himself in a corner, fuming. Observing this, the guru said to his wife, "You said he was mature, that he was ready. Look at his conduct. Now do you understand?"

For two days, the disciple did not eat or do any work. The guru called him and said, "What happened? Who spit on you? Who scolded whom, and who spit on whom? What is all this to you? What is it to me? It doesn't mean anything. If you spit on the earth, it will calmly absorb that spit. Is the earth going to be angry? You contain some earth, don't you? Why can't you be as tolerant as the earth? Do you really have to yell about something like that? Why should you be angry? Now go and eat."

After some time went by, the guru's wife came to the guru and said, "Now he is ready. He is really mature. He has so much love."

"No, he should become a little more mature. There is time yet," said the guru.

"He is ready now. We should not hold him back any longer," she replied firmly.

184

The guru said, "No. Let him become a little more mature."

"He is ready," she insisted.

"Well then, send him to the store again. Tell him to buy some things and scold him for being late when he comes back. This time, hit him really hard with your shoes, four times," the guru instructed his wife.

So she did. Picking up her shoes, she shouted, "What is this? What took you so long? What did you do?" and she hit him four times. The disciple howled in fury and stormed off to sit all by himself. He didn't take any food or do any work.

"What was his reaction?" asked the guru.

"I did what you asked, and he did the same thing as before," replied the guru's wife.

"That's all right," said the guru. "He is my son, and he will mature in his own time. That is his state of wisdom. Do not be mad at him. He is your child, too."

For a whole week, the disciple would not eat. As before, the guru went to him and said, "My son, who beat whom? Who scolded whom? Who are you and who am I? Who did the hitting and who was hit? When you walk you trample the earth, but does it get angry? How much you hit the earth when you chop firewood, but does it complain? Think of how you beat and splash the water, yet still the water cleanses you. Does it complain? We hurt them so much, but they accept it with *sabūr* and tolerance. To accept everything with patience, tolerance, and forbearance is divine wisdom, or *gnānam;* and to understand and extract the true meaning is the heaven of *gnānam*. Go and eat. Do your duties."

Two years went by. This time the guru called his wife and said, "Two years have passed. Today we must open his innermost heart and implant the seed of *gnānam*. Tell him to buy the same things you told him to buy before."

"Why do you say this?" she asked him. "Am I to hit him with my shoes or hurt him in the same way I did before?"

The guru said, "First tell him to chop a lot of wood, and then tell him to go to the store and buy the things. When he returns, hit him really hard with a broom, push him to the ground, and trample him with your feet. Hit him really hard. Then you will know his true state."

When the disciple returned from the store, he was scolded for being late, thrown to the ground, and beaten with the broom.

The guru's wife trampled on him, hitting him repeatedly. But this time the disciple caught hold of her hand. "Mother, don't your hands hurt? Don't your feet hurt? Who is hitting whom? Who is hurting whom? *Aiyō,* don't your hands and feet hurt?" He kissed her feet and her hands. "Don't shout, mother," he told her soothingly. "It will hurt your throat." Covered with welts and bruises, the disciple bowed to the feet that had trampled him. "Mother, please do not hurt yourself like this."

The guru's wife ran to the guru in surprise and related how the disciple was not at all angry, but instead was more concerned with her pain than with his own. The guru said, "Now do you see what the true state of maturity is? You thought he was mature earlier, but this is the right time. Now he is capable of looking after that valuable treasure of *gnānam.* We can entrust it safely to his hands."

He summoned the disciple and said, "My son, bathe yourself and return to me. The time has come." When the disciple came back, the guru opened his heart, his love, and his *gnānam.* Placing the disciple within his heart, he initiated him with these words, "You are I and I am you. You will speak my words. You will perform my actions. Our sounds will become one, our speech will become one, and our prayers and actions will arise from the same state." He embraced the disciple and the two merged, one with the other.

If a disciple attains this state of maturity, he will receive what is within the sheikh. He and the sheikh will merge, and after the sheikh disappears into the disciple, the disciple will begin to do the work of the sheikh. But until the body, wisdom, and divine analytic wisdom of *gnānam* are impressed within him, the disciple must keep his heart open and persevere in his service to the sheikh.

## 480.

There was a wise Sufi. A scientist came to visit him and said, "O wise one, the whole world talks about miracles, prayers, and hypnotism. The world says if you do these things you can become a god and attain liberation. The swamis, rishis, sages, yogis, and the *siddhars,* those who perform miracles, all say this. Those who know the *purānas,* or scriptures, the poets, and the pundits all talk like this. They all talk about miracles. They walk on water and on fire, fly in the air, live in the sky, jump from one body into another, possess the minds of others, and bend the heavens into a bow. They give their devotees money, wealth, gifts, paradise, and children. They even change their birth. O wise one, can you give me things like that?"

"No, I am only a small man," answered the Sufi.

The scientist began to boast. "I studied a few miracles. I know how to do some of those things. I am even going to write a book, a scientific book about the death of miracles. When I write scientifically about all the miracles, science will rise in stature and the miracles will die. Can you tell me anything about miracles? Can you tell me who receives liberation? You believe in God's creation, do you not?" asked the man.

The Sufi answered, "Yes. And if you also believe in God's creation, you will know that it is filled with miracles. The snakes, eagles, and vultures all perform miracles. Earth, fire, water, air, and the illusion of *māyā* perform many miracles. They fly in the sky, beat against mountains, make the oceans rise, and catch hold of and fascinate men's minds. Their miracles are indescribable."

"Do you know about these things, O wise one?" asked the scientist.

"A little," said the Sufi.

"O wise one, you know that vultures, eagles, bats, and birds all fly in the sky. Do they receive liberation, paradise, or *gnānam* because of this? Tell me, wise one. You seem fairly intelligent. Tell me, what is the limit of all these things? What use are they? According to your *purānas,* how can one achieve liberation and reach God?" the scientist inquired.

The Sufi replied, "Money, wealth, and miracles may take you high, but anything that flies must eventually come back to earth, fire, water, and air for the food that enables it to fly in the sky. No matter how many miracles any of the *siddhars* perform, no matter how high they fly, they must all return to the earth for food and water. They contain arrogance, karma, and *māyā,* and they have to come back to it. They need those things. None of them can live indefinitely in the sky.

"Your science is like that, too. Your inventions need petrol, batteries, air, gas, current, water, and oil. No matter how fast your spaceships fly, no matter how high they go, they must come back to their base. They must have the fuel which comes from the earth or they will fall. The people who perform miracles are like that. They are all bound to the earth. Scientists are like that, too. Nothing can live without a connection to the earth.

"You went to the moon in your rockets. You put your satellites into orbit and did your research. When you went into space, you said that God was not there. Well, that's all right. Now you are going to write a book which you will call a scientific miracle-death book.

"But whoever does miracles, whoever enjoys miracles, whoever experiences miracles is still bound to arrogance, karma, and *māyā*. Those people go into space to search for God, and they record all the sounds and things that happen. They do so much research, but their records won't reach paradise, their scientific instruments won't reach paradise, their planes won't reach paradise, their astronauts won't reach paradise, nor will their *siddhars* reach paradise. The *siddhars* do in fact fly in their own way, but God is not reached by flight. *Gnānam* does not come in that way.

"It is a disaster for the spaceship when there is no petrol or electric current, and it is disastrous for you if you have no food or water. It is dangerous to perform miracles. There is no use in it. Miracles are bound to the earth, and anything bound to the earth has hunger, illness, old age, and death. Everything must come back to the earth. All creations perform their miracles, but in the end they disappear into the earth. No matter how high you fly in the sky, if something goes wrong you will fall to the earth. That is how miracles end, and they will subject you to tens of millions of rebirths. It would be good for you to think about this.

"You certainly should write a book, but in the world there are legions of scientific books and books about the miraculous. Man has left the cause and is holding on to the effect; man places his trust in his body rather than in the essence of life. All the miracles and scientific inventions have disregarded life and are holding on to the body; they have left truth and are holding on to symbols. Your books, your body, your miracles, the *siddhars* who fly in the sky, and the scientists—they will all come to an end. You are a great man, indeed. Go and write your book."

"O wise one, what religion are you? What scripture do you follow? What is your race? Tell me," the scientist insisted.

"I am of the male race," answered the Sufi.

"What kind of religion?" asked the scientist.

"I am of the kind that has gone beyond all religion," said the Sufi.

"What scripture do you follow?"

"I am of the scripture that sees what mind and desire cannot see," the Sufi replied.

"But what do you recite, what do you read to reach salvation?" demanded the scientist.

"I recite one thing," the Sufi answered.

"What is that?"

"I recite of the time when you and I will be dead. That is what I recite," replied the Sufi.

"O wise one, you must be mentally deranged! You should be afraid of me. You don't understand what kind of person I am. I have rifles, bayonets, bombs, revolvers, and all kinds of weapons. You should be afraid."

"I am not afraid of people like you," the Sufi said. "I am not afraid of you nor of the things you have. But I am afraid when I see men."

"Why are you afraid of men?" asked the scientist, puzzled.

"Because man's tongue, his thoughts, and his gaze have so much power to cause harm. That power has so much force that if a man tries to hurt someone, the result is truly terrible. I am afraid of man because his words can hurt so much.

"You scientists have all your weapons in your hands. Your revolvers, rifles, knives, bombs, and swords are out in the open so they are visible. Man's weapons are all in his heart. Since they are on the inside, it is a little difficult. Did you say you were going to write a book?" the Sufi asked him.

"Yes," replied the scientist. "A scientific book about the death of miracles. Science is a higher pursuit than miracles. After I write my book, all the previously known miracles will die. They will be degraded and science will rise. That is what I am going to write. What do you think of it?"

"Oh, that is good, my brother. Go ahead and write it," said the Sufi. "There are many like you. *Siddhars* and scientists like you have written a lot of books.

"Let me tell you a story. If you write this story in your book, it will be a very good book, a book such as no one has ever seen before. All the people who read it will fall over with laughter and become very happy. Get ready. Get your ink, your pen, and your paper, brother."

"What is the story?" asked the scientist.

"Listen, I will tell you," replied the Sufi. "It is a story which is very appropriate to your greatness and to your learning. You must not cover too many different subjects in your book. That would not be good. You should write about one subject, one story. Write your book about frogs—then it will be a good book. Do not add any snakes or things like that.

"Get a table and a pen and some paper. Then go and get a frog. Put it on the table, tap it, and say, 'Jump, frog, jump!'

"As soon as you tell it to jump, it will jump. Measure the length of its jump and write it down. Let us say, for example, that your frog jumped a foot. Write that down. 'A four-legged frog jumped twelve inches.'

"Then cut off one of its legs. Again, say, 'Jump, frog, jump. Jump!' and tap it.

"Since one of its legs is missing, it will probably jump nine inches. Write down in your book, 'The frog with three legs jumped nine inches.'

"Cut off one more leg and say, 'Jump, frog, jump!' Tap it. It will jump six inches. Write down, 'The frog with two legs jumped six inches.'

"Cut off one more leg and say, 'Jump, frog, jump!' It will jump three inches. Write down in your book, 'The frog with one leg jumped three inches.'

"Cut off its last leg and say, 'Jump, frog, jump! Jump, frog, jump! Jump, frog, jump!' The frog won't do anything. Say, 'Jump, frog, jump! JUMP, FROG, JUMP!' as much as you want, but the frog won't move. Write in your book, 'The frog with no legs has gone deaf.' After all, the frog must be deaf if it won't do what you say.

"This is an excellent story about the subjects of science and miracles. It is a good story to show how the frog jumped and how scientifically miraculous all the measurements and conclusions were.

"It is in the same way, brother, that science has cut off the legs of mankind, which are the four religions. After the religions have been cut away one by one, the scientists then say, 'God is dead. God has gone deaf. He has no ears. We must be God,' and they will attempt to turn the world upside down.

"This is the kind of story, brother, which is highly valued by current standards. Go and write your book," said the Sufi to the scientist.

481.

"What is most needed in a man's life?" asked a young boy. "My son, you asked a good question.

You need gratitude to your parents, love for them, and trust in them.

You must pay due respect to your parents, to those who are your elders, and to those of wisdom who have good qualities, proper conduct, and actions.

Your tongue must always speak the truth, never falsehood.

Always live in the company of those who are good and those who are wise.

Learn the virtuous qualities of modesty, sincerity, reserve, and fear of wrongdoing.

You must not harm another in your thoughts, in your intentions, in your words, or in your actions.

Acquire God's qualities. Just as God shows compassion and love to all lives, you too must show the compassion and love of God to all lives.

Faith and certitude in God are essential to your life. They will give you strength, determination, and support. You must develop that steadfastness.

Do not be hasty under any circumstances. Develop patience, the inner patience known as *sabūr*, the contentment known as *shakūr*, the trust in God known as *tawakkul*, and always say, '*Al-hamdu lillāh*, all praise belongs to God.'

"Acquire God's qualities in this way and praise Him always. If these qualities appear in you, if you develop and utilize them, your life will become exalted. No matter where you may be, stay in the company of one who is wise and learn wisdom. Then you will understand the connection between you, your life, and the One who created you. If you understand this, you will understand the correct way to pray and the true state of prayer. This will give you victory in your life."

## 482.

"Which is the sound most sweet to the ears and to the heart of a man?" asked a man.

"The sweetest sounds in a man's life are the words of a baby. The baby's words are God's words. They do not contain deceit or treachery. They are words of peace, the sounds of God's grace," answered the sheikh. "They do not have the world or feelings of divisiveness in them. Those sounds and words of God will be loved by everyone."

## 483.

"Which vision is most cooling to a man's eyes, the vision which gives beauty to the *qalb,* the inner heart?" asked a small boy.

The sheikh answered, "The vision of the eye which dawns within the state of compassion, the gaze of the radiant wisdom of grace, is the most cooling and refreshing to the *qalb* and to the eyes of man."

## 484.

"What hurts the heart of a man and makes him suffer?" asked a girl.

The sheikh answered, "Arrogant words and ignorant actions. Actions which do not contain modesty, sincerity, reserve, fear of wrongdoing, and good conduct hurt the heart of man. Behavior which is opposite to the truth, speaking evil of others, slandering others without knowledge of the truth, telling lies, coveting and stealing the property of others, suspicion, deceit, treachery, and lack of respect to elders and parents and to those of wisdom—these and many similar actions are the ones that most wound and hurt the heart of man."

### 485.

"Which is the taste most sweet to the tongue of a man?" asked a man.

"The sweetest and most wonderful taste," replied the sheikh, "is the taste of the honey of pure wisdom in a perfectly pure heart, the honey of love which flows from man's good thoughts, and the maturity of his state of wisdom. That honey gives the sweetest taste to his tongue, to his heart, and to his wisdom."

### 486.

"Who has attained the state that gives tranquillity, peace, and happiness to the heart?" asked a young woman.

The sheikh replied, "Through the companionship of good people who have the qualities of God, and through listening to the teachings of wise sages who have learned the wisdom which has no attachment to the world:

One who does selfless duty

One whose heart dwells within God's grace, love, and goodness

One who fills his heart with patience

One who makes *sabūr*, or inner patience, the staff with which he walks in life

One who sees faith in God as the strength in his heart

One whose absolute faith in nothing other than God is the protecting umbrella for all the difficulties and troubles in his life

One who hands over all responsibility to God in doing his duty

"One who does these things will attain the state that gives tranquillity, peace, and happiness to the heart."

### 487.

What best adorns a woman's beauty?" asked a young woman.

The sheikh said, "The beauty of good qualities and the loveliness of good conduct and good actions is the most beautiful jewelry for a woman."

### 488.

"What can give us the splendor of a life free of sorrow?" asked a man.

"If a man gives happiness, sadness, and everything in his life into God's responsibility and then acts accordingly—that is the peace which contains no sorrow," replied the sheikh.

"Man must use his wisdom and conduct his life in this way: For everything that happens in the present moment, say, *'Al-hamdu lillāh,'* and give all praise to God. For what will happen in the next moment, say, *'Tawakkul-'alallāh,'* and place all your trust in God, knowing that He knows. If you can then do your duty without attachment, just as God does His duty without attachment, selfishness, or pride, that will become the splendor of a life which contains no sorrow or grief."

### 489.

A ten-year-old child asked, "What is God? What is the true meaning of that word? People say, 'God! God! Give all responsibility to God,' but what does that mean?"

The Sufi sheikh replied, "God is a power, a light of perfection. He has no form, no body, no color, no race, no religion, no wife, no children, no relatives, no attachments, no selfishness, and no sensual enjoyment. God is a power who can control all forces and all *shakthis,* keeping each one in its place and subduing those which are excessive.

"He embraces and protects those who are on the right path, and forgives and sustains them when there is a fault. He has fathomless qualities of grace. He is the power which shines as the resplendent light of wisdom within wisdom."

### 490.

A small girl asked a Sufi, "Illusion, or *māyā,* is mingled in everything. God is also mingled in everything. If both are everywhere, what is the difference between *māyā* and God?"

The Sufi answered, "God has created a pair of opposites called light and darkness so that we can know the difference between the two. Darkness exists everywhere, and so does light. Each is revealed through its opposite.

"In the same way, God is the light of perfection and *māyā* is darkness; we understand light through the contrast of darkness, and good through the contrast of evil.

"God is mingled within everything. *Māyā* also exists within everything in the form of darkness, so that the perfect light of God may be understood in contrast. But does darkness remain when the light comes? No. As soon as light comes, darkness leaves. The power that can dispel the darkness is God. *Māyā* is the darkness of manifested creations and is subject to change, whereas God is the effulgence which exists forever.

"Light can dispel darkness, but darkness cannot dispel light. What is driven away is *māyā,* while the power that dispels is God. This is the difference."

### 491.

A disciple asked, "They say it is good for man to cut off rebirth, but how can it be cut? What is reborn, and what does it mean not to be reborn?"

The sheikh said, "My son! These are good questions. The whole world is asking the same questions.

"Man is a subtle wonder. The body which he believes in is not his true form. When man develops the wisdom which is capable of understanding this, he will give up the outer form of earth, fire, water, air, and ether, and the qualities of each, and enter into his true form, the resplendent light form which is inside the visible body.

"To leave this outer body and enter the inner light form is the meaning of being reborn. And once man is reborn in that light form, he will never be born again into a body made of the five elements.

"The elemental body contains four hundred trillion, ten thousand qualities. If man believes that the body made of the elements is his real body, he will retain his connection to elemental qualities and will have to be born over and over again.

"If, however, he cuts away his connection to the qualities of the elements and becomes the light form, he will be connected with the power which is God. Then he does not come back."

## 492.

"Among mankind, who is good?" asked a man.

The sheikh said, "One who does not kill, murder, hurt, or cause sadness to any life whatsoever is good. One who clearly sees the sadness in the lives of others as his own sadness, and helps others, is good."

## 493.

My son, all the things you see and place your trust in will one day fail you. Land, gold, women, relatives, blood ties, attachments, property, possessions, titles, honors, races, religions, and philosophies will all leave you. Even your body will desert you. All the praise and blame you earn will forsake you. All those you trust will give up on you.

While you are lamenting in this desperate plight, when everyone has abandoned you, the One who comes to comfort you is your true friend. He will save your life. He will embrace you with love. He is God, the friend who will protect your life.

If you reflect on this, my son, and if you hold on to your companion, the One who will never give you up, then you will always be comforted. He will never leave you and go away. You must believe this with certitude. This power called God dwells within you, even though you are not aware of it. Place your trust in Him, and you will attain peace and tranquillity in your life.

## 494.

"Does man want to become satan, or does satan want to become man?" A man posed this question to the sheikh.

The sheikh answered, "Satan would never want to become a man, but man very much wants to become satan. Although darkness can never become resplendent, it is possible for light to become darkness. How? If it is reduced in power, if the level of wisdom begins to wane, light can gradually turn to darkness.

"Man has both the resplendent light of wisdom and the dark qualities of satan. If he persists in utilizing darkness and ignoring the light, his light will gradually wane until he becomes completely dark. On the other hand, if he utilizes the light to its full capacity he will become resplendent light.

"In this way, if he reflects with his inner wisdom and eliminates the evil within him, he will become a true man."

### 495.

A man asked a Sufi *gnāni,* "What does it mean to say that man becomes satan? How does he change? Does he actually take the form of satan or is it a formless change?"

The Sufi *gnāni* replied, "You have asked a good question. When we say satan, we mean the qualities and actions which are opposite to truth, the darkness which is opposite to light. All evil things are satan's qualities: darkness, murder, lies, intoxicants, drugs, treachery, gambling, deceit, and millions of other evil qualities and actions which hurt the lives of others. Satan's qualities are qualities that hurt others. If man holds on to satan's qualities, he is satan. That is how he changes.

"However, when man's qualities become God's qualities, that is God's truth. Satan does not like qualities of truth; he does not want to change. He does not like light. He is a liar; he will not speak the truth.

"When falsehood grows within a man, he changes into satan. But when the truth of God dwells in him, he is transformed and becomes God."

### 496.

A woman asked, "People speak about courts of justice and we see them in the world. But they also say there is a court of justice within man. Which one is better? Which is the right one? Which one will most benefit man?"

The Sufi sheikh answered, "One who has been born a man has a court of justice within his *qalb,* or heart. This inner court is not built of earth, fire, water, air, or of the ether which is *māyā.* It is built with the grace of God who is justice, and it exists within a tiny piece of flesh which is smaller than an atom. God is the only One who dispenses justice in that court. Neither falsehood nor the hypnotic delusions of torpor can perceive it. Only a person of truth, wisdom, faith, certitude, and determination, one who has surrendered to God, will have that court open to him. Heavenly beings, angels, and prophets serve there. And inside the place in which they serve, God dwells as the emperor and judge. That place is also a place of worship; it is both a church and a mosque.

"One in whom all the actions of God are present, one who can reach the inner court of justice, open it with his wisdom, and pray to God, will not hurt any life. The judge who sits in that court knows every breath, every word, and every thought of every life. He presides over each case. There are no lawyers. He is both judge and prosecutor, speaking directly to the defendant. This is the highest court, and it is found within man.

"God has also given man the wisdom to understand the four kinds of justice in this inner court: divine justice, king's justice, human justice, and human conscience. If man realizes and understands these four kinds of justice and applies them properly in his life, there is no court for him outside. He will pass judgment on his own thoughts, on his own faults, and on all the qualities within him.

"There is a vast world within man. He contains the eighteen thousand universes, filled with snakes, scorpions, tarantulas, lions, tigers, men, monkeys, and elephants. If even one monkey in that vast world performs its pranks, man himself must give the judgment and the punishment.

"But if one does not have inner judgment, he must go to the outer courts. They are built of earth, fire, water, air, and ether. These courts hear cases which involve love of land, gold, women, worldly possessions, and property. These are the courts for those who claim the kingdom of God for themselves and who fight over God's property as though it belonged to them. The outer courts have many lawyers. There are 'my lawyers' and 'your lawyers', and they too fight over God's property, claiming it as their own.

"A man who submits to the inner court will not need to rely on outer courts. And one who is caught up in the outer courts will not go to the inner court.

"If you understand these two courts with your wisdom and pass judgment on yourself from within, that will be the victory of your life."

497.

"What is most intoxicating to man? Which is the worst of all intoxicants? Which makes man most insanely drunk?" asked a disciple.

"The intoxication of lust," replied the sheikh.

198

The sheikh told his children a story:

There was a king who was very devoted to God. Because of his devotion, he wanted to leave his kingdom to meditate on God. He said to his minister, "I must give my kingdom into the hands of an *insān,* a true man, and then I must meditate and pray to God so that I too may reach the state of *insān.*" He told his minister to find a true man.

"But it is impossible to find such a one," replied the minister.

"In that case," declared the king, "we must post the following proclamation everywhere in my kingdom:

### THE PROCLAMATION OF THE KING

1. WHAT DOES GOD DO?
2. HOW MANY STARS ARE IN THE SKY?
3. WHAT IS THE CENTRAL COURT OF JUSTICE IN THE WORLD?

WHOEVER ANSWERS THE KING'S THREE QUESTIONS CORRECTLY WILL BE GIVEN THE KINGDOM AND THE HAND OF THE PRINCESS IN MARRIAGE. BUT IF ANYONE TRIES TO ANSWER THESE QUESTIONS AND FAILS, HE WILL LOSE HIS HEAD.

The king's ministers proclaimed this to the world, but no one came forth to answer the questions. They were all afraid. Everyone wanted the kingdom, but no one wanted to die.

One day a fourteen-year-old shepherd boy, who was an orphan, heard of the proclamation. "Ah! I will try to answer the three questions. Even if I do not answer them correctly, at least once in my life I will see the king. Then I will be content. That will be enough for me."

He told his friends of his plan and then departed, taking with him a goatskin and the staff he used to herd the goats. "Do not tell anyone where I am going," he cautioned his friends and then went on his way.

Carrying the staff and the goatskin and wearing a loincloth, he went to the palace and rang the bell of justice. In those days, a person who felt he had not been dealt with justly could ring the bell of justice and could himself present his complaint to the king. No one had ever come to ring that bell before. Surprised, the king looked out from above. "What do you want?" asked the king.

"I want to answer the questions of the king," replied the boy.

"What questions?" asked the king.

"I want to answer the king's three questions," the boy stated.

"You do? Do you know what will happen to you if you do not answer the questions correctly?"

"Yes, I do. I will die."

"All right, come at eight o'clock tomorrow morning." So the boy went to spend the night in the forest.

Meanwhile his foster parents and friends heard that he had rung the bell of justice, and they became very frightened. They were afraid the king would kill them also, because of the boy's audacity. "We must catch him before he returns to the king. We must search for him. *Aiyō*! The king might kill us, too. He might get angry and ask who raised the boy."

But the boy heard them coming and hid in the thicket. He overheard them saying they wanted to beat him and force him to return to their village. So he stayed hidden in the forest until eight o'clock the next morning.

When morning came, all the king's ministers gathered in the court. The king entered the audience hall, sat down, and said, "I called all of you together because a boy wants to answer my three questions. I told him to come today. He may be outside. Call him. Call in the boy who wants to answer the questions!"

Everyone laughed as the young boy came into the king's presence wearing only a loincloth and carrying a stick and a goatskin. They mocked him, saying, "Look at the one who has come to answer the questions!"

The prime minister asked stiffly, "Have you come to answer the questions?"

"Yes. I am ready."

"Do you know the consequences if you do not answer the questions correctly?"

"Yes, I know that, too," answered the boy.

"All right then, these are the questions," said the king to the minister. "What does God do? How many stars are in the sky? What is the central court of justice in the world?"

Then the prime minister proceeded to ask the first question. "What does God do?"

The boy stood on the floor, below the king and his prime minister who sat on their thrones on a raised platform. "Maharaja," said the boy, "please forgive me. May I beg your gracious permission to ask one question before I answer your question?"

The minister grudgingly conveyed this request to the king, who nodded his assent. The minister then replied, "Yes, you can ask your question."

"Who is more clever, the one who asks the question, or the one who gives the answer?" asked the boy.

The king looked at his minister and nodded his head.

The minister replied, "The one who answers the question is more clever."

Then the boy asked, "Is it right for one who is less clever to be seated above one who is more clever? Is it proper for one who is more clever to have to stand below while the one less clever sits on an elevated throne?"

The king signaled the prime minister to give his seat to the boy. The boy climbed the steps and sat on the prime minister's throne. The prime minister was furious at having to stand. He scowled, gnashed his teeth, and clenched his fists to see his fine throne occupied by a boy who was practically naked.

Laying the goatskin and his staff beside him, the boy sat up very straight. "Now, ask your questions and I will answer. If I have to die now, I will lose nothing. I am a destitute orphan, but I have seen the king's court, I have seen the king, and I have sat upon a throne. I am ready to die now. Ask your questions and I will answer."

The minister yelled out the first question. "What does God do?" He was eager to see the boy die with the very first question.

"This is what He does," said the boy.

"What do you mean?"

"He puts those who are down up, and those who are up down. This is His work. He made you climb down, and He brought me up from the floor to your throne. If I had done this myself, you would have had me whipped or executed. But God did this. This is His action."

The minister turned toward the king. The king nodded his head in approval and looked affectionately at the boy.

The outraged minister asked the second question in a loud and angry voice. "How many stars are in the sky?"

The boy tossed the goatskin onto the floor. "Count the hairs on this goatskin. My Master and I counted them, and He has given me the exact number. The number of hairs on the goatskin is equal to the number of stars in the sky."

"How can we count the hairs?" the minister asked.

"Then how can I count the stars?" countered the boy.

"But you just told me that you and your Master had counted the hairs," said the minister.

The boy replied, "My Master is the Creator. He created the hairs on the goatskin and He also created the stars in the sky. And He is the One who told me to show you the goatskin and give you this answer.

"Just as Allah created the stars, He created the hairs on this goatskin. If you do not know one, you will not know the other. It is all His responsibility. Allah is the only One who knows the number of stars in the sky and the number of hairs on a goatskin. Anyone who accepts Allah with faith will understand that He is beyond all numbers. Anyone who knows the account of Allah, who is limitless and infinite, will not waste his time counting the creations. It is for the king, the minister, and his courtiers to decide which count is more important. If you had known, you would not have asked these questions. But since you are so concerned with this, He directed me to bring you the goatskin."

The king's eyes filled with tears. The boy continued, "I feel our king has great wisdom and devotion to God, and that he has been striving hard to find the path for the liberation of his soul. The reason he has posed these three questions is to seek out a true man to whom he can entrust the kingdom. He wants someone suitable, someone responsible, to take over his kingdom so that he can go on his spiritual quest, to meet God face to face."

The king was so moved that he wanted to embrace the boy and hand over his kingdom immediately, but the third question remained.

The minister asked, "What is the central court of justice in the world?"

The boy said, "There are two meanings to this question. One

is that the throne in the king's court of justice is the central court of justice. But there is another meaning. Your court is for those who have strayed from justice; only those who have strayed need to come here. But for all the eighteen thousand universes, there is a central station, the *qalb*, or inner heart, where God dispenses justice. This is the central court of justice.

"Those who do not follow the justice of that central court in the inner heart must go to the king's court of justice which lies outside. But those who stay within the dictates of their inner court of justice have no need for a decision to be given in the presence of an assembly. In the inner court, the inquiry and the judgment are experienced face to face in the presence of God alone. That is the best judgment of all."

The king said, "The boy has answered the questions correctly. Give him the kingdom." He embraced the boy, kissed him, and gave him the kingdom and the hand of his daughter in marriage. "He is a true man," said the king.

Then the king addressed the boy. "As you said earlier, the reason for my asking those questions was to find a true man to relieve me of my responsibility to my kingdom so that I could find my way to God's kingdom. God has brought you to me. You are the man for whom I was searching.

"Please accept the kingdom. Rule it with true justice." He presented his minister to the boy and said, "Keep this man as your prime minister." He then introduced his courtiers and his assembly to the boy and said, "Advise all of them to improve their state according to the inner central state of justice."

Having handed over his kingdom and his daughter, he went to find his way to God.

★

The sheikh then gave the explanation: If we understand, we will realize that there is no high and low or large and small in the world. Those who have greater wisdom, devotion, and determination in their search for God are the greater ones, the representatives of God. The one who dies in God after having completed his search is a *gnāni*. One who has disappeared within Him is a *qutb*. One who is merged in Him is man-God.

My children, the king did not know the number of stars in the sky. Yet he posed this as a question, did he not? In the same way, people in the world ask question upon question to intimidate others and think they are very clever.

One who asks this kind of question should know the answer before asking it. A person of wisdom will only ask questions for which he knows the answers, and thus he will be able to instruct others. He is a teacher, while one who asks without knowing the meaning is a fool. We must not waste our lives. We must understand before we speak. That will be best.

To ask questions because you want to learn is different. If you do not understand you must clearly say, "I do not understand. Please explain." You must ask as a student who wants to learn and receive instruction. You must ask with reverence and humility. Only then will you gain wisdom.

499.

A man asked a Sufi, "What should a world leader be like?"

The Sufi answered, "If one is to be a world leader, he must be a treasury to the world. He must be a treasury of the wisdom of grace which comforts all lives by dispelling the darkness in their hearts and making them resplendent with light. He must be able to comfort the hearts of all the people in the world. He must be able to teach them the wisdom which discards what is wrong and carries out what is right. Only if he is filled with those good qualities will he be a leader to the people in the world.

"There are countless leaders who show the way to darkness, hell, desire, passion, selfishness, lust, anger, miserliness, bigotry, envy, arrogance, karma, and *māyā*. But leaders of the first kind are very, very rare. If you discover the difference between these two kinds of world leaders and choose to follow the first kind, it will be very helpful to you."

500.

"How can we find a man of wisdom, a *gnāni*? What will he be like?" asked a man.

The sheikh replied, "A *gnāni* will dwell among the people, doing his duty, but he will have no attachments or blood ties. He will be in the world but the world will not be in him. His love will permeate all lives, and his justice will never fail.

"The integrity and goodness of one who is a *gnāni* must not falter and his duty must be unfailing. Desire, mind, and evil thoughts must not exist within him. He must see the sorrow of other lives as his own, he must see the happiness of other lives as his own, he must experience the illnesses of other lives as his own, and he must feel the hunger of other lives as his own. He must teach the happiness of his own life to others, showing them how to experience that happiness.

"In a state without any attachments at all, he must do duty to God, duty to the people, and duty to the soul. He must have God's qualities and live without any separations or differences.

"Existing in the form of compassion, he has dispelled all evil within him and he has destroyed all the karma of his birth. With God's qualities, he will perform God's duty as his own, dispelling the hunger and disease of all lives and the suffering in the minds of the people. He will teach the way to dispel the illnesses of birth and karma. He will make the people understand the grace of God and teach them wisdom and the way to rid themselves of their own darkness. He will make their wisdom resonant and help them to attain the liberation of the soul.

"He will have the qualities of patience, *sabūr* or inner patience, and *shakūr* or contentment. He will place all his trust in God, *tawakkul-'alallāh,* and give all praise to God, *al-hamdu lillāh.* His heart will be filled with compassion. To give love to all lives will be his life. He will not deviate an atom from faith in God. Such is the state of a *gnāni.*"

### 501.

A man asked, "A king is a leader to his people; the people are subjects in his charge. What should be the nature of the relationship between a king and his people?"

The sheikh replied, "One who is a king must be the wealth which satisfies the needs and wants of the people. The body of the people must be his body, the health of the people must be his existence, the freedom of the people must be his life, and the qualities of God must be the scepter with which he rules. The happiness of the people must be his food, and the contentment of the people must be his palace. The growth of the people will be the growth of his kingdom.

"The state of the king must be such that his kingdom is like God's kingdom and his rule like God's rule. What he sees must be what God sees. The judgment he gives must be God's responsibility, as though God were giving the judgment. In such a kingdom, the three thousand gracious qualities of God will form the basis of the relationship between the king and his people."

## 502.

A man asked, "For a nation to flourish, what should its people be like?"

A wise man answered, "If all the people of a nation will destroy their own animal qualities, their arrogant and demonic qualities, their lust for titles, their conceit, jealousy, and envy, religious differences, the egoism of the 'I', and the separations within themselves, then their nation will flourish with the wealth of the grace of all three worlds.

"Such a nation will be like the kingdom of God. It will never be afflicted by poverty, famine, or pestilence. All the people will be united as one family and as one life, without fighting, wars, or divisions. If people can live in this way, they will have the state of unity which exists in the kingdom of God."

## 503.

A man asked, "What must be done so that a nation can progress?"

The sheikh replied, "Cut away the differences of the 'I' and the 'you'. Cut away your selfishness, pride, ambition for titles, and the frenzy of racial and religious bigotry.

"Establish the state of God's love, and there will be peace and equality. Then all the people will live as one family, and the nation will progress."

## 504.

"The world talks a lot about socialism. Many say that if socialism comes, everyone would be happy. Where can we catch hold of this socialism so that we too can be happy?" a man asked.

A Sufi answered him, "In the Tamil language, 'Soh! Soh!' is what you say when you chase away birds, chickens, goats, cattle, and other animals from the farm so that they do not ruin the crops and cause famine in the land.

"You asked where you could find and catch hold of socialism so that you can be happy. But true socialism is within each man; it relates to the peace which brings liberation.

"In the same way that a farmer chases away birds and animals which attempt to destroy his crops, if you can chase away the evils which come to destroy the truth within you, you will see the qualities of God, which are the true socialism. God is the only true socialist. He alone looks after everyone equally, showing no partiality or discrimination.

"The socialism you mentioned is like the birds and animals that threaten the property of a farm: it threatens your freedom and your life, and enslaves your soul and your existence through guns and oppression. Do not be deceived into believing that the beauty of animals or the flutter of birds' wings is the real nature of that kind of socialism. It is actually a state in which the stronger man is a dictator, suppressing and controlling the weaker men.

"True socialism is God's state, a state without attachments, pride, fame, the egoism of the 'I', anger, or impatience. The justice that God imparts, combined with freedom of speech and movement, is true socialism. When the socialism of God comes into you, then you are really a socialist. If you want true socialism, do not carry chains or sticks; carry only wisdom, God's qualities, and the perfect faith of *īmān*."

505.

A man asked, "What are the benefits seen in a land which enjoys the freedom of God, whose people live as children of God?"

The Sufi answered, "In true socialism, if man intermingles with God in the form of compassion toward all lives, then temples, prayer, worship, and devotion to God will exist; there will be courts and justice, a free press and free speech. Everyone in such a nation will have the right to speak what is in his heart. People will be free to marry, have children, own land and possessions, and live a life without slavery. Each man will have the right to lead the kind of life he wishes, and God's duty will prevail.

"In this way, man can perceive the exaltedness in his life and establish a connection to God and to man, whereby mankind may live as one race with one God. When these are all one, there will be no want in the lives of the people. Such a nation will be the kingdom of God, and the people in it will be His children. His freedom and the freedom of the people will be one. God will dwell in everyone, and all lives will live in unity."

## 506.

A Sufi sheikh said to his disciple: Son, there is a little something you must think about. God has placed within man the analytic wisdom that enables him to consider the state of his life.

With that wisdom, if we discern and analyze the appearances of God's creations and the explanations within them, we can see that the entire world exists within each creation. We can see it in two sections: one is the world in the sky, and the other is the world on the earth. In these two worlds there are many creations—things that move and things that do not move, things with bodies and things without bodies, things with shadows and things without shadows, things with form and things without form, things which speak and things which do not speak.

There are many such things to be understood. There is night and there is day, but even when the night falls, the light of the moon appears so that the world can see. When day comes, the sun parts the clouds and darkness to show its light.

Thus light is given to those who live in the day as well as to those who live in the night. There is no time in which there is no light.

God has made this evident in His creation so that we can see it and realize its meaning with divine analytic wisdom. Because there is light, creations are able to live, walk about, and search for food and water. Some animals rest in the day and feed at night: man rests at night and seeks his food by day. Every one of the six kinds of lives need light.

In this world, no matter how many houses or palaces a man builds, he still needs a light in each of them. It can run on oil, current, chemicals, magnetism, or anything else which will give light. All places need light.

Son, there is another kind of house we must build within the cage of the body, the house of God's prayer, and we need a light for that as well. We cannot worship God without light. That house must be built with all of God's three thousand gracious qualities, His ninety-nine *wilāyats,* or powers, and all of His good qualities and good intentions. The door of the house must be made with the faith, determination, and certitude known as *īmān.*

When the house is completed, we must place the lamp of *īmān* within, pour the oil of wisdom into it, set the wick of God's grace within the oil, and light the flame of prayer to God. Cutting away the 'I', realizing that there is nothing other than Allah, *lā ilāha,* and that only God exists, *illallāhu,* we must place Him before us. We must become slaves to God, give our inner hearts and all our intentions in surrender to Him, and lose ourselves within Him.

When this light and this state are made complete in the house of prayer, then man can commune with God and can see the unity of man within God and God within man. Then he will understand that God protects him from within.

However, if this state is not established, man will see differences in his prayers, his life, his actions, and his behavior. He will be subject to happiness and sorrow, laughing at one time and crying at another. At one time he will praise God and blame Him at another. He will blame God for his own acts of ignorance. He will lack the connection to God.

If, instead, you think of this and light the lamp of *īmān,* you will never be separate from God and God will never be separate from you. Do it like this with the certitude of *īmān.*

### 507.

The sheikh said to his disciples: Children who perform duties and service to God, no matter where they may be—whether in a jungle, in a house, under a tree, or at the foot of a mountain—must carry out the duties which are His qualities, His actions, and His conduct.

Allah has given each of them an account book. There are two bookkeepers: one to record the profits and the other to keep account of the losses. That book is kept within each child's *qalb,* or inner heart. Every moment of the day, this account must be furnished to the accountants who are the representatives of Allah, with the qualities of patience, inner patience or *sabūr,* contentment or *shakūr,* trust or *tawakkul,* and giving all praise to God, *al-hamdu lillāh.*

Each child's duty, effort, and wages, as well as his profits and losses, must be calculated from the time of the early morning prayer of *subhat* to the *subhat* of the following day. Every twenty-four hours, any profit earned must be deposited in Allah's bank of *īmān,* the bank of perfect faith.

You must understand this: What are your duties? What profits have you earned from these duties?

There is duty to God, duty to the sheikh, duty to the people, and duty to all creations in the world. I will give you an example to illustrate this.

If four shiploads of goods worth $400,000 are unloaded and sold for $800,000, there is a profit. The bookkeeper and the accountant must check this and calculate the taxes. If there is any discrepancy, if the methods used were not quite right, there may have to be a government inquiry. The accounts would be submitted and reviewed step by step, showing the books, the bills, the receipts, and all details. Such matters come up for reckoning when people do business.

In the same way, some people say they are performing the four kinds of duty, but the only thing they do is sign their books. Such people may even turn up every morning at *subhat,* but they will only write their names on the appropriate lines, saying they have done this work and that; but as soon as they sign, they go away. They do not do any duty. They do not care to look into what needs to be done and to do duty for the sheikh. They are only concerned about signing their names in the book. Such people are in the majority.

The entries in the account book will be audited four times: in the *qalb,* in the grave, on the Day of Reckoning or *Qiyāmah,* and in the final court in the presence of Allah. Since Allah is the Ruler of all the universes, the final reckoning will be in His presence. There we will be questioned about our duty, wages, profits, and losses. It is there that the caliber of our duty will be revealed. The book will be examined and we will also be questioned directly. According to what we have earned, the final judgment will be given at that court. We must realize this.

Before the Day of *Qiyāmah* arrives, we need to understand in our *qalb* the duty we do and the wages which will accrue from that duty. If man performs the duties of God, he is the perfect purity of *Īmān-Islām,* an *insān kāmil* or perfected man, and a true believer, *mu'min.* Of the seventy-three groups of people in the world, such people make up only one group; all the rest of the people form the other seventy-two groups. The people in those seventy-two groups are the ones who will have to face the Day of *Qiyāmah.*

My son, as we do our duties in serving the sheikh, serving Allah, and serving all lives in the world, we must act with the qualities of God. If we live in a state in which we understand what our wages are throughout all twenty-four hours of the day, if we avoid what is wrong and do only what is right for God, then we will have victory over Judgment Day.

Allah knows our every word and every breath, my son. He lives with us. Since He dwells with us and we dwell with Him, we have to think. Do not try to deceive Him by merely signing the duty roster and then going away to indulge in evil actions. Do not try to steal a certificate, thinking He cannot see.

God has created you out of the twenty-eight letters that form the Qur'an. The Qur'an is mingled with your *surat,* your true body. God will raise every one of the twenty-eight letters, infuse them with light, and ask them directly about their actions. And each of the twenty-eight letters will repeat what it has done.

Therefore, you must reflect and carry out the true duties. Do *tasbih,* prayers of praise, glorifying His name twenty-four hours a day. Love all lives as you love your own. Truly open your *qalb* and worship God. Whether you serve the sheikh or the people, you must do it with an open heart without attachment. Then God will give you a place in His kingdom.

## 508.

In Jaffna, Sri Lanka, a poet asked M. R. Bawa Muhaiyaddeen, "Is there a treasure which transcends intellect? Does such a thing exist?"

Bawa Muhaiyaddeen replied, "Yes, there is such a treasure. The scriptures extend only up to the limit of intellect. They cannot understand anything beyond physical vision, beyond what the eyes see. They talk only about what is already known to intellect.

"There is, however, a treasure which resplends as wisdom within wisdom, as the all-pervasive omnipresence, as the effulgence of the inner heart. Resonating as the grace of God within man's heart, this treasure is a brilliant resplendence which knows and understands all the universes. It shines, pulsates, and scintillates, explaining from within. You must realize this.

"O poet, let me explain something to you. In the same way that a seed is covered by a skin, everything you look at is covered by a form. To know what is inside, you must open the covering. It is important for wisdom to open and understand the minute and subtle aspects within.

"The most subtle of all subtleties exists as the explanations of wisdom within wisdom, as the soul within the soul, as perfection within perfection, as clarity within clarity, as man within man, and as God within the grace of God. You must split open and analyze each of these with divine luminous wisdom, just as a scientist splits an atom in order to analyze it. Then, O poet, you will understand the mysterious power of the exalted treasure which controls everything."

509.

The poet Selvaratnam, son of the poet Selladurai, posed another question. "Jesus *(A.S.)* has said, 'The glory of the son of man will be seen in the clouds.' May I be given an explanation of this, please?"

Bawa Muhaiyaddeen answered, "To say 'son of man' means that all men are the children of Adam *(A.S.)*. The clouds are the sorrows, the illusions which overshadow man. Only when the clouds of sorrow come can we know whether one is a man, a beast, or a satan, whether he trusts God or whether he has thrown God away. It is then that the son of man becomes visible. The clouds are like waves. One who can make the clouds part and stand resplendent, radiating His brilliant light everywhere, is the Father of man. He is easily recognized.

"Man is the light of the grace of God from which Adam *(A.S.)* was created in heaven, and sorrows are natural to the children of Adam *(A.S.)*. For when Adam *(A.S.)* was cast away from heaven through the actions of satan, sorrows fell with him like clouds and colors in the sky. But if the one who was cast out of heaven regains his lost resplendence and stands shining as the radiant light of the grace of God, parting the clouds of his sorrow, then he is the sun of God.

"When the son of man dispels the clouds of his sorrow and regains his original connections, he becomes a sun, a power, and the power of God shines from within him. The power of that light is the power of God."

510.

"People say that when a disciple is ready, the sheikh will be by his side. What is the meaning?" the poet Selvaratnam asked Bawa Muhaiyaddeen.

Bawa Muhaiyaddeen replied, "O poet, although this question can be answered in one word, let me explain something to you.

"The outside world is merely an example which illustrates the worlds and universes within us. Every human being, whether it be you or anyone else, carries many worlds and many disciples within himself. Within your mind you confer with kings, ministers, representatives, and messengers. You carry within you princely palaces with towers, infantries, artillery, cavalries, soldiers on elephants, navies, air forces, and many demonic forces, and you depend on their help. As long as you depend on the world, you are relying on these forces within yourself. But they are changing and perishable, and they can let you down.

"You must place your faith in the one indestructible, imperishable God. To do this, you must stop depending on the kings, forces, and armies within you. When you give up all this and stand defenseless and alone, saying, 'O God, it is all Your will!' the sheikh will stand by your side. It is only when you surrender to Allah that the sheikh, who is the explaining wisdom of the *Qutbiyyat (Ral.)* which guides you on the path of God, will come to stand by your side. 'Son,' he will say, 'now you are ready. Come, let us go.'

"When that time comes, you will no longer be the firewood, you will have become the fire; you will not be the gem, but the light within the gem; you will not be the sun, but the light of the sun; you will not have the world within you, but you will bring resplendence to the world."

511.

A learned man asked, "O sheikh, people talk about wisdom. They always say, 'Use your wisdom,' but what is the meaning of that word?"

Bawa Muhaiyaddeen replied, "There are six kinds of lives within you, are there not? Five of them relate to the five elements: earth, fire, water, air, and ether, which are the shadow lives of *māyā,* or illusion. The sixth kind of life is human life, the life of light. Each of these lives has a soul. The soul of human life is the power which comes from God; it is the superintendent of all the other lives. Corresponding to these six kinds of lives are six levels of wisdom.

"For example, suppose there is an itch somewhere on your body. The first level of wisdom is feeling, the sensation of the itch. The second level, awareness, tells you the nature of the feeling: it is an itch. Intellect, the third level of wisdom, tells you what to do: scratch. These three levels of wisdom are found in all creations— plants, insects, reptiles, fish, birds, mammals, and so forth.

"Creatures with these three levels of wisdom can experience fear and apprehension, they can reproduce, and they are able to protect their newborn. But they do not have the discrimination to know right from wrong. Thus every created thing has feeling, awareness, and intellect. Human life, however, has three additional levels of wisdom.

"At the fourth level, judgment or evaluation, a human being takes stock of his life: Where was I before? Where have I come to now? How long will the house which is my body last? What is the foundation on which this house has been built? Is it built on *māyā*, on water, on dirt, on marshy land, on fire, or on air? Is it a strong, solid building or will it break down easily? Evaluation inquires, estimates, and finally decides: this house has a weak foundation; it will fall apart easily.

"The fifth level, subtle wisdom, analyzes the report and finds that the house is in danger of perishing where it now stands—through fire, hurricanes, tidal waves, earthquakes, or the hypnotic fascinations of *māyā*. Subtle wisdom decides that if a house is to be strong and stable it must be built on a solid site.

"The sixth level, divine analytic wisdom, the awakening wisdom of the *Qutbiyyat* which discovers what is right and what is wrong, analyzes the report further. It decides that to be durable a house must be built on the firm, unshakable rock of perfect faith, or *īmān*. It tells us that in constructing a house, we must avoid using materials which will decay and thereby cause the building to fall apart; for example, earth, fire, air, water, the printed colors of *māyā*, and magnetic energies must not be used. We must use the imperishable materials which are God's actions, God's plenitude, God's three thousand gracious and compassionate qualities, His ninety-nine *wilāyats* or powers, His virtuous conduct, His patience and tolerance, His justice, His integrity, the inner patience called *sabūr*, contentment or *shakūr*, trust in God, *tawakkul-'alallāh,* and praise to God for everything, *al-hamdu lillāh*. Divine analytic wisdom understands that if these are the materials used for constructing that building, and if everything perishable is left out, nothing can destroy that building. None of the elements will be able to attack or destroy it.

"Once the building is completed, divine luminous wisdom, the resplendent light of *Nūr*, has to be placed inside. As soon as that light is installed, it will reveal all the universes and all of everything. Its power of perfection and the One who is within that power will be revealed. The house becomes a house for that power: God's house.

"For your life, this is the house of glory, the house of heaven, the house in which God will dwell, the house in which you will do service to Him. If you build that house, you will understand the eighteen thousand universes, *sirr* and *sifāt,* or the secret and the creation, *dhāt* and *sifāt,* or the essence and the manifestation, and *khair* and *sharr,* or good and evil. You will understand all creations and see them directly.

"Therefore, my son, wisdom is that which analyzes, understands, and builds that house of God, revealing everything that comes to dwell within it."

### 512.

A man asked, "O my sheikh, what is needed to make a country prosper?"

The sheikh answered, "That is a good question. In order for a country to prosper, God's justice must become the justice of the leader, the justice of the leader must become the justice of the common man, and the justice of the common man must become the conscience in each man. The hearts of the people must be soothed, and compassion must be made to grow within them. The four qualities of modesty, sincerity, reserve, and fear of wrongdoing must be nourished within the leader. If God's compassion comes to the leader and to the people, the country will prosper."

### 513.

A man inquired, "What is needed to make the house of man's body peaceful?"

The Sufi replied, "It is necessary to have good behavior, good conduct, love, compassion, patience, tolerance, peacefulness, justice, and honesty, and to serve others selflessly, performing the exalted duty of God. If you nurture these within your body, then Allah, the One who is within good qualities, *Kunamkudiyan,** will come to dwell within you, tasting their sublime nectar. That is the state of peacefulness."

### 514.

The sheikh speaks to his child: Son, the world is a book, and

---

* *Kunamkudiyan*—God is the One who drinks *(kudi)* the intoxicant of your good qualities *(kunam).*

215

creation is the history which is written in the book. It contains the full story and all the explanations of everything that has ever appeared.

In these stories are all the hells and heavens, wisdom and ignorance, happiness and sadness, difficulties, losses, devotion, miracles, arts, sexual games, sciences, the waves of the mind which obscure wisdom, wandering desires, jumping monkeys of the mind, howling dogs of desire, hidden demons, poison-spitting snakes, hole-chewing rats, swallowing pythons, stinging scorpions, blood-drinking tigers, and hooting foxes. There are donkeys carrying the burdens of the world, chickens scratching at the earth for worms, the qualities of what is called love—which are like a cat that rubs against good and bad alike, arrogant elephants which throw down and trample whoever tries to ride them, the qualities of poisonous insects and demons, and the vulturous quality of feeding on the dead.

In these stories are worms and insects that gnaw at man, evil demons who drink his blood, enticing lusts, overwhelming sadnesses, laughing mind-monkeys, and the millions of births, deaths, shapes, and shadow forms within man's dreams. All these qualities are within the sculptured statues that form the secret story of the world. This is the world of creation.

This history is in the cage of your body, where it is clearly explained. The world is a book, and you are a story within that book. It is for you to differentiate between the right and wrong within your story and take what is right. After you have learned to do that, you must live according to these words: "If you miss your chance in this birth, in what birth will you ever reach God? This is the unique birth of man."

If you understand the depth of meaning in these words, if you live your life taking in only what is good and always rejecting the bad, you will attain the exalted state of never having to be reborn. If you fail to attain this state, you will be subject to millions of rebirths, one for each of the worldly qualities which you have enjoyed.

### 515.

Mohammed Haniffa asked about Islam. "People cry, 'Islam! Islam! I was born in Islam!' I say it too because my forefathers said it, but how can one understand its real meaning?"

Bawa Muhaiyaddeen replied, "What you say is true. It is easy to talk about Islam. But Allah is the only One who knows Islam, and Prophet Muhammad, the Rasūlullāh *(Sal.)* is the only one who knows the secret or *sirr* and the *khair* and *sharr* of God's creations. *Sharr* is what is wrong, what we can see, the manifested creations. *Khair* is the unseen, Allah. Anyone who attains the state where he knows the difference between *khair* and *sharr,* and who then excludes what is *sharr* and accepts what is *khair,* is in Islam.

"Islam is a vast mystery of Allah, impossible to describe in its totality. Understanding even one drop of it will earn us the limitless wealth of the three worlds. Such is the infinite nature of Islam. However, because you have asked the question, let me give a small explanation, which is only an atomic fraction of that truth.

"Islam means the perfect, spotless purity of God. The state of Islam is so exalted that through it appeared all creations and lives in all the universes everywhere. Within that appearance were manifested all the bounties of Allah, and within those bounties was manifested the treasury of grace.

"Within the treasury of grace was manifested the *rahmat,* the infinite benevolence, and within that infinite benevolence appeared Allah's limitless grace.

"Within Allah's unfathomable grace was manifested Allah's incomparable love, and within that love was manifested the perfect, completeness of Allah. Allah's actions were manifested within that completeness, and within those actions were manifested Allah's duties. Within those duties were manifested His qualities of patience, inner patience, contentment, trust in God, and *al-hamdu lillāh,* praising God for everything.

"*Al-hamdu lillāh,* praise to God, is formed of the five Arabic letters *alif, lām, mīm, hā,'* and *dāl.* In these letters were manifested the representatives, messengers, saints, *qutbs,* and prophets of Allah. Within those prophets were manifested Allah's powers, His completeness, the mirrored ocean of His grace of wisdom which is known as *'ilm,* His radiance, His justice, His ways of absolute truth, and His selfless duties.

"The might of the benevolence bestowed by Allah exists in the manifest and the unmanifest and is revealed within these Arabic letters, aspect by aspect: the *alif* is Allah; the *lām* is the light of the Triple Flame which gives the explanation; the *mīm* is the beauty of Muhammad *(Sal.),* the beauty which bears within it the three worlds—*hayāt,* which is life, the soul, *dunyā,* this world, and *ākhirah,* the next world, the world of God. The might and the essence have been placed within the *lām* and the *mīm.* The resplendent beauty of Allah's Messenger was placed in its completeness within them. That light was made of *ahmad,* the beauty of the heart. *Muham,* the beauty of the face, was made the beauty of the inner form of man. The beauty of that form, or *sūrat,* was made the beauty of the light of the perfect *Nūr Muhammad.* The light of *Nūr Muhammad* was made into the resonance and the explanation of *Allāh Muhammad.*

"That power exists as Allah, and the beauty of that power exists as *ahmad.* The shining explanation of the resonant resonance and the radiant radiance was given through His messengers and His prophets.

"If we want to understand the meaning of Islam, we need firm faith in Allah, certitude in that faith, and determination. This is known as *īmān.* This is the full weight of the meaning of Islam, and the form of Islam is the word of God, the *Kalimah.* When the *Kalimah* and *īmān* become one, that is Islam, the light of purity. When the completeness of that light shines forth, radiant and perfect, that is Allah.

"Islam is the wealth which never diminishes or perishes. It is the wealth of prayer, the wealth of worship, the wealth of meditation, the wealth of *īmān,* the wealth of true man, *insān,* and the wealth of this world and the next. This is the wealth which *insān* must attain. One who discards what is *sharr,* takes what is *khair,* and attains this wealth is in Islam. For such a person, Allah is his only treasure.

"Islam is heavy only until one understands its beauty and its subtlety. Allah is not a burden; He is the essence mingled within all lives. Allah's benevolence is not heavy; the things we have gathered in this world, the *sifāt,* are the burdens. The secret is not heavy. *Sharr* is heavy, not *khair.* If one can give up *sifāt* and *sharr,* it will be very easy for him.

"As we gather more and more worldly things, our burden becomes heavier and heavier. But if we unload them, if we take all the things we have and throw them into the garbage truck of the world, it will be easy. The garbage truck will pick up the dirt and carry it away to the dump.

"If we collect all the gold and silver objects around us and put them in a bag, they will be heavy. But if we empty the contents of that bag back into the earth where they came from, saying, 'Come, take it all,' the earth will dissolve them and take them back, and the bag will become very light.

"Nor should you carry the bag of gold and silver to the market, looking for praise from people of wealth and titles. Give it back to the earth. Do not look for the world to praise you for what you are carrying. Look for the praise of God. If you throw away everything else, then the burden will be less. Anyone who holds onto the things he has accumulated in the world is not truly in Islam, he is only talking of Islam.

"Carry only Allah, His qualities, His actions, the value of the 6,666 verses He sent down as the Qur'an, and the qualities of the Rasūlullāh *(Sal.)*. Understand these and understand the Rasūlullāh *(Sal.)*, and your faith, your *īmān,* will become complete. When one's *īmān* is perfect, he will accept only Allah and Allah's qualities. Then he is Islam; he is the light for all three worlds.

"I have given a small explanation according to my small level of wisdom. There are others with higher wisdom who may tell you more about Islam."

516.

A child asked, "Someone said that the meaning of Islam is to eliminate impurity and become pure. Is that right, my sheikh?"

The sheikh replied, "I told you that it is easy to talk about Islam, but very difficult to act accordingly. What that person said was right, but the one who heard it merely listened; he did not do anything about it.

"Someone did say that, but our birth and existence themselves are impure. The place from which we emerged and the place in which we grow are impure. Everything until the very end is impure. When impurity is discarded, man will indeed be pure. When all attachments are cut away, only purity remains. That is Islam. The body, the world, and our attachments are the impurity.

"The person you spoke of said that the meaning of Islam is to end impurity and become pure. What he said was right, but how can we get rid of impurity when everything we see is tainted? The body, possessions, and the elemental spirit are all impure. When they are all dispelled, purity will remain. This means that the world must die away from us. Only then does one become pure."

A sheikh tells his disciple, "Son, in the world there are three kinds of children: the children of the world, the children of the sheikh, and the children of God.

"The children of the world are those who are formed from the playing and intermingling of blood ties, the pleasures of sexual games, the pleasures of the arts and sciences, and the pleasures of lust and desire. They are born with and enjoy the sounds, voices, colors, bodies, and faces of those games, appearing and disappearing within them. Their five-element body is nourished with food, blood, fluid, and the milk of *māyā,* or illusion, which is extracted from blood. In this way, attachments to blood ties are poured into these children. This is how worldly parents give birth to and raise their children. This is one group.

"But the sheikh makes his children cut away those attachments. The sheikh's children are formed in his *qalb,* in his inner heart, existing in the state of wisdom with the beauty of compassion. Theirs is the body of faith, determination, and certitude. They receive wisdom and the qualities of God from the sheikh, who nourishes them and raises them with the splendor of their right to eternal life. Their father, the sheikh, will make them children of resplendent wisdom, children with the clarity of the absolute faith of *īmān,* children of absolute truth. He will feed them with the milk of love and the honey of grace, with patience, with *sabūr, shakūr,* and *tawakkul-'alallāh,* or inner patience, contentment, and trust in God, and with the qualities of God's grace. He will raise his children without ever deviating from the path of justice. He will raise them within his heart of *īmān,* feeding them with the milk of *īmān* and the honey of wisdom, and make them worthy of receiving the wealth of all three worlds, which is called *mubārakāt.*

"Then he will tell them, 'The father you saw when you were born was made of flesh and blood; he belongs to the world. I am your father of wisdom, the father of the essence of grace. And now you must find the Father of your soul, with whom you were earlier.'

"He will open their wisdom, saying, 'Look at your Father's brilliant light: that is your true body form; it is the form of His essence, the resplendent light body you had when you came from the world of the souls. Do you see your rightful body? That is the body in which you must meet the Father of your soul.'

"He will say, 'I have brought you to this stage. Now you must take on the body of light which you had before.' Then he will take you and hand you into the care of your original Father in heaven, saying, 'My son, this is Allah, the Creator of all the universes, *Rabbil-'ālamīn*. Go and reach Him! Such a child is a baby to the sheikh, light to wisdom, clarity to faith, and a representative of God.

"God will accept the child given by the sheikh, and He will teach the child His qualities, His actions, and His ninety-nine powers. He will demonstrate the difference between this world and the next, and raise the child to His own state, so that the child will serve Him and the people who have reached His kingdom. God will make the child His representative in the performance of all His duties.

"Thus there are three kinds of fathers who bring you up in three different ways. My son! Children who relish the pleasure of worldly desires are children of hell. Those who learn and receive divine knowledge in the world are the children of the sheikh. Those who receive Allah's benevolence, qualities, and grace, those who lose themselves in Him, are the children who serve Him as His representatives and messengers."

518.

It's all false.<br>
It's all a dream.<br>
It's all crazy.<br>
It's all over.<br>
It's all right.<br>
Let's see what's next.

519.

A *hadīth:* Hell awaits those who know of Allah yet do not pay obeisance to Him.

520.

One who desires what is forbidden by God, while knowing the difference between *halāl* and *harām,* what is permissible and what is forbidden, will face punishment on Judgment Day.

521.

To establish the absolute faith of *īmān,* to determinedly believe the laws and conditions related in the Qur'an and in the *ahādīth,* and to hand over all responsibility to Allah at every moment is the real treasure of contentment.

### 522.

A *hadīth:* One who is a *mu'min,* a true believer, must make his faith steadfast and say, "*Lā ilāha illallāhu Muhammadur-Rasūlullāh,* none is God except Allah and Muhammad *(Sal.),* who is the beauty of the face and the inner heart, is the Messenger of God."

### 523.

One who has the intention of conducting himself with Allah's good actions will never come to ruin in the world.

### 524.

In the words of the Prophet Muhammadur-Rasūlullāh *(Sal.):* One who has forfeited justice in his life falls prey to the fiery ocean of injustice.

### 525.

The sheikh says: There is no purpose in fighting a *jihād,* a holy war, against those in the world outside you who do not accept Allah. Within you there are creations that do not accept Allah. If you can wage *jihād* on them, eliminate them, and strengthen your absolute faith, certitude, and determination in Allah alone, you will attain the excellence of a *mu'min,* a true believer.

### 526.

Do not fight holy wars, seeking to kill other creations of Allah because of their religions. Fight a holy war to destroy religious hatred within yourself. That will bring glory to the inner religion spoken of by Allah and the Rasūlullāh *(Sal.).*

### 527.

Do not serve God with the motive
Of gaining titles, honors, and praise.
Realize with the firm conviction of *īmān* that Allah is your Lord, bow in obeisance to Him, and perform His duty as His slave. This will be the magnificent treasure you will receive in this world and the next.

### 528.

Do not set out to capture
The kingdom of Allah
And the wealth of His grace
Thinking in your arrogance
That they belong to you alone.

Your arrogance will become your hell. Allah, the wealth of His grace called *rahmat,* and His kingdom belong to all of His creations. Understand this.

### 529.

"What does a person need in order to live in peace?"

"Give up your desire to capture and own the things of the world. Search for Allah, the one God who is the Ruler of all the universes, *Rabbil-'ālamīn.* Then you will find perfect peace."

### 530.

Seek the qualities of Allah. Let yourself be filled with the perfect faith spoken of by Allah and His Messenger, the Rasūlullāh *(Sal.).* That is your greatest wealth.

### 531.

O man, if you catch a thief in the world, you might scold him or hit him. But if you search carefully, you will find a bigger thief within you who is stealing all your valuable treasures. Catch him, punish him, and drive him away. Then you can safeguard the true wealth of your life.

### 532.

O man, do not wander around shouting, "My race, your race," praising one and disparaging the other. Do not nurture the fire of racial differences. That same evil fire of arrogance will one day consume you.

Adam and Eve *(A.S.)* and all men and women belong to the same race. For one who has the perfect faith of *īmān,* there is only one Creator and one race. If you realize this with your wisdom, you will understand Allah and His *rahmat,* the benevolence of His grace.

## 533.

O man, we have a duty to strive to acquire the grace of divine knowledge called *rahmatul-'ilm*. The Rasūlullāh *(Sal.)* said, "Go even unto China to learn *'ilm*."

But no matter how much we study, we need wisdom to understand the inner meanings of our learning. Knowledge without wisdom is like rain falling into the ocean. No matter how much rain falls, it turns into saltwater and is unsuitable for drinking.

## 534.

When one man wrongs another, the one who is wronged must forgive the one who wrongs. This is the exalted state of the forgiver.

## 535.

The sheikh says: My son, people complain about those who slander and carry tales. But man must realize that within himself his mind and desire are slandering him, others, and even Allah.

Rather than finding fault with others, if man can expel the slanderer within him, he will be a man of *īmān,* a man with perfect faith. Then he will not slice and eat the flesh of those outside himself as though he were eating carcasses.

## 536.

The sheikh says: My son, if a man evaluates his own actions with justice, inquires into the state of his own heart, and carries out the judgment of Allah on everything within his own heart which is guilty of causing him to do wrong—that will be more exalted than seventy times of prayer and worship.

## 537.

A *hadīth:* If one learns, knows, and understands *'ilm,* or divine knowledge, from a sheikh, from *rasūls,* from men of wisdom, from the prophets, or through the *ahādīth,* he will attain a state more exalted than if he performs fifty times of prayer.

## 538.

A man who has no compassion toward other lives will lose the wealth of God's grace in all three worlds.

### 539.

My children, treat your babies with goodness, love, and compassion. Feed them with the milk of the grace of divine knowledge known as *'ilm,* and they will attain an exalted life.

### 540.

My children, the family of mankind is God's most sublime creation. We must do only what is good for them, no matter who they are or what they may do to us. All of us must nurture the gracious qualities of God within ourselves and give of that goodness to all mankind.

If you plant the seed of goodness in the house of your heart, you can live as the tree of the undiminishing wealth of God's grace. The fruits that grow on that tree can be given to all your brethren, and those fruits will help them grow in His beneficent love.

### 541.

The sheikh says: My son, any man who is truly willing to help all humanity, whether with his hands or mouth or body, is most exalted among mankind and among all God's creation. Such a man is a *mu'min,* a true believer, with the perfect faith of *īmān.*

### 542.

A man who causes pain and suffering to his neighbor will not live in the house called *Īmān-Islām.* The Rasūlullāh *(Sal.)* brought the forbearance of inner patience, or *sabūr,* to bathe all mankind in the water of perfect faith, embrace them with the heart of compassion, and feed them with the milk of the *Kalimah,* the word of God. This is the crown of the qualities of *Īmān-Islām.* The Rasūlullāh *(Sal.)* would always comfort his neighbors, even if they were hostile toward him.

### 543.

My son, give charity in your life, and your wealth will never decrease.

### 544.

My son, if you are a man of wisdom, do not tell others to do something that you yourself would not do. If something is harmful to you, do not mislead others by saying it is desirable or worthwhile.

Even if you cannot bring yourself to do good for others, at least avoid guiding them on the wrong path.

### 545.

If you fail to bring your house to a state of peacefulness, then even if you acquire titles by memorizing the Qur'an, the Bible, or other religious philosophies, your learning and titles will be like oil poured onto the fire of hell.

My son, if you correct yourself and transform the qualities and actions of your heart into those of a loving and beautiful baby, that will become the plenitude of the perfect faith of *īmān*.

### 546.

O you who are men, charity given unwillingly is like blood squeezed out of a dark, compassionless heart. To give in that state is not charity. It will give no comfort to the heart of the receiver.

### 547.

O you who are men, true fasting is to destroy the fire of arrogance, the fire of anger, the fire of the base desires or *nafs ammārah,* and the hell within each of these.

### 548.

The sheikh says: My son, fasting is observed in many ways in the various religions and languages. Human beings fast for different lengths of time and for different reasons. But we must reflect on this with wisdom.

*Allāhu ta'ālā,* Almighty God, created the food for each being 70,000 years before it was created. There is no one other than Allah who can feed His creations. This truth was told by Allah to His prophets, and thus to all people. Any man who has the faith to absolutely accept this truth will not covet or plunder the wealth or nourishment allotted to another, either in this world or the next. Why? Because he will understand that each creation has already been given his own share of the treasure of all three worlds: the world of the souls, this world, and the next world.

There are some men, however, who will steal the wealth, home, and food allotted to others. This quality of stealing exists only in man and not in animals. In the *qalb,* or inner heart, of man are craving, avarice, selfishness, pride, conceit, and countless such evil and base desires. Because man plundered the possessions of his brethren and thought he could live happily with this world as his hunting ground, *Allāhu ta'ālā* sent down to the Prophet *(Sal.)* the *furūd,* the five obligatory duties.

The first *fard* is to have *īmān,* or perfect faith in Allah. The second is to observe the five times of prayer each day, affirming that there is no one worthy of worship other than God, *Allāhu ta'ālā.* Third is to give charity. The inner meaning of charity is to keep only the nourishment that Allah has given you for your own and to share the rest. Allah is the only One who supplies nourishment.

It was to explain and make man understand them that *Allāhu ta'ālā* sent the laws by way of the Prophet *(Sal.).* But the people could not observe them properly because of their pride, avarice, and jealousy.

Then Allah sent the explanation of the fourth *fard,* fasting, to the Rasūlullāh *(Sal.),* and said, "Tell your followers to observe fasting which will make them feel hunger, fatigue, and loss of strength. Make them experience this so they can realize the suffering of those whose food, houses, and other God-given things they might think of taking." This *fard* was given in order to make man understand that he must not take others' property and wealth, but that he must return to others what belongs to them.

The fifth *fard* is to perform the *hajj,* the holy pilgrimage. To fulfill this duty you must distribute your property to your wife, your children, and to the poor and needy, and go to Allah in the state of death. That is, you die to the world and make your pilgrimage clad in a shroud-like cloth. Kill your *nafs ammārah,* your base desires, by returning all the wealth and property you took from others. Make your passions die and make the world within you die.

In this way, if you make all your thoughts die and take only Allah with you, if you discover the way to pray to Him, if you fulfill the *hajj* and find Him, you will receive the wealth of the next world.

Allah did not lay down these *furūd* to cause suffering, but to make people realize and understand. Allah gave the *furūd* so that each creation would be content with whatever it is given. But we have forgotten this explanation.

To have a clear understanding of this, to realize the thoughts within you that are selfishly trying to take what belongs to others, and to make these thoughts die away from you—that is real fasting. All lives must be allowed to experience and enjoy the wealth of the three worlds given by Allah.

To value the happiness and comfort of everyone is Islam. To be happy at seeing unity and peace in yourself and others is Islam. Those who live happily and share their food as one congregation, praising and praying to Allah, are the true believers in *Īmān-Islām*. Those who have no doubt in their hearts, those who receive the resplendent light of *īmān,* those who live in the infinite benevolence of Allah, praising Him in every moment and placing their trust in Him for the next moment—they are the ones who will have the perfect purity of Islam.

If one has eliminated his desires, his fast is praiseworthy and his heart will receive Allah's wealth of grace. We must understand the significance of fasting and act accordingly.

### 549.

The sheikh says: My children, using the perfect wisdom which exists in your hearts, understand good and evil and do the duties which are good. That is exalted.

### 550.

O mankind, every part of your body has desires, and every part thinks of and looks for the essence of the world and evil. Therefore, ask for God's forgiveness with every breath and every word.

### 551.

O you who are men, do not search for faults in others. The faults you see in others are really within yourself. Search for your own faults, eliminate them, and achieve purity. To do that will be best for your faith and for the house of your inner heart, and it will bring happiness to Allah.

### 552.

The sheikh says: My son, let us reflect on prayer. Prayer is that which eliminates all our suffering. What makes us suffer? Everything we see in the world!

One who truly wishes to pray must see only Allah. Before his death, he must go to Allah and die in Him in the state of prayer. Then Allah will accept him, lift him up, and embrace him.

Some meet Allah only after death, when they must face the Day of Reckoning and Judgment, but true prayer is to die in Allah while you are still in the world. If you can understand this with your wisdom, you will realize the wealth of prayer which is the wealth of the three worlds, and you will not have to face the Day of Reckoning or Judgment.

553.

The sheikh speaks to his disciple: Son, here is a treasure. Within Allah is the seed of His benevolence. Its outward manifestation is creation.

Son, if you open the creation and look within, you will see the secret. If you open the secret, you will see the heart. If you open the heart, you will see Allah's essence. If you open the essence, you will see Allah's majesty. If you open Allah's majesty, you will perceive His taste. If you open Allah's taste, you will perceive the beautiful fragrance of the flower of divine wisdom. If you imbibe that fragrance, you will perceive the brilliant fullness of the light of Allah's *Nūr*.

If you open the *Nūr*, you will perceive the resonance of Allah. If you open the resonance, you will see the explanation. If you open the explanation, you will see yourself. If you open yourself, you will see Allah's mystery which is intermingled with and dwells in all of everything. You will see all of Allah's powers, actions, qualities, and conduct. As soon as these are seen, the created will be the Creator, and the Creator will be the created.

When you reach that state, He will be within you and you will be within Him. You will be the flower and He will be the fragrance. You will be the fruit and He will be the taste. You will be the current and He will be the light. You will be the Qur'an and He will be the treasure within the Qur'an. You will be the knowledge of grace and He will be the ocean of that knowledge. You will be paradise and He will be the beauty of paradise. You will be truth and He will be the life and the light of truth. You will be the baby and He will be the One who embraces and praises you. When you embrace Him within your heart, He will be the baby and you will be the one who tenderly cares for Him.

This, my son, is the exaltedness of the world of the soul, of this world, and of the next world. This is Allah's wisdom and His grace of benevolence.

## 554.

A man asked the sheikh, "People seize kingdoms, possessions, and countries which belong to others. Why doesn't God punish them?"

The sheikh replied, "Son, God has given His kingdom, His property, His grace, and hell and heaven to all of His creations. Because God has given wealth and a place to each being in order for it to live in freedom according to its own needs, the house of hell awaits anyone who tries to take away the freedom and possessions of others. Such a one will become food for hell.

"For a man who has the absolute faith called *īmān,* Allah alone is his treasure. This treasure will give him peace and enable him to give peace and show love and equality to all lives.

"Those who do not understand this will plunder God's property, rob the freedom of others, and cause suffering to their well-being. Allah does not punish those who have lost their wisdom. He laughs at these wicked animals with human faces and says, 'O mankind, I created you as the most beautiful of My creations. Do not fight. I made the apple tree and gave it countless fruits to be eaten by all. Do not uproot the tree fighting over what it has been given. If you claim it is yours and destroy the tree, the suffering and loss which follow will torment you. Realize this.'

"O disciple, conduct yourself as a true human being! Allah laughs at selfish people and He waits. When the food and water decreed for them in this world are finished, His judgment will be given. You must understand this, my son, and conduct yourself as a true human being."

## 555.

Leading a deer he had caught, a hunter passed by the Holy Prophet *(Sal.).* With great respect and obeisance, the deer cried, "O Rasūlullāh! This hunter has caught me, and it is time for me to give milk to my two babies. O Rasūlullāh, please free me. Let me give milk to my children and tell my husband what has happened. Then I will return and give myself to the hunter."

The Rasūlullāh *(Sal.)* called to the hunter, "Please come here. This deer has children; let her go to feed them and speak to her husband. She has promised to return."

The hunter cried out, "Are you insane? I underwent so much difficulty to trap this deer, and now you tell me to release her! I know only my hunger. If I set her free, she will never come back!"

"The deer has the quality of honesty. Release her and let her give milk to her children. She will come back," replied the Prophet *(Sal.)*.

"I cannot release her," declared the hunter.

"Please set her free. If she does not come back in half an hour, I will give you four deer," said Muhammad *(Sal.)*.

Reluctantly, the hunter agreed to let the deer go. He sat near the Prophet *(Sal.)* and waited.

The deer went home, fed her children, and told her husband what had happened. "The Rasūlullāh was my surety. He said he would stay with the hunter until I returned. I have given you milk, children. Now I must go."

"We are coming with you," they cried.

"No. You must stay. I must keep my word to the Prophet even though I am going to become food for the hunter. If you go with me, the hunter will eat you also. You must stay," said the deer firmly.

"No, mother. We must go wherever you go. If the hunter wants to eat you, let him eat us, too," her children replied.

Her husband said, "I too must come. We must all go together as one family and satisfy his hunger. Then we can all fulfill your promise to the Rasūlullāh."

Meanwhile, the hunter was furious. The half hour had passed. "Where is the deer? Where is the deer?" he yelled.

"Wait a little," said the Rasūl *(Sal.)*. "You will get four for your one. Be patient for a while longer."

The deer appeared with her family. "O Rasūlullāh, forgive me. I am five minutes late. I was telling my husband and children of how I was caught and of my promise to return. They wanted to come with me and offer themselves as food for the hunter. I am late because I was trying to dissuade them. Now the four of us are here. Please accept us."

The hunter stared at the deer in disbelief. "I released one deer and now I have four. What a wonder!" He turned to the Rasūlullāh(Sal.). "In truth, you are the Rasūlullāh. The deer knew you, but I did not. I did not possess the faith or certitude that the deer has." Saying this, he fell at the feet of the Rasūlullāh and begged, "Please teach me the word of God, teach me the *Kalimah*."

The Rasūlullāh *(Sal.)* taught him the *Kalimah*.

Then the hunter said, "O Rasūlullāh! The deer trusted you. I cannot take them. Their faith in you has saved their lives. If I too put my trust in you, I will be saved from the fire of hell. Please forgive my sins."

"Have faith," the Rasūlullāh *(Sal.)* told him. "Show compassion to all lives and help them. Praise God and eat only the food of Allah's love, the food which is *halāl,* the food which is permissible for you."

The Rasūlullāh *(Sal.)* then told the deer to go back to the forest and live happily.

The sheikh told his children: Strengthen your faith. No matter how hungry you are, be content. Show compassion to other lives and place your trust in God alone.

556.

A *hadīth:*

While some Bedouin Arabs were tending their goats on Mount Hirā', a huge tiger caught one of the goats. Its owner chased the tiger away and retrieved the goat.

The tiger then ran back to the top of Mount Hirā' and began to speak. "O Arab, you have taken my food! I didn't take all your goats, did I? I only caught the one that Almighty God destined for me. But you hit me, chased me away, and took my food. Why have you done this? Is it right? How can you do such things? Have you forgotten Allah, O Arab?"

The Arab was amazed. "Come! Come, brothers!" he shouted. "This is a wonder. A tiger is speaking like a man!" All the Arabs came running.

Again the tiger spoke. "O Arabs, my speaking like a man is not a wonder. But there is indeed a wonder: Muhammad, the Messenger of God the light of Allah, is in the city of Mecca. He has been born as the son of Āminah. But you do not know, realize, or accept the Messenger of God; isn't that a wonder? He is the

Rasūlullāh, the Messenger to the world of the souls, this world, and the next world. He puts out the fires of those who are burning in hell and helps them ascend to heaven. Isn't it a wonder that you do not know him?"

"Where is he? We must go to him! Tell us," cried the Arabs. The tiger replied, "He is at the foot of the mountain."

When they reached him, they found the Rasūlullāh *(Sal.)* mending his clothes. They asked him, "Where is the Rasūlullāh?"

"What is the matter? Why are you inquiring about him?" asked the Rasūlullāh *(Sal.)*, smiling.

The Arabs related what had happened. "There was a tiger who spoke like a man. It told us that in the city of Mecca there is a prophet called Muhammadur-Rasūl who is the child of Āminah. The tiger said that Muhammad is the Rasūlullāh to all three worlds. We came here to search for him. Do you know who he is?"

"I am Muhammad," said the Prophet *(Sal.)* very softly.

"You?" they asked. "But the tiger spoke of majesty and splendor, and here you are—mending clothes!"

The Rasūlullāh *(Sal.)* said, "All praise is to Allah alone. I am His slave. I serve Him and do His duty. Doing His duty and paying obeisance to Him will put out the fire of hell within us and bestow upon us the beauty and resplendence of heaven."

The Prophet *(Sal.)* smiled, and the Arabs saw the luminous radiance of his face. They said, "O Rasūlullāh, please accept us. Show us the right path and teach us the word of God, teach us the *Kalimah*." He taught them about the absolute faith of *īmān*, and then he taught them the *Kalimah*.

The Rasūlullāh *(Sal.)* asked them, "Do you know who the tiger was? Angel Gabriel *(A.S.)* himself spoke to you in that form. He opened your hearts and melted them; the hell that surrounded you has left. Now your hearts are radiant with the resplendence of the *Kalimah*, and the brilliance of Allah is in your hearts."

### 557.

The sheikh said to his disciple: Son, who will receive a letter without an address? If the address of the one who wrote the letter and the address of the one who should receive it are missing, neither of them will get the letter: in the end, it will be thrown in the trash can.

Charity that is given without faith in God and without a compassionate understanding of both poverty and hunger is like a letter without an address. Likewise, prayer done without melting faith, open-hearted reverence, and fear of God is like a letter without an address.

If you understand this and surrender yourself to Allah, your prayer will reach Him. When you give charity with an open heart, that is food given by Allah, food which will give peace to all, and the benefit will come back to you.

558.

The sheikh said to his disciple: Service done selfishly is the service of satan. Prayer which asks on behalf of oneself is the prayer of satan.

Duty and service which is done unselfishly, with a melting heart which is surrendered to God, will receive Allah's treasures in the next world.

559.

A man asked a Sufi sheikh, "Is it better to teach the people, or is it better to teach oneself?"

The sheikh said, "Son, a wise man must first learn to improve himself and bring himself to a good state. Then his good actions, good qualities, and good conduct will teach the world. When the world sees this, it will learn by itself."

560.

The sheikh said: Son, a certain man who loved music bought a violin. He tapped on the instrument but no music came.

A visitor came to his house and asked him what he was trying to do. The man who loved music said, "I've heard others play, so I bought a violin and now I'm trying to play, too. But I don't seem to be able to make music like the others do."

The visitor looked at the violin and said, "It has no strings!"

The man who loved music bought strings, fixed them onto the violin, and was then able to learn to play music. He was overjoyed. "This is the music I love!"

Even though the man had a violin, the sound he desired was not in the violin, but in the strings. No matter how many violins you may have, they will not produce music without strings.

Similarly, no matter how much you love your body, no matter how many things you buy for your body, it will not have real beauty. Only when the strings of wisdom are placed across the bridge of faith, certitude, and determination and played with the bow of absolute faith will you know the beautiful resonance of, "*Lā ilāha illallāhu.* There is nothing other than You, O God. Only You are Allah." It is the resonance in your inner heart, or *ahmad,* which lights up and produces beauty in the face, which is Muhammad *(Sal.).*

561.

The sheikh says: Son, there are millions and millions of mantras in the world. Many people learn to recite them like parrots, and think they can reach God and heaven through them. Some even come forward to teach mantras to others. But their hearts have not been made clear and their wisdom has not emerged. They are entangled in darkness and are suffering in agitation. You will understand this if you open your heart and look with wisdom.

It is better to catch your mind, lock it into the cage of faith, and teach it with your wisdom. Discard the parroting of mantras. Instead of this, acquire the knowledge which will teach you the truth, and act accordingly.

562.

The sheikh says: Discard the desire to become a guru or a sheikh so you can teach the world.

Instead, become a true man. Live as a true man, acquire the qualities of Allah, bow down at His feet, and surrender yourself to Him. This is exalted.

563.

A wise man says: It is easy to become a guru. It is easy to say you are meditating. However, before man can really meditate, he must be at peace. In order to be at peace, he must cut away the monkey of the mind, and cut away desire, deceit, treachery, fraud, falsehood, envy, all the selfish thoughts of this body, the thought of wanting to ruin his neighbor, and the thought of taking revenge and torturing other lives.

He must discard the quality of hypocrisy with which he destroys the unity of other lives; the quality of anger which is like fire; the quality of having one justice for himself and another for others; the poisonous quality of the snake; the quality of separations and the differences of religions which are like the torturing, blood-drinking tiger and lion; and the rat-like quality of making holes in the lives of others.

If man can tie up his mind of *māyā* and control the tricks of the monkey which mimics everything it sees, and lock them into the cage of wisdom, he will find peace. Then if he sits and meditates, forgetting himself within that peace, his voice will be heard by God and God's voice will be heard by him.

If, however, he tries to be a guru and, as a guru, does meditation, that will be like the meditation done by a stork which stands for ten hours on one leg in order to catch a fish. His meditation will be done with the selfish intention of catching the world and the tricks of the mind.

Son, realize this state. Before you can meditate, you must make yourself the meditation. Clear your heart. Before you do your prayers, make your heart a prayer. This is the victory of meditation.

### 564.

The sheikh says: Son, there are fools who think that the robe makes the guru. They are the ones who do not comprehend the grandeur of the wisdom taught by the sheikh. My son, do not be like them. Always remain a student. Stay on the straight path. Learn to be alone, awake, and hungry.

Lose yourself and die in the One. Then you can learn more and more of Allah's benevolence, His *rahmat*. When you become a slave to God, you cannot be a guru. If you try to become a guru, you will not receive the *rahmat* or the wealth of the three worlds. You will have arrogance, karma, and pride, and day by day, you will sink lower and lower. Think of this with certainty. Be the slave of God. Do not try to be a guru.

### 565.

The sheikh said to his disciple: Before time takes control of man and hands him over to the Angel of Death, it is better for man to take control of time and give himself to God, the Creator.

### 566.

A man asked the sheikh, "O sheikh, one cannot exist in the world without money. What can be done about this?"

The sheikh answered, "Yes, that is true. If you do not have money and wealth, you cannot have this world; and if you do not have grace, you cannot have that other world. See this clearly with your wisdom and decide which of the two worlds you want."

"You are the sheikh, please advise me," said the man.

"You are a man, are you not? Both worlds are under the control of man. If his heart is filled with the absolute faith of *īmān,* he will have the wealth of this world and the next. If man dispels the wants of mind and desire, he will want for nothing; he will have in plenitude the wealth of the world of the souls, this world, and the next world. This explanation is given by the *Tiru Qur'ān,* which is the inner Qur'an inscribed within the heart."

### 567.

The sheikh said: These are the prerequisites for one to be a true believer, or *mu'min,* in *Īmān-Islām.* Know them, my son.

1. *Patience.* No matter what one suffers in the world, no matter what difficulties or losses may come, one must have patience.
2. *Sabūr* (Inner patience). One must have forbearance within forbearance at all times.
3. *Shakūr* (Contentment). One must have contentment within contentment under all circumstances.
4. *Al-hamdu lillāh* (All praise is to God). One must accept whatever is given to oneself, praise God, and give Him all responsibility for the profit and loss, happiness and sadness that come at any moment. This is man's most exalted wealth in this world and the next.
5. *Tawakkul-'alallāh* (Trust in God). One must surrender to God whatever will happen at the next moment, and do His duty as a slave within Him.

Know these as the prerequisites of *Īmān-Islām* in your life and you will know the plenitude of praising God for what happens in this moment, and you will have trust in God for what will happen in the next moment. If you acquire this wealth, Allah will conduct your life. Your soul and your body will grow in His protection, and God's wealth will be your wealth and your grace.

### 568.

A man asked his sheikh, "O sheikh, one must be grateful to the land in which he was born, is that not so?"

The sheikh said, "Yes, that is right. You must have gratitude. You must be grateful to the land in which you were conceived and nourished for ten lunar months. You must indeed be grateful to the land into which you were born.

"You were born in this world, and you will die in this world. But there is something else to consider: Where will you go after your death? Think of that.

"In order to know this, you must go to the land in which you dwelt before you came here and understand the good and evil in both worlds. You must know your Father, the One who created you and sent you here to learn the secrets of both worlds, the One who sustained you in these two worlds, the One who will ultimately protect you in the land to which you will go.

"If you understand this, if you have gratitude toward your Father and the kingdom which is His land, and if you serve Him with that gratitude, you will not die, nor will you be born here again."

### 569.

"What clothing is most beautiful for the life of man?" asked a disciple.

The sheikh said, "Man must weave the fabric of modesty, sincerity, reserve, fear of wrongdoing, good thoughts, good conduct, God's compassionate qualities, patience, honesty, and the actions of truth, forbearance, equality, and treating other lives as his own. If he adorns his body and his heart with that fabric, it will give him the most beautiful clothing for his life in both worlds. Everyone will be enchanted by those qualities.

### 570.

"What things are needed to make the body happy?" asked a man.

A man of wisdom answered, "The body is very happy when it finds the things it experienced earlier. It likes the things from

238

which it was created, the things which joined to form and shape it, and the things in which it grew. These are the things that will make the body happy.

"However, the very things which make the body happy now will later cause its destruction and suffering. Think of this with wisdom, and understand the One who created and nourished you. Then suffering will leave you, and your body, mind, and qualities will experience everlasting joy."

571.

A man asked, "The Communists say there is no God. Is that right or wrong?"

The sheikh said, "Son, one who says there is no God has no God. But if God did not exist, creation would not exist; nothing would move. He has always existed and always will exist. People with wisdom must think of this.

"If you put water into a pond without banks, what will happen? Will the water stay there? No. Such a pond is just a depression in the ground. Though some water may collect in puddles, this would hardly be sufficient to water the crops on a farm or to supply water to a town.

"The heart, life, and learning of a man who has no faith and certitude in God is like a pond without banks. He tries to lead his life without God, saying, 'I belong to nature. I am the doer.' Such is the ignorance of his arrogance.

"The people you spoke of could be like that. They can never protect the world; they can only cause destruction and war because such people are like puddles with very little water. The instruments of those who have no faith in God are destructive instruments. They have weapons and guns to kill each other, but they have no tools to make the country prosper. Just as a pond without banks cannot supply enough water for the crops on a farm, people without faith in God who try to rule the world with their destructive weapons cannot bring peace.

"You cannot raise fish in a pond without banks. One day the water will dry up and the fish will die. Know this with your wisdom and trust in God. He is the shore to the ocean of life. Go to the ocean with banks; that will benefit you. Entrust the exaltedness of your life to Him. He alone can make it grow."

"Is there no judgment for the evils in the world? If there is a God, a judgment will come, will it not?" asked a man.

The sheikh said, "Son, you asked a good question. A huge ocean surrounds the world, and the fish in it are God's creations. God gives food to them and protects them. He does not kill or eat the fish; He nourishes each of the countless fish.

"Fish eat fish. Two-legged fish also catch them. The water which God created does not punish or kill the fish. On the contrary, one might say the fish cause a lot of discomfort to the water by jumping and rolling around in it. When the tide comes in, the fish run along with it. When the tide goes out, some of the fish remain on the shore and die.

"Creations judge and punish themselves. God does not punish them. The world punishes the world. Water punishes water. Fish punish fish. Man punishes man. And God looks on.

"However, there is a Day of Judgment, and on that day God gives His judgment. Man brings about both exaltedness and destruction in his own life. All destruction is within him. He kills and is killed. If you think about this, you will know. God sorrowfully smiles at the ignorance of people who punish themselves. They punish themselves even before His judgment arrives. God feels sad. 'With your ignorance, you are killing yourselves. Did I create you like this?' He asks. And He laughs, too. If you look with wisdom, you will understand."

573.

A wise sheikh spoke to his disciple: Son, plant the seed of human wisdom within God's grace, and it will grow and bear fruit. When the fruit is mature, the divine wisdom called *gnānam* will come. From that *gnānam* will come the wisdom of grace. From the wisdom of grace will come the resplendence of *gnānam*. From the resplendence of *gnānam* will come plenitude.

Within plenitude, man's torpor and birth are cut away, and he will experience the resplendent *gnānam* taste of a birthless and deathless state.

A human being who can live as a true man and understand this with clarity is exalted and divinely wise.

574.

Let me tell you a story from the Tamil *Purānas* as an illustration:
There was a *munivar* named Vasistar. He was so exalted in meditation that even the *dēvas* praised him.

Arunthathy was his wife, and duty to her husband was her sole
purpose in life. One day before sunrise, while her husband was
in meditation, she went to the river to get water. On the other
side of the river she saw another *munivar* in meditation, but no
one served him. Arunthathy thought to herself, "He must be
hungry," so she went home, got some food, and carried it across
the river to him. This continued for some days. When she gave
the pot of food to the *munivar,* he would tip it into his mouth
and swallow it. She would always return before her husband
finished his early morning meditation.

One day when she set out to take food to the *munivar,* she found
that the water level in the river had risen so high that she couldn't
cross. She returned to her husband and waited silently. When he
opened his eyes, he asked, "What is the matter?" She explained
how she had been doing service for a *munivar* and how the water
level had risen so high that she couldn't take his food to him.

Vasistar said, "Tell the river that the *bramachāri* says it should
give way to you."

Arunthathy thought, "He is married to me and yet he says he
is a *bramachāri.*" Still, being a devoted wife, she went unquestion-
ingly to do as she had been told. Sure enough the river opened
and made way.

The *munivar,* Visvamitra, tipped the pot of food into his mouth
as usual and gave it back to Arunthathy. When she went back to
the river to return to her home, again the water was too high. So
she went to Visvamitra and stood quietly in front of him. "What
do you want?" he asked. She told him that though she had been
able to cross the river earlier, the water level had risen once again.

"What did you say then?" the *munivar* asked.

She replied, "I said, 'The *bramachāri* says to give way.'"

"Now go tell the river, 'The one who never eats says to give
way.'"

As she walked back to the river, Arunthathy thought, "My husband says he is a *bramachāri,* and now the man I feed daily says
he doesn't eat. What a wonder!" When she came to the river,

241

she said what she had been told to say and, sure enough, the river made way. Arunthathy crossed it, went home, and continued her duties without question, but she was troubled by the thought of all that had happened.

Some time passed. The king of the celestial realms, Devendran, decided to conduct a *yāga,* a ritual of sacrifice. But since there was a curse that made it likely that the head of the one who officiated at the *yāga* would split into a thousand pieces, no one was willing to do it. Finally, Devendran requested that Vasistar do it, and he agreed. The condition of the curse was that only a chaste woman could save her husband.

The day of the *yāga* drew near. Vasistar told Arunthathy, "You must come, too. Bring two pots, one of which must fit into the other with just the width of a thread between the two. And bring some water and a small stick." A chariot came for them and they went to a celestial world called *Indra-lōka.*

As the *yāga* began, Vasistar told Arunthathy, "Fill the big pot with water and place the other pot into it. Then you must rotate the inner pot with the stick without allowing it to touch the outer pot. My life is in your hands. If you stop, or if you let one pot touch the other, my head will split into a thousand pieces. Only if you carry out these instructions successfully until the end of the *yāga* will my life be safe."

The *yāga* continued for eight days. Arunthathy did exactly as she was told, although all around her *Indra-lōka* was rollicking with dramas, music played by the *dēvas,* and dancing by the celestial maidens Rambay, Ūrvashi, and Mēnaka.

At last the *yāga* was over. Still Arunthathy continued to turn the pot with the stick. Vasistar called, "Arunthathy! Arunthathy! Arunthathy!" but she was so absorbed in what she was doing that she did not hear.

He touched her hand. She looked up and said softly, "Swami?"

Vasistar said, "I called you three times. Didn't you hear me?"

"No, Swami. Forgive me," she replied.

Then he asked her, "How did you enjoy the music of the *vīnas,* the dancing of Rambay, Ūrvashi, and Mēnaka, and all the dramas that went on here?"

"Oh Swami," she replied. "What are you saying? I was not aware of any of those things. As you started the *yāga,* I began to rotate this pot, and I was not aware of anything else. My only concern was to save your life, so I concentrated on only this one task. I was doing exactly what you told me."

Vasistar said, "The whole of the heavenly worlds was turned upside down with music, dancing, and fun, but because of your state of concentration, you did not notice any of it. Similarly, you say that I married you.

"Did I know that I married you? From that day to this, I have not known it. I have given up land, women, and gold. I have made mind, desire, and thought die, lost the self, and melted and meditated on the one point of God. So I am indeed a *bramachāri*. If I tell the river to make way, it will do so. Why should you have any doubt about that? Why did you worry about it all these days, Arunthathy?

"Visvamitra's meditation is in the same state. You thought you fed him daily, but just as you did not see the dancing and music in this hall, he did not know that you went to him and gave him food. He did not know that he had eaten; therefore, he is a man who continually fasts, and the river will give way at his command too.

"You must give up the thought that I married you and the thought that he ate the food you gave him. You must stop worrying about this. Your state during the *yāga* is the state of the meditation of true *gnānis;* just as you forgot yourself, they too forget themselves in the one thought of prayer. That is true meditation. To surrender in that one thought and die in that one love is true prayer. To lose one's mind, words, and body in God and give all responsibility to Him is prayer. Think of this, Arunthathy.

"One who has nothing other than God, one whose life disappears in Him, is in the state of true prayer. Just as a tree is hidden in a seed, for man to disappear in God and God to disappear in man is true prayer. If meditation, prayer, and worship are done in this state, that is true prayer. One in this state will not know the world or what is happening in the world."

### 575.

The sheikh said to his disciple: Son, the world is the magical, mesmerizing torpor of illusion. You must think of this a little. Let me give you an example.

An ant-eating lizard went in search of its food. It stretched out its tongue reaching inside an anthill and waited patiently. The ants attacked its tongue, thinking it was their food, but no matter how much they bit, the lizard bore it all patiently. Then, when its tongue was completely covered with ants, it pulled it back in and swallowed all the ants. Again it put out its tongue and again the ants bit. No matter how painful the bites, the lizard persevered in order to get its food.

Like that, my son, ignorance, the world, illusion, torpor, money, gold, possessions, poverty, illness, and disease will all try to eat you if you intend to go to the real God. They will bite your mind in the way the ants bit the lizard.

And in the way the lizard forbore all that pain until it got its food, you too must bear all your suffering with *sabūr,* with inner patience, until you obtain your real food. You must bear the suffering just as the lizard did. You must know that Allah is your real food, the food that dispels hunger, disease, and old age. If you take this food into yourself with wisdom, placing it within your heart and your soul as food, light, and divine wisdom, it will appease the hunger of your heart. It is the food of the benevolent grace of Allah.

Until you obtain this treasure, the sufferings of the world will continue to assail you. If you hold onto Allah's food for your soul with faith, certitude, determination, and perseverance, and withstand the suffering, you will certainly receive Allah's benevolence and the wealth of the three worlds: the world of the souls, this world, and the next. However, if you run away in fear of that suffering, millions and millions of more terrible afflictions will follow. Understand this. Hold on to Allah steadfastly with absolute faith and patience, and you will be victorious.

### 576.

A fox who was very cunning stole chickens from around the countryside. Every day he would bring the chicken to a banyan tree by the pond and eat it. A crocodile who lived in the pond was watching the fox day after day. Then one day, while the fox was feasting, the chicken's intestines fell into the pond. The crocodile snatched them into his mouth. The fox said, "Brother, the intestines belong to me. Please give them back."

The crocodile thought, "The intestines are a trivial thing, but the fox has been eating chickens for so long that their essence must be in his liver. If I eat the fox's liver, I will get the essence of all those chickens. I will give the intestines back for now and await an opportunity to eat the fox's liver." With this thought, the crocodile charmingly returned the chicken's intestines to the fox, saying, "These are yours, indeed."

From then on they became good friends, but the crocodile still had other ideas. One day he said, "Brother fox, I have told my wife and children many things about you, and they are very anxious to meet you. They have lovingly asked that I bring you home to visit them. Won't you please come and satisfy their wish?"

"Oh yes, elder brother," replied the fox. "I would love to come, but how can I go in the water?"

"Brother, why should you worry about that? You can ride on my back. Come," said the crocodile, lying next to the bank of the pond.

The fox climbed onto the back of the crocodile, who then carried the fox to the center of the pond. There his desire overcame him, and he said, "Brother, you have been eating chickens for a very long time. All the essence and strength of what you ate must certainly be in your liver."

"Oho! I am in trouble," thought the crafty fox. "He wants to eat me." But aloud, he asked, "Would you like to eat my liver?"

"Why do you think I brought you here? I have been waiting for so long to eat your liver," said the crocodile.

The fox thought for a moment and said with apparent concern, "Brother, why didn't you tell me earlier? Everyone wants my liver, so I carefully leave it at home when I go out. But since you are my dearest friend, I must satisfy your desire. If you take me back, I will get it for you."

The foolish crocodile turned back, and as soon as it came close to the bank, the fox leaped to the shore, crying, "Oh stupid crocodile! You deceived me and tried to eat my liver. Oooh, oooh. My liver is within my body. I will never fall into your hands again." So saying, it ran away howling.

This is the way everything is in the world. The attachments, religions, blood ties, relatives, relationships, the body, and all such connections of the human-animal are the crocodiles which tear your body apart, eat your liver, put you in the bottom of the pond to rot, and consume you at their leisure.

In the way the fox escaped from the crocodile, you too should escape with wisdom from these human-animals who live in the pond of *māyā*. This is the way to save your life.

577.

There was a guru in the east who had many disciples, and a sheikh in the west who had only one disciple. Both spent their time in meditation and prayer. The guru from the east went with his many disciples to see the sheikh of the west and his one disciple.

The guru asked the sheikh, "What do the two of you pray to?"

The sheikh explained, "We pray to that which must be prayed to."

Then the guru turned to the disciple, "What do you pray to?"

"I pray to whatever my sheikh tells me to pray to, in the way that he teaches me," answered the disciple of the west.

The foremost disciple of the east then exclaimed, "We don't see any gods on your side, but look how many gods we have!" The guru's disciples brought forth one hundred thousand different idols. "We have so many gods, and we can speak to them directly. These gods give us whatever we need. And you will be wonderstruck at the miracles our guru does: he can bend the sky into a bow; he can weave sand into rope; he can walk on water and fly in the sky; he can become invisible to the eyes of others; and he can create countless idols, giving them life and the *shakthis* with which to drink the blood of enemies who do not respect us, then drive them crazy and destroy them. He can do so many miracles like this."

The guru's disciples then proceeded to display various wondrous feats. They made water appear from nowhere, they manifested fire from nothing, they made the wind to blow and storms to strike.

Then the guru asked the sheikh, "What does the God you worship do? Where is your God?"

The sheikh answered, "We pray to the one God who is worthy of worship. That is all. After I die in God and only God is in God, you can come and get your answer from Him. That is all I can say at this time."

The eastern disciples continued to mock them and laughed, saying, "Two fools have joined together. They have a God who cannot be seen by the eyes or held in the hands. We have wasted our time with these mad people," and they went away.

The sheikh and his one disciple were not disturbed by this. They simply carried on with their usual duties. The sheikh taught his disciple all that was necessary. "My son, before you can meditate, you and your intentions must disappear within the sheikh. You must be immersed in the sheikh, and the sheikh must be im-

246

mersed in God. Only then will it be possible for you to dwell with God. Only then will His protection be with you. No matter what else you may do, no matter how much you may achieve or what miracles you may perform, when the power which is God appears, everything else will be burned. Therefore, to receive that protection, you must immerse yourself in the sheikh."

The sheikh taught his disciple to lose himself within the sheikh. The disciple's body was separate, but his mind, his heart, and his meditation were within the sheikh.

"My son, we must now meet the disciples of the east," the sheikh said. "Tell them that an accident will soon befall them, and when it does, they will understand the answer to the question they asked earlier."

The disciple from the west hastened to the disciples of the east and told them, "Look over there. A brilliant light is approaching. It is not like any light you have ever seen before. If you can escape destruction by its resplendence, then all your meditations and gods will have proved to be worthwhile."

When the sheikh's disciple said this, all the guru's disciples jeered at him. These were the disciples who had performed the mantras and miracles. Each had control over a particular *shakthi*.

Suddenly, with a thundering resonance, the resplendence drew near. The disciples of the east ran to their gods and clutched at them, frantically chanting their mantras. As each deity was consumed in flames, they ran to another. One by one, all their gods were burned by that resplendence. The guru of the east also stumbled from one idol to another, and he too was consumed. When all the idols were burned, the disciples ran to the sheikh and his disciple.

"Our guru is gone! Our gods are gone! How did you and your sheikh escape?" they screamed in fear. "The resplendence is still coming with a terrible resonance!"

As the resonance drew closer, the sheikh stood facing the approaching resplendence. Because he had disappeared within God, when the resplendence reached the sheikh, it gently entered him. The light stayed within him and radiated brilliantly from within his heart. The sheikh spoke, "O disciples, all your gods, your learning, your miracles, and your meditations are gone. The moment they were confronted by the light, they were consumed.

"This power has no form, no mantra, and no shape. It does not contain any of the things you were doing. This is God. This power alone is worthy of prayer and meditation. Only one who merges with and meditates on this power can escape from it. One who prays to anything else will be burned when the resplendence appears."

The sheikh then turned and revealed the resplendent light to the eastern disciples. They looked around for the solitary western disciple but he could no longer be seen, because he was hidden within the sheikh. The disciple had merged with the sheikh who had merged within the power and the resplendence.

"Now do you understand?" the sheikh asked. "First, the true sheikh must be immersed in the power which is Allah, and then the disciple must lose himself within the sheikh. Only then is he truly protected. One who has not attained that state will end as you have. Your guru is gone, your gods are gone, and all the miracles you displayed have been consumed by fire.

"If I had not been here to protect you through my meditation, and if I had not been merged in this power, all of you would have been burned. Only if we are immersed in that power can it benefit us. All the things you have done for so long can be destroyed in one instant by the power which is God.

"So, instead of wasting our time, our lives, and our breath, it would be better if we were to understand what is right. To know what truth is and to lose oneself in it is the wealth of wisdom. None of the things we see is true wealth. Everything we see is torpor and illusion. This body which is nourished through the slaughter and consumption of so many millions of lives ends up as a handful of earth. No matter how much wealth we may amass in this world, this body will end up as fuel for the fire of hell.

"But if the one who is a handful of earth receives the grace and wealth of God, then all the treasures and grace in the eighteen thousand universes will be his. Those treasures will never diminish.

"This is what we must try to obtain. This alone is true peace. Even kings live in misery. Everyone in the world suffers. Since everyone in the world always wants something he does not have, his wealth will always be incomplete, and he will never have peace. Only when one dwells within the undiminishing and complete wealth does he dwell within peace.

"With wisdom, understand God in your heart and worship Him with absolute faith, saying, 'Lā ilāha illallāhu: There is nothing other than You, O God. Only You are Allah.' This will benefit you." So said the sheikh to the guru's disciples.

248

The sheikh tells his disciples the story of Mansūr al-Hallāj *(Ral.)*:

Mansūr al-Hallāj *(Ral.)* thought there was no one greater than himself. He was a saint, but he had pride, egoism, and arrogance, and he thought his prayers were most exalted.

One day while he was praying, a voice came from a distance, "Mansūr! Mansūr!"

Mansūr al-Hallāj *(Ral.)* looked around to see where the sound had come from, but he saw only a small boy.

Again Mansūr al-Hallāj *(Ral.)* heard the sound, "Mansūr!"

He turned around and asked, "Who called me?"

"I did," said the small boy.

"Why did you call me?" asked Hallāj *(Ral.)*.

"You are praised and respected by people as a great saint. I want to ask you a question," the boy said.

"What is the question?" Hallāj *(Ral.)* asked.

"Allah has created everything. He gives all of His creations food and wealth. If one has wealth, what should he do? If one does not, what should he do? If one gets food, what should he do? If one does not get food, what should he do?" asked the small boy.

Mansūr al-Hallāj *(Ral.)* thought, "What is this? He must be a crazy boy." But he replied, laughing, "If one gets food, he should eat it happily and praise God; if he does not, he should have *shakūr,* contentment."

"What do you do?" asked the boy.

"That is what I do," answered Mansūr al-Hallāj *(Ral.)*. "If I receive food or wealth, I praise Allah and enjoy it. If I don't receive anything, I have *shakūr.*"

"Really? Is that what you do?" The boy laughed and laughed.

"What are you laughing at?" demanded Mansūr al-Hallāj *(Ral.)*.

"I am laughing at what you said. We have a dog in our house that happily eats when it gets food, and contentedly goes to sleep when it does not. What is the difference between what a dog does and what you do?"

Mansūr al-Hallāj *(Ral.)* did not know what to say. "All right then, what would you do?" he finally asked the boy.

"Me? If I get food, I give it to those who are hungry. If there is any left, I praise Allah and I eat. If I do not receive anything, I have *shakūr.* For any wealth I receive, I praise Allah and then I give it to widows, poor unmarried girls, and orphans, keeping only the undiminishing wealth of Allah," answered the small boy. Mansūr al-Hallāj *(Ral.)* bowed his head and said, "People call me a saint, but what is the use of all my studies? I could not even correctly answer the questions of a small child. What have I received from God? All I have is arrogance and vanity. One who receives the benevolence of doing what you do will never lack anything."

Then the small boy said to him, "All wealth is Allah's and must be shared among His creations, but *shakūr* belongs to you. That is what you must keep. That is a prerequisite for the perfect and pure splendor of *Imān-Islām*."

Mansūr al-Hallāj *(Ral.)* bowed his head. "I will cherish what you have said and act accordingly."

After that the boy disappeared. On that day, the arrogance and the pride of Mansūr al-Hallāj *(Ral.)* left him; his heart opened fully, and he surrendered to Allah's ocean of benevolence.

## 579.

A man asked the Sufi sheikh, "Some Sufis who lived in the past gave their disciples certain explanations, such as, 'A real mystery, a real meaning, should not be spoken of to one who cannot understand. It must remain hidden and withheld from them.' What is the meaning of that?"

Bawa Muhaiyaddeen answered, "What they said is right. The mystery known as truth does exist. That mystery created all lives. The basic unit of all creations is an atom of that mystery, the real power which understands every created thing and which exists as the mystery within it. Without that power, nothing, not even an atom, would move. This is one explanation.

"It has been said that this mystery should not be spoken of to one who does not understand. Even though a man appears to have a human face, if he does not have the wisdom and qualities of a man, he has no faith in God. You cannot tell him the truth about the mystery. He is worse than satan, because even satan accepts God and the truth, although he might not accept certain other things. Satan had pride of self and wanted to be the leader of heaven and earth. He was jealous and deceitful and treacherous toward those who were placed above him. Because of that, God created Adam *(A.S.)* above satan and decreed that satan and the others must stand behind him to pray to God. It was for this reason that he became jealous of Adam *(A.S.)*. Satan accepted truth and God, but he would not accept anyone else as superior to him.

"But the actions and ideas of a man who is not a true human being are much worse than satan's. Such a man has egoism, pride, jealousy, treachery, deceit, trickery, vengeance, hypocrisy, selfishness, intoxicants, lust, theft, murder, falsehood, backbiting, arrogance, karma, illusion, craving, hatred, miserliness, greed, fanaticism, and envy. If one who is filled with these evils has the form of a man, his heart will be darker than the darkness of satan. He will never be able to look you in the eye; his expressions will be deceitful. He is one who has sold the wisdom and the faith in God within his heart to darkness. That is why mystery and truth should not be told to one in this state."

## 580.

"One must have peace and freedom in order to meditate. Where can I go to do this?" a man asked the Sufi sheikh.

The sheikh thought to himself, "This man thinks that if he goes to the jungle he will have the necessary peace and freedom to meditate. Because he came here with this thought, he will not listen to any other advice. He must be made to experience certain difficulties before he will accept the correct way."

So the sheikh replied, "If you go to the jungle, it will be very peaceful. There are no people there, and it will be very easy for you to meditate."

Happily the man ventured into the jungle, and as he walked, he thought, "The place in which I meditate must have trees, stones, and a river so that I will have water for drinking and bathing. I must also have a cave to protect me when the rains come. These are comforts I really need." He went deep into a dark jungle and searched all day. Finally, he found a cave with a pond nearby. To him, it seemed a lovely and peaceful place, but he was not aware that the cave was full of lions and that poisonous snakes lived in the pond.

When night fell, it became very dark. Snakes hissed on one side, while tigers and lions coughed and growled on the other side. Peering into the dark depths of the cave, the man cried out, "O God, save me from the lions and tigers! They might eat me before dawn. Where can I go? I cannot go into the cave. It is their house. Protect me!" He climbed to the highest branch of a tree, trembling and wailing until dawn, "O God! O God!"

When the day broke, the lions and tigers crept back into their caves and all the other animals went back to their places. The man climbed down from the tree and thought while he ran all the way home, "I didn't have even one night of peace in the jungle!"

When he reached his sheikh, he threw himself at his feet. "My sheikh! I cannot describe how much I suffered in the jungle. The tigers, bears, lions, snakes, and elephants made noise all night long. I had no peace. All through the night I suffered in terror. I thought of God and screamed all night."

"Is that so?" said the sheikh. "How did you manage to escape?"

"If I hadn't climbed a tree they would have eaten me! Did you tell me to go there because you wanted me killed?" asked the man."

The sheikh answered, "I told you to go there so that you could kill that which killed your peace, not because I wanted you killed."

"What was it that killed my peace, O sheikh?" asked the man.

"The comforts you wanted: the pond, the cave, water for drinking and bathing. You ended up where you did by searching for things to give comfort to your body. Those comforts are your lions and tigers and poisonous snakes; they are the things that killed your peace. If you kill mind, desire, and thought, and the fear of things that could kill you, you will have peace wherever you may be. What were you scared of?"

"Lions! Tigers! Bears! All kinds of poisonous creatures were there," exclaimed the disciple.

"Little brother, they are all within you; you raise them formlessly inside yourself. Outside, they exist in form, but the beasts inside are worse than the animals you saw. If you chase away the beasts of mind and desire within you, then wherever you are, whether in the jungle or the city, it will be a peaceful place, a place that is conducive for meditation. Understand this." So said M. R. Bawa Muhaiyaddeen.

### 581.

"Where is the best place for man to meditate?" asked a child.

Bawa Muhaiyaddeen answered, "The best place for meditation is the place in which the 'you' and the 'I' do not exist.

582.

"Who meditates upon whom?" a child asked.

The sheikh answered, "The one who meditates and the one who is meditated upon should be one. The one who meditates should become God and meditate on God. That is true meditation."

583.

"How can the world be overcome?" asked a man.

Bawa Muhaiyaddeen replied, "If you overcome your attachments to the world within you, the outside world will be like an atom which will disappear on its own. To your eye of wisdom, it will become like a speck of dust, and it will fly away.

584.

"When will I attain peace?" asked a man.

Bawa Muhaiyaddeen said, "You will attain peace when the arrogance and the bigotry of the 'I' are destroyed."

585.

"How can one think of all lives as one's own life?"

Bawa Muhaiyaddeen said, "When the thoughts of ignorance, selfishness, hunger, blood ties, fanaticism, arrogance, falsehood, jealousy, envy, anger, pride, theft, treachery, deceit, and the differences of the 'you' and the 'I' are destroyed, your analytic wisdom will emerge and show you that all lives are like your own. You will then realize the state of equality."

586.

"Who is good for the country, O sheikh?" asked a child.

"The one who is good for the country is one who knows himself, one who controls his tongue, one who has overcome desire for land, gold, and women, one who has dispelled selfishness, one who grows up on God's qualities, one who has God's actions, one who is nourished by God's compassion and grows up in His patience, and one who does God's duty."

587.

"Are there animals more terrible than the lions, tigers, poisonous snakes, vultures, and eagles which torment, torture, kill, and eat the lives of others, O sheikh?" asked a man.

Bawa Muhaiyaddeen answered, "Do you not know? Of all the lives that God, the Creator, has made, the one who was born as man but changed into an animal-man of arrogance, pride, jealousy, selfishness, and conceit is the worst beast of all.

"He is the beast which murders, torments, and drinks more blood than any other. There is no animal as horrible as he. It is easy to escape from the other animals, but it is extremely difficult to escape from the animal-man. If you can escape from him, that alone will give you peace in life."

### 588.

"What is the greatest happiness?" asked a child.

"My child, to gain freedom from this world and to return to the One with whom you existed earlier is the greatest happiness," said the sheikh.

### 589.

"What is best for love, O sheikh?" asked a child.

"Truth is best for love, wisdom is best for truth, grace is best for wisdom, and God is best for grace. A man who understands this and acts accordingly is best for God."

### 590.

Children, God creates, protects, and nourishes. He has created lives with six levels of wisdom. According to its level of wisdom, each creation seeks the food God has destined for it. God has created the food on the earth—in trees, grass, weeds, leaves, ponds, and everywhere.

God has created man with divine analytic wisdom, thus making him the most exalted of all His creations. He has placed all of creation and the eighteen thousand worlds within the body of man. With his divine analytic wisdom, man is capable of understanding the secret of God and the secret of man.

Man progresses by analyzing and discovering what he needs for his eyes, nose, ears, body, neck, and hands. If any of those parts needs anything, he tries to obtain it.

To satisfy his hunger, he has discovered incredible varieties of food; he has discovered how to plant seeds and make them multiply. He has discovered countless things to feed his one-span stomach and nourish his body—houses, property, comforts, money, and wealth.

Man has learned to live comfortably in the world. He has also studied many religions and scriptures. He has learned about everything but himself. He has not learned of his own state, nor of how to know himself or his Chieftain. He has not studied the explanation of his soul or how to receive grace. This is the wonder of one who has been born a man.

He has collected the things seen in his dream, believing they are real. But he has failed to learn about the resplendent daylight of his life, the treasure which is the freedom of the soul, and the means to obtain the fullness of the infinite wealth of grace from the One of limitless grace. He has not learned of the crown bestowed by God which gives him the right to live eternally in God's kingdom without ever being reborn. Because he has failed to study these, he has lost them.

All the things he has collected here, hoping they would make him happy, are merely part of the dream of his life. But when he goes to the next world and opens all the bundles of his supposed treasures, he will find them empty. Only then will he realize that his life was an empty dream.

If a man will take only the essence—the photographs—and leave all the bulky, heavy structures behind, if he will take the eternal things mentioned earlier, he will receive the wealth of God, the kingdom of heaven, the kingdom of the soul, and the kingdom of this world, and he will live as the representative of God in all three worlds. One who is a man must realize this.

591.

Hunger knows no taste.
Lust knows no caste.
Desire knows no shame.
Sleep knows no comfort.
Intoxication knows no good conduct.
Anger knows no sin.
Status knows no compassion.
Bigotry knows no justice.

Attachment to scriptures knows not the
    peace of other lives.
Blood ties know not the truth of justice.
Money knows no good qualities.
Arrogance knows no peace.
Falsehood knows no truth.
Pride knows no patience.
Wealth knows no poverty.
Fame knows no mercy.
The bow and arrow know not the act
    of killing lives.
Acting knows not the good conduct of
    modesty, sincerity, reserve, and fear
    of wrongdoing.

## 592.

The sheikh says: Son, there are many thoughts which appear in the mind of man; they appear and they change his form, killing his good qualities and good thoughts. They turn him into a demon, an animal, a dog, a monkey, a devil, a snake, and a scorpion. With divine analytic wisdom, you must examine what the five elements, the mind, and the desire in your body have gathered and brought to you. You must analyze the good and the evil in what they have brought, and cut away the evil with the sword of wisdom. The evil in what they have brought is capable of destroying you, so you must take only what is right and keep it safely in your real treasure chest.

Within you, there is One who is wisdom within wisdom, One who shines and explains as truth within truth, One who is the radiance of the soul within your soul. If you know this One through the radiance and the explanation, wisdom will show you the path that leads to the liberation of your soul.

Walk on that path of freedom, knowing and accepting the meaning of freedom. Pray with surrender in your heart. Pray to that One, you within it and it within you, as truth and light.

So said M. R. Bawa Muhaiyaddeen to his child.

## 593.

There are many types of insanity in the world. We will talk about five common ones:

The insanity originating in the brain,
The insanity for women,
The insanity for money,
The insanity for intoxication,
The insanity for wisdom.

At a crossroads near a park, there was a shady tree. Five people with these five forms of insanity were sitting beneath the tree. They were talking to themselves. To the passersby, the five crazy people looked alike, but there were different reasons for their craziness.

The man who was mentally insane picked up all the scraps of paper and dead leaves on the ground and turned them around in his hands, jabbering to himself, "You went this way, you went that way."

The one who was obsessed by women picked up all the scraps of paper thinking they were love letters. He muttered, "She wrote this, she wrote that. She said, 'I will come to you!'"

The one obsessed by money picked up all the scraps of paper, looked at them, turned them this way and that, and mumbled to himself, "This bank, that bank. This amount, that amount. My bank."

The one who was insane from drink stood up and staggered onto the road, bumping into people and things. Finally, he fell unconscious by the roadside, and robbers took his clothes. When he came back to consciousness he was ashamed, so he went home, fought with his wife, and blamed his family for his own faults.

But the one who was obsessed by wisdom took up a dead leaf and smiled wistfully. "What beauty you had when you emerged as a tender shoot. At first you were a lovely green color which soothed others. Then you became yellow, and now you are the color of earth. You are a dried leaf and you will go into the earth as fertilizer. Everyone and everything will suffer the same fate. Everyone and everything becomes food for the earth." He laughed and cried, but not on the inside.

The man obsessed with wisdom laughed at his own explanation. He said, "What a life this is! O God, I search for You and become crazy. You are the only doctor who can cure my craziness. If You do not come, I will die like the leaf. You are the One who creates, protects, and sustains me. You are the One who understands and knows me. Give me Your medicine of grace, wisdom, and love and fulfill my needs. I am Your slave in this world." His heart opened, and he surrendered to God.

The other four did not realize this. They were speaking of what was within them. But to the world, all five people looked crazy.

Son, understand these states. Do not follow the ways of the world. If you see one who truly understands himself, loses himself in the obsession for wisdom, and dies in God, you should respect him and learn good words and wisdom from him. That will make you exalted.

594.

The sheikh said: Son, here is an explanation of creation and how it took place in the miracle of God's qualities and actions.

The power called God existed alone in *anāthi,* the dark time before creation began, and in *āthi,* the time immediately preceding creation. Two radiances, the *Nūr* and the *Qutb (Ral.),* emerged from within God, paid obeisance to Him, and said, "*Bismillāhir-Rahmānir-Rahīm,* in the name of God, Most Merciful, Most Compassionate. O Allah, You are a power. You are alone, and yet all of everything is contained within You. O Allah, look!"

Rays emerged from the *Nūr* as atoms and scattered throughout all the universes. In the atoms which came from the ray, there was earth. Within the earth was water, within the water was fire, within the fire was air, and within the air were the colors of ether. There were seven types of resplendent rays, and within every atom of energy were millions of cells. Within the cells were the five elements and their energies, within these energies were the creations, and within the creations were countless changing colors and forms, existing as cells. These cells were scattered as millions of viruses. Within the viruses were vibrations; within the vibrations were feeling, awareness, and intellect; and within intellect was the atom of the power of grace.

The light of the soul was there, and a sound came, "All of you, look at God! Pay obeisance to Him. Look at what we see before us. Look at the power of light which is wisdom, the plenitude of the light of *Nūr.*"

Without realizing the full wonder of this, man lives his life thinking that the qualities, actions, and potentialities of each creation are in themselves miraculous.

When God created forms, four hundred trillion, ten thousand

energies arose from the mind. Men made the forms into gods and offered them the mantras of the five elements, thereby filling them with life. To those gods they sacrificed cows, goats, blood, alcohol, and humans. Through these sacrifices, demonic forms were created. The creation known as man desires these energies and uses them to perform miracles.

If we understand the energies, we can receive the plenitude of grace which is the wealth of wisdom that controls everything. Thus we can control and destroy all the energies and miracles. God said to the saints, "I have created the food and the statue-like forms in creation. Take the food, but discard the idols; take the essence of grace from My creations, but discard the forms of the creations; take what is permissible, but discard what is forbidden."

Analyze all these energies and forces with the resplendence of *Nūr Muhammad* in your heart. With the wisdom of the *Qutbiyyat*, make them obey the resplendent light with absolute faith in God. God has placed within us the light which emerged from Him. Let us bring forth that light. And then, when the two lights emerge from us, we can understand all explanations. Realize this.

### 595.

"What is necessary for the world?" asked a disciple.

"The truth of man living as man and the compassionate qualities of God are necessary in the world."

### 596.

"Who must rule the world?" a child questioned.

"Allah and His justice must rule the world from within the heart of an *insān kāmil,* a perfected man, who has lost himself within Allah's justice as His slave."

### 597.

"What is the benefit of the distinction money gives to a man?" asked a child.

The sheikh replied, "Son, the distinction that money confers will be revealed by the shroud on a man's corpse. The shroud will give him distinction and earn him praise. Money will turn him into a corpse and become his shroud."

A disciple asked, "What is needed to become a true man?"

"Good conduct, God's compassion, God's good thoughts, the perfect faith in God known as *īmān,* God's actions and qualities, and man's pure wisdom are needed for one to become a true man," replied the *kāmil sheikh.*

Son, if the vision of the eyes is occluded, a doctor can prescribe glasses to improve it.

Like that, if the eye of the heart of perfect faith, *īmān,* is occluded, go to an *insān kāmil,* a perfected man, and get some glasses for your heart. Buy the lenses of *īmān,* polish them with wisdom, and wear them. They will dispel the darkness of your heart, and you will be able to see all of everything.

Do not cry for money,
It will ruin your qualities.
Cry and search for God's qualities,
The qualities that will destroy
The corpse of the karma of your birth
And make your life eternal.

Son, let me tell you something. Listen. Even if you smell all the fragrances of all the flowers in the world, every flower and its fragrance disappears within a week, does it not?

If you realize this and look with your wisdom, you will see an indestructible flower of incomparable beauty which has an unforgettable and endlessly sweet fragrance: the flower of the *qalb,* the heart. In this world or the next, you will never see a flower which can compare to it. Nourish it until it becomes mature and it will bloom with good thoughts, good actions,˙and good conduct. Imbibe and praise its fragrance. How exquisite it will be for your life! Then there will be no other joy for you.

Furthermore, son, in this world there are many tastes, fruits, foods, and sweetnesses, are there not? But there is not one of those things that will not change in taste and become the taste of hell as soon as it passes down your throat and goes below. Such is the extent of the taste, sweetness, and praise and blame you have been able to perceive.

Son, beyond worldly taste there is a wondrously beautiful taste that is ripe and sweet and joyous. It is the taste of the grace of the mirrored ocean of divine knowledge called *'ilm*.

To partake of this taste, you must plant the tree of inner patience. Feed it with the fertilizer of contentment and pour onto it the water of certitude, determination, and absolute faith. Placing your trust in God, do your duties, giving all praise to Allah. When you act with the qualities of Allah, you will reap the fruit of the *Kalimah*, the word of God. Taste this fruit on the tongue of wisdom, and your heart will resplend with beauty; the joy of the taste of that fruit will flow throughout your whole body. Even on the Day of Judgment, this unchanging purity of sweetness will bring beauty to your heart and your face, and it will protect you.

602.

Listen carefully, there is something I must tell you. There are many kinds of poisonous snakes, and they have millions of colors and hues. Their poisons accord with their qualities, the places in which they dwell, and their size. Each kind of snake has a different kind of venom. When snakes bite, their victims can die in several ways, can they not?

Compared to other snakes, the cobra (in Tamil, *nalla pambu,* literally meaning good snake) has the quality of thinking a little. Some cobras will bite only when stepped on, hit, or hurt in some way. There are other cobras whose qualities are even subtler. If a man steps on such a cobra, it can realize whether or not it has been stepped on by accident; if so, it might hiss and spread its hood, but it will not bite. If someone says to that kind of cobra, "I stepped on you unknowingly; this happened without my intention," the cobra will not harm him. Such cobras do exist. There are snakes much worse than the cobra, snakes that seek out human beings in order to bite them. But even those snakes do not maliciously bite animals.

Why? Because it is against the nature of animals to intentionally hurt other lives. An animal does not think, "I must kill that snake, I must hit that snake, I must crush it." Goats, cows, horses, and other creatures do not intend evil toward other lives. If an animal steps on a snake by mistake, the snake might bite it reflexively, but it will not bite maliciously.

Man, however, has the quality of always causing evil to other lives, of always hurting others. Man is selfish, jealous, revengeful, arrogant, impatient, and hypocritical. He has many evil qualities. The evil smell of the sins he commits toward other lives is on him.

If he hits an animal, the smell of that animal will be on him; if he kills or eats a cow, the smell of that cow will be present in his sweat; if he murders, the smell of that murder will be on him. As soon as a snake perceives that smell, it will think, "Ah, he is a murderer!" and it will bite him. It will think, "He has come to beat me!" and bite. If a wild bull perceives that smell, it will either run away or attempt to gore the man. A goat might do the same.

Everything a man has done is apparent in the smell of his sweat. As soon as any being perceives the man's odor, it will either run away in fear or attempt to destroy him. If these evils and sins did not dwell within man, no being would ever harm him. Any being would bow to him, pay obeisance to him, and worship him. This is one thing we must consider.

Here is another point. There are eight kinds of poisonous snakes which are normally prey to an eagle, or a garuda, the king of all the birds. When these snakes are struck by the talons and beak of the garuda, or even if the shadow of the garuda falls on them, they will die. In the way the snake has the strength of its poison, the garuda has the strength to kill snakes.

When the garuda flies in the sky, it glides in perfect poise and balance, looking for snakes or small animals. It concentrates on what is on the ground while maintaining a perfect balance in the sky, gliding in circles.

When it spots its prey, it swoops down from the sky and carries if off. A snake dies as soon as it is caught; other creatures fall unconscious. The garuda carries its prey into a tree and eats it. We can see this with our own eyes, can we not? We need to reflect upon how the garuda catches and kills snakes.

In the same way, in man there are millions of poisonous snake-like qualities. His poisonous qualities are worse than the venom of snakes, worse than the qualities of any animal. Those poisons exist with many different colors in man's qualities, words, actions, vision, speech, thoughts, intentions, and behavior.

When man takes on snake-like qualities and actions, whatever he bites will die. There are as many different kinds of poisons in him as there are in the various kinds of snakes. He has the qualities of the cobra which thinks a little, has compassion, and waits for some understanding before doing harm. But there are also snakes within him which bite without hesitation or reflection, and snakes which actively seek to do harm.

Therefore, son, when you are amidst the snakes that are within man, you must walk very carefully in order to avoid their venom. If you want to be rid of the qualities and poisons of these snakes, you must be like the garuda: with patience, you must take on the body of the absolute faith called *īmān* and fly in the heavens on wings of determination and certitude, gliding silently with the balance of divine luminous wisdom. Balance yourself with: *Lā ilāha*—there is nothing other than You, O God; *illallāhu*—You are Allah.

When you are balanced in this way, if the evil snake qualities come, they will be killed as soon as the shadow of that sound touches them; the poison of their evil thoughts will die. Dive with wisdom and strike the evil. Like the garuda, you must fall on those evil qualities, strike them, kill them, tear them apart, and throw them away.

You must be the garuda of wisdom, and with the might of grace, you must kill all the poisonous creatures dwelling within you. If you do this, the forms taken by the poisonous qualities of the millions of human snakes in this illusory world can be conquered. If not, you will become food for the evil qualities and poisonous actions of man in the same way that many lives become the food for snakes. You must know their capabilities. In the way that the snake has the strength of its poison and the garuda has the strength to kill snakes, there is a strength within wisdom which can kill the poison of the evil qualities within man. Kill these poisonous snakes and escape. Then you can attain completion for your soul. You can exist as God within God, speak to Him, and mingle with Him.

### 603.

In earlier times, nomads journeyed across the desert on camels. Stopping to rest at night, they would make a fire and cook their meals. In the desert there are ostriches that eat limestone and fire; the smell of the fire would attract them. When the nomads tried to catch them, the ostriches would run very fast for a while, but when they became tired they would bury their heads in a pile of sand, thinking they had hidden their bodies entirely. Naturally, the nomads would find them, chop off their legs with axes, and bring them back to cook and eat.

Though the ostrich is huge in size, it has no intelligence. When it puts its head into a pile of sand, it thinks its whole body is hidden. It is this ignorant thought that endangers its life.

The men in the world are like this. They have the arrogant strength of the 'I'. They have pride, learning, titles, honors, wealth, religions, scriptures, religious stories, *purānas,* and science. They study all these things intensely, thinking no one is more clever than they are, no one has learned as much as they have. Just as the ostrich carries its huge body and sometimes even a rider, these humans carry the weight of the world in their bodies. When the world climbs onto these people, they have enough strength of ignorance, arrogance, karma, and *māyā* to carry it and run. Such is the strength of what they have studied in religions, scriptures, and science.

When fate and death overtake such a man, he will run to the mantras and knowledge he learned in the world and think he has escaped, just as the ostrich runs from men in the desert and hides its head in a pile of sand. And in the same way the nomads killed the ostrich, 'Izrā'īl *(A.S.),* the Angel of Death, will take him away to hell where he will receive his due punishment.

Man has lost his faith, trust, and true prayer to God. He has lost tolerance, equality, patience, contentment, the qualities of placing all his trust in God and praising God for everything. Instead of taking on God's three thousand gracious qualities, he takes on the world and worldly qualities and carries them inside himself. He buries his head in what he has gathered and learned in the world, thinking he has escaped. At that time, the Angel of Death takes him.

Son, you must not have the qualities of the ostrich. You must understand your life. You must trust God, acquire His qualities and actions, treat all lives as your own, regard the suffering and hunger of others as your own, and perform service to other lives as God does. If you do this, God will give you a life of freedom from burdens and take you to Himself, bestowing on you His grace and His light.

## 604.

Sages of times gone by have spoken of the following points:

*To be born a human being is rare.* One born a human being has no fault or blemish and no animal qualities.

*To be born a male is extremely rare.* One who is not fascinated by the torpor of the world is a male.

*To be born without blindness or a hunched back is even more rare.* To be born without blindness in the eye of the soul's wisdom, and without the hunched back of the desire for the torpor of illusion is rare.

*Rarer is it to be born a man with analytic wisdom.*

*Rarer still is it to be born with the qualities and actions of God.*

*To be born a king is even more rare.* To be born as a king who rules the kingdom of his mind, which consists of the four hundred trillion, ten thousand occult energies, elements, animals, monkeys, dogs, and foxes, is very rare.

*To be born a gnāni is the rarest of all.* A *gnāni* is one who, with the gnostic eye of wisdom, sees all lives as equal to his own, who sees the hunger and suffering of all lives as his own. To know the qualities and actions of others and show compassion according to their needs, to show love and teach wisdom are God's duty. One who sees the three worlds on the inside as well as the outside is a *gnāni.* Seeing the resplendent beauty that is never destroyed, seeing God's qualities within himself, doing God's duty without selfishness, seeing nothing other than God, accepting no other wealth but God's wealth, the *gnāni* disappears into God, resplends in the wisdom of all hearts, and dispels their darkness, hunger, disease, old age, and death. Such an exalted one gives peace and shows equality to all.

## 605.

*Bismillāhir-Rahmānir-Rahīm,* in the name of God, Most Merciful, Most Compassionate.

My precious children, jeweled lights of my eyes, all of us have come to this world, have we not? But this is only one world; as one looks deeply with wisdom, three worlds will be seen.

The first is *awwal,* the world of the souls, the world seen first in *āthi,* the time before creation began. The second is *dunyā,* this world, in which man's body has appeared. The third is *ākhirah,*

265

the world in which everything is known and understood, the world of the kingdom of God, the world of God's undiminishing benevolence. In *ākhirah,* men are given their rightful status and live a birthless, deathless life in eternity.

These are the three worlds that appear in man. Two of these are completely internal and not understood by men. They exist as a mystery, a secret.

This earthly world is seen both inside and outside man. The arts, the sexual games, and the four hundred trillion, ten thousand energies and miracles exist as man's inner and outer world, and they control him.

In this world of creation are many visible differences and separations. Man has countless languages, deities, religious teachings, and occult energies. He has different kinds of intellectual knowledge and methods of learning. Within him, the energies take many different forms: elemental, illusory, and artistic.

These things change man's nature and his qualities; they divide one man from another, section by section; they divide man from God and truth and then control him. When man leaves God and truth to hide in the fascinating darkness of birth and illusion, he loses the original, natural qualities of wisdom that realize the truth of the one family of man and the one God. He leaves wisdom and travels on the illusory path of mental torpor. While he lives in his body, his mind is reborn into various energies and illusory forms. Forgetting the exaltedness of his life, he begins to believe in time and to live subject to the influences of the planets which make him dance and shake. These planets rule him and cause him to fall into the hands of the Angel of Death. After his death, he takes countless rebirths, according to the energies to which he surrendered earlier in his mind.

We who have taken the form of man must understand and study the three worlds within ourselves and find clarity. We must understand their good and avoid their evils. The explanation and the learning is all here as the world in which we live: outside it exists as a show, and inside it exists as a shadow.

The world in which we see things is the dream world. The world in which we live is the visual world of the fascinating illusions of the mind. The world in which we study is the world of differences, separations, and killing, the world of tens of millions of occult energies.

Because we have been given the capacity to understand this, we who have been born as men must know the real point. There is real truth, and it is inside us, not in books. Truth exists in a place that mind and desire do not see.

The world of the souls is the world of light rays, a secret mystery world. The universe of the soul emanates from the grace of Allah as rays of light. When the soul and the perfect power of God merge, it becomes a mysterious secret: man who came from God merges back into the power of God.

This power will look at the world of illusion and explain the sights, appearances, and aspects of all the energies. From within the mystery, it will reveal the story and the knowledge which exist as a secret, not within the mind, but within man's inner heart, his *qalb,* which is beyond earth, fire, water, air, ether, mind, and desire.

This is the eighth level, the eighth heaven, *firdaus,* which has been built for man by God with God's qualities, conduct, and actions. If man can be in *firdaus,* from there he will be able to see all of everything and receive the wealth and divine knowledge of the three worlds. Then he will accept nothing other than Allah.

### 606.

Let me relate to you a *hadīth* which the Messenger of Allah *(Sal.)* told to his companions and to his followers:

First, prepare your hearts with faith in Allah and pray only to Him. With the light of the *Kalimah,* the word of God, make your hearts radiant with the resplendent faith of *īmān. Sabūr, shakūr, tawakkul-'alallāh,* and *al-hamdu lillāh,* or inner patience, contentment, trust in God, and praise to God, must always resonate in your hearts.

Second, all of you must come together as one. Wherever you may be, you must intend to be one and live in unity, as one race. Everyone's heart must be in the same state.

Third, do not consider worldly feasting, weddings, food, or celebrations exalted. Do not seek happiness in those things, carrying mind and desire with you to satisfy their craving for rich food.

However, when there is a funeral, you must attend. You must pay your respects to the dead. If you go, take *sabūr, shakūr,* and your love, and pay your respects. No matter what race, religion, or caste the dead person might have been, you must not see any of those differences. He is one of the children of Adam *(A.S.),* and he is a creation of Allah. He is your brother. *Allāhu ta'ālā Nāyan,* Almighty God, is the only One who can give judgment, the only One who knows the individual heart. You must not judge. On the last day you are able to see him, you must go to pay your respects and send him off on his last journey. Each of you must have this state in your hearts. If someone dies as a destitute, you must inquire and take care of the necessary arrangements to help give him a good burial. Remember this in your heart. No matter how rushed you may be, if there is a funeral procession, you must walk in the procession for at least seven steps or pause for a few moments to show respect for the dead.

Fourth, wherever *hadīth* are spoken about Allah, you must search those words for wisdom and divine knowledge, or *'ilm.* This is most important.

Fifth, whenever anyone is suffering from an illness, you must go to him, assist him, make him happy, and give him peace of mind. You must do this no matter who the person may be, without considering his caste, status, wealth, or relationship to you.

Sixth, go to those who are troubled in mind, those who are mentally disturbed. Give them peace appropriate to their mental suffering, comfort them, show them Allah's love and His state, and teach them the wisdom which can end the sorrows in their lives. Show them love and make them happy. This is an important duty for those who have *īmān,* absolute faith in Allah.

Seventh, you must observe the state of others. Look for the signs of hunger, unhappiness, or suffering in their bodies and faces. Understand the reasons for their suffering and then render whatever help is needed. Do this. If someone is hungry, you should give your own food to satisfy his hunger, even if you have nothing extra. Do not hide your food thinking of your own hunger. Control your hunger with contentment, satisfy his hunger, and make him peaceful.

Doing these things will be the exaltedness of *īmān.* This is what the Rasūlullāh *(Sal.)* has said.

Bawa Muhaiyaddeen says, "All of us who are human must think of this and bring it into our actions."

### 607.

The sheikh says: Son, listen to this explanation. The cobra has a jewel in its mouth, and it also has poison. But the cobra does not wander around proclaiming, "I have a jewel and I have poison; if you harm me, I will kill you." Instead, it hides itself in places where no harm will come to it.

It is also like that with a true sheikh. He has *gnānam,* the divine wisdom of God's grace, yet some of his words are like poison. Both are in his mouth. And like the cobra, a true sheikh will hide himself. He will not say, "I have *gnānam.* I perform miracles. I can do this and that. I belong to God's family. I am the light. I have come from a resplendent family. I have confidence that I can do everything. I can destroy you in an instant. Do not oppose me." A real sheikh will not say any of these things. Both the gem and the poison are in his mouth, but he will hide himself where he will not harm men.

Where there is danger, the snake will give out poison; where there is love, it will give the jewel. In the same way, if the time comes when a sheikh cannot tolerate what is happening, fire might be in his words; but the light of *gnānam* can also come from his words. When his beautiful words come, they give true benefit. We must pay obeisance and receive the jewel for our lives: the benefit of good words from the sheikh.

We who are men of wisdom must know this and think about it a little.

### 608.

There are many kinds of fruit trees and many kinds of fruits. They have beautiful colors, beautiful shapes, and lovely fragrances which can be very attractive to man. But the flavor and sweetness of the fruit is on the inside: the flavor is not in its beauty, color, or shape, is it?

Only one who eats the fruit will know the flavor. Then the fruit can be identified. "Ah! This looks like a lovely fruit, but it is sour. That one is sweet, but this one is bitter," he can say and put the bad one aside.

Similarly, there may be many gurus, sheikhs, yogis, and *gnānis* in the world, and they may have many religions, scriptures, doctrines, and beliefs. They may adorn themselves with robes, beards, jewelry, and gems and look quite beautiful. As with fruits, there may be many varieties; they may appear in many colors and hues and perform all kinds of singing and dancing.

But you must know the flavor in their hearts, their qualities, actions, conduct, and wisdom. Only when their hearts are tasted can it be known whether the flavor within them is the flavor of the honey of *gnānam,* the honey of illusion, the honey of torpor, the honey of lust, the honey of craving, or the honey of demons. All these can seem like honey, but their very different qualities can be known only through their flavors.

When a man who is wise examines the flavor within them, he will say, "Ah! These are not good. These are things that can kill us, are they not? They may seem quite beautiful on the outside, but they are not tasty. They can cause suffering to our lives." A man who is wise will not look at colors, hues, shapes, or outer beauty. He will turn his attention to the flavor of the fruit.

In the same way, one who needs truth and wisdom will not look at religions, races, colors, hues, high status, or low status. He does not need them. Instead, he will focus on what is in the heart and taste it to see what flavor exists there, what qualities, love, goodness, sweetness, grace, and beauty exist there.

He will find the sheikh who has the flavor of these good qualities and follow him. Once he finds the true taste, he will stay with it. This is the real flavor and the real state to which a man must attain.

609.

Food gathered from the world
Is hay for the fire of hell.
But the food of love for God
Which comes from the inner heart,
Will satisfy the hunger of your soul,
And nourish the freedom of your soul.

610.

Trivial friendships endanger your life.

611.

Friendship that is excessive,
That is beyond proper limits,
May be harmful to your wisdom
And may end in disaster.

### 612.

Too much teasing
Can separate even close friends
And may endanger your life.

### 613.

A sharp knife will become dull
From cutting things that are hard;
The sharpest point will one day be blunt.
Even fine and subtle wisdom
Can be ruined by the arrogance of the 'I'.

### 614.

Tricks and a sharp wit
Can bring you disaster.

### 615.

One who keenly feels his own hunger
And labors to satisfy it,
Will never realize the hunger
And the suffering of others.

### 616.

One who is greedy will not realize
The difficulties felt by others.

### 617.

Justice and compassion
Cannot dwell in the heart
Of one who has selfishness,
Or one who has hypocrisy.

### 618.

Worse than the poison of a deadly snake
Is the poison of one who seeks vengeance
For wrongs that were done in the past.

### 619.

One who sees joy
In the fulfilment of desire
Will lose the joyous life
Of the freedom of his soul.

### 620.

The praise sought by mind and desire
Is one of the billboards for hell.

### 621.

What is tasty to the mouth
Is not always acceptable to the stomach.

### 622.

What is tasty to your tongue
Is opposed to wisdom,
To inner patience and contentment,
And to the giving of all praise to God.

### 623.

Allah's love is tasty
To one who has wisdom.

### 624.

What is tasty to one who does good
Is the compassion which loves and protects
All lives as carefully as his own.

### 625.

Self-pride
Will kill the self.

### 626.

The arrogance of the 'I'
Will lower and corrupt the self.

### 627.

Jealousy
Is the fire that consumes life.

## 628.

Doubt
Is the cancer in life.

## 629.

Patience
Is a most rare treasure in life.

## 630.

One who acquires God's qualities
Will lead a life of undiminishing wealth.

## 631.

The Prophet *(Sal.)*, whom Allah sent as the eternal and last prophet, was chased from Mecca to Medina. From that history, can we not understand that as long as we are loved by God and as long as we love God, the world will not accept us? Our parents, our children, our brothers and sisters, our relatives, and our people will all drive us away.

When Allah loves us, the world will drive us away. But when the world accepts us, we will not be acceptable to Allah. This is a sign we can see. If you desire and accept the praise of the world, truth will not accept you, and if you desire truth, the world will not accept you. All who have wisdom must realize and understand this.

Those who praise the evils which can be seen with the eyes are in the majority, while those who love and praise Allah are in the minority. The majority will hound and chase away the minority, just as the Holy Prophet *(Sal.)* was chased away from his land.

However, if you discount your sufferings as trivial and accept only God, maintaining your connection with Him, He will give you His treasures and His kingdom. Realize this.

## 632.

My son, there is only one happiness for us, and that is Allah. He is our treasure and our happiness in all three worlds, the world of the souls, this world, and the world of God. He is the treasure of undiminishing wealth in the treasury of our inner hearts, our *qalbs,* and the one and only state of peacefulness for man.

The treasure exists in His qualities, actions, and conduct. If each of us takes on these qualities, and if we give all responsibility to God, saying, "All praise is to God, *al-hamdu lillāh*," it will bring peace to all mankind. We will have no want or suffering if we can have absolute faith in Allah and make that state steadfast in our *qalbs*. One who attains this state is called a *sayyid*.

633.

The sheikh speaks to his children: When the Rasūlullāh, Prophet Muhammad *(Sal.)*, was living in Medina, there lived in distant Baghdad a man of wisdom called Uwais al-Qarani *(Ral.)*. Although he had never seen the Holy Prophet *(Sal.)*, he was one of the few who truly knew the Prophet *(Sal.)*. But the people of Baghdad were not aware of his greatness.

He spent his time taking the cattle in the streets out to graze, and when he brought them back in the evening, he would eat whatever crusts of bread someone gave him and spend the night under a tree, on a rock, or on a hillside. The people knew him only as a crazy man.

One day, shortly before the Prophet *(Sal.)* was due to leave this world, he held out his robe to 'Alī *(Ral.)* and 'Umar ibnul-Khattāb *(Ral.)* and asked them to give it to Uwais al-Qarani *(Ral.)* in Baghdad. 'Alī *(Ral.)* and 'Umar *(Ral.)* inquired about Uwais from all the travelers who came from Baghdad, but no one had heard the name. So they put the robe aside and forgot about him for a time.

Some months later they came upon the robe and remembered what they had been asked to do. They traveled to Baghdad, but the people there said they knew no one by the name of Uwais al-Qarani *(Ral.)* in their city. 'Alī *(Ral.)* and 'Umar *(Ral.)* searched without success. Finally someone said, "There's a crazy man called Uwais who takes the cattle out to graze and accepts whatever food is given to him. He must be somewhere in the forest. He usually comes back at dusk. But he's not a great person—he's crazy. Anyway, he's the only one whose name is similar to the name you mentioned."

So 'Alī *(Ral.)* and 'Umar *(Ral.)* went into the forest. There they found Uwais *(Ral.)* seated under a tree, watching the cattle graze. He did seem quite crazy.

They all greeted each other with the *salām*, the greeting of peace.

"*As-salāmu 'alaikum,* may the peace of God be upon you."

"*Wa 'alaikumus-salām,* may the peace of God be upon you also."

"Are you Uwais al-Qarani?" they asked.

"Are you 'Umar?" he asked 'Umar *(Ral.)*.

"Yes, I am 'Umar," he replied.

"Are you the son-in-law of Muhammad *(Sal.)*?" Uwais *(Ral.)* asked 'Alī *(Ral.)*.

"Yes, I am," replied 'Alī *(Ral.)*.

"What is it? What has brought you here?" asked Uwais *(Ral.)*.

'Alī *(Ral.)* and 'Umar *(Ral.)* were amazed that he knew their identities. As they stood there puzzled, Uwais *(Ral.)* continued, "You, 'Alī, are the son-in-law of the Rasūlullāh *(Sal.)* and you, 'Umar, are one of his closest companions.

"I want to ask a question of both of you," Uwais *(Ral.)* said. "One of the teeth of the Prophet *(Sal.)* was broken in the battle of Uhud. Which tooth was broken?"

Both 'Alī *(Ral.)* and 'Umar *(Ral.)* were stunned. They could not answer. "Don't you know which tooth?" asked Uwais *(Ral.)*. "How can you be called his companions if you do not know even that?

"I did not know which tooth he lost or on which side, so I pulled out all of mine. Look, aaaaaaaah!" Uwais *(Ral.)* opened his mouth and showed them. He had no teeth. "What did you do?" he asked 'Alī *(Ral.)* and 'Umar *(Ral.)*. "You, 'Alī, saw only your father-in-law; you did not see the Rasūlullāh *(Sal.)*. And you, 'Umar, might have been a close companion, but you did not see O Sayyid Muhammad Mustafar-Rasūl *(Sal.)*, the resplendent light."

Then he asked, "Can you tell me if the Rasūlullāh's *(Sal.)* eyebrows were joined at the center of his forehead?" They did not know the answer.

"This means you have not seen him," said Uwais *(Ral.)*.

'Alī *(Ral.)* and 'Umar *(Ral.)* began to tremble and one said, "The Rasūlullāh *(Sal.)* asked us to give you his robe." Uwais *(Ral.)* bowed in reverential prayer. He prayed for a long time. 'Alī *(Ral.)* and 'Umar *(Ral.)* waited and waited, but still Uwais *(Ral.)* continued to pray. They began to worry; night was falling and they had to get back. But Uwais *(Ral.)* was still doing *sajdah;* he was prostrate before God for such a long, long time. Finally they said softly to Uwais *(Ral.)*, "We must go."

Uwais *(Ral.)* lifted his head and said, "You have ruined it. I was doing *sajdah* and begging Allah that all the followers of the Rasūlullāh *(Sal.)* should be accepted into heaven and that no one should be sent to hell. I was told by Allah that out of the seventy-three groups of people in the world He would accept into heaven without any questions on the Day of Judgment only the seventy-third group, those who have fully accepted the Rasūlullāh *(Sal.)* and Allah.

"Then I begged again, 'O Allah! Please accept the other groups also. No matter what mistakes they have made, forgive them and accept them.'

"And Allah replied, 'Of the seventy-second group, on the Day of Judgment I will inquire into their right and wrong actions, give them the rewards and punishments according to what they have done, and then accept them.'

"I begged yet again, 'O Allah! Please accept the seventy-first group.'

"Allah said, 'On the Day of Judgment I will inquire into their right and wrong actions and reward or punish accordingly, as I did for the seventy-second group.'

"Later when I asked Allah to forgive the other seventy groups, He said, 'These groups have completely rejected the Rasūlullāh and Me. I will give them the place they have earned for themselves. They have sought and gained hell, so I will give that to them.'

"While I was pleading on behalf of the other seventy groups both of you interrupted me with your impatience. This was the correct time to plead for their salvation, immediately after I was offered the robe of the Rasūlullāh *(Sal.)*, when I was offered that *rahmat,* that benevolence. Now I have lost the opportunity to ask for their deliverance. You have spoiled it."

Uwais *(Ral.)* accepted the precious gift. He kissed it and held it to his heart.

My son, Uwais al-Qarani *(Ral.)* was one who knew and understood the Rasūlullāh *(Sal.)* in his own time. It is said in the *hadīth* and by those who are wise, "One who has seen the Rasūlullāh *(Sal.)* even once will never see hell." We must reflect on this.

They say the Rasūlullāh *(Sal.)* was born in Mecca and buried in Medina. They say his mother was Āminah *(Ral.)* and his father 'Abdullāh *(Ral.)*, that his grandfather was 'Abdul-Muttalib *(Ral.)*, and his great grandfather 'Abd-Munāf *(Ral.)*. People speak of his genealogy as his history. However, my son, we must understand the real history of the Rasūlullāh *(Sal.)*.

Allah has said, "O Muhammad! I would not have created anything but for you!" Therefore, what was his ancestry? When did it begin? Who was he? To whom does he belong? Is there anyone to whom he does not belong? Who was that Rasūlullāh, the Muhammad *(Sal.)* referred to by Allah? If we understand the brilliant light of the *qalb* called *ahmad* reflected in the radiant beauty of the face, Muhammad *(Sal.)*, hell will be far from us. That is the resplendent form of the Rasūlullāh *(Sal.)*, the benevolent grace of Allah.

My son, the Rasūlullāh *(Sal.)* we saw was merely the robe that he wore. If we had opened the robe and looked within, we would have seen the light which is the real Rasūlullāh *(Sal.)*. Anyone who sees that light will never go to hell; for him, hell has become *harām*, forbidden.

If we understand this and follow that light of Muhammadur-Rasūl *(Sal.)*, we will never see the house called hell. We will always live in the house of *mubārakāt*, the wealth of the three worlds which is Allah's *rahmat*, His benevolence. Realize this and understand with wisdom.

### 634.

My son, when the sheikh speaks, it is the responsibility of each child to explore what is said for something that might apply to him. When the sheikh speaks in the presence of his children, his words are like the rain of benevolent grace, *rahmat*.

When rain falls from the sky, each creation takes up the water in its own way, according to its own needs. Trees, grasses, and tubers take what they need, and so it is with every plant in creation. The balance of the rainwater flows to the sea by way of lakes and rivers. The rain does not fall for the sake of only one creation, one tree, or one shrub. It falls equally on all, and it is the responsibility of each creation to take its own share according to its needs.

In the same way, when the sheikh's wisdom of grace rains in the presence of his children, they should not think it is meant for any one person alone. The words of the sheikh are the grace of divine knowledge, *rahmatul-'ilm*. Just as the trees, grasses, and weeds take what they need from the rainwater, everyone must take his share of that *'ilm* according to his state, his wisdom, and his intellect. His words are not meant for only one person. Having received them, each child must realize, understand, and correct himself.

This is what the sheikh does in his effort to protect and bring up his children. In his prayers to God, he says, "O God, protect all the children. Give them a long life, a life without illness, and give them the fullness of the wealth of grace."

635.

To a sheikh who is a perfected man, an *insān kāmil,* this world is just an atom within his *qalb,* his inner heart. The world is so tiny for him that he can observe all his children within that atom, no matter where they are. No child is far from him. Therefore, you must not worry, thinking that the sheikh is not here, that he is in another country, that we cannot see him, or that he does not see us.

The world may appear vast to your eyes, but to the eyes of the sheikh, the world is only a dot. If you too will open that eye which is within your *qalb,* you will also see the world as a tiny dot. Then you will understand.

636.

The *gnāna sheikh* speaks to his children: The father of your soul who gave birth to you from his heart knows all your roguish tricks. He can detect what is hidden within you. He can detect all your faults. He may be here in this room, but he can see you wherever you are. By observing your faces, the way you look at something, your actions, and your conduct, he can see what is in your hearts. He has the camera and the pictures. In this way, he understands each one of your qualities. You cannot hide anything from him. My children! Do not do things with the thought that the father is someplace else and cannot see you.

When you stand in front of a mirror, you see yourself, do you not? Similarly, he is a mirror; in him, you will see your faults and be able to correct yourself.

Therefore, correct yourself before you go into his presence. Then the father, the sheikh of wisdom, will always embrace you to his heart.

A child asked the Sufi sheikh, "Would you tell me the state I am in?"

The sheikh replied, "A seed must be planted at the correct time. When it begins to grow, its roots creep into the earth, embracing it in all directions. Soon the plant grows into a tree, and the tree grows bigger, flowers, and bears fruit. When the fruits emerge, they have no real connection to the earth; although the tree is connected to the earth, the fruits have a connection to man and to all of creation.

"My child, your life is like that, too. Though you have grown so tall, like a tree, the connection and attachment of your mind, thought, and desire is to the earth and the world. This is your present state.

"However, my child, you have a connection in your *qalb*, in your heart, which thinks of and seeks God. Let me describe to you the means to develop that connection. Follow this direction clearly.

"No matter how many connections you may have to the earth, if you want to search for God, if you want to go on the path to God, you, your prayer, and your worship must be in a state similar to a tree: although a tree is attached to the earth, it gives its fruits to all. Even though you are fixed to the earth, like a tree, your intention must be like the fruits in the tree: your prayers, devotion, worship, qualities, and actions must be connected to God, and you must perform the unselfish duty that benefits all lives. Then you will fare well on the path to God."

638.

A boy inquired, "In telling fortunes, some study charts, some do it without charts, and some read from the palm. Do they speak from intuition, from the mind, or from the light of wisdom?"

The Sufi master answered, "In astrology books, words are repeated over and over in cycles. There are twelve signs to the zodiac: the lion, the bull, the goat, the ram, the scorpion, the crab, the fish, and so on. But there is no sign for a human being. Is a man denoted by any of these signs? No.

"There is no astrology for *insān*, for true man. Astrology is about animals and their history. Since man's history is not found within astrology, there is no need for human beings to take advice from astrology. When wisdom dawns, and when you use that wisdom correctly, no wrong can come of it. Only what is right will exist. When the light comes, the night automatically recedes Only the light of truth remains. Then there is no fear or agitation.

"Fear comes from doubt. Doubt occurs only when there is duality, when you cannot make up your mind one way or the other. Of the multitude of things that go through your mind, one thing may come out right, or maybe two. Such is the mind. Only the monkey mind depends on intuition.

"But if what is said comes from wisdom, only one thing is seen—truth. Then there is no doubt as to the origin of anyone's words. When you reach the state where there is no duality, that is the wisdom called *gnānam*. Try your best to attain this state. Do not waste your life on other things."

### 639.

A man said to a Sufi, "Sometimes when I want to speak, I feel it would not be right to say anything. Though I want to say it, I cannot, because if I did I feel it would betray what I was thinking."

The Sufi replied, "In that case, the thoughts in your mind and intellect must be wrong or evil, or the doubt in your mind must be whispering to you that it is unwise to speak what you are thinking. If you can eliminate the doubt, only truth will remain.

"My son, reflect on this and realize. Cut the inherent qualities of your mind with wisdom, reject what is wrong and use what is right. That will be the light which will cast out all the darkness in anything you see. When you understand the good and the bad in each of your thoughts, you can speak without fear."

### 640.

A child asked his sheikh, "I would like to know if the poverty, misfortune, or illness that may befall the children of God is a test by God. Does that misfortune in any way involve the karma of those particular children? Is it something separate, or is it because they are on the path to God?"

The Sufi sheikh answered, "If you are poor, it is because you are poor in intellect as well as in your qualities. That is why you experience misfortune. The reason for the poverty or the illness you speak of is that your good qualities are not growing. When they do not grow, the result is karma. That is what karma is.

"When the good qualities grow, there is no karma and there is no unhappiness. Karma is connected to earth, fire, water, air, ether, dirt, filth, and all the things that are in the body. The animals and the qualities and actions of the animals, the birds and the actions of the birds, the dogs and the actions of the dogs, the donkeys and the actions of the donkeys, the horses and the actions of the horses, the elephants and the actions of the elephants, the rat and the cat—these actions and qualities are spread throughout the body. Along with *māyā* and darkness, they cause difficulty and unhappiness to man. They are the karma of the body.

"They will make you think, 'I am poor. I am unhappy. Money comes to other people but not to me. Other people are happy, but I am not.' Your connection to these thoughts is the cause of your unhappiness.

"When we come into the world, we do not bring anything. When we leave the world, we do not take anything away. That is the extent of worldly wealth. What is real wealth? Real wealth is the grace of God, which is light. As long as this divine wisdom of grace does not grow within us, we will feel hurt.

"When, due to ignorance, our thoughts change like the changing seasons, that is karma. However, when we overcome this and receive the wealth of God, misfortune will not affect us, because there will no longer be any karma to make us suffer. Then we will dwell in the plenitude of God's grace."

### 641.

My son, the world we see on the outside is a show. It is only an example. Our mind is the world. The angles in the mind are what we see as curves and angles in the world outside. If each of us would straighten the angles within himself, the world would appear straight.

For example, when doing art work, if a straight line is needed, you must draw a straight line. When a curve is indicated, you must draw a curve. Similarly, if you see a wicked man, a lion, or any other obstacle or danger, you must take a curved path to avoid it. If you are crossing a river and a straight crossing is not possible, make a curved crossing. But if the path you are going to take is supposed to be a straight path, you must cut a straight path and not a crooked one. If everyone would make a straight path for himself, the world would be heaven.

Sometimes, however, when the path is crooked, or when it turns to the left and the right, we blame the world instead of looking into ourselves and accepting the blame for our own faults. It is our responsibility to find the faults within ourselves, correct them, and make them straight. If we make our goal clear and cut a straight path to that goal, according to the correct map, we will not see faults in the world.

Similarly, the noise in the mind is what we hear as the noise in the world outside. Actually, the world is mute; it makes no sound at all. Whether the sound is like the braying of a donkey, the roaring of a lion, or the trumpeting of an elephant, it is our minds which make all the sound. We cause all the noise, and then we bellow some more while we suffer the consequences.

Stop the noise of your mind, and you will know the silence of the world.

### 642.

My son! Are you on the straight path? Is anyone on the straight path?

When a woman comes to stand beside you, winks, and shows you attention, you might leave the path to look at her. If you see a deer playing with its fawns, you might be drawn away from the path. Or you may see a flower with a sweet fragrance along the way and become distracted by it. Seeing any of these works of art might divert your attention.

If you can conquer these visual and mental scenes, cast them away, and look carefully at God's domain with wisdom, His beauty will be manifest. Once you see that beauty, you will be so entranced by it that you will want nothing else, and you will seek it always.

Then, my son, no matter what other wonder the world shows you, you will not desire it. When that strength of certitude emerges within you, all the dangers, fascinations, and darknesses that threaten you will go away. Understand this.

### 643.

The *gnāna sheikh* speaks to his children: Children! Whenever you are worried or troubled by difficulties at home you should read a good book about God or a divine subject, or you should give prayers of praise and worship in the name of God.

However, when you do put your disturbances aside and devote your time to something good, satan will come to make you fall asleep. You will start snoring and the book will fall from your hand.

Whenever you attempt to go on the straight path to God, satan will try to disturb you in some way or other. He will say, "Oh, you are going to do this work, are you? I'll see what I can do about that!" He may make you feel tired or bring other things to your attention. He might make you feel a pain here or there. If he cannot do that, he might make you itch or bring you a headache or a fever. When you try to focus on goodness, satan will always come to distract you. If you say, "I am going to pray," he will make you exhausted.

Despite all this, if at that moment you say, "Get out, satan! Do not disturb me!" if you get up quickly, wash your face, and return to your prayer, satan might still watch you for a while, but he will finally go away, disappointed. However if you become concerned with this pain and that tiredness, satan will tap you on the head and say, "You are my friend. Come. Come, and I will be with you."

Therefore, my children, if your certitude and faith are firmly fixed on God, satan will not approach you. As long as your *qalb*, your inner heart, is resplendent, satan who is darkness will not come to you. Understand this and make your *qalb* resplendent with firm certitude in Allah, and it will provide you with undiminishing grace.

### 644.

A father's responsibility is to bring up his children. The children must obey the father and follow him. Still, if a father of ten children embraces them and asks them to come with him, he might find that one of them has strayed toward the seashore. When he goes to bring that child back, he may find that the other nine have gone somewhere else. And as he brings each child back, he finds that each comes according to his own qualities.

It is the same way for a sheikh. The children might try to project their qualities onto the sheikh, or to draw the sheikh onto their paths. How much a dog suffers when it gives birth to ten puppies! My plight is the same, now that I have given birth to my children.

My precious children, listen to your father's words. Reflect on them. Take them into your hearts and follow them. Then your father can take you with him without trouble, and he can take you home very easily.

### 645.

The sheikh speaks to his children: A brass pot tarnishes easily and must be constantly polished. When polished, it looks like gold. When not polished, it discolors and eventually turns black.

The minds of some people are like brass. They have to be polished every day or they will become tarnished, or even crusty. They do not listen to the words of the sheikh; though he polishes their minds today, they will become tarnished again tomorrow, and they will have to ask the same questions again.

The words of a sheikh, however, must fall every day, and they must be absorbed with faith and certitude. If the children polish their *qalbs,* their hearts, every day, the crust will go and the pot will turn to gold. In the same way, we must join a sheikh and remain in his company with the absolute faith called *īmān.* With the polish of *'ilm,* the polish of divine knowledge, he will scrub away the crust which is the karma of our birth and transform our minds and *qalbs* into gold.

### 646.

My son! God is unlearned in the world. He has not gone to college to study, yet He is far above you. He is a scholar in the school of *gnānam.* He has no home, yet He resides in your hearts. No flag flies over His kingdom, yet He reigns in every heart, flying the flag of *īmān,* of absolute faith, certitude, and determination. He has no external court of justice, yet He has a seat of justice in each heart. He has no world, yet He rules the world within every heart, nourishing and protecting each with compassion.

He has no wife, yet He is mingled with the love within the heart of each created being. He has no child, yet all lives are His children. He has no hunger, yet the hunger of each creation is His hunger. He has no distress or difficulty, yet He accepts with tranquillity and tolerance the adversities of all creations as His own, bringing comfort and peace to all.

One who has these qualities and actions is called God.

647.

My son, do you understand what *dīn* is? *Dīn* is patience, inner patience, and contentment. *Dīn* is to place your trust in God and to praise Him, accepting with patience any difficulty which might come to you. *Dīn* is purity. It will be good if you conduct yourself according to this explanation.

648.

My son! This is a *hadīth* of the Rasūlullāh *(Sal.)* about Islam:

Brothers in Islam! You who are *Īmān-Islām!* You must not see differences between yourselves and your neighbors. You must not discriminate against any religion. You must not oppress or harm any man, no matter what religion or race he may be. Islam is one and Allah is one; just as we in Islam see Allah as one, we must see all mankind as one.

All the prophets brought the words of Allah, and all the words they brought are true. Allah sent His messages through each of the prophets, and they brought His commandments step by step. In the revelations contained in the Qur'an, Allah has given the entirety of His teaching. The Qur'an is the ultimate and final teaching, showing everything in its fullness.

All the children of Adam *(A.S.)* are brothers and sisters. They are not different. Although they may stand on different steps of the teachings brought by the prophets in their respective times, you must not discriminate against any of them. You must not harass their places of worship, their bodies, or their hearts. You must protect them as you would protect your own life.

To comfort the hunger of your neighbor, no matter who he is or what religion he belongs to, is Islam. When someone dies, to join together and give him a decent burial is Islam. To realize the pain and suffering of others and offer your hands in assistance, helping to alleviate their suffering, is Islam.

To see division is not Islam. To see other men as different is not Islam. In this world and the next, there must be no prejudice in our hearts, for all will come together on the Day of Reckoning and the Day of Judgment. All of us will come together in heaven. Therefore, we must not see any differences or create any divisions here. Where Allah does not see a difference, we must not see a difference. We must not despise anyone whom Allah loves—and

Allah loves everyone. He belongs equally to everyone, just as Islam belongs equally to everyone. Islam is unity, not division.

Hurting another is not Islam. Failing to comfort the hunger of your neighbor is not Islam. The purity of Islam is to avoid hurting others; you must regard others as you regard yourself. You must accept Allah's word totally. There must be no discrimination in your heart against the children of Islam.

You who are Islam must understand what is *halāl* and what is *harām*, what is permissible and what is forbidden. You must understand that there is only One worthy of worship. You must understand *Qiyāmah*, the Day of Reckoning, and the Day of Judgment.

To understand this world and the next world is Islam. Because Islam is the wealth of grace, you must use that grace to wash and comfort the hearts of others. To truly understand this and see all lives as your own life, without any differences, is the way of Islam. To see your neighbor as yourself, to heal the suffering of others, to share food from the same plate in harmony and peace, to live unified in food and in prayer, in happiness and in sorrow, is the way of Islam. To live separated and divided is not Islam. You must reflect on this.

O you who have faith! Do not compare anything to Allah. Do not hold anything equal to Allah. Do not make distinctions between men; king and beggar must be equal in your sight. There must be no difference between rich and poor. No one is rejected by Islam. Islam is one. You must realize this.

This is what the Rasūlullāh *(Sal.)* has said. He has given countless *ahādīth* with his divine lips of grace, from the flower of his divine mouth, his mouth of faith, his mouth of Allah's grace, and his mouth of Allah's divine knowledge.

O you who have received the wealth of faith! May you understand and act with the clarity of these teachings.

649.

Each of us is bringing up a baby inside called mind and desire, which cries for everything it sees in the world. Not only does it cry, but just as the ocean waves come rolling in, this baby brings waves of thoughts which roll over us incessantly; as each wave passes, the next one and the next one break. The mind begs ceaselessly, and there is no end to the waves of thought. The interminable howling of the mind will not let you pray in peace or even merely sit in peace. As long as you carry around this noisy baby, you will never know peace in prayer, in reflection, or in any aspect of your life.

The baby of mind and desire will deceive you. It can take the form of a beautiful girl, an old woman, a toddling baby, and four hundred trillion, ten thousand other forms. As a baby it asks for baby things, as an old lady it asks for pretty things, as an enchantress it asks for the things a demon needs, and as a schoolchild it asks for shoes, clothes, and books.

My son, you must sever your attachment to the baby mind. Let go of the baby. Only then will you be able to perform your duties without fear. As long as you hang on to your attachment, you will show partiality and prejudice. Your justice will be lop-sided: one law for yourself and another for someone else. You will have a tendency to favor those you love and want to please.

Therefore, know with your wisdom that the baby mind is the cause of your suffering and throw it back to where it was formed, to the place from which it came. The moment you throw it away, you will be successful in your actions, in your duties, and in your life, and you will be free of fear.

### 650.

The sheikh said: My son, there are certain things which are vital to man's understanding of life. No matter how a man thinks, no matter how he lives, he will still have the fear of illness and death. But if he can live as a real human being, if wisdom dawns in him, if faith in God develops within him, there will be no room for fear.

If wisdom and absolute faith are firmly established within us, we can reach the state of death before death. Before the Angel of Death visits us, we will have cut all our attachment to the world; we will have become 'dead' to the world. If we can establish the certitude that God alone exists, then God alone will dwell within us. If we retain only God's treasure within us, we will have no fear, because the Angel of Death can capture us only if the treasures of the world are within us. If we keep the treasure called Allah, the Angel of Death will not enter.

As long as you have the world within you, there is fear. But if Allah is within you, neither suffering nor death will visit. It is the connection to earth that brings suffering, because suffering is natural on the earth. If you had no connection to earth, even if suffering and death were to come, they would not affect you, because you would no longer be dwelling within the elemental body. For when Allah is within you, you will be dwelling within the body of resplendent light.

651.

## WORTHLESS THINGS

An ax without a handle

A knife without a hilt

A razor without a sharp, straight edge

A nose without the sense of smell

Eyes without light

Ears without hearing

A tongue without the sense of taste

Faith in God without determination

A heart without light

A brain without clarity

A body without blood

Love without compassion

Giving food without inner love

Intellect that teaches without self-correction

A rose without fragrance

A woman without good conduct

A man without tolerance

A fruit without flavor

A cow without milk

A horse without the ability to run

A dog without gratitude

Music without sound

Learning without understanding

Prayer without purity of heart

Walls without a foundation

A house without a roof

A sun without resplendence

A moon without coolness

Stars without glitter

A life without purpose

A house without worship of God

A king without justice

Wealth which does not feed the hunger of others

Learning without a sheikh

A sheikh without wisdom

A disciple without faith

A crop without rain

Bathing without water

Clothing without cleanliness

Duty without selflessness

The property of an ungenerous man

Beautiful fruits that contain poison

A fruit that does not ripen on the vine

Worship and learning that do not bow to God's love

A life in which the love of a man and a woman
cannot join as one

A house without occupants

Food without salt or taste

Sugarcane without sweetness

Land without fertility

Water that does not quench thirst

Food that does not satisfy hunger

A child who does not help his parents in times
of danger

A wife who is unaware of her husband's financial
difficulties

A king who cannot control his anger

A minister who works without wages

A disciple who does not listen to the words of
his sheikh

Seed that is sown without knowledge of the soil

A body without awareness

A wife without respect for her husband

Preaching religion without the truth

Duty done without a melting heart

A town without a place of worship

A country without water

A fish without water

A man without life

A gem without radiance

Gold that does not glitter

Business without profit

A bird without wings

A tree without shade

A rosebush without flowers

A well without water

Wealth accumulated by a childless man

A vegetarian who does not realize the equality of all lives

Charity given without a melting heart

Paddy planted on a mountaintop

The life of a man who likes a woman for her makeup

The life of a woman who marries a man for his elegant clothes

Silver without luster

A bow that does not bend

A hunter who cannot take aim

An arrow without a point

The beautiful fruit of a strychnine tree

An automobile without gasoline

Tires without air

A driver without a steering wheel

A donkey that does not carry burdens

All these are like the life of a man who journeys through a dark jungle filled with dangerous animals. No benefit will come of it. His life will be futile, a desert where nothing lives or grows; there will be intense heat, no water, no wind, no crops, no inhabitants. Think of this with wisdom and understand. Before you make use of anything, you must understand it. This will serve you well.

### 652.

A man who cannot control his lust
Forfeits good conduct.

### 653.

The life of a man who cannot control anger

Becomes the fire which will kill him.

### 654.

The life of one who has no determination,
Of one who acts without a firm plan,
Is like a pond without a shore.
Though there is water in plenty
It flows away,
Rendering his life worthless.

### 655.

A house without protection for its wealth
Becomes the property of thieves.

### 656.

Unearned, undeserved wealth
And charity given without compassion
Are like sea water:
Unable to quench thirst.

### 657.

Charity given with compassion
Is the duty of God;
The one who gives and the receiver
Will know the joy of complete satisfaction.

### 658.

If one who cannot find liberation from his own life preaches for the liberation of others, it is like rainwater falling into the sea; his teaching will not give any benefit.

### 659.

One who does not see the truth while preaching to himself will not see truth in the lives of others.

### 660.

If you place your trust in what you have not seen with your own eyes or what you have not tasted with your own tongue, it will not last. One day it will desert you. With wisdom, try to see what must be seen. Search hard. Take with wisdom what must be taken. Then the taste of God will never leave you.

### 661.

When one expects shade from a cactus or fruit from a barren tree, his life becomes like the reflection in a mirror placed before a monkey: he continually tries to embrace his own image, thinking it is someone from his own family. Placing all his trust in that reflection, the monkey even forgets to eat and eventually dies. Through trusting in non-existent things, his life runs out in vain.

### 662.

The world is a field for cultivation, a farm.
The world is a stage for drama.
The world is a prayer mat.
The world is a school of history.

Because the cage which is the body
Is a school filled with stories,
One who knows these four aspects of life
Can reap from his life
The imperishable harvest of truth,
And knowing the drama of life,
Take from it what is right:
The qualities and duties acceptable to God,
The qualities and duties belonging to Him.

Find the way to truly pray to God. He dwells within each creation, and He has made a place for Himself within our *Ka'bah,* the place in which we can worship Him. Open the *Ka'bah* within you and you will see Him. At each time of prayer, hand all responsibility over to Him, and die within Him. This is true prayer. With clarity, find the way to prayer, worship, and the remembrance of God which is called *dhikr: Lā ilāha*—there is nothing other than You; *illallāhu*—You are God. Know the One who is eternal and surrender to Him.

With the explaining wisdom of the *Qutbiyyat,* understand the history school of the world to find the one thing that will remain forever. With clarity, sift, analyze, and extract the imperishable that is within the Creator and His creation.

To one who has the wisdom to study the four aspects of life and their benefits, the world will become:

> A world of flowers,
> The kingdom of God
> And the resplendent world of *gnānam*.

To attain liberation from the four aspects of life, it is not necessary for a man to hide and meditate in caves, jungles, trees, or bushes. When real wisdom dawns, he will understand them. Then, within the society of men, he will be able to understand God, the happiness of life, the acting in his life, and the clarity of prayer which can see God. He will be able to understand God's story, our story, and the exaltedness of our true state, as well as the study of wisdom, the history school of the body in which it must be learned, and all the explanations of God's creations. These are the *purānas,* or scriptures, of the great and pure history which is man's life. The agreement which limits his life and determines his disappearance from the world can be understood with the divine analytic wisdom of man.

If one who has the face of a man does not learn the meaning of his existence, there is no purpose in his living, and his life will end as a dream. However, in this school, if we understand God's qualities, actions, and duties and learn to do our duties in the same way He does His duties, we will reach His kingdom, and one who reaches His kingdom reaches Him. This is the final result of all the explanations within explanations that we came here to study.

### 663.

My son! A cat creeps stealthily in order to kill. A bow bends in order to shoot. In the same way, when a man's mind begins to creep stealthily, it is to harm someone else. When anyone speaks lovingly on the outside, pretending to be affectionate like a purring cat, while being bent like a drawn bow on the inside, it is to harm someone else.

If you see anyone in this state, it is good to have the wisdom to recognize his qualities and avoid him. Otherwise, you will lose your life, just as you can die by eating a poisonous fruit because it looks beautiful or drink venom thinking it is nourishing.

It is better to live with a tiger than to live with one who has the face of a man but not his qualities.

My son! Just as a desert might say, "Come, I will give you shade. I will make you cool," one whose wisdom has not reached maturity will tell you he will give you the divine wisdom called *gnānam*. Do not believe his words. If you do believe them and act according to them, you will become like oil for the fire of hell.

The fruit of the strychnine tree has a beautiful yellow color, but it contains a deadly poison. It waves in the wind, inviting everyone, "Come, come. See how pretty I am!" If you are seduced by its beauty, your inner wisdom and truth will be destroyed, and you may even die.

With divine analytic wisdom, look at that tree and think, "This tree is loaded with beautiful, ripe fruits, yet no one seems to be eating them. There are no human beings around. Some fruits have burst and fallen to the ground, but even the birds and animals are not eating them." Realize with your wisdom that the tree and its fruits must be poisonous. No matter how beautifully it waves in the wind, leave it and go your way.

Like that, do not be taken in by the beauty of words, body, or dress. Do not be lured into tasting them. They are hell-fire.

After you understand Allah, the One, take His qualities for your own, act according to His actions, and search with wisdom. Then a true sheikh will be shown to you.

He will be like a ripe fruit hidden and protected by leaves. If there is one precious fruit on a tree, it will be concealed by a cluster of leaves, unseen by the world. You will have to part the leaves and look carefully to see that precious fruit.

This is the way to discover the original truth. The flavor you must discover is in him. The flavor you must taste and know, and the state you must attain, will be in him.

Find him and taste him for yourself.

## 665.

My son, let me tell you a story: There was a very learned man in a certain village who was renowned for his miracles. He had many titles, and everyone went to him for advice.

One day a goat was trying to drink water from a brass pot that was used for drawing water from the river, and it got its horns and head stuck in the pot. The owner and many of the villagers tried to pull the pot off the goat's head, but it would not budge.

"The goat will die! What should we do? Oh, yes! If we ask the learned one, he will tell us what to do," they said, and they ran to get him, because he was supposed to be the wisest of them all.

"All right," he said, when they told him what had happened. "Let us go." When he got there, he tried to pull the pot off the goat's head. He tugged and twisted, but the pot would not come off. "All right," he said, "if you have a long knife, bring it."

He told them to cut off the goat's head. The head fell to one side and the body to the other. "Now try," he told them, but they still could not get the head out of the pot.

"All right," he said, "bring an ax." He hit the brass pot with the ax and it split into two pieces. "Now take the head out," he told them, and they did. "Now it is done, is it not?" he said.

"Yes, O guru of gurus, O wisdom to all wisdom! You alone can solve all our problems. How can we find words to praise you?" They showered him with presents and conducted him back to his house with great pomp and ceremony. The goat was dead and the pot was broken, but they did not think of that.

Like this, when disciples who have faith without wisdom and a guru without the explanation of wisdom meet to meditate and live together, they will suffer the fate of the goat and pot. Not only was a fifty-rupee pot broken, but a goat was lost as well. But in their ignorance the people praised him for having released the head of the goat. They did not realize the loss of the pot or the loss of the goat's life.

There are many gurus and wise men like this in the world. Understand this, and find a teacher of wisdom who will understand the debt of your birth, one who will understand what has gone before and what is to come in the future, one who can extricate you without loss. Otherwise you, too, could suffer the fate of the goat.

### 666.

My son, a high-caste man, one who was very titled, came to a certain village and married a girl who lived there. He was very happy. After the wedding, the new bride and groom set out to return to the man's village.

Walking a little distance ahead of them was a man very low in caste, one who killed animals, ate their flesh, and used the hides to make shoes. The low-caste man was chewing a very fragrant leaf called betel with immense enjoyment and spitting betel juice as red as blood on the ground as he walked. The new bride smelled the fragrance and developed a desire for the betel.

When the bride and groom came to a river, the man who was chewing betel was already there, waiting for the ferry. As soon as the bride saw him, she ran to him and took his hand. Even though he was low-caste and she was high-caste, she clung to his hand. Surprised, he bowed to her and exclaimed, "Oh my lady, please let go of me!"

"Why are you telling me to let go? I am your true wife," she replied.

Her high-caste husband stared at her in disbelief. "What is this? How has my wife degenerated to such a state?" He was a man who had never eaten flesh. He was so ashamed of what she had done that he turned his back on her and went away.

The low-caste man asked her, "Why did you come at me like that?"

"Please give me some of your sweet-smelling betel. I saw the trail of your spittle on the path. It smelled so good that I decided you would be good for me. You smell wonderful," she said. But when she actually went home with him and saw the skins lying out in the sun, she realized that he lived in a place where cattle were slaughtered.

He was a shoemaker and so he soon taught her to stitch leather shoes. He also asked her to cook the beef, knowing she was a vegetarian. "Just eat a little beef and you will see," he said. "You will like it, my lady."

It did taste good to her, so she ate it and praised it. "I have never tasted anything so delicious in all my life. You are definitely the most suitable husband for me. Never have I experienced anything like this before." She embraced him and kissed him with fondness. And so she began to eat beef and stitch shoes.

But after some time she realized that her previous life would have been better, and that now she was no more than a shoemaker. She had left a potentially happy life with a wealthy and titled high-caste man who did not eat flesh, merely because of her desire for betel spit.

Like this, when people in the world lack wisdom and follow their minds, reaching out for whatever they desire, in the end they can only lose their modesty and their exalted qualities, as well as the happiness, freedom, and truth in their lives.

667.

My son,
Time deceives the body
The body deceives your eyes
The monkey deceives the mind
Death deceives desire
Illusion deceives man
Lust deceives your feelings
Hatred deceives intellect
Doubt deceives peace
Intoxicants deceive good conduct
Fanaticism deceives the unity of mankind
Hastiness deceives the wisdom of the senses
Anger deceives good thoughts
Sin deceives and destroys maturity.

Acts like these destroy the truth in man's life. Therefore, he must seek divine luminous wisdom and through this wisdom receive the light to chase away the dark torpor of bad qualities. Then he will perceive the grace and wealth of God, the open space, and the light of the soul.

When you understand man's explanation, resonance, and resplendence, you will understand our Father's charity, compassion, and duty.

668.

A car without brakes
The driving of a blind man
A friend without love
A wife without good conduct or good qualities
Physical beauty without clothing
The life of one who has no control over his mind
Current without a switch
Climbing a mountain without a staff
Learning without wisdom

Entering the sea without knowing how to swim
Desiring to pluck the topmost fruit on a tree
　　without knowing how to climb

These are dangerous. Each action in a man's life must be considered and acted upon with care. A man of wisdom must understand and realize this.

### 669.

One who lives believing in the pleasure and happiness of physical beauty, one who praises his own beauty, will end his life like a monkey.

Small birds will build nests for themselves and four-legged animals will find caves in which to dwell, but a monkey does not know how to build a house for itself, even though it has hands and legs like a man. It gets wet in the rain, scorched by the sun, and beaten by the wind. Like this is the man who will not seek truth in order to realize his life.

### 670.

A beautiful woman seen in a dream
The mirrored images seen in water
Writing on water

A man with wisdom must realize that these three cannot be held in his hands, and that he must throw them out of his mind. He must understand what must be done, what must be seen, and what can be written on. If he acts accordingly, he will receive the benefit.

### 671.

A gem hidden within a hard rock
The pearl hidden within the sea oyster
Gnānam hidden in the qalb, the heart

Even if one knows of the existence of any of these things, he will not be able to find them through superficial efforts. When he is faced with difficulties, he will give up his effort immediately, assuming that the treasure he seeks is not there. Such things must be searched for with perseverance; those who are lazy will not be able to find them.

One who breaks the hard black rock of the mind will be able

to obtain the jewel of wisdom; one who breaks the mountain known as the ignorance of the mind can take from within it the truth of the soul's light. One who swims across the ocean of illusion which is *māyā* and dives down to the bottom can take from it the pearl of the soul's radiance. One who knows about and uses the light which can penetrate the *qalb* will be able to obtain the light known as *gnānam*. One who has the ability, wisdom, and faith to make the effort will succeed.

## 672.

One who learns from a book and then preaches from a stage will never read or know his own story. He will not know his own faults and correct himself. One who seeks the praise of the world will never understand the value and wisdom of a truly wise man.

## 673.

Rain without a sky,
Crops without land,
And the beauty of those who do not have
Good conduct or good qualities,
Will be of no benefit
Do not believe in them
For they will not bear fruit or truth.

## 674.

The learning of one who has no truth
And the wealth of one who has no faith
Are like the attempt to prove the identity
Of a body without a head.

## 675.

Those who desire benefit
From compassion given without a good heart
Will suffer the same fate
As worms thrown into fire.

## 676.

A judge who nods his head like a chameleon

To everything he hears
Will never be able to extract the meaning
By which he can analyze what has occurred.
He will never understand the difference
Between right and wrong.

A lawyer whose mental stubbornness
Is like the grip of an iguana
Will never let go of his own opinions.
He will always insist that only he is right.

A witness giving evidence for both sides
Is like the tail-wagging of a grateful dog
Who will go anywhere to get its food.

The actions of these three will never result in justice or truth, for the right and wrong in a person's words must be understood for the execution of proper justice.

677.

The sheikh says: Son, the country in which these three exist
A land without water
A king without justice
A man without truth
will be a hell filled with fire. Man must live in a place where there is water, justice, and truth. These will protect him and quench his thirst.

678.

The sheikh says: Ministers who give evil advice to the king can destroy the kingdom, bringing humiliation and disgrace to him and to the people.

679.

The One who does not have the six evils of lust, hatred, miserliness, attachment, fanaticism, and envy, the One who has no connection to the world, is our true partner.

The One who comes to help us when we suffer from poverty, illness, and difficulties is our friend. God is our only real friend.

### 680.

One who has a friend with the evil qualities of intoxication, lust, theft, murder, and falsehood will face a fate similar to being thrown from the summit of an icy mountain.

### 681.

If you have to feed milk to a snake, do it carefully and with wisdom. If you forget the snake's qualities, you will die. Understand this.

### 682.

The sheikh explains: Son, you are constantly taking different births within the same body through the countless thoughts, actions, and qualities arising in your mind. If you change these qualities into His qualities with your wisdom while you are still in this body, then you will not have to undergo rebirth into another body. Understand this.

### 683.

Transform the qualities in your body and be reborn into the qualities of God. There is a light within you; be reborn into that light form. When you are reborn into the form of God, you will be God's representative, and His kingdom will be yours.

### 684.

Do not harm others
Even in your thoughts or dreams
Or greater harm will come to you.

### 685.

Do not make an enemy of your neighbor
Or it will create sorrow in your life.

### 686.

Do not make an enemy of the neighborhood
Or it will kill the roots of your life,
Bringing ruin to your family
And everything you have.

### 687.

Do not accept as truth
What your wisdom knows is false.
Your life has no permanence in the world
And there will be a day of death.
Know this and
Believe the Day of Judgment will come.

### 688.

Do not advertise your charity
For the sake of praise from the world.
This will not give you any benefit
At the time of judgment in the grave.

### 689.

Do not make fun of the poor
Or one day the world will make fun of you.

### 690.

Do not kill any life in thought or in deed. If you do, one day, either in this world or in the world of hell, all the lives you have killed will join forces within your body. They will kill and eat your mind day by day as mental illness, insane thoughts, ghosts, and desires. Understand this with wisdom.

### 691.

Act with true justice and faith
And it will give you eternal life.

### 692.

Show kindness toward all
And all lives will love you.

### 693.

Do not ridicule the weak
Or tomorrow the Mighty One
Will ridicule you.

694.

Do not curse anyone
Through the use of black magic.
The deceptions and curses
Will turn back on you,
Striking you like a thunderbolt.

695.

Do not live trusting in your relatives.
Realize that they will one day desert you,
And resolve to trust the one God alone.

696.

Do not rejoice in acquiring money.
Rejoice in acquiring God's qualities.

697.

Do not cry because you are poor.
Cry to eliminate the poor qualities
Which torment you from within.
The greatest wealth is within,
The wealth of God's grace and God's qualities.
Spend that wealth freely, with wisdom.

698.

Do not look at the world and wonder.
Look at yourself and wonder.

699.

Before you try to transform animals
Into human beings,
Strive to transform the animals within you.
That will benefit them and you.

700.

Do not be a snake charmer
To the snakes of the world.

Charm the five-headed cobra of your senses (sight, taste, smell, sound, and feeling). Extract its four hundred trillion, ten thousand poisonous teeth, lock it within the cage of your wisdom, and make it dance. Then you will be a real snake charmer.

### 701.

Do not try to win prizes from the world
By swimming in the ocean.
Swim across the ocean of your mind,
The ocean of illusion which is the mind,
And win the indestructible prize from God.

### 702.

Do not mount and ride a racehorse
To win a prize from the world.
Mount the horse of the breath of your soul,
Ride around the world of your mind,
Conquer it with wisdom,
And receive your prize from Allah,
The prize of Allah's endless grace.

### 703.

Shaving the hair off your face every day
Does not make you beautiful.
But shaving away the hair
Of the evil qualities within your heart
Will give you the beauty of God.

### 704.

Do not store food in your house like a crocodile that lets its food rot at the bottom of a muddy pond. Do not take the karmic, sinful, stolen possessions of the world and hide them in the pond of your mental hell to eat later on. If you do, you will smell and experience hell before you actually go there.

Instead, happily accept and eat the *halāl,* permissible, food God gives you whenever He gives it, and praise Him for it. Then whatever you receive will be yours. Eat it with inner patience and contentment, placing your trust completely in God, and day by day your suffering will decrease.

## 705.

Do not be arrogant.
Arrogance is a tiger that will kill you.

## 706.

Making the mind peaceful and tranquil
Will grant equality and perfection
To the life of a human being.

## 707.

The help you give to others must be your happiness. It is good if that help is returned, but it is not good to expect it. If you help a snake and then ask for its help in return, the only thing it can give is its poison. Do your duty with a perfectly open heart, and it will elevate your life.

A crane has a selfish motive when it stands in the water for hours and hours; it is expecting a fish. Standing on one leg, it holds its wings, body, and shadow perfectly motionless for as much as a whole day.

Similarly, no matter what kind of yoga exercises he does, the meditation of a man who expects any profit, miracle, praise, glory, title, or honor will be like the meditation of a crane. Real meditation is to lose the self, destroy selfishness, and discard from oneself desire for land, gold, and sexual pleasures. First, control the mind so that it is perfectly motionless, and then meditate on only the one God.

## 708.

Son, an eagle can remain balanced in the sky, even when there is no breeze. You too have a balance. When you fly through the air of *māyā,* you must hold on to the state of surrender and balance.

To hold the body of wisdom in a state of balance, to observe and push aside all that comes to kill him—this is the balance of a wise man.

## 709.

It is good to raise a watchdog; however, it must be properly trained. But don't you begin to do the work of the dog and search for discarded food. To a dog, feces is like sugar. No matter how

306

well you raise it, the dog will retain its feces-eating qualities.

Similarly, all the evils of the world and all the treasures of hell are joy to the dog known as desire. Though the dog of desire exists as a part of the cage of your body, you must control it properly with wisdom and train it to do good work. It will cry, howl, bark, and beg you to let it out. But if you do let it out even once, it will immediately go for feces. If you feel sorry for it and take it out for a walk, it will drag you around, searching for the food it likes. It will not let you go on the good path.

Therefore, do not take the dog of desire with you on your journey. It will bark, knock you down, and lick your nose and mouth. Chain it at home and go where you have to go. When you go to prayers, tie up the dog. When you go to learn good wisdom, tie up the dog. Then you can complete your mission peacefully.

### 710.

During a certain season, a special kind of magnetic, silvery rain falls over the ocean. Although they are deep in the ocean, the pearl oysters know when this rain is falling by the coolness and movement of the water. They rise to the surface, knowing that a drop of this rainwater will form valuable pearls inside them. They keep their mouths open, and as soon as they receive a drop of this water, they go to the bottom and hold on to a rock or the sand on the ocean bed and stay there until the drop of water matures into a pearl.

Similarly, the embryo which is your life dwells in the ocean of *māyā,* the world of illusion. It eats and grows on illusory earth, illusory air, illusory fire, and illusory water. The rain of *rahmat,* the benevolence of grace, falls from certain wise men who come to the world, but only rarely. When the rain of the wisdom of *'ilm,* or divine knowledge, falls from them, just as the pearl oysters catch the silvery rain, you too must catch the words of wisdom with absolute faith. Attaching yourself to the rock of faith, certitude, and determination, breathe, saying, "*Lā ilāha illallāhu,* but for God, there is nothing; only You exist, O Allah." Then the pearl of pearls, the Pearl of Muhammad, *Muttu Muhammad (Sal.),* will mature within you.

In the same way that the oyster dies when the pearl matures, the differences of the 'I' and the 'you' will die when wisdom matures in you. Then Allah, who is the mercy and compassion of all the universes, will collect this pearl and keep it in His treasury.

Understand and realize this. This will be your *rahmat*.

## 711.

My son, when a cat sets out to catch a rat, the cat walks so stealthily that only the sound of the rat can be heard.

It is like this that the cat known as the mind comes to grab man. It comes so stealthily and silently that no one perceives it. The cat of the mind grabs the senses of the body, releases them, jumps on them, releases them, and jumps on them again. The cat of the mind clings to your thoughts. It creeps silently until it suddenly grabs you and causes you untold suffering. It kills you without killing you and destroys your life without destroying it. The cat of the mind with its magnetic *māyā* catches your life and tortures you. It creeps and creeps, but you do not know it is coming; no matter how careful you are, it will still catch you.

But if you ring the bell of wisdom, the cat of the mind will run when it hears that sound. If you hold the light of wisdom properly, the cat of the mind, which can see only in the dark, will stare in fascination, dazzled by the light—and then you can escape. Hold up the light of wisdom and chase away that tormenting cat. Then you will find peace. You need the clarity of faith, determination, and certitude to avoid that torment and torture.

## 712.

When you go to fetch water from a pond, do not take a vessel that already has water in it; you will be unable to fill it with fresh water. When you go to the supermarket, do not take a bag that is already filled with old things; you will not be able to fill it with new things.

Like that, when you search for wisdom, do not take with you what you learned earlier. Do not fill your mind with arrogance, karma, *māyā,* lust, hatred, miserliness, attachment, fanaticism, and envy.

If you wish to acquire God's qualities, actions, conduct, compassion, truth, and patience, you must cleanse your heart and be receptive. If you throw away your preconceived ideas and proceed with an open mind, you will be able to receive the wisdom which will end your karma.

### 713.

Do not try to grow crops on a rocky mountain; you will not be able to irrigate them. The rain and the water you pour over them will wash away the earth, and the hot sun will parch the seeds.

Like that, you must understand each man's thoughts, actions, and qualities. Once you know his nature, let him go the way he wants to go. Do not try to teach wisdom to one whose ignorance has hardened. Wisdom will not grow in the hard rock of the ignorance of man's mind and desire. If you split that rock, you will not find even a drop of moisture.

### 714.

O man, make your desire like a plow
Your thoughts like a bull
And your mind like the land.
Plow the land with wisdom and sow a good crop. Share the harvest of that benevolence of grace with your brothers, and it will benefit you.

### 715.

Do not conduct your life
Believing in what your eyes see.
Conduct your life by fully analyzing, reflecting upon, and understanding everything. Otherwise, you will meet with accidents.

### 716.

Place the truth in front of you,
Follow it,
And it will reveal to you
The path to the liberation of the soul.

### 717.

Do not think everything that is white is milk. Some intoxicants are milk-white, but if you drink them they will drug your wisdom and ruin your virtue. Think of this. Protect yourself by knowing which is milk before you drink it.

Similarly, do not think everything you have learned is *gnānam,* or divine wisdom. With clarity, analyze and reflect upon everything you learn and extract from it the truth of *gnānam.*

## 718.

My son, do not be deceived into trying to drink water from a mirage in the desert. It is composed only of heat waves. If you follow a mirage, you will grow hungrier and thirstier, you will suffer, and finally you will die.

Similarly, do not trust what your physical eyes see. Do not trust the mirages in the desert of ignorance, the heat waves of the desire of the mind in which illusion shows itself as truth.

Do not believe that the miracles and prayers of your mind and desire can benefit you. They will only lead you to an empty hell. Hunger will come to your soul, and disease will come to destroy your life. Understand this.

## 719.

There are flowers, such as the *neerāmbal* and *allitthāmaray,* which grow in water and resemble the lotus, but do not mistake them for lotuses.

If the water evaporates, the false lotuses will die, but not the real lotus; its tuberous roots survive and new shoots will come up.

Like that, do not think everything you have learned is the truth, do not think all your prayers are genuine, do not think everything you sing is devotional, and do not think everything your mind brings to you is real. These are all the false lotuses that grow in the ignorance within the pond of illusion which is your mind. Miracles and such things are all false lotuses.

When your strength decreases, your blood thins, and your nerves become weak, all the wisdom of your mind, all your learning, and all the miracles will evaporate, sending you to the hell of death. But like the lotus, true prayer will keep you alive through any difficulty, and it will grant you eternal life.

If you pray, knowing what real prayer and meditation are, that will give exaltedness and the radiance of wisdom to your life.

## 720.

When you pray to God, do not make a list of the things you want, as you do for the supermarket. Leave your shopping list behind. Be alone, be hungry, and be awake. Take these three kinds of attentiveness with you and pray only to God. Keep God within your inner heart, be within God, and pray. Then all the forces

310

ruling from within will leave you. In that state, the lone treasure becomes one with the Lone Treasure, and that is true worship.

### 721.

Do not imagine that you are deceiving the world and all the people in it. Realize that your mind is deceiving you and ruining your life. If you understand this with wisdom and disentangle yourself from this deception, you will be a wise person.

### 722.

Do not take up a knife, a gun, or an ax
And set out to kill others.

For without knife, gun, or ax, you are being tortured and killed by the enemy of your mind, day by day, hour by hour, minute by minute, second by second, atom by atom. The mind is the enemy you must try to kill. Only then will you be wise and clever.

### 723.

Do not resolve to kill others
With curses, black magic, or plots.

Day and night your mind and desire and the five elements are plotting against you. Day and night, through plotting, curses, vengeance, trickery, treachery, and thought, they torment you atom by atom, spreading throughout your body as energy, dividing and spreading as viruses and cells, and becoming a cancer in your body. In the end they will deliver you into the hands of the Angel of Death.

### 724.

If you wish to bathe in a forest grove, do not try to carry the bathwater from your house. It would be very difficult to carry enough water to cleanse yourself properly. On your way, if you look for a place where there is already water in which to bathe, it will be easier.

Similarly, if you wish to cleanse the karmic dirt from your body, you must find a place of wisdom and wash away your dirt with the water of grace. Do not take with you what you have already learned; it will not be enough. Go to a place of wisdom and bathe in wisdom. Then you can be free of karma.

## 725.

Do not carry apples to a fully-laden apple tree and try to attach your apples onto it. Temporary apples grafted onto the branches will fall off. It is easier to simply pick the original apples. They will taste better, too.

Similarly, do not carry what your mind and desire have collected and graft it onto the truth. Truth is beyond mind and desire. Throw away your mind and desire and search for truth with wisdom, and you will find the original taste.

## 726.

There are four kinds of terribly infectious diseases in man, four kinds of inherited cancers: the selfishness of religion, the selfishness of race, the selfishness of desire, and the arrogance of the karmically dark ego. These are the cancers which cause tremendous pain to everyone in the world. They disrupt equality, destroy peacefulness, hide the truth, spoil good conduct, burn man's good qualities, destroy peace of mind, tolerance, and patience, and bring the diseases of poverty and destruction.

These cancers can be cured only with the power called God which is within man. If man acquires the power which is the good qualities, good conduct, good actions, patience, tolerance, equality, and compassion of God, if he takes that power as a medicine and allows it to spread throughout his body, those malignant diseases will be consumed. That is the only good medicine.

## 727.

As long as one has a head, his nose will run. Where does the water come from? The head.

Similarly, as long as you have mind and desire, your thoughts will run, oozing worldly karma. In the way that water comes from your head, what is in your heart will show in your face. If your heart is clear, your face will be clear, and your life will also be clear.

## 728.

The vessel of the mind has twelve holes: arrogance, karma, *māyā;* the three sons of *māyā* known as *tārahan, singhan,* and *sūran;*

312

lust, hatred, attachment, miserliness, fanaticism, and envy.

Do not take this vessel with you to receive the grace of Allah until you plug the holes with your wisdom. Then go to the ocean of the knowledge of grace which is within a perfected man, an *insān kāmil,* and receive the water of the grace of Allah's benevolence. Fill the vessel of wisdom with this water, drink it, and say, "*Lā ilāha illallāhu,* there is none other than You; You are Allah." Then you will see the light and the open space, and you will receive the grace and wealth of Allah.

729.

Do not try to inject flavor into a fruit.
The real flavor is already there.

Like this, if you want to search for God, true wisdom, and liberation for the soul, do not think that you are the greatest of all miracle workers, that you are better than anyone else, or that you are God. Do not take the flavor of your ignorance and pride and try to inject that into the fruit of God. That would be like a monkey being let loose in an orchard: it would ruin the fruit and break the branches. Your prayer, your miracles, and all that you have gathered will end up like that.

If you try to put the thoughts, the flavor, and the tricks of the monkey mind into the flavor of God's truth, do not think the result will be tasty. The fruit of God's truth contains an eternal and changelessly sweet flavor. Throw away the flavor you have brought with you and taste the eternal flavor of God's truth.

730.

One who wishes to climb a mountain of ice must use special equipment.

Similarly, if you wish to climb the slippery mountain of mind and desire in order to speak with God, you must take the appropriate equipment. You must have:

> The qualities of God
> The actions of God
> The behavior of God
> The patience and tolerance of God
> The peace of God
> The compassion of God

The selfless duty of God
Faith, certitude, and determination.

This is the equipment you will need to climb the mountain of mind and desire. With it, you can transcend the slipperiness of the mind and speak to God.

If you do not proceed in this way and then blame your failure to talk to God on the mountain, or on the sheikh, or on his teachings or his actions, that is wrong. But once you realize that it is your own fault, and once you discover the proper equipment which must be used, then you can climb up, reap the benefit of your search, and speak with God, the Good Truth.

### 731.

The beautiful fragrance of the rose announces the flower's presence, but it is surrounded by thorns. If you want the rose, you must pluck it carefully so that the thorns do not prick you.

Like that, in the body, too, there is a very beautiful and fragrant flower, the sweet-scented truth which is God. It exists in the heart, surrounded by the many thorns of desire. If you wish to obtain this flower, you need total determination and careful, subtle wisdom to pluck it without hurting yourself. If the thorns injure you, it is not the fault of the flower.

The orange also grows amidst thorns. If you want to eat it, you will have to pick it carefully.

In your body, there are four hundred trillion, ten thousand spiritual and karmic thorns. In the midst of these is the beautiful orange of truth. Avoid the thorns, pluck the fruit, and taste it. It has the flavor of the resplendent light of *Nūr*, the one hundred flavors of grace. These flavors contain the quality of the one hundred resplendences of God. Within these resplendences is the flavor of the ninety-nine *wilāyats*, or powers of God. If this spreads throughout your body, your body will become the flavor of these resplendences. You must avoid the thorns with analytic wisdom and enjoy the flavor of the fruit of divine wisdom.

### 732.

The ocean is salty, but are there grains of salt in the water? No. The salt is dissolved in the water; it is mingled with the water. If you want salt, you must put the water out in the heat of the sun and let it evaporate. Then the grains of salt will appear.

The saltwater in the ocean cannot quench the thirst of men or animals. It can only sustain the lives in the sea. However, when the ocean water is evaporated and made into salt, all lives can make use of it. It can be used in all kinds of medicine: homeopathic, ayurvedic, and western medicine, as well as in home remedies. It can also be used to make fireworks and chemicals. Salt crystals can be used in countless scientific ways to make or destroy things in the world. Man uses salt to enhance the flavor of his food. Nevertheless, though his body does need a certain amount of salt, if taken in excess, it not only spoils the taste of the food, but also becomes dangerous to the body.

Like the salt in sea water, the *māyic* essences of the earth, fire, water, air, and ether are dissolved in the body and in the illusory ocean of the mind. If man can boil these with divine analytic wisdom, changing them into divine luminous wisdom, that can be used for many beneficial purposes. With divine luminous wisdom, he can give to all the different lives the things they need in exactly the right amount.

In making salt by letting ocean water evaporate, man makes a useless thing into a useful and essential thing for life. In the same way, if man can find the way in which he can use his body and mind with wisdom to help others, it will elevate his life.

### 733.

A dog has enough awareness to find its master through its intellect and its sense of smell. Whether asleep or awake, it also knows when a thief is nearby, and it will bark and reveal his presence. Then with its sense of smell, it can even follow the thief's trail if necessary.

If a dog which has only feeling, awareness, and intellect can do so much, how much more should a man who has feeling, awareness, intellect, judgment, subtle wisdom, divine analytic wisdom, and divine luminous wisdom be able to do toward finding his Father. He should be able to follow the scent with his nose of wisdom and by barking, chase away and frighten his Father's enemies which are mind, desire, and the illusions of the world.

If he can do this, he will become a child of God and a *gnāni* in the midst of men.

## 734.

Son, let us look at the body. If a piece of dust is about to enter the eye, the lid will automatically close to protect it. If we begin to slip on one foot, the other foot will help us to regain our balance. If we slip down even more, the hands will reach out to protect the body. All the sections in the body of man protect each other and live in unity. If an illness comes to one of them, that pain is felt by all. All of them will shout. If the stomach aches, the whole body has a stomachache. If hunger comes, the whole body feels hungry. Even though the limbs and the various sections of the body are separate, they share everything that comes. They have unity even though they have different qualities, even though they have different actions.

Similarly, truth, God, wisdom, and light exist within the body, protecting each other. The light and the essence exist within us in the way that the parts of the body help each other, the power which is God's actions, God's compassion, God's equality, God's peace, God's justice, His unselfish duty, and all His qualities protects and helps the truth within the body—the light form. If danger threatens one, the others come to help.

If we understand with deep wisdom what it is that protects us, we can overcome all danger. Human beings must understand this.

## 735.

The cobra may be beautiful, but it is poisonous by nature. A wise man will not wear it on his body just because of its beauty.

Like that, if a man looks with wisdom and understands the qualities and actions of the beautiful things in the world, external beauty will not enchant him. Once he realizes what is on the inside, he will avoid outer beauty and its hazards. You too must understand with wisdom and avoid the beauty which can lead to evil.

## 736.

Although a crow is black, it regards its own children as gold and brings them up with great attachment.

Similarly, mind and desire which live within the five elements consider their children as gold. Their children are evil qualities, blood ties, worldly attachments, jealousy, fanaticism, racial differences, religious differences, separations, and all such things.

Those without wisdom, those whose dark minds are full of selfishness and ignorance, perceive God's qualities, God's actions, wisdom, divine wisdom, divine luminous wisdom, good thoughts, equality, regarding all lives as one's own life, helping everyone equally, peace, tranquillity, justice, and charity as black, while they regard their own state as golden. They are the enemies to truth.

But gold is gold and brass is brass. Gold needs no makeup, while evil qualities cannot appear beautiful without a lot of make-up. We need to inquire into and understand both sides.

If you want to remain golden, you must first chase away the black and ignorant mind and establish good thoughts and good qualities. Chase away the mind and you will be victorious; you will forever be that original gold.

### 737.

The wood from a mature teak tree can be used to build handsome houses, beautiful furniture, and many other objects which will last for generations.

Although we spend so much time and thought in bringing up the body, man's body is much less useful than the body of a teak tree. When man's body is cut, all we find is flesh and blood. If we keep a dead body for three days, it begins to smell foul; the whole place in which it is kept will reek.

Man must realize the impermanence and uselessness of his body and take on God's form, God's qualities, God's duty, good actions, and good behavior. He must raise within himself that which is permanent. If he then makes himself useful to other lives, he will become a king to the three worlds.

### 738.

Do not attempt to purify water by putting fire into it; the fire will be extinguished.

In the same way, do not attempt to preach wisdom to one who has no faith in God, or you will suffer the same fate as fire that tries to purify water.

Hidden within a seed is that which can bear fruit: the tree, the branches, the leaves, and the flowers. When the fruit ripens, its flavor and fragrance emerge.

Similarly, there is a seed of truth within you. The flavor of grace is within it. The man of wisdom who will taste it is also there. If you taste the fruit of truth with wisdom, and if you understand the honey, the resplendent light, and the perfection of Allah which is the flavor of the soul resonating, radiating, and shining brilliantly within you, you will attain a glorious victory in life. Think of this.

### 740.

When a fisherman throws a net into the sea, all kinds of fish will be caught in it. When he draws in his catch, he will take the edible fish and throw the sea snakes and the other creatures he does not want back into the sea.

Like this, when you spread out the net of your life in the ocean of illusion, everything that lives in that ocean may be caught in your net: the treasures of mind, desire, ignorance, and the five elements. Many of these things have the evil qualities of snakes and crocodiles; throw them back into the ocean of illusion like a fisherman throws back what he does not want.

The five elements (earth, fire, water, air, and ether) are certainly necessary, and they can stay with you. But you must discard the evil they bring and preserve the good. This will provide you with the explanation of the grace and wealth of Allah, and it will appease the hunger of your soul.

### 741.

The sandalwood tree has a naturally lovely and cooling fragrance. If you simply smell the tree the fragrance is less obvious, but if you rub a piece of its wood the fragrance increases, does it not? Not only that, but the trees which grow next to the sandalwood tree, the trees whose branches and roots are intertwined with it, begin to smell like sandalwood too, though the sandalwood never takes on their fragrances.

Similarly, within man there is an original treasure that contains the very beautiful and lovely fragrance of God's truth and essence. This fragrance and the fragrance of the completeness of God's compassionate qualities are mingled with His wisdom of grace and exist within man as an original treasure.

The truth within man, the truth within his good qualities, is surrounded by and intertwined with the evil actions of the five elements. Man should not change his nature toward that of the elements. Instead, without taking on their odors, he must give them the true fragrance of God and transform them. Then he will have exalted qualities and the completeness of wisdom.

Like the sandalwood tree, even though evil qualities are intertwined with our being, we must not change the truth; the truth must change the evil qualities by giving them its fragrance, but their qualities and their fragrance must not be taken on by man. He must take on only the fragrance of the qualities of truth. Truth is truth only when it is not blemished by these evil qualities.

### 742.

There are two types of cells in the blood, the white cells and the red cells. When the white cells begin to destroy the red cells, a man's body becomes weak, his strength decreases, and he approaches death.

Similarly, the evil qualities within man destroy his eternal life and devour all the good qualities within him. For this disease, we must take the medicine of the word of God, the *Kalimah. Lā ilāha illallāhu*—There is nothing other than You; only You, O God, are Allah. Then we must fill the resplendent vessel of plenitude called *Bismillāhir-Rahmānir-Rahīm* and drink with wisdom, saying, *"Illallāhu."* If we remember to do this diligently, then this evil disease that eats the good qualities will die and we will know the plenitude of the *Kalimah*.

### 743.

If you dissolve earth in water, what is it you smell? There is a fragrance that comes from earth when it is dissolved in water, a fragrance that can fascinate all mankind. Man does not suffer because of it, nor is he harmed by it. However, if you dissolve a man in water, you will faint from the smell of his blood and body fluids. As long as earth remains in the form of earth, you can endure its odor, but as soon as man made of earth becomes a corpse, its odor becomes so unbearable that it can knock you down. Therefore, which is better, the earth or the body of man? You must think of this.

Similarly, even though you have a connection to the earth, the odor that is really horrible is the odor that arises from the connections to *māyā,* the mind, blood ties, karma, and demons. That stench can kill; it can make wisdom fall into a faint. Do not associate with it.

If you take on the earth's qualities of patience and tolerance and discard evil qualities, you will not harm other lives. You need wisdom to distinguish between good and bad connections.

### 744.

The sheikh said: Son, there are many wonders in God's creation. God created millions of four-legged animals, two-legged men, birds, reptiles, and countless other beings. Some men do not take fish or meat and say they are vegetarians. They say, "We are close to God. We will go to God's kingdom." They pray and dance and perform rituals. They call themselves *saivam,* or vegetarian. We have seen and heard of this.

But cows, goats, donkeys, and some birds are natural vegetarians. Some do not even drink milk. They certainly do not take cooked food or tea and coffee. They also perform service for the world. But they do not go to heaven; they end up in the butcher shop. If even such natural vegetarians do not receive heaven, how can man, who takes eggs and his mother's blood in the form of milk, go to heaven? At best, he is a temporary vegetarian. Is this *saivam?* He will receive only what the cow received. The cow goes to the butcher shop, and man will go to hell. This is what will happen if he does not understand the truth.

Son, man will not reach heaven through words or by eating vegetarian food. He must analyze with wisdom and understand. If he understands, he will not hurt any heart or eat any part of any being. He will not steal another man's food, hurt another man's life, or take away another man's freedom. He will consider the suffering of all lives as his own and help them; he will consider everyone's hunger as his own, sacrifice his own food, praise God, and serve others. No matter what he suffers, he will acquire God's qualities, do the duties God does, and make the mystery of God his. He will forbear with patience and be content regardless of all the suffering that comes to him in performing his duty. At every moment, he will say, "All praise belongs to God, *al-hamdu lillāh*," and do whatever has to be done. For what is to happen at the next moment, he will give all responsibility to God. He will do duty without arrogance or anger, without praise, titles, karma, sin, or hatred, without taking the intoxicants of the world, and without losing his faith. With faith, certitude, determination, and surrender to Allah, he will pay obeisance to God, praying to Him in every breath and in every word.

One who is pure, one who has cut away his birth, one who will not be reborn, one who has the undiminishing wealth of Allah, one who disappears in Allah, is called *saivam*. One in this state is called Islam. *Lām* is light. But the words and deeds of men who merely talk of it are like fuel for the fire of hell. What benefit is there in that?

Son, one who understands with wisdom, and knows what is *saivam* and what is Islam, is *Īmān-Islām*.

## 745.

Let us look at the water in a pond. In it there are fish, mud, snakes, crocodiles, crabs, and turtles. Many animals come to drink the water; they urinate and defecate in the pond and then they leave. Eventually, the water becomes full of dirt, viruses, and germs. Before a man can drink that water, he must either mix it with a chemical, filter it, or boil it to kill the germs and make it clean. Animals do not do this, but human beings do.

Similarly, within man are many kinds of dirt. The dirt comes through mind, desire, thoughts, and the five elements; it comes through what the eyes see, through what the ears hear, through what the nose smells, through what the tongue tastes, through food, and through drink; many things come in many ways. Evil odors, filth, sins, accidents, dangerous poisons, and many such things come into the body of man. Because of this, you must use the sieve of wisdom every moment of every day to filter what comes to us.

Once this has been done, you can give the water to the soul and to truth; you can use the water for prayer and for worship. The water will be good only if you filter away the earth, fire, water, air, ether, mind, and desire with the seven levels of consciousness: feeling, awareness, intellect, judgment, subtle wisdom, divine analytic wisdom, and divine luminous wisdom.

Drink with contentment, saying, "*Bismillāhir-Rahmānir-Rahīm. Al-hamdu lillāh*. In the name of God, Most Merciful, Most Compassionate. All praise is His." Pray, "*Lā ilāha illallāhu*. There is nothing other than You, O God. Only You are God." Only then will all that is connected with the karma of your birth leave you. Only then will you be free of illness.

### 746.

Son, let us think about the unity of men and women. Though unity is exalted in the life of a human being, husbands and wives find fault with each other and separate. Both husbands and wives must think.

Women have a magnetism in their minds and qualities to attract men in the same way a magnet attracts iron. With this magnetic quality, a woman can attract any kind of man, even an unbending one. God has given women magnetism, beauty, love, good qualities, and good actions. If a woman uses her magnetism in the correct way, she can pull an uncontrollable man together, just as a magnet can pull together rigid or irregular pieces of iron. The pieces will not come apart as long as the magnetism lasts. If a woman uses her magnetism properly, there will be no separation between husband and wife in this world.

Female children must observe and understand this, bringing it into their qualities, minds, and love, and conduct their lives with patience.

### 747.

A pot to fit the lid
A lid to fit the pot

When people see a united married couple, they say, "This pair is like a pot and a lid." The connection between a husband and wife should be like this.

Man must think. Pots vary in size and shape; the middle may be wide and the bottom narrow, or the bottom may be wide and the top narrow. But no matter what the shape of the pot, the lid must fit the mouth of the pot.

When we cook food, the heat, weight, and pressure are felt by the pot. The whole weight is in the pot, not in the lid. The lid is the man, and the pot is the woman. When the pot suffers with the heat, and the food in the pot boils up, the lid will lift.

At that point, instead of complaining about the minor difficulty he is undergoing, the man must realize the weight, suffering, and pain felt by the woman, who bears the burden of the family.

The lid must be lifted when the pot boils and the contents stirred with a spoon to ease the heat and keep the food from boiling over into the fire. Only then will you have food to appease your hunger.

The woman bears the family's burdens, sorrows, mental depressions, and physical illnesses. When she begins to boil with all the difficulties and sufferings, the man should lift up the lid and stir with the spoon of wisdom to keep the pot from boiling over. When she comes to talk to her husband, he must comfort her with wisdom and love by listening to her complaints, thereby easing the boiling heat within her and giving her peace. As the spoon was used to stir the boiling pot, a husband must use his wisdom and love to ease the mounting sorrows of his wife, thereby maintaining the unity of the pot and the lid. If he continues to stir, releasing the heat, there will be unity. If he does not, a heart filled with mounting suffering will break with the excess pressure, and the unity of their life together will be destroyed.

Men must think of this with wisdom and give love and comfort to their wives, who bear so much suffering and trouble in life. To give a wife to a man who fails to conduct himself in this way would be like giving a flower garland into the hands of a monkey. Just as a monkey crushes a flower, unaware of its value, he too would crush the life of a woman without understanding her true worth. Then there would be no unity in his life. Men must think of this.

### 748.

Now let us look at a banana tree. Suppose we raise it with love and tender care. As it grows, it looks cool and very beautiful; it is a lovely shade of green. Within six months, a stem bearing a flower emerges from within the banana tree, and people say that the banana tree has given birth to a child. As soon as the 'banana child' emerges, the beauty of the mother tree begins to fade, day by day. Three months after the banana bunch emerges, the mother dies and is cut down. The mother tree is killed by the child that comes from within it. We have seen this with our own eyes.

It is like this also for those who are human beings. We are the original story of God. God created man as the basic meaning and the explanation within the story of creation, so that the meaning of creation could be known. Man is called wise. God created man as a very exalted being. He comes into the world with purity and beauty and the light of God's beautiful qualities.

But in spite of his beauty, there are things that emerge from within man to kill him. In the same way the banana fruit grows from within a banana tree, man blooms and bears fruit; he begins to show racial and religious differences. When arrogance, karma, *māyā,* the beauty of ignorance, the arts, and the sexual games of *māyā* emerge, they kill the original beauty of man.

In the way the banana fruit emerges from the banana tree and kills it, sin and karma emerge from within man, who came from God's grace, and kill him. They destroy his beauty, kill him, and hand him over to the Angel of Death. We must realize this.

If man would kill with wisdom the illusory beauty of praise and the arrogance which will kill him, if he would prevent their growth within him, he would remain beautiful. Unlike the banana fruit that kills its mother, he would be one who does not kill his Creator. He would cherish his Father, grow in that beauty, and acquire His gracious qualities.

If anything other than God emerges in man, it will kill him. The only thing that can save man from this calamity is to act with wisdom.

### 749.

A disciple asked the sheikh, "How can we put the right (the path to God) and the left (the material world) together?"

The sheikh answered, "You have two eyes, a left eye and a right eye; you have two hands, a left hand and a right hand; you have two legs, a left leg and a right leg. Both eyes look forward to see one thing, both hands move together to do things, and both legs move when you walk, first one foot then the other.

"As you go forward, your attention and your wisdom must go ahead of you, discerning what is wrong and what is right. Your eyes must see the wrong and right in everything. When you see what is wrong, you have to avoid it or put it aside, and when you see what is right, you can go on. If you avoid the wrong path and go along the right path, everything will be right.

"The right path is the path to God; the left path is the path to the world. Analyze with your wisdom and seek the right path, which leads to the truth, while avoiding the path on the left, which leads to the world of illusion."

### 750.

The sheikh said: Son, a banyan tree grows into a huge tree which can cover an area of nearly a mile. Though this tree grows from only a tiny seed, its taproot goes very deep, and the supporting roots spread out and fix themselves firmly. When the tree is firmly rooted, its weight does not affect it, and no matter how big a gale or storm may come, the roots hold on firmly because the taproot is strong and straight. The supporting roots give additional strength to the taproot.

You are a man, are you not? Similarly, if the taproot of *īmān,* the taproot of faith, certitude, and determination in God, goes straight down within you, and the supporting roots of patience, inner patience, contentment, surrender to God, and praise to God spread out to strengthen it, even if the weight of the whole world comes on you, even if poverty, illness, elemental ghosts, and all the troubles of the eighteen thousand worlds come to attack you, they will not be able to dislodge you. If you have fixed your balance in the proper place, you will see God within you and yourself within God. None of these states will shake you up or make your mind waver.

It is because you do not have this balance, because you do not have the firm taproot of *īmān,* that suffering is affecting you. Because of this, even if you know there is a God, you are unable to derive any benefit from it.

### 751.

The sheikh said: Son, here is an example. Say we want to grow some paddy. If we sow it and cultivate it well, it will grow healthy and high. But paddy cannot be harvested while it is still growing. And even after it is cut, there will be dust and dirt and chaff in it. So what must we do? We must winnow it in the wind. The dirt, dust, and chaff will be blown away and what remains will be good. The outer husk must then be broken in a mill and the grain converted to rice. And even then we have to wash the rice and pick out the stones before we can cook it or turn it into rice flour.

You must cleanse yourself in a similar manner. Winnow yourself with wisdom and realize that within you there are things which are good and things which are not so good. You have to pound them, clean them, and take what is good. Winnow with wisdom everything the mind brings. You need to do this to your inner crops, both the good and the bad. This is what you must do in your life.

## 752.

A child asked the sheikh, "When I tell you I'm not progressing quickly enough or that I'm going up and down, you tell me not to worry about it because I am still young. At what point is youth no longer an excuse for ignorance?"

The sheikh replied, "As long as wisdom has not developed within you, you are still young. As soon as wisdom emerges, you are older.

"Thus, even if one is small, his wisdom might be big. Those who have wisdom are great. Until wisdom comes, however, you are a very small child though you may be old in years. This is the way it is. Because the question arose, it signifies that wisdom is yet to come and that more clarity is needed. Until then, you will be a small child.

"This body belongs to the earth, and it is bound by an agreement which limits its time. The life span of the body is the time of ignorance, but there is a time of wisdom which belongs to an indestructible, endless life. Wisdom is a huge section that grows from the world of the souls, through this world, and high into the next world. Until it becomes complete, you are a small person. 'You are young' means that there is still room for you to learn. As long as we need to study in school, we remain students. You are still a student, are you not? And this is a school. My child, continue to study."

## 753.

The sheikh asked the children, "Are there any other questions?"

One responded, "Some people seem to have faith in God and there arises in me a desire to tell them about my sheikh. Is that a good desire? When should the sheikh be spoken of, and when should he not be spoken of?"

The sheikh replied, "Speak about the truth of God. That must be spoken of all the time. The sheikh is a student. If there is anything good in what he says, talk about that. If he has wisdom and good qualities, talk about that. If they accept what you say, it will be beneficial for them and for you. If they do not, it might come back on you and cause you harm.

"A tiger has to be fed with meat. If you try to feed it grass, it will eat you, because you are meat to a tiger. You must understand who needs what and teach accordingly. Know the qualities, actions, and conduct of the person to whom you talk. Understand this and do it this way, son."

754.

The sheikh said: Look at cows and goats when they itch or when an insect bites them. What do they do? Some bite the place that itches. Others flick their tails to chase the insects away. Still others scratch themselves with their hind legs.

But animals do not have an evil itch on the inside like man does. Even though they have attachments, they do not have the thought of hoarding for tomorrow, they do not have thoughts of vengeance, murder, or causing pain to others, so they do not have anything that bites them on the inside.

Man, on the other hand, contains the whole world. His attachments and prejudices bite him, chew on him, suck his blood, and make him itch on the inside. Within him are the sixty-four arts and sexual games. Man has gathered within himself the blood ties of possessiveness, religious, racial, and color differences, falsehood, jealousy, revenge, trickery, deceit, mantras, magic, mesmerism, theft, murder, arrogance, hastiness, pride, my property, your property, and four hundred trillion, ten thousand selfish, wicked, murderous actions.

The sinful qualities of arrogance, karma, *māyā*, lust, hatred, miserliness, envy, and fanaticism are inside man. So, not only does he itch on the inside, but he also contains hell. Those poisonous things are biting and scratching him. This evil itch does not give him peace for even a second; day and night it is eating him inside and out so that he suffers more than an animal. This is the itch that no one can cure. Therefore, man has no peace.

If man can use his wisdom to get rid of these itching qualities that eat at him, he might find a certain amount of peace. A man with divine wisdom will throw away the world. Having rid himself of the itch inside and out, he can be calm and do duty as God does duty for all lives, peacefully. Understand this.

755.

Allah alone knows the hearts of those who praise Him, pray to Him, and worship Him. He alone knows who truly gives charity in His name. Others look at people's clothes and actions and praise and blame them.

The learned have many thoughts. They think about the pride they take in their learning, the worth of their learning, and the praise they have received for their learning. With the learning they have, they will judge others and praise or blame them. Allah will observe them until the Day of Judgment.

However, one who is not learned has only the name of Allah in his heart. He praises Allah at every moment. Because of his faith, Allah always instructs and warns him from within his heart. Allah and the Qur'an are in the heart of an unlearned man, while the learned man has the Qur'an only in his hand. This is the difference between the two.

If we are true believers, we must understand with wisdom and keep Allah's Messenger *(Sal.)* in the house of our hearts. That will benefit us well.

756.

There is a *hadīth,* a traditional saying, that Allah cannot bear it if anyone hurts the heart of one who is a slave of God, a perfected human being, an *insān kāmil.* Whether people are learned or ordinary, if they hurt the heart of such a being, Allah cannot bear it or grant forgiveness. If you ask forgiveness from Allah in such an instance, He will say, "Ask forgiveness from the one you hurt." At that time you will have to ask forgiveness from the slave of God. As soon as his heart is made peaceful, Allah's heart will be made peaceful; when his heart is made peaceful, Allah's love will be peaceful. That is one instance. In all other instances, forgiveness must be asked from Allah.

*Question:* What if we hurt someone other than a slave of God?

*Bawa Muhaiyaddeen:* You do not know who is a slave of God and who is not. Allah alone knows.

*Question:* Still, if we hurt an ordinary person, what should we do?

*Bawa Muhaiyaddeen:* You must ask God for forgiveness. If you realize you have done wrong, you can ask forgiveness from the one you hurt. If you do not, the results of the hurts you cause to ordinary people will come back to you on Judgment Day, while the results of hurting a slave of God will be immediate. Hurting a slave of God is like falling into fire. This is the meaning.

### 757.

A child says, "I have seen a picture in my mind and also in my awareness since the age of twelve. What is the meaning of this?"

The sheikh says, "Son, the mind is a big picture world. The intellect stores in the mind what we see in this thought world. Moment by moment, the intellect presents this picture in the mind as feeling, awareness, dreams, and thoughts. What the feeling and perception take in at one time, the intellect shows and explains later in the world of the mind.

"If you analyze with wisdom, you will realize that you are seeing what was seen by and stored in the mind. When you realize that it is only a picture and throw it away, and if you can find the true explanation which is seen by wisdom, you will see God who is wisdom within wisdom."

### 758.

A child asked, "Is it good to pray and ask God for divine wisdom, learning, wealth, and so on, for yourself, or is it good to pray to God for others?"

The sheikh said, "That is a good question. Child, if you pray with the idea of receiving anything for yourself, that is not true prayer. That is the prayer of the base desires. In this kind of prayer, your thoughts become a veil; they become a mountain between you and God. It is of no use.

"The day you throw away all your thoughts and surrender to the One to whom prayer is due, your prayer will be like the sun. Just as the sun serves the entire world, you too can serve the entire world. When you become a good one, the rain that falls for you will benefit everyone, and you will have no need to ask for anything for yourself or for others."

### 759.

Son, listen to what I say. In the world there are children in many different circumstances. There are children who are hungry, children who are unable to speak, children who have no clothing, and children who have no housing. Those who have should help those who are in need. How can one with a house possibly seek the help of one who has no house? One who has wealth must help one who has no wealth. One who has wisdom must help those who lack wisdom. One who has clothes must give to those who have no clothes. Like this, you should try to help others and soothe them with whatever you have. If you do, you can become good children.

Instead of attaining that state if you keep on reciting requests to God, "Give my wife health, give my children health, give me this, give me a house, give me that, give me a job, give my son a job, give my daughter a job," it is absolute selfishness. No matter how many prayers you recite for such things, they will not benefit you. That kind of prayer is like trying to pick fruit from a tree that does not bear fruit.

To think of God is true prayer. If you acquire God's qualities and do His duties without attachment in the way He does, considering all lives as your own, and if you pray in that state, that is the prayer which will benefit you.

760.

A man studies music in order to make his mind happy. He uses intoxicants to make the music happy. He takes women in order to give happiness to the intoxicants. Then he indulges in sex in order to make his experience with women happy. To fully satisfy his lust, he searches for money. To make money happily, he practices falsehood. To happily indulge in falsehood, he takes LSD and other drugs. To be happy while taking drugs, he gives away his brain and his wisdom, leaving himself with nothing but ignorance. And because his ignorance will not let him sleep, to make it happy he must take sleeping pills and intoxicants. To make his sleep happy, he either commits suicide or murders others. This is the drama of the arts. These are the sexual games of the arts. And this is how they end. This is where these kinds of happiness lead us.

To make himself truly happy, man must search for wisdom and clear his heart, dispelling the darkness of the lack of wisdom in his heart. While he is dispelling the darkness, he will face many kinds of suffering and opposition from the five elements. This opposition must be overcome with faith, certitude, and determination. In order to bear the sorrow, man needs patience, tolerance, forbearance, inner patience, contentment, and trust in God; he needs to give all praise only to God. He needs the compassion of God, and he needs to give all responsibility to God. He must fight the opposition with faith and wisdom. He must fight the enemies within his own body.

If he overcomes these enemies with the weapons of wisdom, it will result in victory in the world and happiness in his life. The blissful song of *gnānam,* the music of *gnānam,* will end man's suffering and sorrows. Those who have wisdom should think a little about what was just said. If they understand, they will have peace in life.

### 761.

In the desert there is a certain kind of tree which does not have leaves, and it would be useless for a man to expect it to give him shade.

Similarly, the tree known as man's desire and mind has neither leaves nor fruit to give him protection and sustenance; therefore it is of no benefit to him. If he sits beneath mind and desire hoping to rest in their shade, everything that comes to him will bring suffering. With wisdom, man must realize that this is a useless, impermanent tree; he must leave it, go to the *Katpaha Virudcham,* the tree of divine knowledge, and embrace the One of limitless grace, saying, "*Lā ilāha illallāhu:* But for Allah, there is nothing; You are Allah."

If you do this, you will receive what you want. He will comfort you and give you peace. If you realize this, establish this state, and fasten your heart on that point, you will never want for anything more.

### 762.

The sheikh said: Son, if your own back itches, you should not go to scratch someone else's back. If you see a donkey scratching itself on a broken wall, you should not go and scratch its back. If you think, "Ah, the back of that donkey is itching," and rush over to help, it will kick you with its hind legs. It will knock out your teeth and break your arm.

The wisdom of some people is like that. Instead of trying to correct their own faults and reform themselves, they approach others, trying to share in their problems and advise them.

This is what the meditation, prayers, and duties of some people are like. It is an act of ignorance to try to correct the faults of another without properly correcting your own faults. It is like taking the donkey's itch onto yourself and being kicked by the donkey. It is like picking up an ax by the wayside and dropping it on your own foot.

Use wisdom in every one of your actions. Correct your own mind and take what is corrected to God. Then others will look at you and correct themselves.

### 763.

Son, the learning of religions, races, and philosophies is like the learning of the parrot. The human parrots learn about 'my religion', 'my race', 'my philosophy' in the same way that the parrot learns to speak. Destruction comes from the language, fanaticism, religions, and philosophies that they learn. The learning from these philosophies destroys the man, his birth, and the truth of his heart. Because he does not understand the truth, his unity and wisdom are destroyed.

When the parrot is left to guard the house and a cat or a thief comes and catches it, the parrot forgets all that it learned and makes its original squeaking sound, "Ki, ki, ki." When the Angel of Death finally comes to the ones who learn these races and religions, they start shouting, *"Aiyō, aiyō,"* their original cry. At that time they do not remember what they learned or anything about God. All they can remember is to say, *"Aiyō."* Humans who learn in this way will be in this state. This is not wisdom.

There is a language that came from the original God. That is the language of truth, wisdom, God's qualities, and His unity. This language gives peace and equality. If you learn this language and if you keep God to guard your house, He will be your protection. God's protection cannot be beaten by any thief. Even the one who comes to steal will receive peace from this Guard. That thief will not steal anymore. Instead, he will find peace and equality. It would be good to learn this original learning.

### 764.

Son, when you go on a journey, if you take with you only the wealth of Allah, that wealth will never diminish, no matter where you go. Allah's wealth of grace, the wealth of the wisdom of divine knowledge, and the perfect plenitude of the hereafter will be yours. No robber, no illusion, no one and nothing can steal that treasure, and no harm will ever come to you.

Son, take this wealth as your sustenance in this world and the next. It will not burden your life, it will eliminate suffering in your mind, and you will have no wants in life. To your wisdom, to prayer, to your soul, and to everything, this is the most essential thing.

765.

The sheikh said: In the past, many meanings were revealed in the *Purānas,* the scriptural epics from the Asian continent. It was said that heavenly beings showered the great ones with flowers, and the flowers fell like rain. The rain of flowers was written about in the *Purānas* and in the recorded histories of the Asian continent. In Africa, America, Europe, and Australia, as well as in Asia and the other continents, that same rain of flowers is falling even now, on both good and bad people.

What falls from the heavens is now called snow. This shows the difference between the way people thought in those days and the way they think now. Then they said rain fell like flowers, but now we call it snow. It is falling on both the good and the bad, and it is very beautiful. When wisdom comes, you will know the explanation. Without wisdom, it will only be a story or a history.

In some of the old stories, they had snakes for gods. In others a half-moon was depicted as resting on the head of the god Shiva, and the people of that time were devotees of Shiva and trusted him. On the Asian continent, this is still the case. According to the *Purānas,* the half-moon was a sign that Shiva was a special god to all the worlds. But when we consider this explanation now that science has already gone beyond the moon, it can be concluded that science has therefore gone beyond Shiva. Since the moon is said to be above Shiva's head, the scientists have therefore transcended Shiva as well as the *Purānas.* The scientists have reached the stage where all the ancient stories have been termed false. They can be accepted only as stories; modern scientists do not accept them as truth. Why? Because they have gone beyond them.

You must realize this and examine it. However, no matter in

what world you exist, if you analyze your own story, you will understand that there are many worlds within you. When you understand your story and the story of truth which is God's story, when you understand what constitutes lack of wisdom, false wisdom, scientific wisdom, and true wisdom, and when the explanation of wisdom comes to you, you will see only God. Nothing else. Nothing else is real; you will see only the power of God.

If you cut the atom of creation, you will see the power of God which continually eludes and surpasses our wisdom. That is the story which will unfold endlessly until we surrender.

You must analyze with the seven levels of consciousness: feeling, awareness, intellect, judgment, subtle wisdom, divine analytic wisdom, and divine luminous wisdom. When you finally look with that resplendent divine luminous wisdom, you will see the one power and nothing else. Anything else that appears and that changes will not be accepted within the description of God. Realize this, search for wisdom, and look into your own story. Your story is a good story.

### 766.

The sheikh gives an example: Son, a man raised a donkey and asked it to do some work. The donkey agreed. When they went on their first journey, the man put one log on the donkey's back. The next time he put two; the time after that, he put four; and finally, on the last trip, he loaded ten logs onto the donkey's back.

They were crossing a desert, and after a while the donkey could walk no further. When the man tried to force him, the donkey said, "I cannot carry this load. You must either carry half the load or throw half of it away. I can carry only half this much." But the man insisted that the donkey carry it all. The donkey refused to move, and there they remained until a hyena came along and killed them both.

Like this, man brings up the donkey known as the mind and loads onto it the burden of the world: the sixty-four arts and sexual games, land, gold, women, lust, hatred, miserliness, greed, fanaticism, envy, selfishness, titles, status, praise, wife, children, property, attachments, and the four hundred trillion, ten thousand mantras, tricks, and miracles. He bundles them up and loads them onto the donkey of the mind, then sets out to make his journey to God.

On that journey he comes across the desert of *māyā*, of illusion, where nothing grows. He and the donkey of the mind fall down, unable to take another step. While they are weeping in the torpor of darkness, suffering from hunger, illness, and old age, and gloating over their gathered possessions, wailing, "Mine! Mine! How can I let go of this?" the Angel of Death comes to take the man, and hell captures his mind. This is the state in which he dies.

Realizing this, men of wisdom must not raise the donkey of the mind and load it with worldly illusions. Give the mind wisdom and God's qualities, show it patience and compassion, soothe it, perform God's actions, and travel on the path of peacefulness. Then the journey to God can be completed in a peaceful way.

767.

A cobra, gazing at a frog, said, "My precious and beloved friend, you are so beautiful to my eyes. Your body and your shape are gorgeous! Your legs are long, your stomach is white, your hands and your feet are delicately shaped. Of all those I have seen, I have never seen anyone as lovely as you! I have never seen anyone who can jump better than you. Come here. Come close. I need to kiss you, even if only once in my life. I want to embrace your beauty. Come out of the water." This is how the cobra wooed the frog.

The praise went right to the frog's head. "Ah! There really is no one in the world as beautiful as I am!" And with two or three hops it left the water and came to the shore. Eagerly, it leaped toward the snake.

The snake was very pleased. It said, "Ah, how beautiful you are. Ah! Stretch out your legs, let me see. Stretch out your hands. Oh! Turn over a little. Turn over on your back. I want to see the beauty of your stomach." The frog turned over. "Ahahaha!" said the snake. "How beautiful you are. God, who created you and me, created us both so perfectly, and He invited you to come to me." And then, "Pop!" it swallowed the frog.

At the moment it was caught, the frog was thinking, "I was listening to his beautiful speech, I was deceived by his flattery, and now my life is in danger!" This is what the frog thought in its dying moments, while it was on its way into the belly of the snake.

★

The sheikh explains: Disregarding God's praise, man spends his life gathering all the praise of the world—titles, status, gold, wealth, house, property, and miracles. Because he has desire for worldly praise, he has the arrogant notion that there is no one in the world greater than he. He even claims to be God, saying, "There is no other god; I am the one who creates and protects." He thinks that the whole world is under his control.

While he is in this state of arrogance, his senses flatter him. "Oh, there is no one as beautiful as you. What titles you have! How the beauty of your heart and face shine! Your actions and conduct are incomparable, your charity is praiseworthy, and your miracles are glorious." His mind and the five-headed cobra of his senses invite him closer. "Look at me, look at my beauty! Come closer, my beloved, my own born, my friend. Come and take the prizes we have brought for you."

They bring him the occult energies of the world and all the illusory, glittering flowers. The praise goes right to man's head, and as he moves closer to take the gifts, the mind and his senses grab him. They swallow him little by little, day after day. It is then that he realizes his plight. At the point of death he cries out, "Oh, where is my gold, my wealth, my status, my title!" Moment by moment, more and more illnesses torment him. All the demons and ghosts that he raised within himself begin to chew on him and eat him. He cries and howls.

Finally, the Angel of Death arrives. "Oh praised one! Where is all your honor, strength, and wealth now? What you nurtured is eating you. They are all waiting for you. Come, we will go to them." Then the Angel of Death carries him to hell, according to God's judgment. Whatever he raised within himself, whatever he thought was great and praiseworthy, he will find in hell in the form of evil worms, insects, and poisons which will devour him.

Son, you must realize this and avoid being entangled by flattery. You must throw away with wisdom whatever comes in this form and make God alone your wealth. Acquire His wisdom as your wisdom and His qualities as your qualities. Pay obeisance at His feet. Praise Him. Kill your pride. That will grant you limitless wealth and undiminishing life.

## 768.

The *kāmil sheikh* speaks: Son, there are two sections in the heart—the jealous dog of desire and the inner heart which contains the light of Allah. One section is the *qalbullāh,* the heart of

Allah, and the other is the *kalu balla,* the black dog of worldly desire. A dog's tongue always hangs out in desire, "Aahah." Have you not seen the difference between the two sections? With wisdom, dispel the dog of desire and open the light of Allah in your heart. There you will see His qualities, His actions, and His kingdom.

### 769.

If you split anything with wisdom and look, you will see an atom. If you split the atom, there will be a light. If you open the light, you will see your original human form. If you open the original human form, you will see Allah's benevolence. If you open Allah's benevolence, His kingdom will be seen. If you open His kingdom, you will see His justice. If you open His justice, you will see Allah ruling within that justice. If you open the state in which Allah dispenses justice, His duties will be evident. If you see this and carry out His duties and actions, you will receive the wealth of the three worlds. If you understand this, it will benefit you.

### 770.

The sheikh said: Son, love is something that brings out many different kinds of actions. It is all called love. If a poisonous scorpion is going to show love, it will embrace you and sting you with its tail. That is its love. What will the love of a scorpion do? It will make you writhe in pain and lose consciousness; it will bring you to a state near death.

But if the love of a wise sheikh, a wise person, a man old in wisdom, one well versed in wisdom, sees something wrong in you and stings you with love born of wisdom, there is no poison in it. It contains medicine for the soul, medicine that will dispel torpor and give you clarity, medicine that will dispel disease and give you happiness. It will give you explanations, peace, and tranquillity. But you will not understand this until later.

All the other kinds of love and attachments could be poisonous either immediately or after some time. Man has millions of animal qualities, poisonous qualities, and qualities of attachment. Whatever love he gives with any of these qualities will ultimately bring you suffering. But the love of a true sheikh is not like that; it is of a different kind. Realize this and understand which kind of love you need.

337

## 771.

Son, when a cat is happy or hungry, what will it do to a rat? It will try to catch it, and when it succeeds it will be very happy. Its happiness is to hit the rat with one paw and then with the other, and, when the rat tries to run away, to catch it in its mouth. Without killing it altogether, the cat torments the rat, little by little. This is joy for a cat; this is the kind of love a cat shows to a rat. But to a rat, it is torture. Finally, the cat kills and eats the rat.

Like this, the happiness of an ignorant person, the happiness of an arrogant person, the happiness of one who has racial and religious bigotry, and the happiness of one who is full of the 'I' will be dangerous to people who have faith and trust in God. We must avoid such people in whatever way we can. They may show love for selfish reasons, but if you believe them and follow them, you will suffer like a rat. Be careful and escape.

## 772.

A dog shows love through gratitude. It wags its tail and wiggles its body. But whatever it might wiggle, its ultimate love is to lick your lips, chin, nose, and mouth. It tries to put its tongue inside your mouth. This is how it kisses. This is the way a dog shows love.

But what kind of love is it? We must think. It is not real love. The food for which it is always searching is inside your mouth. Your mouth has the stench of blood, decay, and saliva. The dog seeks the mouth because it has a desire for bad odors. No matter how much gratitude it has, its love is drawn to evil odors. It licks your feet and hands because they too have that smell. If there is a sore, it licks it. Think about this with wisdom.

Do not give your heart to the love shown by illusion, mind, or the dog of desire. Do not let them lick your heart, nose, mouth, hands, or feet. They show love by drinking blood. The love of desire and mind is selfish love, a love that can ruin you.

If the germs, poison, and acid in the mouth of a dog go into your mouth, they will create diseases. Like that, if desire, the monkey mind, and evil qualities show love to you, do not give them your heart.

The dog of desire shows love to you because of the stench of the worldly things within you: the illusion of *māyā,* the sores of hell, blood, saliva, insects, worms, sexual games, sexual arts, and

338

many more. Analyze and look at this with divine wisdom. There are millions of germs and acid in the saliva of a dog; it eats rotten food and feces. If you allow a dog to lick you on the face, you will become diseased. Day by day your health will be affected, and cancer may develop in your body.

Mind and the dog of desire have the kinds of viruses, cells, insects, and worms that destroy the good in your life and create the disease of karma. Under the guise of love and gratitude, they will feed you with these things, turning you into a dog that eats all the discards of *māyā*. Do not allow your heart to be licked by either the outside dog or by the dog of desire within you.

773.

A man asked a pond, "O pond, who are you? Have you realized yourself?"

The pond said, "Fool, don't you know me? I am the water. I am the chieftain of the whole place. I have all kinds of lives within me. Big creations like crocodiles, and all the little fish and crabs are dependent on me." The pond spoke to him only of its own pride and honor.

Similarly, within man there are four hundred trillion, ten thousand occult energies, the knowledge of the arts, sexual games, gold, gems, land, women, demons, ghosts, poisonous qualities, the eighteen thousand worlds, and the shadows of all the creations in the world. Within man there are countless sinful thoughts and desires, animal qualities, karmic qualities, the differences of the 'I' and the 'you', racial and religious differences, arrogance, karma, *māyā,* intoxicants, lust, theft, murder, falsehood, hatred, miserliness, fanaticism, and envy, as well as pride in titles, status, beauty, and praise. If a sheikh says, "Realize yourself. Know who you are," man will know only his university learning, the visions of the world, and the pride within himself, the pride that no one is greater than he. "Fool!" he will reply. "Don't you know that I know everything!" There are many so-called gurus who talk like this.

But a true sheikh must teach a man with love and wisdom. Daily he must teach his own qualities, his conduct, his duties and actions, and his modesty, reserve, sincerity, and fear of wrongdoing, helping him to understand God's qualities and actions. Dispelling all the bad qualities that are within the disciple and implanting the qualities of Allah within him, the sheikh must make him realize that Allah alone is the mercy and compassion of all the universes and that Allah alone is worthy of praise. The sheikh will teach him of Allah, who is the wisdom within wisdom. With this wisdom, he will help the disciple realize himself and the light within the light which is within him. The sheikh will show him that everything and everyone is contained within that resplendence.

All praise and praising are to Him alone. He is the *Rahmat,* the Benevolence, the One of limitless grace and incomparable love, the One who gives the undiminishing wealth of grace. A perfected man of wisdom would teach his student in this way. That is called wisdom.

### 774.

When gas escapes through the mouth, it does not trouble anyone. But when it comes out through the anus, it can make a man hold his nose and run away, unable to bear the offensive odor.

Like this, man has learned many kinds of knowledge, and he has gathered worldly titles as the honor in his life. There are many learned people who exhibit this kind of learning. They will preach their knowledge to the world and gather praise, titles, and honors. Promising liberation for the soul, they will perform many miracles. They will bend the sky into a bow, weave sand into rope, walk on water or on fire, and fly in the sky. They will even change from one body to another. But it will be very difficult for them to control their minds, to correct their actions, desires, attachments, and intellects, and to know themselves and be still. Their preaching is for the world. They will not know anything within themselves.

Those with this state of intelligence will give off a foul odor to the nose of wisdom, certitude of faith, divine knowledge, and the divine analytic wisdom of the *Qutb (Ral.).* Understand this. The actions, conduct, behavior, and love that comes from the mouth of wisdom will show only Allah and His qualities. Advice that is bountiful, that gives freedom for the soul, is a sign of grace. It is the wealth of the world of the souls, this world, and the next. With wisdom you must try to obtain it.

### 775.

Son, if a man must travel through a jungle, he needs certitude, determination, faith in God, and the courage to handle any problems that may arise. He must also take a light to shine in front of him so that he can avoid danger and accidents. Only if the light precedes him will he know what lies ahead. If there is no light, man will be subject to attack from beasts on all sides. He will become prey to the animals that can see in the night, animals that live and search for their prey in darkness. One who is accustomed to daylight must have a path and a light when he makes a night journey. Only if he has a light can he make it through the jungle. Is this not so?

Similarly, if a man wants to establish his connection with God, truth, grace, and the soul, he must cross through the darkness of birth, transcend the connection to his karmic birth, travel through the beasts of arrogance, transcend the torpor of *māyā,* go through the forces of birth *(tārahan, singhan, sūran,* which are the three sons of *māyā),* transcend the demon of the mind which takes many millions of forms, and transcend *indira jālam, māyā jālam,* and *mahēndira jālam,* the magic tricks of illusion which extend up to the very heavens. He must transcend many forces and energies. He must transcend arrogance, karma, *māyā, tārahan, singhan, sūran,* lust, hatred, miserliness, greed, fanaticism, envy, intoxicants, obsession, theft, murder, and falsehood. He must transcend these seventeen *purānas* and overcome them all.

In order to transcend these *purānas* of darkness, he must focus a light before him. What is the light? It is the light of a true Sufi sheikh, the wisdom of the grace of a good sheikh. The sheikh should be impressed within you as truth. You must be the case for the flashlight, the grace of the sheikh will be the battery, wisdom will be the light, and true faith will be the switch. When you switch on the light and go along the path, holding it before you, you will be able to see everything. All the animals and all that dwells in the darkness will run away, and then you can proceed without danger. The light will have to precede you and you will have to follow behind because you are the case—there is something within you. If you try to go before the light, you will fall victim in the darkness to all the animals and they will devour you. Think of this.

Similarly, no matter what you say, where you look, or what thoughts exist within you, the vision which is the light of the sheikh must develop within you. The speech of the sheikh must be within you, the words of the sheikh must develop within you—the entire state of the sheikh must be within you. Once that state is established, you will not be the one who looks; you will be the case, and he will be the light. If you fail to benefit from the light, you will be like firewood devoured by fire. All your knowledge and all your acquired learning will be burnt up completely. You must think of this.

Imitation truth will not give any benefit. Neither can you use truth for the sake of your own vanity. You cannot use truth for selfish purposes, you cannot use truth in order to obtain flattery, you cannot use truth for the sake of the ego.

Truth cannot be used for any of these things. If you try to use truth in the wrong way, it will be like trying to drink water from a mirage: a mirage will never quench your thirst. Your life will be wasted. If you try to use the truth for any attachment other than God, it will not benefit you. You will see only differences. Justice and truth will not be where attachments are. You must understand this with your wisdom.

### 776.

The eyes of a man deceive him. If your mind deceives you because of the visions seen by your eyes and the learning you acquire from books, you should not find fault with the sheikh. You allowed your mind to deceive you. You did not use your wisdom; you did not use the words of the sheikh to analyze what you experienced.

With wisdom, you must recognize the difference between what you learn from books and what you learn from the sheikh. You might consider your earlier book learning to be wisdom. But is there not a difference between sugar and honey? Is there not a difference between the light of the sun and the light of a candle?

If you clarify your experiences with wisdom, you will find that the teachings of the sheikh are honey, while all your previous learning is only sugar; you will find that the light of the learning from the sheikh is like sunlight, while your book learning is only like candlelight.

With faith, certitude, and determination, you must take in the words of the sheikh and expand your wisdom. If you fail to do it in this way, you must not find fault with the sheikh for what befalls you tomorrow. Every child who comes to the sheikh must think about this carefully.

A blind man and a deaf man went together to see a drama. The deaf man described what he saw to the blind man. The blind man communicated to the deaf man what he heard.

The deaf man could see the movements, the dancing, and the makeup very well. He said, "Oh, how beautiful the acting is! How incredible the dancing is! The costumes and makeup are marvellous!" He raved and raved about what he saw.

The blind man said, "You fool, what are you talking about? No one is dancing. Can you not hear the beautiful singing? How sweetly she sings."

The blind man and the deaf man fought over this and separated, thereby losing each other's help.

★

The people on the stage of the world see the acting of the various races and religions. Enchanted by these worldly religions, the man who has blind wisdom says, "What joy, what beauty, what sweetness!" There is no one to show him the path to God because he does not have the eye of wisdom. The man whose wisdom is deaf looks at the acting, the drama, the dancing, the glamor of the makeup and costumes, and the beauty of the statues and the arts. He is enamored with worldly beauty, but deaf to the subtle sounds of truth, the words of wise men, discourses about *gnānam,* and God's voice.

Those separated from God, justice, and truth lose each other's help; they lose unity, tolerance, and peacefulness. There are many people in the world with this kind of deafness and blindness. Do not spend your time in the worldly dramas, becoming blind to the beauty of God's truth and deaf to His voice of truth.

## 778.

A group of people were standing in a field, arguing. The sheikh passed by and asked them about their dispute. The people said they were trying to decide what crop would grow best on that particular plot of land. They asked him for advice. Four of the men were quite advanced in soil research, and these four men spoke in four different languages.

One man said, "We must plant *kurrakan* on this land." The other man said, "No, *kevor* will grow better." The third man said,

"I disagree. Red millet will do much better on this land." The fourth man said, "*Kepai* is good."

The wise man said, "All four of you must bring what you want to plant so that I can see it." When they brought the seeds, they saw that the seeds were all the same. "You spoke about the same thing," the sheikh said. "Only the names you gave to it and the languages you spoke were different."

★

Like this, all the races in the world belong to one race, the human race. God is also one. He has no form or shape. He is a power. To this power, they give different names in different languages. They carry out different rituals, reciting, "My God, your God."

The children of one father and mother have separated into millions of divisions, and they have separated the one God into many, giving millions of forms to One who has no form. The One who has no equal, the One who is present in all lives, has been parcelled into 'my God', into 'my property and yours', 'mine is right, yours is wrong'. The people fight among themselves and pray to God in the way they want, disrupting the unity of the human race. They have lost the qualities, actions, and conduct of God. This kind of fighting, dissension, sin, and falsehood are flourishing in the world today.

People use the word God, but they do not know that He is one power and that the only place in which He will grow is truth. The God spoken of in all the different languages is the same God. If wisdom grows within, if men stop fighting and go to a sheikh to discover the meaning of God, he will tell them the true point. And when the sheikh asks them to speak of what they believe, each will be speaking of the same primal treasure.

The sheikh will then tell them, "This treasure must be grown within your *qalb*, your inner heart. Plow the *qalb* and prepare the soil. Make it clean."

Then the One without equal or form should be planted in every *qalb*. If you plant this seed and if the crop grows, you can dispel the poverty and illness of all the souls in this world. Then all can live in unity as one race, praying to one God. If you obtain this wisdom, you will receive its benefits, and the kingdom of heaven will be yours.

344

There was a very tiny hole in the ground. A cat, a dog, a rat, a fox, a lion, a tiger, a bull, a goat, and a monkey got together and held a meeting to discover the depth of the hole. "It seems very deep," they said. "It's a small hole but it looks very deep. What can its dimensions be?"

The tiger had the longest tail, so he put his tail into the hole. The tiger said, "It is as deep as my tail is long." Then the lion stuck in his tail and said, "You're crazy. It is only as deep as my tail." The monkey put in his tail. "No, it is as deep as my tail." The bull said the same thing when he put his tail into the hole. Each animal lowered his tail into the hole. The fox said, "Oh! It is only this deep. It's not a big thing." The dog said, "This is only a small hole, no deeper than my tail." The cat concluded, "This is not a deep hole." The rat exclaimed, "Everything you said was a lie! It is only as deep as my tail." Thus all came to their own conclusions and fell to quarreling.

It came to such a state that they all set out to catch and eat each other. Each animal became food for the stomach of another, and the meeting was over.

★

With your ignorance, you try to measure divine knowledge. With your worldly knowledge, book knowledge, and scientific knowledge, with your ignorance and everything else you have learned, you try to measure the truth and wisdom of the limitless ocean of the divine knowledge of grace, which is very, very subtle and exists as wisdom within wisdom and truth within truth. You say, "I am great. What you said is a lie. What I said is right." This is like animals trying to measure a deep hole with their limited tails.

Allah alone knows the ocean of divine knowledge. When man fights without this knowledge he causes only separation and destruction. It destroys racial unity, compassion, peace, and equality. It takes from man the qualities of God's actions, conduct, and behavior, and the qualities of modesty, reserve, sincerity, and the fear of wrongdoing. Finally, it ends in murder and sin. The one race is split into many races and languages. The one God is split into millions of gods; division and antagonism develop. Thus the human race moves toward hell.

We must analyze with wisdom and realize that there is one God and one religion. This will give peace and equality to all lives, and we will know the light and beauty of human life. Grace and divine knowledge are known only to Allah. All praise belongs only to Him. No one else can complete the learning of that divine knowledge. What we have learned is like a handful of earth compared to the whole world of what we have not learned.

### 780.

The sheikh said: Any seed we observe has two sections. Between the two is a point, the atom of the inner point, from which growth takes place when the two sections open. This is the germinal point of the seed; this is what grows and blossoms and gives benefit.

Within the seed known as man, it is the same. If a man really wants to grow and develop, the two sides of mind and desire must open out. It is only when mind and desire are opened that the point will be revealed. That point is the point of the letter *alif* signifying one God. That is what must grow; that is the light. And once it grows, mind and desire will die.

We must reflect on this. The two sections of a seed are covered by an external skin which must split apart in order for the seed to grow. The external skin represents the selfishness of the body, which is the first thing that must be obliterated. Secondly, mind and desire must open, and the light of Allah, the germinal point, must grow. That is true man. It is the emergence of this light that is beneficial. If it grows, physical man is destroyed, the section called the world is destroyed, and there is only light. In that state, God is within man and man is within God. You must understand this. This is the state of divine wisdom in which you die within God.

### 781.

The ocean surrounds and holds the entire world, but the ocean really has no shore. God's grace is the shore. There is a song which describes God:

> The Protector who
> With His grace
> Created the ocean
> With no shore.

In each place, the ocean develops its own shore.

What is the intention of the water when it comes crashing onto the beach? When it swells, the wave says, "When I beat against the land, I will destroy the world. I will destroy those who eat my creations." At its crest it rumbles, "They are my enemies. Arrgh!" As it approaches the beach, it rolls in with a hissing sound, "Huuu." It carries in sand, leaves it on the shore, and silently returns to the ocean. What was its intention? It said, "I will destroy the world." But because God's grace is there as the protection, the sand the wave brings builds up the shore. When the waves see God, their force and their thoughts of destruction dissipate, and when they leave, the shore has been strengthened.

Similarly, there is an ocean of *māyā,* an ocean of illusion, around the inner heart of man. In this ocean, there are countless thoughts, desires, attachments, enchantments, tricks, and four hundred trillion, ten thousand occult miracles. There are gold, women, the feeling of 'mine' and 'yours', racial, religious, and scriptural differences, and differences in learning, worship, and color. Pride, ignorance, selfishness, greed, jealousy, falsehood, arrogance, karma, illusion, and craving are also there. All these grow in the ocean of *māyā.* The waves which come from this ocean try to break man's mind and life in order to overthrow truth, prayer, faith, trust, patience, tolerance, peace, inner patience, contentment, trust in God, and praise to God.

In the way God subdues the ocean, you must stand with certitude, always strengthening your faith in God. Do not give up determination when suffering comes. Holding Allah in front of you, stand fast. All the mind-waves of the ocean of *māyā* and the waves of its animal qualities will lose their force and their qualities and finally recede. Keep faith, certitude, and determination as your protection. Then, even if the whole world comes rolling toward you, nothing will be able to destroy you.

### 782.

A tiger was sitting alone in a cave. A goat passed by, looked in, and said, "O lord, are you not well?"

The tiger replied, "I am very ill. Tell everyone to visit me, and then I will get well very quickly. Tell them to come here to help me!" The goat reported the news to the other animals and then returned to help the tiger. The tiger was very hungry; so it killed the goat, drank its blood, and ate its liver. When the other animals entered the cave to visit the tiger, they met with the same fate.

Finally, a cunning fox came to the cave. It stood outside and asked, "Master, are you ill?"

The tiger replied, "Brother, I am very ill. Come inside and help me."

"You are the king, we are the subjects," the fox said. "We must be respectful and keep our distance. That is the way to show the respect due to a king. I will pray to God for your good health."

The tiger begged and begged the fox to come in, but the fox was adamant, "The ones who went in to see you never came out, so I will stay. The goat that helped you first is now helping you from inside your stomach. At least I will escape!" He ran away.

"Oh, you cunning fox!" the tiger growled.

★

Like this, son, desire, mind, selfishness, arrogance, pride, and praise are tigers within the cave of the body. They are the qualities that separate man from God. When the light of wisdom and truth shines forth these tigers hide in their caves and turn to the lower three levels of consciousness (feeling, awareness, and intellect) for help. These qualities cry out, praising man and his good qualities and begging for help. If man heeds the praise and pleading of these bad qualities and goes to help them, his plight will be the same as that of the goat which went to help the tiger. If, while trying to help these ignorant, arrogant Bengal tigers, you enter the caves of illusion, you will never return. One who enters the darkness of the mind through the gateway of selfishness will never return.

Understanding this with wisdom and analyzing it with analytic wisdom, a man must cleverly escape from the evil qualities. You must know that those who went into the four hundred trillion, ten thousand occult energies, the cravings of *māyā,* and the scriptures never came back. They were devoured.

One who searches for God and the truth, one who has the absolute faith called *īmān,* must try to escape like the fox. A Sufi is one who escapes and then surrenders to Allah, saying, "*Lā ilāha illallāhu,* there is no one other than You; You are Allah." His speech, actions, and conduct will be Allah's, and no matter what happens, he will say, "*Al-hamdu lillāh,* all praise is to God." Before he begins anything, he will say, "*Bismillāhir-Rahmānir-Rahīm,* in the name of God, Most Merciful, Most Compassionate." Whatever he takes in, he will say, "*Illallāhu.* You are Allah." One in this state knows Allah.

## 783.

In the forest, four buffaloes lived together as good friends. A fox saw them and thought greedily, "How fat and healthy they are. The meat of even one of those buffaloes would be enough to feed me for three months, and all four would be enough for a whole year. Now, how can I kill them? I must trick my master, the lion, into killing them for me."

The fox hurried to the lion. He wailed, "Oh, master!" and began to cry and roll around on the ground as if unable to continue.

Surprised, the lion asked, "What is the matter? Why are you crying?"

"Oh, master," the fox said, "I cannot bear to think of it! My whole body is trembling. There are four buffaloes who claim they are the kings of the jungle, and I just cannot bear to hear them say such a thing when you are our sovereign. They have captured the whole jungle. No one can go near them. I shiver to think of them. They must be killed."

"Where are they? Show them to me," the lion demanded.

So the fox led the lion to where the buffaloes were grazing. When the lion saw the four of them together, he knew that he could not fight against them as long as they were united. The lion turned to the fox. "I need your help. You must separate them so that I can kill them."

"I will do my best," the fox said. "Now, as I go up to each buffalo, you must move so that you stand facing that particular buffalo." The lion agreed, and the fox hurried away.

The fox crept over to one of the buffaloes and quietly whispered into his ear, "Don't trust these other three buffaloes. They are trying to move away from you and leave you to that lion over there." And indeed, when the buffalo lifted his head, he saw the lion straight ahead. He believed the fox's story and separated himself from the other three. The fox then moved to each of the other buffaloes and said the same thing. In this way, he separated the four of them, and the lion was able to kill them easily, one by one. The fox was very happy to have gotten enough food for a whole year.

★

Although the children of Adam *(A.S.)* have been separated into four religions, they have only one God and one race. *Māyā,* satan, mind, desire, arrogance, falsehood, jealousy, selfishness, hatred, and

349

lust all came together into a dark, cunning form that separated the unity of the human race and handed it over to satan and the world, just as the fox tricked and separated the buffaloes. The four religions succumbed to the tricks of these dark forms and separated from one another. Finally, when they were separated, gold, women, miracles, and the Angel of Death came to capture them and drag them to hell.

Man must understand this and acquire God's qualities. Realizing that the children of Adam *(A.S.)* belong to one race and one family, and considering other lives as his own, he must show peace and equality to all. He must show patience and love and dispel their poverty and illness. Understanding his birthright, he must pray and surrender to the one God, the precious *Allāhu ta'ālā.*

That is the state in which he must find peace, equality, and victory. Otherwise, time, *māyā,* arrogance, and karma form in his body, enclosing him within mind and desire and killing him. Trust only in unity and Allah. That will be your undiminishing wealth.

784.

The sheikh said: Son, a cat lived in a fish market. He ate the leftover fish and their entrails, but he told the dogs and rats that he was a vegetarian. The world praised him for this. So one day the cat invited all the rats to come and eat whatever they wanted, and when the rats came, he ate them, too.

Like this, there are people in the market of the world who have all the world's sins and karma. They enjoy worldly pleasures and kill many lives. They have separated from God, compassion, and patience, yet they advertise, "I am with God. I am praying to God. I have His grace." For this, they receive titles and fame.

You must think with wisdom and know that the state of these people is like the state of the cat in the fish market. They are not merged with God. You must keep away from such people. Keep away from their actions and the market in which they live. Search for God and merge with Him.

Analyze with your wisdom and develop patience, inner patience, contentment, and trust in God. For what happens in the present, say, *"Al-hamdu lillāh,* all praise is to God." For what is to happen in the future, give the responsibility to God. Saying, *"Illallāhu,* You are Allah," surrender to God and receive the benevolence of His grace.

## 785.

Son, carefully raise a good horse to have good qualities and use it to ride on your journey. That will be good. Do not let the horse ride you, or you will meet with accidents and death.

Like that, O mankind, ride on the horse of your mind, guiding it along the good path. If you control the horse, you will avoid accidents and your life will turn out right. But if the horse of the mind rides you, it will lead you to many accidents and a terrible state. Knowing this, climb onto the horse, hold the reins properly, and direct it onto the right path. That will give you victory in your life.

## 786.

God has given you eyes. But do not follow your eyes everywhere they look. Your eyes go in all four directions and collect visions from far away. Stand where you are and assess with your analytic wisdom all that your eyes see. Distinguish right from wrong, take the good things, and discard the bad. You must focus your attention and examine the work your eyes are doing. For if you act according to what your eyes see, you will meet with accidents and your life will end in disaster.

## 787.

My son, there are different types of people in the world. Each does things differently. They may meditate under trees, in caves, on mountains, at intersections, in public buildings, in churches, or in temples. Some say, "I have seen God and I pray to Him." Others say, "I have given up the land and all my attachments to the world, to my wife, property, and possessions. Now I am on the path to God." But although they claim this exalted state, hunger, old age, illness, and death have not left them. Hunger says, "I have never left you, not even for a day, and you have never left me, either."

My son! You are trying to deceive the world. Give up this deception and realize that you are only deceiving yourself. If you realize that by continuing this deception you will be liable to punishment by God, you will cut your attachments. Until then, no matter where you sit and meditate, you will be deceiving yourself.

Open your heart and give all responsibility to God. Give your house to Him and enter His house. Give your comforts and your qualities to Him and take His comforts and qualities. Give your wealth to Him and take His wealth. Take what belongs to Him and die in Him.

If you pray to Him in this state, you will be victorious. Your world and everything you have belongs to Allah, and your duty is to give Allah's property back to Allah. Then Allah will become your property. This is what you have to understand. You must return what was given to you by Allah. Otherwise on the Day of Judgment, it will be revealed that you were deceiving yourself and the world. Understand this.

*Āmīn*, may this intention be fulfilled. *Al-hamdu lillāh*, all praise is to God.

## 788.

My son, the seven base cravings are always trying to steal the things of the world. The mind and desire enjoy these stolen goods. They are the thieves within your body. Everything they bring is forbidden. Take the whip of *īmān*, the whip of absolute faith, and with the hand of the explaining wisdom of the *Qutbiyyat*, beat these thieves and teach them the difference between *harām* and *halāl*, what is forbidden and what is permissible. With wisdom, cut off the hands of the base cravings. Throw back to the world everything they bring. Teach them *sabūr*, inner patience. Make them tie the stone of *shakūr*, or contentment, to their stomachs and tell them to give all praise to Allah. Tell them to surrender to Allah whatever is to happen next, and to eat the food of Allah's love.

## 789.

Do not wage war to capture lands. That is not the reason you came to this world.

God has given you a beautiful kingdom within. He has given you His beauty and His wealth. But there is a war within you. Satan's arrogance, karma, and *māyā*, the three sons of *māyā* called *tārahan, singhan,* and *sūran,* as well as obsession, hatred, miserliness, attachment, fanaticism, envy, intoxicants, lust, theft, murder, and falsehood are the seventeen *purānas,* the seventeen scriptures which are ruled by demons and ghosts. They are trying to capture the pure kingdom within you, the eighteenth world of pure Islam, pure prayer to God, pure peace and tranquillity, pure unity, pure thoughts, and God's pure qualities. They are eating and destroying everything pure. Wage war on the demons of religious differences.

This is the war you have to fight in shadow form within you. Miracles, cells, viruses, energies, the *indira jālam, mahēndira jālam, māyā jālam,* and mesmerism are performing tricks within you in their shadow forms in order to deceive you and destroy God and the kingdom of God.

With the *Qutbiyyat's* hand of grace, hold the sword of firm certitude and the discus of faith and determination in Allah and cut off the magic tricks of these evil forces. Attack and defeat those who are tormenting you from within. Destroy and burn the forces within you that are disrupting the unity of the one race and trying to destroy the knowledge that God alone is God. With the power of God's qualities, you can defeat those forces.

### 790.

All of God's creations belong to the same group. Live for that one group. Because God belongs equally to all, you must be equal in truth and show that equality to everyone in your actions and conduct. Call them to a life of love, and with wisdom, teach them to have the absolute faith called *īmān.* Show them the way to reach Allah, to understand Allah as the One and only, and to receive His grace.

### 791.

Son, the blade of a knife must be made sharp so that you can use it. But do not test the sharpness on yourself or you may end up in the hospital.

Similarly, do not use the benefit of the praise and prayer you offer to God to gain worldly titles, fame, and praise for yourself. It would be like testing the blade of a sharp knife on yourself; you would end up in the hospital of hell. To pray is to surrender all responsibility to God.

### 792.

Son, look at an ant. When it knows there is sugarcane nearby, it searches for it. It finds the location by following the fragrance.

It does not go alone, but leads its whole tribe in one single line. This is unity.

Like this, discover the fragrance and the taste of Allah. The family of Adam *(A.S.)* is your family, and the whole human race belongs to it. Understand this. If you can do what an ant does, if you can lead your entire family to Allah in that kind of unity, you will discover the taste of Allah and acquire His qualities. Then you will not see any differences.

You are a man, are you not? You have analytic wisdom. The work that an ant without analytic wisdom can do should not be difficult for a man. Think of this and try to do it.

### 793.

Son, a camel is called the ship of the desert. If you want to journey across the desert, take a camel, for it can bear the heat and suffering. This ability has been given to the camel by God.

But do not beat it with your hastiness, uncontrollable anger, or the arrogance of the ego just because it walks too slowly. Nor should you become a camel and try to do the camel's work. You cannot walk across the desert. Your anger and hastiness would be hazardous to you.

With wisdom, you must acquire patience, inner patience, contentment, trust in God, and the quality of giving all praise to God. Acquire these qualities and conduct your life with them. This will give you peace and tranquillity.

### 794.

Son, do not try to swallow a banana, skin and all. You must peel it first, if you want to know the taste.

Similarly, there is a beautifully sweet fruit in your mind. You must peel off the skin of the mind and eat the sweetness of God. This is the state of true prayer. To fill yourself with that taste and appease the soul's hunger, acquiring peace and tranquillity, is the prayer of the heart. To pray is to accept Allah and keep Him in your heart as the complete treasure. To make hunger, illness, old age, and death non-existent is the exalted taste of real prayer.

### 795.

Do not write on water all the learning you have acquired. Even

354

before you lift your finger out of the water, the writing will have disappeared. Not a single word will remain.

In the same way, do not write what you have learned from the sheikh or from experience on the desire, arrogance, vanity, or selfishness of your mind. It would be like writing on water. There are waves, and the writing would be instantly erased.

But if you wish to learn with *īmān,* with the determination and certitude of absolute faith, then open your heart and write on the heart within the heart. With the hand of wisdom, write the words of your sheikh and the words of Allah on the plaque of the *Kalimah,* and it will be like writing etched on stone. Never in any age will it be erased. It will be a radiant light. That state will become the *'ilm,* the profound knowledge of the mirrored ocean of God's grace, of your *īmān.*

796.

When birds hatch their eggs or other animals give birth to their young, within half an hour the little ones stand up and begin to walk. Within half an hour of its birth, a calf staggers to its feet, searches for its mother, and starts to suck milk. Human babies, however, take many months to walk. Is this not so? We have seen this. What is the reason for this difference?

For these creatures, the world is not heavy. They are not carrying the weight of the world. Because they do not have the thoughts, the mind, and the connections to the world that man has, they get up from the earth immediately. The only quality they have is to accept with gratitude whatever food God gives them at whatever time He gives it. Though they are only animals, they do not carry the weight of mind, desire, or selfishness.

On the other hand, when a human child is born, it takes a year for it to begin to walk. Because it carries the weight of the earth, it is difficult for a child to get up. Before it can stand, it shows the positions and the qualities displayed by its father and mother during conception, the actions they performed and how they whispered. If the father and mother were on four legs, the child walks on four legs. When it does get up, it does so with a great deal of effort because of the avarice, desire, selfishness, and craving for the world which are in the mind. The wonder is that man, who is born so rare, is unable to do even what an animal does.

If he would think about this and cast off the weight of the

world, he would be able to rise up immediately and speak with God. And then, whenever God gave him anything, he would accept it with patience, inner patience, contentment, and trust, saying, "*Al-hamdu lillāh,* all praise belongs only to God."

797.

Son, when you plant a beautiful fruit tree which can bear delicious, sweet fruit, plant it with perfect purity of heart. Plant it in the name of God, *Bismillāhir-Rahmānir-Rahīm.* Intend it for Him and praise Him. Then it will grow with great subtlety and beauty, and one of its seeds will produce a thousand fruits.

But if you plant it with selfish thoughts, if you plant it only for yourself and your children, the growth of the tree will be stunted by ninety-nine percent, its yield will be reduced by ninety-nine percent, and its beauty will be diminished, too. What is planted with selfishness is *harām,* or forbidden, because in selfishness you are forgetting Allah. Food that is grown in forgetfulness of Allah is not permissible to those who are true believers.

When the seed is given to you, the benefit from that seed should be given to all the children of Adam *(A.S.).* When you plant it in the state of surrender to God, it becomes permissible for all of Allah's creations: birds, insects, cows, goats, men, angels, fairies, prophets, and saints.

Duty should be done in the state of surrender, not only when you are planting a tree, but always. This is how God does His duty, and this will be beneficial to you. *Āmīn.* Allah is the Ruler of all the universes. *Āmīn.*

798.

Son, *Allāhu ta'ālā Nāyan,* Almighty God, has given you the wisdom with which to analyze and understand that God has placed within the earth millions of varieties of soil. There are sands of many colors. There are desert areas and marshy areas, rocky soil and soft soil. There are places where the earth contains gold, salt, gems, mercury, oil, minerals, and lead. The earth always has an open and giving nature. You must never complain that the earth did not help you to grow a good crop.

With your wisdom, you must find out what will grow where. Saying, "*Al-hamdu lillāh,* all praise is to God," plant whatever has to be planted in the right place. If you do this, Allah's benevolence will make your crop flourish one hundred percent.

Without wisdom and an open heart, if you try to plant crops in just any soil, nothing will grow. This is not the fault of the earth; it is your fault. For if you had looked with wisdom, you would have known what to plant.

Correct your mind with wisdom. With surrender to Allah, find the right place and plant your seeds. Then if the gold, gems, oil, and other things within the earth, as well as the crops grown on its surface, are reaped in God's name, praising Him, it will be beneficial to you.

### 799.

Son, if you want a house that can be lived in for generation after generation, you must plan it well before you start building. First, you must consult an engineer and an architect. Next, you must get a survey map and a plan, estimate the expenditures, and engage a contractor and many workers. But even when a house is built with all that care, there is a time limit beyond which it cannot survive. It can last for only so long; it has a fate. This is the way it is. You build a house and prepare to live in it, but it is a house bound by an agreement as to its life span no matter how well you plan. Is this not so?

Therefore, since the soul will live eternally, you must strive to build a beautiful house for it, a house which is not subject to time or to external conditions. For this house, you are the engineer, you are the contractor, and you are the architect; you draw the plan and you set up the system. And when all the planning is completed, you are the one who must construct that house. You must build it alone; no one else can build it for you.

The materials you need for such a house are the qualities of God, the actions of God, the behavior of God, the duties of God, and the unselfishness with which God performs His duties. You must gather the three thousand beautiful and gracious qualities of God and build your house in the way that God performs His actions.

This house of meditation is not built with earth, fire, water, air, and ether. It is built with His light, His grace, His wisdom, His compassionate gaze, His thoughts, His intentions, and His prayer. If you build the house correctly, it cannot be destroyed by time or external conditions. Such a house will benefit you throughout all the ages; you will be able to live in it eternally. That will be the house of perfect purity in which you and God dwell in unity. Far, far better than building a house bound by time and external conditions is to build a beautiful, eternal house, a house of heaven in the kingdom of God, a house of prayer, a house of divine wisdom, a house for your soul, a house in which you will dwell forever.

If you build a house like that, it will receive the benefit of Allah's wealth in all three worlds: the world of the souls, this world, and the next. Tomorrow, on the Day of Judgment, Allah will give you the house you built. He will give you the benevolence of His grace. You will not want anything after that. Understand this, and build your house with God's qualities.

800.

The black and white skunk is very beautiful to the eyes, but the stench within the skunk is horrible. Its smell is so disgusting that you cannot be within three hundred feet of it.

In the same way, man may also look beautiful on the outside when he wears beautiful clothes and jewelry, or when he has money and property. But the stench of arrogance, karma, *māyā*, selfishness, anger, pride, jealousy, vengeance, deception, scheming, fanaticism, bigotry, and the other evil qualities within him is far worse than the smell of a skunk. When this odor emanates from man, Allah and His benevolence, good qualities, compassion, and truth will quickly fly away.

If man peels off and throws away the skin of external beauty which has such a repulsive odor, the resonance of Allah, His qualities, His fragrance, His actions, His unity, His peace, His equality, and His justice will come looking for him. Many lives will come to him in friendship, and he will be a cooling fragrance to the hearts of all God's creations. Cast away the external beauty which smells so awful inside, and acquire the inner beauty which is fragrant everywhere.

A man must strive to develop inner rather than outer beauty. A beautiful fragrance must exist on the inside, a fragrance which can attract and enthrall everyone. Inner beauty is God's beauty, God's love, God's compassion, and God's unselfish duty. If you can develop that beauty and fragrance within yourself, it will be good.

Son, have you seen the dangerous discoveries man has made in the world? Ultimately, the energies and forces he discovers will destroy him and all other lives.

*Allāhu ta'ālā Nāyan,* Almighty God, has given to man all the potentialities of the world of the souls, this world, and the kingdom of heaven. He has given him the inner secret and the outer secret of these worlds. Man is free to do what he wants, but it is important for him to discover and understand these secrets and all the potentialities.

Because God has given him wisdom, it is possible for man to discover and understand everything, but his intention must be for God. Giving all responsibility to God, he must use his discoveries to help the growth and prosperity of all lives. Rather than harming others, if man can use his knowledge to help the world—with devotion, faith, peace, equality, and unity—he will never cause any accidents or danger to anyone. One who discovers this will be wise and respected among men, a representative of God, and God will give him his due reward.

There are those who have made valuable discoveries recently, but how are they using their knowledge? First, they claim they can prove that there is no God. Second, they use energies and atomic rays to make bombs, rockets, missiles, and other deadly weapons which they use to murder people, destroy lands, and conquer and torture human life. With these weapons, they are trying to prove the strength and superiority of their own nations.

Some deny the existence of God and say that everything comes from nature. Did man come from nature? No. Men are born, they suffer from illness, and after some time they die. Their bodies are bound by a time agreement. But some have illnesses and some do not; some suffer and some do not. If it were all according to nature, all bodies would be the same, would they not?

There is a truth and a power above all. That power is God, who dwells beyond all our research. As we continue to cut into everything we research, that power is endlessly beyond it. Whoever understands this must believe in and have certitude in God and give Him the entire responsibility for everything that happens.

There are some things we can do, but there are things man cannot prevent. He cannot stop the rain, the lightning, a hurricane, an earthquake, a volcano, or a tornado. We must understand that these and similar things are controlled by that power of God.

Realizing this, we must trust in God and know that there is a difference between good and bad. We must realize that the suffering or illness of another is as great as our own suffering, no matter what his color: black, white, yellow, or brown. Man must have the thought that he should not hurt other lives. Whether he studies science or true wisdom, he must understand unity and the suffering of others, and he must have compassion for all lives.

Furthermore, man must realize that even tiny birds can fly in the sky; God created them that way. There are stars that fly in the sky. The sun and the moon fly between east and west. Water and air encircle the earth; they are above and below it. This is how God created them. So it is not a big wonder for man to travel in a rocket; such a long time ago God made things that fly. He is the Causal One who rules everything.

Man must realize this and understand that our Creator existed before anything else existed. He must understand that there is an atom within him that will eventually destroy him. He must reflect on this, find the atom bomb within himself, and fling it away from him. He must praise God for the atoms he discovers on the outside and use them for the benefit of all mankind. This will save the world and all the lives in it from danger.

802.

If a man stands in a garden filled with beautiful flowers, he will experience their cooling fragrance. But if a man stands beside a lake into which all the drains and sewers of the town empty, he will experience the stench of all that flows into it. The place in which he stands and the things which are present there will determine whether he experiences stench or fragrance.

In the same way, if man contains God's qualities, actions, thoughts, and intentions, he will perceive only the fragrance, the peace, and the sweetness of God. In other people, he will perceive only peace, tranquillity, and good thoughts. But if man goes to the place in which tigers, dogs, foxes, demons, ghosts, devils, and the five elements live, if he takes on their qualities, he will see their fighting. All he will see is one animal killing, eating, and drinking the blood of another animal, claiming, "I am greater than you." He will praise them, become one of them, and finally die with them.

Like this, the qualities and actions which man experiences will depend upon whether he has wisdom, devotion, and faith or whether he has the qualities he has acquired from his elemental life. What he experiences will depend upon where he chooses to stand. He who lives with the qualities associated with God, he who lives with love and God's compassionate qualities, will see the qualities and the actions of the kingdom of heaven, the qualities and actions of God's love, beauty, and light.

Man must know this. With wisdom, he must discover in which place he should stand and what he must acquire. He must form good thoughts and God's qualities in his life. If man acquires God's qualities, he will receive the unending fragrance and benevolence of God.

## 803.

A dog encountered a pack of foxes. He did not actually join the foxes, but as he ran near them, he gradually began to mingle and move along with them. Even though there is a slight difference between dogs and foxes, and even though they make different sounds, when the foxes began to howl, the dog also made a valiant effort to howl in the same way, "Ow ow oooh ooh oooh oohooo!"

Like this, no matter how pure a man is, if he decides to follow the fox known as the mind and walk by its side, when the mind starts to howl, man will also make a valiant effort to howl. If he joins satan's realm of mind and desire even to a small extent, gradually he will be dragged toward that side. However, if man joins with God, he will acquire God's qualities and sound.

Man must understand with wisdom that his place is in the kingdom of heaven and that bad qualities belong to the kingdom of hell. He must escape and gain his freedom, filling his life with Allah's resonance. The friendship of bad people is very harmful even if it is only for a split second; they will drag you down. You must understand this with wisdom.

## 804.

Do not expect a small pond to give you drinking water forever. When the rain falls, a little water might collect in the pond, but when the sun shines, it will dry up. Then it will be very difficult for you to obtain water, for drinking or for other purposes. It may even become necessary for you to move to another location.

Therefore, you must use your wisdom to search for a spring. Where can springs be found? Under the earth. You must dig in the correct spot so that the eye of the spring can be opened. After that you must build a well, fashioning its walls carefully so that they will not cave in. Then you must clean the water which flowed into the well during the digging and construction; all the mud and cement must be cleaned out. Finally, when clear water flows, you will no longer have a water problem, and you will not need to rely on rain.

Similarly, when through your efforts you find the benevolent grace which Allah has kept for you, you will have water wherever you are, not only to satisfy your thirst, but for all purposes. If you fail to do this, there will be difficulties. So do not rely on the pond; dig a well in the proper place. That will truly benefit you.

Within you, there is a spring. Therefore, do not rely on the waters, the springs, and the mirages of the world, expecting them to comfort you. Just as you have to dig deep to find clear water, you must dig deep into the earth of the five elements within you. You must dig deep into your heart, throw away the five elements, and reach the light of the spring of grace which flows from God. The water of divine wisdom must flow; the water and the light of grace must flow.

Once the spring of grace is laid open, you must wash away all the dirt and impurity within you: the dirt of arrogance, karma, and *māyā*. Sift away the dirt and make the spring clear. Then, if you build the walls of the well properly with faith, certitude, determination, and the qualities of God, in all three worlds you will have an undiminishing source of the water of Allah's benevolent grace flowing from the spring of wisdom. When you drink from this well, your thirst will be quenched, and you will receive the light of completeness. Then the world in which you dwell will be the kingdom of God, and you will live in freedom.

If you do not do this, you will have lived your life in vain; your life will be as bleak as a man who relies upon a pond for water.

### 805.

Do not rely on food from a restaurant. The manager is a businessman, and he seeks money. All different kinds of people go there asking for all different kinds of food, and he will cater to all their needs. Meat, fish, beef, pork, and vegetables will be cooked there, but he will not use different pots for each kind of food. Only the serving bowls will be different. He might have four or five pots and six or seven spoons for cooking. The same pots and spoons used to cook the meat will be used for the vegetables. Permissible and forbidden foods will be combined.

Food like this is not acceptable to your body, your heart, or your faith. But the restaurant keeper is not at fault. He needs money; he is only running a business. If you go to his restaurant, he will give you the dish you asked for. But you must think about this. You could lose your faith by eating that food, you could develop a desire for it, and it could also make you ill.

If you want to lead a healthy life, eat clean food, live with faith, and clear your heart. Try to cook your own food. Give all praise to God, saying, *"Al-hamdu lillāh,"* and eat your food with the contentment known as *shakūr.* Food eaten in this manner is good for your body, for your prayers, and for your wisdom. Think about this. Understand what is permissible and what is forbidden and eat only what is permissible. That will be exalted for your faith. Buy the food you need, cook it, and take it with you when you go to work. If you do this without giving in to laziness, it will make your life beautiful.

806.

Do not preach to the world with the idea of creating revolution or acquiring power and position.

Make every speech to yourself. There is a revolution within you, and insurgents have taken over your kingdom, your freedom, and your life. The revolution of satan and his followers has taken over your entire life. Demons and ghosts and spirits, *māyā,* darkness, arrogance, and karma have created a revolution within you and captured your independent life. You must subdue and capture them. You must fight that war, executing a counter-revolution so that you can exile them all and rule your own kingdom once again. That is true socialism.

Capture the evil and banish the satans within. If you can do this, you will have peace and freedom. If everyone can achieve this state, there will be no war at all because there will be true socialism—no war outside and no war inside. True socialism is to live with the belief that every life is as precious as one's own.

This is the life which will give peace, unity, and tranquillity. You must safeguard the inner realm, keeping it in the same state in which Allah gave it to you. This is the way you must conduct your life in the world of Īmān-Islām.

## 807.

O man, you must think. All the universes are kingdoms of God. All kingdoms belong to God: land, women, gold, oceans, everything. God is the emperor of all kingdoms.

He has given you two of His kingdoms to use for as long as you live. But you have forgotten them. You must identify and resume control over those kingdoms within you—the kingdom of heaven and the kingdom of hell.

The justice of God is within you, and you must become the judge who dispenses God's justice. You must become the commander of both kingdoms. You must control hell and then discard it, keeping heaven inside and ruling it as your paradise.

Do not forfeit the divine justice which has been given to you by Allah, and do not intend to kill Him, capture His kingdom, and make it your own. If you do, you will become an enemy to God. You must rule the inner kingdom and live as a representative of God, a divine messenger of God, protecting and looking after the kingdom of heaven and discarding the kingdom of satan.

O man, understand this. Whichever kingdom you rule in the world is the kingdom that God will give you in the next world. If you control and rule your inner kingdom here, you will receive the kingdom of heaven there.

## 808.

O man, you must put forth effort in order to grow the crops you need for the hunger of your life, and you must plant those crops in the appropriate seasons. Do not be lazy; do not expect to be supported by the earnings of others. God has given you good limbs. Use them to work for your own living.

## 809.

The Sufi sheikh says to his disciple:
            O disciple, my son,
            What you see is the world,

What you like in it is hell,
And what you desire to eat changes
Into foul smelling feces.
Whatever you desire is a poison,
What appears must disappear,
Whatever you see now will change.
All you have seen is a dream,
And all you have learned,
In this world of illusion,
Is like a pumpkin drawn on paper
Which you can never eat.

This is called the world of creation, and the scenes of creation are the shows of birth and death displayed by the energies and miracles of the world. All the scenes you see are lovely, but each of the scenes is eating another. But do any of them retain what they eat?

Look at the food you eat. See how many kinds of fruits and flowers there are, each with its own nectar. The tongue and the throat relish the taste, but once the food slips past the throat, the food turns to feces. Everything is eventually defecated, is it not? No one retains the things he eats.

When you look with wisdom, this is what has been happening all along and will continue to happen. Whatever is born and grows will die; the scenes you look at, praise, and enjoy will disappear. All of them will end as dreams and thoughts. Your body, what you have acquired, and everything you have seen is all a dream. Do not live relying on these. That would be like building castles in the air. You will have wasted your time.

Think instead: "Why did I come to this world? What must I do here? Where will I go?" Make a decision. Understand and learn the secret of where you were, and strive to return there.

### 810.

There is something within you which cannot be seen by mind, desire, or physical vision. That is the food and water of grace which you cannot eat or drink with your mind and desire. Take it with the hand of faith and eat and drink that grace with the mouth of faith. It is grace. It is His nourishment. That is the food of grace which does not become feces or urine, the food that truly makes you grow.

Truth does exist. It is the power of Allah. You cannot learn it from books, nor can you understand it through the visions of your eyes.

If you wish to understand this power, you must know that there is a Qur'an and a sheikh of wisdom within you. It is with his wisdom that you must open your *qalb,* your inner heart, read the inner Qur'an, and understand the benevolence of grace. But until you attain that state, you must find a Sufi sheikh on the outside, ask him, and learn.

812.

There is a treasure of grace within you
Which will never diminish:
Take from it.

There is a complete perfection within you
Which was never born and will never die:
Try to reach it.

813.

There is unseen light within you
Which the eyes cannot perceive
It dwells within you
And you within it
In unity.

Resolve to live in the kingdom where God lives within you and you live within God. That is the kingdom of freedom. That is God's kingdom, the world of grace, the world in which there is no darkness, the world in which there are no seasons and no time at all. Morning, noon, evening, and night do not exist in that kingdom. Where these states do not exist, you will have no aging, no death, no rebirth.

In striving to attain that state, you will become a human being. And on that day, you will receive the beauty which merges with God and attain the state of the non-duality which merges with God. You will achieve the unity of a life in which you are within God and God is within you. My son, try to achieve this state.

## 814.

A Sufi *gnāni* speaks to his disciple: You have said the world is a prison, and you have asked how one can laugh in prison. My son, if what you have perceived is a prison to you, it is because you live in sorrow, amidst difficulties. That is why you are sad and do not laugh. Your father, the Sufi *gnāni,* says that if you look at the world as a jail, if you feel you are imprisoned, if you feel you are unhappy, that thought itself puts you in prison. If you free yourself from that thought, you can laugh.

As long as you have that thought, no matter where you are, whether in a palace, in the world, or in meditation, you will be imprisoned. But when wisdom shines forth and you see God, there will be no prison. Until then, sadness is a prison, problems are a prison, selfishness is a prison, and even your happiness is a prison. When you destroy both happiness and sadness, you will have freedom. Then you will see nothing other than the state of union with God. That is freedom.

You must think about this. There is much more to be said. When your wisdom grows a little more, we will tell you more. You are the one who laughs and cries. When you understand who you are, both laughing and crying will leave you.

## 815.

There are many who came to rule the world. They came, they ruled, and they died. Many came to rule possessions and property. All who came to rule land, women, gold, forests, and kingdoms ruled for but a little while, then left everything behind and disappeared.

This world is a rest house, a hotel. There is a billboard listing the names of all the people who came here, their lineage, when they were born, and when they died. They all came for a nighttime picnic, to live in the glitters of the darkness of the world. And then they left.

One who begins to rule himself will never die. Do not rely on rest house guest lists. Do what you came to do. Understand who sent you here and you will know your Father; when you know your Father, you can return to Him. Your real property is there. This rest house is not your permanent dwelling place.

When we stand on the bank of a pond and look into the water, we see ourselves upside down. The trees and surroundings appear upside down too.

Similarly, if you place a mirror above your head and look into it, you will find that your feet are up and your head is down. Or place a mirror above you and look at the cars on the road. You will see them upside down, with their wheels in the sky.

The intellect can take in only what it sees. It can assess only what philosophies say. The limit of intellect is philosophy, but God is beyond intellect. He is the wisdom within wisdom, the truth within truth, and the mystery within mystery. The understanding of this is within man.

The learning about this power, the real Bible, and the real Qur'an are within. The inner Qur'an has no form, it has only grace. It has no writing, only light. It has no ink, but it does have sound. It has no speech, but it has resonance. It has nothing to conceal. It has the resplendent light called *Nūr,* and Allah's benevolence, His actions, and His conduct. It has no selfishness, but it has equality. It has no pride, but it has peace and tolerance.

It has no form, only contentment, trust in God, and the quality of giving all praise to God. It has no comparison, nor can it be explained. It has no equal. It stays alone. It is not contained within anything, but it contains everything, understanding and protecting everything. It has no weariness. It understands the hearts of all, comforts them, teaches them justice, and gives them the explanation. That is Allah's Qur'an. That is Allah. The wisdom of an *insān,* a true human being, can understand that this is a mystery.

One who understands this mystery will understand the complete resplendence of God. The explanation is the profound knowledge called *'ilm.* One who understands and learns this is *Īmān-Islām,* the one who swims in the ocean of *'ilm.* He is Allah's slave. He is a Sufi. Except for Allah, he has no wealth. Whatever may happen, he says, "*Al-hamdu lillāh,* all praise is to God alone." His life, wealth, speech, and all he has is *al-hamdu lillāh.*

The Qur'an is within his heart, and absolute faith is the light by which he reads it. He never puts the inner Qur'an where earth, fire, water, air, ether, mind, and desire exist because those places are unclean. He will touch it only with the clean hands of faith, certitude, and determination. The inner Qur'an must be put in the *'arshul-mu'min,* which is the throne of the true believer, the place where Allah dwells.

One who keeps the Qur'an where it should be kept, holds it in the hand in which it should be held, and has it read by the One who should read it, praising the One who should be praised and praying to the One to whom prayer is due, is a real Sufi. If we do not have this understanding, it is no use to recite from the Bible or Qur'an.

817.

A young woman said, "I've been doing a lot of crying to God and a lot of yelling at the dirt that surrounds me all the time. I am wondering if that is correct."

The sheikh said, "That is very good. But if you sit under a barren tree and ask for fruit, will you get any? No. If you want fruit, you must go to a tree that bears fruit.

"Like that, with determination, certitude, and absolute faith in God, go to a man of wisdom, a good father, and cry to him. Then you will receive a reply."

818.

A child asked, "Our father sometimes asks us to talk about God and wisdom. But if we are to speak of wisdom in the presence of our father who is wisdom, it will be upside down speech. How does it benefit us on the path?"

The father said, "That is very good. Your father dressed you, put your shirts on, and washed your backsides for a long time. But now he is watching to see whether you are able to dress by yourselves, whether you have modesty, sincerity, reserve, and fear of wrongdoing, and whether you have the focus and good conduct to correctly maintain that state. He is watching to see whether that state is developing within you or whether ego, pride, selfishness, vanity, and love of titles are growing within you.

"He is watching to see whether you are lecturing the country-side or whether you are lecturing to your own hearts. Are you teaching the world or are you teaching yourselves? Are you correcting the world or are you correcting yourselves? Are you relying on the world or are you relying on the only One? The reason for asking you to speak is to judge with clarity your answers to all these questions and to see whether you can be taken on the journeys which lie ahead.

"From your words he assesses your state and teaches you the wisdom appropriate to it, giving you further explanations about God's state and your relationship to Him. This is why your father asks you to speak in his presence."

819.

A king had thirty-two ministers. The thirty-second minister carried their commands to the outside. The first minister stayed with the king, made policy decisions, and did the more important work.

The thirty-second minister began to complain, "I do so much running around and I work all the time, yet I am paid only one thousand dollars while the first minister receives ten thousand dollars for just sitting with the king."

When the king heard about this, he called the thirty-second minister and told him, "Find out if a ship has come to our harbor."

The thirty-second minister went and asked the people at the harbor, "Has a ship come?" When they told him yes, he came running back to the king and reported that a ship had arrived.

The king asked, "Where did the ship come from?"

The minister went to find out and returned to say, "The ship came from Rome."

The king then asked who sent the ship.

The minister again went to the harbor, came back, and gave the king the name of the person who sent it.

Then the king asked, "What did the ship bring?"

Again he ran to the harbor and this time came back with the information that they had brought crockery.

Now, the king told the thirty-second minister to sit next to him, and he called for the first minister to whom he said, "Has a ship come to our harbor?"

The first minister went to the harbor, investigated, and wrote down all the details about the ship, who had sent it, and what the cargo was. He had the cargo unloaded and sent to the warehouse. Then he came back and gave a full report to the king.

The king looked at the thirty-second minister. "I gave the same instructions to both of you. Do you see the difference between your work and his? How many times you went back and forth! The difference in your salaries is due to the difference in how you carry out your duties. The day you reach his state, you will get his salary. Now go and do your work."

Son, God's work is also like this. Whether you prostrate yourself a thousand times, perform a thousand prayers, or say eighty thousand times that you are going to remember God, only one who is on the true point of the state of prayer and meditation, only one with the connection to God, one who is surrendered to God and truth, performs true prayer. One who keeps God within himself and who remains in prayer within God is doing the true prayer that will benefit him.

Any other kind of prayer would be like the lowest minister running back and forth a thousand times, complaining, "God has not given me His grace. He has not given me His light. I am doing so much work, I am praying so much, I am crying and crying for God." If you talk like that, you will be like the lowest minister, performing endless work for low wages. The wages you receive are in line with the quality of the work you perform. It is like this with God's work. Your worship, your prayers, and your actions must be done correctly.

820.

The sheikh does not hit you with a stick or scold you with harsh words. His work is to hit you with wisdom and embrace you with love. However, without understanding this, you say that the sheikh has scolded you.

When you deliver a quantity of aluminum pots to a shop to sell, some may be dented in transport. Those dents must be repaired in order to restore the value of the pots, to make them saleable.

The sheikh taps the pots gently, using two blocks: one of love for support on the outside, and one of wisdom on the inside to beat out the dents. The pot might feel hurt during the process, but it has to be made valuable. The sheikh will keep beating until there are no more dents. Then the beating will stop.

Like this, the sheikh will hold love within himself and beat your five elements with wisdom. He will beat your mind and remove the arrogance, karma, *māyā*, selfishness, hastiness, pride, anger, and the 150 million dents of the birth of karma. Once that is done, he will stop beating you. When the dents are removed and you are made valuable once again, he will give you to God.

You must understand this. The sheikh beats and repairs the dents of mind and desire in his children, makes them valuable, and hands them to God. That is his work.

821.

When a pond is full of water, everyone comes to either bathe, wash their feet, or quench their thirst. But the pond should not become proud, thinking, "If not for me the world would end and everyone would die of thirst," because a pond depends on rain for its water. It also depends on a spring, and the spring feeding it might become blocked.

Like this, no matter how much a man may have learned, no matter how much wisdom he preaches, no matter how much he has grown, he must not become proud and begin to think like the pond. He must realize that he too is dependent like the pond, and he must give all responsibility to God for the learning he has acquired.

The sheikh has the connection to God; God's words flow through him. When you receive wisdom from the sheikh, you should not be proud like the pond. You must realize that the sheikh is guiding you. If you let him lead you and always keep the sheikh in front of you, the connection to God will come through him. If, however, the pride of the ego comes into you, the spring of 'ilm, the profound knowledge of grace, will become blocked, and you will be like a dry pond.

822.

If you plant a tree, it is your duty to water it and help it to grow. God gives the fruit to the tree, and the tree gives the fruit to everyone. A tree does not eat its own fruit.

Just because you watered the plant, you should not think that you are providing the fruit. What you think you are giving others is what the tree is giving you. You may think, "I am giving charity." This is like taking another man's property and giving it as charity or picking up a coconut from the wayside and offering it to the nearest Pillaiyār (a Hindu elephant deity, also called Ganēsha). Think about this.

On the path of God, water the plant of truth and help it to grow. Do your duties without attachment just as God does His duties. Give like a tree gives of its fruit. Dedicate your life to helping others. Allah has given you so much fruit, so many good gifts; use them to benefit others. Comfort those who suffer and need help. That will be the exaltedness of your life.

823.

Son, fish live in water and they take their food from the water. Man lives on land and his food is on the land. But even if a man learns to swim in water like a fish, he cannot become a fish, nor can he live like a fish. If he has the arrogance to think he can do that, it will destroy his life.

Like this, you must try to learn to swim in the *bahrul-'ilm,* God's ocean of profound knowledge; you must learn *'ilm* from a sheikh. That sheikh is a *mīm*★ in the ocean of *'ilm; alif* represents Allah, *lām* represents light, and *mīm* represents Muhammad *(Sal.).* The sheikh is the light of Muhammad *(Sal.).* He lives in the ocean of divine knowledge. You must swim with the sheikh in that ocean and try to learn *'ilm.*

If you think you have learned a lot from the world, if you have that arrogance, your plight will be like the plight of a man who tries to live in the ocean like a fish. Pride, arrogance, and love for titles and status bring about a man's destruction.

Think about this with your wisdom. Give the speech of your mouth to God, give the hearing of your ears to God, give to God your happy smile, and give your heart into His responsibility. Give to Him also the responsibility for the *'ilm* and wisdom you have learned, and establish absolute trust in God. This will bring triumph to your life, endowing you with the benevolence of *'ilm,* the power of Allah, and the wealth of the sheikh's divine knowledge.

824.

There are two very narrow pathways. On one is a sign which carries the words, "This path is open to all." On the other path it is written, "This is a subtle path. Two cannot go together on this path. It is meant for one."

---

★ In Tamil, *meen* is fish. In Arabic, *mīm* is a letter of the alphabet which, in the mystical sense, refers to Muhammad *(Sal.).* *Alif* and *lām* are also Arabic letters.

Within us are two pathways. One is the path of the pleasure of the world, and it is open to all. The other is the path of the worship of God, where one worships alone. On this path, you have to go alone. Discarding your mind, desire, and thought, you have to go alone. You must be within God and God must be within you. On this path, you can go only in one form. Only then can you reach the destination.

If two want to go together, they must take the other path, the path of the world of hell, the path of gold, property, possessions, livestock, houses, and wealth. It is the path which leads to material possessions and other such things. If you go on that path, you will return to the place of your birth.

If you go on the path meant for one, the path which has the connection to God, you will return to the original place from which your soul came. There you will hear two sounds: the resonance of "*Lā ilāha,* there is nothing other than Allah," and "*illallāhu,* You alone, O God, are Allah." This is the world of the souls, the place in which you existed before, the place in which you were free. The other path will bring you here, to the world, to the place in which your body was born. We must give all responsibility to God, immerse ourselves in Him, and reach His place.

825.

Son, the most important action of one who has come to this world as an *insān,* a man, must be to have firm certitude in God. He must have faith, certitude, and determination in Allah. He must understand God's laws and justice and observe them in his life. God's justice must prevail for everyone, from a world leader to a beggar.

Man must reflect on three points. First, divine justice must become executive justice; a leader must make divine justice his justice. Then, the people must make executive justice into their justice, the justice of man. After that, each person must make that human justice the conscience which rules his life. He must form his life with inner patience, contentment, and surrender to Allah, and he must give all praise to Allah alone. Whatever happens, this must be observed, because this is the state of Allah's justice.

Second, you must never dwell in a country which has no temples, mosques, churches, or other places of worship. For a human being, there is no purpose in dwelling in a country where one cannot worship God with devotion. Any country where there is no devotion to God is a desolate, ruined country, not worth living in. You should not stay there. Do not join those who have no certitude and faith in Allah.

Third, anything learned without a sheikh is like the reflection of the discarded shell of a pearl oyster. If you want to study the truth, you need a *gnāna sheikh*.

There are two places in which proper worship to God can take place: in the outer prayer and within the inner heart. The inner place of worship must be built within the heart with divine justice, executive justice, human justice, and conscience. If you establish this state, if you make the sheikh your *imām,* your leader of prayer, and stand behind him in prayer, you will hear Allah's sound. When the sound of the sheikh resonates in your heart, you will understand Allah's sound, and you will know Allah's power and the benevolence of His grace.

### 826.

Do not try to live
By depending on the changing seasons.
Try to live by depending on God
And that will give you the highest victory.

### 827.

Do not try to measure with your intellect
The depth of the ocean of divine knowledge.

For your intellect is only as long as a rat's tail. It is better to try with wisdom to fathom the vast ocean of your heart, the ocean that has no length or breadth. That will truly benefit you. With the analytic wisdom which is the *Qutb (Ral.),* understand the secret of your inner heart and pray to Allah there.

### 828.

Do not follow your hunger.
Place *sabūr,* inner patience, in front of you
Give all praise to God
And then go forward.
That will be your plenitude.

### 829.

Do not move toward death.
Move toward Allah
And you will overcome death.

### 830.

Do not feel sorrowful about your poverty
And languish in despair.
Turn away the very thought of poverty,
Turn toward Allah,
Praise Him and look inside.
God's treasure is within you
And it is rightfully and eternally yours.

### 831.

Do not think that you must go
Into the jungle to meditate.
There is a vast jungle within you;
Destroy it and chase away the animals.
Be alone and meditate,
And you will have serenity.

### 832.

Do not kill other lives
Continuing to supply flesh and blood
To the lions, tigers, cats, rats,
Dogs, foxes, ghosts, and demons
Dwelling within you.

You should feel sad, not only because they are eating the flesh
you supply, but also because they are eating you; they are eating
your own flesh and blood. Chase away all the tigers you are raising
within yourself and develop compassion for other lives. This is
one of God's qualities.

### 833.

Follow people who are good
And you will understand and know
The good and evil of your life.

## 834.

There is a bird called a crow. Crows always live in groups. When one crow dies, all the others gather. When they see something black on the ground, they will not fly close enough to determine whether it is a dead crow or whether it is a piece of black cloth from an umbrella. Fearfully, the crows think, "I might also die. If I go near, I will be killed, too!" The crows are afraid, and they caw from a distance; they will not go close to investigate. This is a quality in the relationship between crows. They will circle around cawing for a little while and then they will disperse, leaving the dead crow or the rag where it was.

It is like this with the racial hatred, the religious bias, and the blood ties we call the world. Do not rely on such groups. Do not live your life depending upon them. When you are dying, the crows of racial and religious differences and blood ties may see the signs and hover around you. If you have some money, they may even put on a show of wailing, but if they do come, they will come only for the money. If you have no money, they will caw a bit, but keep their distance, without helping you or sharing in your suffering.

Do not waste all the days of your life relying on these hordes of crows. They are frightened to die with you, frightened to stay with you, and frightened of the illness you have. Therefore, reflect a little and love only our one God who is eternally complete. Live with God in unity. He will be with you and suffer with you.

## 835.

Do not put on the garb of a guru
As fools who have never known the sheikh
Put on their robes.

Only when you walk on the right path with the right sheikh will you derive any benefit. The sheikh will disappear within you and you will disappear within the sheikh. When the two become one, you will become the sheikh. That is the right path. Understand and establish that state.

## 836.

Do not roam the hills, valleys,
Jungles and parks
Searching for God.

This is the craziness of the wandering dog of desire in the mind, the roaming of a doubting mind. Do not roam. If you stay with a true sheikh, he will show you the horse of the *dhikr* of the two breaths. The wisdom that rides this horse can run faster than the wind and the mind. It can know and understand all that must be understood. The sheikh will reveal to you the horse of the *dhikr* and the clarity that comes out of this understanding.

### 837.

Son, if the one who sits for a shave sits properly, the one who shaves can shave carefully and satisfactorily.

Similarly, if with faith in your sheikh you clear your heart, with his wisdom the sheikh will shave away all your karma and rid you of the dirt of your birth. If you do not establish this state of faith properly within you, when the sheikh tries to shave you of your dirt, you will receive cuts which will cause pain to your mind and body. When you see the cuts and experience the pain, you may run away from the sheikh only partially shaved.

You must learn to sit properly. Then the sheikh will shave away everything with his wisdom, and you will not experience pain.

### 838.

Do not waste your time in useless talk. Silently learn to speak the wise speech which exists within speech. That will give you tremendous peace.

### 839.

Do not laugh at or ridicule God's creations. The very trees, plants, shrubs, creepers, woods, and animals within you are laughing at you and calling you a fool.

### 840.

Do not say that creation is crazy. All of creation is within you, calling you crazy and feeling extremely sorry for you. It says, "O God, give him some wisdom and make him realize."

### 841.

O man, while you are happily raising a dog on the outside,

the desire within you is making you bark. Tie up the dog of desire within and become a man.

### 842.

People often bring up cats to catch the mice in their houses. We have seen this, have we not? They carry on their lives depending on their cats.

Just as the cats on the outside continually rub against you, does the cat within you ever leave you alone? No. The cat on the inside is always rubbing, scratching, and mewing. It constantly pulls you toward the world with its magnetic energy. Cats have static electricity in their hair, just as the cat within you has the magnetic current of illusion which magnetizes your attachments. Catch that cat and put it out. You are like iron, and that magnet is pulling on you. Realize this with wisdom.

The cat mewing and scratching at you from the inside asks you to give it cow, goat, and pig meat, milk, rice, bread, rat, and mouse. "No matter what murder or other harm you have to do, give me food," it demands, pulling at you with its magnetism. Hit the cat with your wisdom and you will be released from karma; you will give up murdering other lives and learn compassion.

### 843.

A sheikh must know the qualities of his children. He must know their hunger and the states in which they exist. He must know how much of each thing each child needs. The sheikh must treat the children according to their qualities and bring them to the proper state. One who can do this is a true sheikh. He will comfort each child according to the child's level of wisdom, according to his state, and according to his conduct and actions.

No matter what the disciples may do, the sheikh does not consider their behavior inimical to him. Opening his heart, he embraces them to his chest and continually feeds them the milk of wisdom until they reach the state of true wisdom and maturity. He has no anger or hatred toward his children. He protects them with care, concern, compassion, patience, and responsibility. This is how he brings up his children. Such a one is truly an *insān kāmil,* a perfected man.

### 844.

Do not waste water just because there is a lot of water in the pond. Use the water for good crops and good purposes.

Leave the water in the pond until you have plowed and planted a crop which will be beneficial to you. If you then use the water properly and put it to good use, it will last for season after season.

In the same way, even though you have filled yourself with many kinds of acquired learning, even though you have learned about God, you must first understand which crops need the water of the benevolent grace of divine knowledge and then give it accordingly. Open out the water of grace for the purpose of nurturing useful crops. It is then that your learning and wisdom will be of benefit.

### 845.

Son, the people who are living in this world are trying to carry it with them as they go on their journey. Can they do it? That is my question.

Due to his ignorance, man is carrying the world. This is why he suffers so many losses, this is why he is crying. If he rids himself of ignorance and searches for wisdom, he can unload the world. Then he will no longer experience the sorrows which are the cause of his illnesses. He will gain the undiminishing wealth of a life free of illness. He will receive material wealth, the wealth of grace, and the wealth of the soul. A man of wisdom must think about this and unload the huge burden of the world so that he can receive his real wealth.

### 846.

Do not try to grow by raising cows and goats, milking them, and drinking that milk, thinking that you have reached the heights of happiness. Do not think that you could go on drinking that milk forever!

While you are drawing and drinking the milk of cows and goats, the illusion known as your mind and desire is drawing out your blood, your flesh, your tissues, your strength, and your wisdom.

Mind and desire are milking you, weakening your nerves, draining your beauty and youth, reducing the days of your existence, and showing you the way into the hands of the Angel of Death. They will bring you to the state in which a man who walks on two legs is made to crawl on all fours.

Therefore, first of all, catch those who are milking you and throw them away. If you can do that, you will remain eternally youthful. Ridding yourself of them, if you can draw in and drink the milk of God's grace and wisdom instead, you will live at the age of sixteen forever. Now, when we say sixteen years old, do not think it is an age. Sixteen refers to the state of the full moon, the state of completeness.

Whether you drink cow's milk or human milk, anything you drink of the world will drink your life. Mind, desire, and thought will drain you and cast you into the cemetery. Understand this and drink only the milk that will give you an eternal youth; drink the milk of Allah's grace.

### 847.

O man, do not even think of stealing someone else's property. If you steal, you will be labeled a thief for life. You will no longer be referred to as a man.

Try to live like a human being. Stop stealing from the world and rid yourself of the thief within who is stealing from you, the thief who is eating you. Then you will become a good man.

### 848.

O man, you must think. We came from God, from the world of the souls. When we came here, we did not bring anything with us other than God; and when we go back, we can take with us only God. We came here to know God and His history. All else must be left behind, and you must be ready to leave on the ship the moment it arrives. Do not pack the burdens of desire and sin to take with you. Be ready to take only what you brought with you. One who does this is a man.

The journey of those who dally here, trusting the world and packing worldly things, will take them to hell. Whereas one who is ready to go at any time, taking with him only God who is the weightless treasure which he brought with him to this world, will go to heaven. He is a wise man.

### 849.

Do not allow the world to trample you; you must walk on it.

You will be crushed if you try to carry the world when you walk. It is your attachments that make you carry the world; when you do duty without attachment, then it will be easy for you to walk on the world.

850.

A man came to the Sufi sheikh, crying, "O sheikh! I am undergoing many difficulties. I have no means to eat."

The Sufi asked, "Son, why are you crying? Come, sit down and learn.

> What is eating you?
> What do you eat?
> What you eat is eating you
> If you stop eating it,
> It will stop eating you.

"This is what you are eating: desire, mind, attachments, blood ties, selfishness, anger, hastiness, karma, arrogance, illusion, treachery, deceit, robbery, vengeance, jealousy, ignorance, lack of wisdom, obsession, hatred, miserliness, greed, fanaticism, envy, intoxicants, lust, theft, murder, falsehood, and everything else that is prohibited. Every day you continue to search for and devour the things which will one day turn around and devour you.

"Give them up. Discriminate between good and bad, permissible and forbidden. Eat only what is good. At every moment, you must praise Allah and accept with contentment whatever He has set aside for you. For whatever is to come at the next moment, give all responsibility to God.

"The day you eat in this manner the food He has given you, that is the day the wealth of God's grace will blossom within you. On that day, the darkness that was eating you from within will leave automatically."

851.

My son, you must understand. What is most exalted in your life? What gives splendor to your life? You must understand whether you are one who has *īmān*. *Īmān* means purity, and purity means light. Islam means light: *lām*—the light of life, the light of your actions, the light of your prayer. The One to whom you intend to pray is Light.

There are five points in Islam: first, patience; second, inner patience; third, contentment; fourth, absolute trust in God; fifth, giving all praise to God.

These relate to *khair,* or that which is good. Islam is the state of understanding *sharr,* or evil, and then establishing that which is *khair.* These five points are the introduction to becoming a human being and becoming Islam, becoming light. If you lose them, you will be in a dark room, a room without light.

852.

The Sufi *gnāni* tells his disciples:
> My children, come here.
> Sit in the presence of the One who is forever,
> Pray in the presence of the One who prays,
> See in the presence of the One who sees,
> Speak in the presence of the One who speaks.
> This is prayer. This is meditation.

853.

There are two eyes in your face, but there are four hundred trillion eyes in your body which are the pores of your skin. There are nine mouths: the two eyes, the two ears, the nose, the mouth, the navel, and the two below. How can you think you are meditating with your eyes closed when you have all these eyes? You must close all of these and stop the speech of the openings of the body. Though you close your physical eyes, you allow all the other eyes and mouths to open and meditate on whatever they like. This is not meditation.

By this, you are deceiving yourself, your birth, and your life. To others you may seem to be in meditation, but for you it is hell. All the nine mouths are screaming, all the millions and millions of eyes are howling, wanting everything they see. How can you meditate in such a state?

Learn to meditate properly. Plug the nine holes in your body, close all the eyes, stop your speech, control your self, dispel the earth, and chase the woman of illusion away from your mind. Then you will know the benefit.

## 854.

Son, in the cold countries of the world, during certain seasons, the leaves fall from the beautiful trees and leave them standing there stiff and bare, as if they were dead. Then in the spring, the leaves, flowers, and fruits appear again. People do not go near the trees when they are bare, but when the leaves, flowers, and fruits emerge, they return once again to enjoy the trees.

It is the same way with man, too. In the years of his prosperity, when he has worldly titles, money, and beauty, he is like a tree in full bloom. The world praises him, and he enjoys it. Later, just as the leaves fall from a tree, poverty and old age come to him, and no one will accept him.

People and birds come in flocks when there is fruit; otherwise, they stay away. Observe the trees and learn. When you see that joy and sorrow come and go like sprouts, fruit, and falling leaves in the changing seasons, throw them both away from you. Die before death. Receive the grace of Allah which gives undiminishing and undying fruit, endless wealth, a source of water which will never become dry, an indestructible house, a light that never goes out, and life without death. If you trust Him, if you say, "*Lā ilāha illallāhu*: There is nothing other than You; only You are Allah," with faith, certitude, and determination, and if you conduct your life accordingly, you will receive His grace.

## 855.

Son, there is snow in the northern countries. It falls like white cotton upon the trees, houses, and the ground, making everything white and beautiful. In a few days it turns into ice, then finally melts into water. When it is snow, people like to look at it, but when it becomes ice, they are frightened to walk on it.

The story of man's creation is also like this. It is a secret. When man was created, he was pure. In all of Allah's creation, the part which is the soul is white and pure. After coming from the world of the souls, the soul is placed in a piece of flesh made of the five elements: earth, fire, water, air, and ether. The luminous white ray of the soul exists within that piece of flesh as the heart within the heart, and that is the grace. God created the body in this way. He created man with a ray from the world of the souls, beautiful and pure, just as snow is beautiful when it first falls to earth. He created mankind as one race, as beautiful and pure flowers.

384

After some time, just as the snow changes into ice, man is changed by anger, desire, arrogance, satan, and all of satan's qualities, which are rolled together and made hard. Just as it is dangerous to walk on ice, these qualities cause accidents to people when they walk on the path to Allah. One eats the other. Divisions in color, race, religion, and language cause difficulties. Because of this, no man is free. Many have slipped and fallen on the ice of illusion, doubt, jealousy, arrogance, and evil.

Man must realize this and reflect on his original state. Just as snow comes in a beautiful form, hardens into ice, and finally melts away, the elements that make up man's body will also melt and return to their respective sources. Man's body, beauty, flesh, and all that he has collected will melt away.

A wise man will think and realize that the beautiful, pure, white form that came first, the form that will never die, is the essence which belongs to Allah. Creation will die. Understand this, take the essence, and say the call to prayer:

*Allāhu akbar, Allāhu akbar, Allāhu akbar, Allāhu akbar. Ash-hadu al-lā ilāha illallāh. Ash-hadu al-lā ilāha illallāh. Ash-hadu anna Muhammadur-Rasūlullāh. Ash-hadu anna Muhammadur-Rasūlullāh. Hayya 'alas-salāh. Hayya 'alas-salāh. Hayya 'alal-falāh. Hayya 'alal-falāh. Allāhu akbar, Allāhu akbar. Lā ilāha illallāh:* God is great, God is great, God is great, God is great. I witness that there is nothing other than You, O God; only You are Allah. I witness that there is nothing other than You, O God; only You are Allah. I witness that Muhammad is the Messenger of Allah. I witness that Muhammad is the Messenger of Allah. Come to prayer. Come to prayer. Come to success. Come to success. God is great, God is great. There is nothing other than You, O God. Only You are Allah.

Call the Rasūlullāh *(Sal.)*, the *Qutb (Ral.)*, the *olis,* and the prophets to your prayer. Make the Rasūlullāh *(Sal.)* the leader of prayer, the *imām,* and look to Allah, asking that your prayer be fulfilled and that you receive His wealth. If you understand this state, you will receive the eternal grace of God.

### 856.

Do not be fascinated by the call of *māyā's* illusory beauty.
Do not desire the world that desires your body.

Do not desire those who beckon you for your
physical beauty.

Do not fondle the worldly joys that fondle you.

These are deadly diseases; they will kill you. But there is One within you who is formless. Realize Him within you and you within Him.

857.

The Sufi *gnāni* says: My son, you can learn some things by looking at the world. You can learn from religions and religious scriptures. You can also learn from looking at mind and desire and creation.

But no matter what you learn, not all of it can be called wisdom, not all of it is *'ilm,* or divine knowledge. Most of it is like a blind man learning by touch. It is not complete, and it will not be beneficial.

This is why the Rasūlullāh *(Sal.)* has said, "Go even unto China to learn *'ilm.*" There is a very broad meaning to this. Allah bestowed *'ilm* upon His Rasūl *(Sal.)*. *'Ilm* is to learn without learning, pray without praying, understand without understanding, know without knowing, see without seeing, hear without hearing, eat without eating, and taste without tasting. The learning of God's three thousand gracious qualities, the learning of His ninety-nine powers, the learning of His actions, conduct, behavior, and duty, is like this.

It is the learning of Allah's essence, the wealth of the ocean of profound knowledge. The learning and understanding within this ocean is the explanation of the learning of *rahmatul-'ālamīn,* which is the mercy and compassion of all the universes. Allah is the One who rules with mercy and compassion, and the learning is about this. It is not written in books, nor is it a show. It is found in wisdom within wisdom, light within light, faith within faith, certitude within certitude, determination within determination, heart within heart, soul within soul, resplendence within resplendence, and in Allah within Allah. This is what we have to learn.

The Rasūl *(Sal.)* repeatedly said that we must go even unto China to learn *'ilm.* What is *'ilm?* That is what we must learn. From time to time it is taught by prophets, sheikhs, *olis,* and *qutbs.* Learn it from them. One with wisdom and faith should teach wisdom and faith. You must learn about light from *olis,* who are the lights of God. If we learn in this way, we can learn about the ocean of divine knowledge. If we can get even the taste of one drop of this ocean of divine knowledge, we will be very fortunate; we will become good. This is the only way one can ever learn *'ilm.* It is the only way one can reach Allah, who is within *'ilm.*

### 858.

Do not harm another
Even in your thoughts,
For it will result in greater harm to you.

### 859.

Do not analyze
The right and wrong in another,
Finding fault with his life.
Analyze and understand the right and wrong within your own life. That will be of greater benefit to you.

### 860.

Your intention to hurt the feelings
In the hearts of others
Is killing you without killing you.
If you cut away this intention, you will be free of mental pain.

### 861.

When you are looking for a job with status and a high position which will earn you the praise of the world, directors of companies will interview you for jobs which befit the certificates you have acquired: birth certificates, religious certificates, school certificates, certificates of learning—all kinds of certificates. Then they will all call out to you, "Come to my store." "No, come to my shop." "No, come to my company! I will give you a job as an engineer." Many people will offer you jobs according to the certificates you have, and you will be able to acquire status, praise, merit, titles, and money.

You may have to sign a contract agreeing to work for one, five, or ten years. When the contract expires, you may move to another company and then another, receiving better and better positions according to your credentials, and each time binding yourself to an agreement.

If you take all you have studied, all the certificates you have obtained—prayer certificates, religious and racial certificates, doctrine certificates, school certificates, meditation and miracle certificates, philosophy certificates, and doctor-of-this-and-that certificates—to the supermarket of the world, you will be given a job appropriate to them. If you wear the right sort of dress, hat, robe, insignia, or medal, you will obtain the right position. But when all this is over, you will go to the cemetery. You will even get a certificate for that, too. These are the certificates the world gives you for your worldly study and learning; but after all this, you do not know exactly what awaits you or what wages you will receive for what you did here, in this world.

However, there is another realm. In that place certificates are unnecessary. An entire kingdom is in your hands. Your job is to rule the kingdom in the right way, avoiding what is wrong and doing what is right in the right way. If you can do that, the rightful leader, the One who gave you the kingdom, will also give you whatever you need at any particular moment. He will talk to you when you need to talk. He will have an intimate connection with you. You will not lack wealth. There, you can rule the kingdom in comfort.

But here in the world man takes so many certificates; like a chameleon changing color, he changes his makeup and dress to suit the occasion, acting out an impermanent drama in an impermanent world to build a victory which will end up in the cemetery. All his titles and glory are the advertisements which are leading him to hell. Only things that cannot otherwise be sold need advertising; valuable things, such as gold, need no advertisement. God's treasure needs no advertisement.

Realize this. God has given you the kingdom of hell and the kingdom of heaven. If you discard hell and rule God's kingdom of heaven properly, His kingdom will become your kingdom, and you will lack nothing.

862.

A man asked the sheikh, "Wherever you turn, people are saying, 'Islam, Islam!' But is it Islam for one man to kill another while reciting the name of God, for one to hurt another's heart, for one to destroy himself and the world? Is Islam merely a matter of talking about worshiping God while still indulging in such actions? Is that correct according to conscience?"

The sheikh replied, "Son, it is not Islam to hurt the body or the heart of anyone. Killing is not Islam. Islam is to make others peaceful and call them to the light of absolute faith. Islam is to stand on the mat of inner patience, open the umbrella of faith in God, and give the water of the word of God, the water of the *Kalimah*, praising God and inviting all to join together with love. Islam is to give all responsibility to God. This is Islam. This is the victory of the real *jihād*, the real holy war."

863.

Here is a *hadīth:*
Abu Jahl chased the Rasūlullāh *(Sal.)* and his followers from Mecca to Medina and then wanted to chase them away from Medina as well. He disguised one of his men and sent him to Medina to kill the Rasūlullāh *(Sal.),* promising him a large reward.

The man hid where the Rasūlullāh *(Sal.)* and his followers were praying. Gradually, he crept up to the Rasūlullāh *(Sal.),* who was in meditation. Taking up the Rasūlullāh's *(Sal.)* sword from the ground, he said, "Muhammad, you sorcerer, don't make a sound. You are a magician and a deceitful person. You say your God is in an unknown place. Tell that God of yours to come and save you now!"

The Rasūlullāh *(Sal.)* softly replied, "He will come!"

"Tell him to come!" sneered the man, struggling to raise the sword. But he found he could not. He sweated and shivered, and the sword dropped to the ground.

"The Rasūlullāh *(Sal.)* picked up the sword and said to the man, "Now you tell your gods to come and save you."

The man fell at his feet and cried out, "Oh please, you must help me!"

The Rasūlullāh *(Sal.)* lifted him up with both hands. "You and I are brothers. What fight is there between us? The fight is between truth and falsehood. You came to kill me with my own sword and challenged me to call my God, who is in an unknown place. He came. Though God is in a place unknown to you, He knows everything and He is everywhere. He came immediately. Your thirty-three million, forty-eight thousand gods are nearby, in Mecca. I told you to call them, but you are holding onto my feet instead. This is the only difference between us; my God came, your gods did not. The fight is about that failure."

The man said, "O Rasūlullāh, I realize my fault. Please teach me the *Kalimah*. I will have faith."

The Rasūlullāh *(Sal.)* embraced him and taught him the *Kalimah,* the word of God.

★

The sheikh says: Son, if we look at the Prophet's *(Sal.)* words, we will see that the real war is against the inner forces and energies which try to rule us and separate us from God. Islam is to believe that these forces must be stopped from attacking us and from keeping us away from God. To merge with God is Islam. Islam does not advocate man cutting man; Islam advocates cutting away the many tens of millions of so-called miraculous energies and forces within us. This is Islam. This is what the Rasūlullāh *(Sal.)* has shown us in this *hadīth*. For each of us to cut away the evil within us is Islam.

It is Islam for people to live as one and merge with God. For anyone to be hostile to anyone else is not Islam. There is no other holy war, no other *jihād*. The only holy war is to cut away the energies and forces and evil within ourselves. This is *jihād*. The battles are within the self. This is the meaning.

## 864.

No matter where the sun is in the sky, if a man has a magnifying glass in his hand, he can catch its rays and make a fire. He does not have to worry about the sun's position.

In the same way, it does not matter where God is; it does not matter where the light of God's truth is. As long as a man has within himself the magnifying glass of wisdom and absolute faith in Allah, he can catch the rays of the light of truth and draw them into himself. That will be of great benefit to him.

## 865.

A fish spends its life in the water; it cannot live without water. Its food, its play, and its life must be obtained within water. Can a fish live on the shore? If a fish were to decide to leave the depths of the ocean and live in a place without water, it would surely die; if it leaves its rightful place, it cannot survive.

Similarly, truth is the life of anyone who is a man. God's qualities, actions, and grace are man's real life. In these, man can swim, live, play, see, hear, taste, smell, and do many other things. The qualities of God form his life and the exaltedness of his state.

When a man decides to leave his exalted state, that becomes the lingering illness which causes him to suffer and die. In the same way that a fish encounters death if it decides to leave the water and live on the shore, as soon as a man makes the decision to live outside God's qualities he experiences sorrow, illness, poverty, and all the suffering associated with them.

But if a man decides to continue to live in his rightful station, death cannot reach him, nor can suffering afflict him. As long as the fish realizes that water is its life, it will not suffer undue affliction. Even if suffering were to approach, the fish would be able to avoid it and escape. Man must realize this. Each man must strive to live in his rightful station.

### 866.

Although he has tens of millions of eyes, man sees through only two kinds of eyes. At night, one kind of eye sees the thoughts of his mind as dreams. In the daytime, the other kind of eye looks at his thoughts as daydreams. Man looks at these two types of dreams every second of every day in his life—the dream of the night and the dream of the day.

If he were to think with wisdom, he would know that what he sees in both his wakefulness and in his sleep are dreams. If man would dispel the thought-dreams which are his mental visions and the mind-dreams of the night, his life would become the permanent and original life of wisdom.

### 867.

It is good for people to live where there is water; it is good for their health and their comfort.

Like this, if you are with a good sheikh, it is possible to gain freedom for your soul and to learn about prayer and devotion, thus cleansing the inner body. Just as the outer body is cleansed by water, the inner body is cleansed by association with a good sheikh.

## 868.

If there is a hole in your clothing, you need only a small needle and some thread to mend it. No matter how big the tear is, it can be mended with a tiny needle.

Similarly, in man's body there are four hundred trillion, ten thousand holes: the eyes, ears, nose, and mouth, the two below, the hair follicles, and all the torn spots in his thoughts and in his mind.

Thread the needle of wisdom with God's qualities, actions, and conduct and, sitting with inner patience and contentment, mend the holes and tears in your life. Then God's speech and actions will not go to waste. A man who will do this will be victorious in this world and the next.

## 869.

A dog said to a cow, "I want to go to a place where I can find enough water to satisfy my thirst, enough to drink in big mouthfuls. So far I have only been able to lick water from puddles, and my craving has not been satisfied."

The cow led him to a huge lake and watched as the dog lapped at the water. The cow was surprised. "Why are you still licking the water? There is plenty of water here. Why don't you take big mouthfuls?"

The dog replied sadly, "Only today have I realized the truth of the saying: No matter where a dog goes, it has to lick in order to drink water."

★

Man has come here with the wealth of all three worlds: the world of the souls, this world, and the next. He has come with the benevolence of Allah's grace. He has everything necessary for his life. Yet, once he sees the illusory creations of this world, man loses his wisdom and forgets everything God has given him. Within him, the dog of desire and his seven base cravings lick all the evils of illusion in the world, causing him to lose the undiminishing wealth, the *mubārakāt,* of the three worlds. He roams around, preferring the fate of the world.

On the day man decides to throw away worldly evils, he will regain his original wisdom and his life of plenitude. Those without wisdom will continue to lick at the world like dogs, even though they have an ocean of wealth within them.

870.

A tiger thought to himself, "Though I roam all over the jungle, I still cannot catch enough animals to fill my stomach. If I go into the village, there will be so many goats, cattle, and dogs, which I can capture and eat to my heart's content. Then I can live happily. I can eat as much and as long as I want; I can eat new and interesting kinds of food."

So the tiger left the jungle, moved to the village, and roamed around, running here and there. The people panicked. The goatherd locked up his goats, the cowherder locked up his cattle, and the dogs hid in terror. Men came with guns and bows and arrows to kill the tiger. The tiger was frightened, and so were the men who lived there and so were the goats, cattle, and dogs. The tiger could neither obtain his food nor live in peace. A month went by like this. The tiger had not been able to find any food, the men could not sleep, and the goats and cattle could not go out to graze.

Finally, the tiger went to a tree and said, "O tree, if I were in the jungle I might have captured and eaten at least one animal by now, but my greed drove me here. Now my life is in danger and, what's more, I am causing trouble to everyone. What has happened? I have gone hungry for a whole month. What do you think I should do?"

The tree replied, "O tiger, I grew from a single seed. I was a tiny seed, and see how far I have grown! I am growing right up to the sky. See how many fruits I have. See how many birds, animals, and human beings come to partake of my fruit. Though I was once only a tiny seed, now I get my peace from giving of my fruit to all these creations.

"What God provided for you in the jungle was enough to satisfy your hunger. Your greed in wanting to take more lives was due to ignorance, and that ignorance has caused you so much trouble and suffering. You set out to cause suffering to many lives and, as a result, you yourself are suffering. Therefore, return to the jungle and obtain your peace and tranquillity from the food God provides for you day by day. Be satisfied with that, and you will have contentment."

*

This is what the tree told the tiger, and the same is true for man. If he can find the one seed which can grant him fulfillment, he will never intend harm to others. If within himself he can find the seed that is good and correct, the harvest that comes from him will give peace to all. He will not want any of the fruits for himself. All the good things which blossom from him will go forth to bring peace and happiness to others, and mankind will exist as one race.

If man gives as the tree gives, his wealth will never diminish—just as a tree bears new fruit every year. If he can find that one point of the truth, which is to give to others with faith in God, certitude, and determination, and if he can give all the praise to God, that will give him peace.

871.

The sheikh speaks to a disciple: Anyone who hits you when you are telling the truth is a fool. But if you talk in ignorance, the one who hits you and gives you the explanation is wise. Try to clearly see the ignorance within you, instead of deceiving yourself by calling it truth.

872.

Son, all the trees, shrubs, and plants in the world have a strong taproot which firmly binds their lives to the ground. In addition, they have supporting roots to help hold them firm.

Similarly, man's life also needs a taproot to hold it firm. For this, he must first plow the soil of his *qalb* with the enlightening wisdom of the *Qutbiyyat*. Having prepared the soil, he must then plant the seed of *Allāhu* with absolute faith and wisdom.

He must nourish the seed with faith, certitude, and determination, pouring the water of the *Kalimah* as his prayer: *Lā ilāha illallāhu Muhammadur-Rasūlullāh:* There is nothing other than You, O God. Only You are Allah, and Muhammad is the Messenger of God. The water of God's benevolence must be poured with certitude so that the seed will germinate. From the seed of Allah, the taproot of *lā ilāha illallāhu* must grow with such strength that it cannot be shaken by anything.

The supporting roots for this principal root are faith in God, certitude, determination, inner patience, contentment, trust in God, and praise to God for everything. Then neither storms, tornadoes, mantras, *tantras,* darkness, torpor, illusion, cells, the countless poisonous and demonic energies, nor the four hundred trillion occult forces can harm the tree in any way.

If a man plants the seed of *Allāhu* in his heart, making the *Sidratul-Muntahā,* the tree of paradise that bears the fruit of grace, grow with the trunk of absolute faith, then the words of the prophets and *qutbs* will become the branches of the tree, and the truths in the teachings of the 124,000 prophets will emerge.

From these branches, the flowers of Allah's speech, actions, and conduct, His three thousand gracious qualities, and His ninety-nine powers will bloom and bear fruit. All the qualities and truths given to the different prophets, up to the 6,666 verses of the Holy Qur'an given by the final prophet, Muhammad *(Sal.),* will flower and bear fruit on that tree.

If man becomes *insān,* a true man, he will pluck and taste each fruit and then give it to all people to soothe their hearts and make them happy. To everyone, he will give Allah's love, His countless expressions of grace, His benevolence, and all the fruits of divine knowledge, dispelling the blemishes and darkness in their hearts. He will light up their hearts, make the wisdom of divine know-ledge grow, and place the resplendence called *Nūr* in their hearts. This is the natural way of a Sufi.

### 873.

An empty vessel rolls and clatters in the wind, but not a vessel that is full. The slightest wind will topple an empty vessel, making it clatter down the road, "Gada-gada-gada-gada." Because it weighs nothing, it is bound to roll whichever way the wind blows. But if it were full, the wind could not push it about.

Similarly, man's mind and body are pushed around by the wind of his base desires. But if his heart is filled and strengthened by the completeness of absolute faith in God, by the determination and certitude of faith in God, by the truth of faith in God, by patience, inner patience, and contentment, then he will not be upset by the waves of the mind and the winds of illusion, illness, poverty, sadness, desire, lust, envy, blood ties, and racial and religious differences. He will derive strength from the power of God which fills him, the power of perfection, equality, peace, and tranquilli-ty. Instead of these qualities, if he has selfishness, blood ties, and other self-oriented states, he can never be full because they are empty things; they are always lacking something. One whose heart is an empty vessel will roll and break in the slightest breeze.

The garbage of 'my religion, your religion', 'I am great, you are great', 'I am god, you are god' has no weight. It will roll around, causing the vessel which is man to roll with it. The things he gathers in the world are his diseases. He is rolled around and all that he collects here is blown away with him.

If man can fill his vessel with the treasure of truth, he will not be toppled by the shaking of the world, the wind, or blood ties. If he has that fulfillment within himself, he will not be affected by the connections to the earth, by blood ties, or by religious and racial bigotry. They will never be able to knock him down. Man must realize this.

874.

Man builds enormous fortresses, but the doors he makes for them are small. And just as the door is never as big as the fortress, the lock is smaller than the door. And just as the lock is smaller than the door, the key is smaller than the lock. And even smaller than the key are the little tongues on the key which move the tumblers in the lock. Only if the little tongues click the tumblers can man enter the fortress, where he can be free of danger from the winds of the world.

Anyone who trusts the world and his body, desiring all that he sees, saying, "I! I!" and collecting impermanent things that are really rubbish, will not be able to fit it all into that tiny keyhole.

In the same way, a man may have great titles, he may be a king, he may rule the whole world, he may have a huge body—but the door through which he must enter is small. For the huge fortress, for that beautiful house within, the door is faith, certitude, and determination. The lock is wisdom, and it is more subtle than the door. More subtle than the lock is the key of wisdom. And even more subtle than the key of wisdom is the tongue of divine analytic wisdom which turns the tumblers of divine luminous wisdom. Divine analytic wisdom is what clicks the tumblers and opens the fortress.

The *qalb,* or inner heart, is a fortress which contains all of everything, and Allah is the king of this fortress. If you want to see Him, you must use the key of subtle wisdom to open the door. You must clothe yourself in His actions, wearing the robe of His qualities and adorning yourself with the serene beauty of the light of *"Lā ilāha illallāhu* (There is nothing other than You, O God; only You are Allah). *Lā ilāha illallāhu. Lā ilāha illallāhu.*

*Lā ilāha illallāhu Muhammadur-Rasūlullah* (There is nothing other than You, O God; only You are Allah and Muhammad is the Messenger of God). *Allāhu akbar* (God is great), *Allāhu akbar, Allāhu akbar."* If you resonate with the sound of *ilāha,* He will come forward, and you can speak to Him. Man must think about the subtle key to this huge fortress.

875.

The lemon is liked by kings and commoners alike. All kinds of people plant lemon trees in their gardens, for lemons are used for many different purposes. But when the fruit is used, the juice is squeezed out and the skins are thrown away.

*Allāhu ta'ālā Nāyan,* Almighty God, created man, placing within him the essence of His own qualities and actions, which everyone likes.

In the body are the world, hell, thoughts, desires, arts, sexual games, and countless other things. With wisdom, man should extract the essence of the truth of God and throw away the worldly dirt, in the way the skin, seeds, and pulp of the lemon are thrown away after the juice is extracted. Then taste the essence of God's truth with the tongue of wisdom and faith.

But do not cut up or throw away your body. Accept it and use the good qualities within it. Throw away only the bad qualities. When all the waste matter has gone, when everything the desires have collected has been thrown away, you will possess the most valuable thing in your life—the taste of Allah. Wisdom searches for Allah, and Allah alone will be there. His taste is the taste of the undiminishing benevolence of grace called *rahmat.*

876.

God created man as the supreme being, the being to rule over all other beings, the one to understand right and wrong. But man comes to this world and absorbs what he sees, thinks, and intends. He studies what mind and desire bring to him and places it within his ego. He hangs up the flag of pride, "There is nothing like me," and displays his titles and honors.

Man considers what he has learned in the world equal to the profound knowledge of Allah's benevolence. "I can do everything," he says. "There is no one greater than I." This is like flinging a handful of salt into a huge lake and claiming to have made the lake salty. Such is the arrogance of man's ignorance, and this is the way he wastes his life. Unless that arrogance is eliminated, man does not truly pray, even though he bows in prayer a million times.

Man must accept God as the One of limitless grace, undiminishing wealth, and incomparable love. With His ninety-nine powers, His actions, His conduct, and His qualities, God performs His duties without selfishness, dwelling within all lives and understanding every heart. According to the qualities, actions, conduct, and wisdom of these lives, He will give of His powers and protect them. Allah is the One who gives peace without the ego, without pride, and without anger. He is the One who has contentment and peacefulness.

If man will absorb these qualities, keep Allah in front of him, surrender to Him, and acknowledge that Allah is the One who is doing everything, he will have wealth in the world of the souls, this world, and the next. Man must realize this.

## 877.

A disciple asked his sheikh, "What is the intellectual understanding I need to be able to have certitude in God?"

The sheikh answered, "God made this world so vast and created man with such subtlety. God has made many kinds of creations, and He has made their eyes, noses, and other features just right, placing them symmetrically on their faces. He did not make them lopsided, did He? No matter in what form God makes men, the eyes and the nose and the mouth and the ears and the face are centered and symmetrical.

"God centered man's *qalb,* his inner heart, in the same way, and He placed wisdom in the center of the *qalb.* In the center of wisdom is God and His justice.

"You can realize this with your intellect, can you not? The features of the face are not crooked. God did not place them randomly. There is a certain symmetry. Though the elephant's trunk is quite long, it has been placed in the middle of its face.

"Son, you must not find fault with any of God's creations. You must realize that the center is within you. If you open your wisdom, stand in the center, and look intently at yourself, you will understand the point. Do not waste your time trying to analyze other people: if you look at others and try to figure out what they are like, everything will go wrong, because each person sees his own faults in others.

"You must try to see your own faults within yourself. If you recognize your faults and force them to leave you, you will not find fault with anyone else.

"When your photograph is taken, the shadow of your image goes onto the paper. If you had not been there, would your shadow have gone onto the film? No. There would be no photograph. Is that not so? Like that, the faults you see in others are faults you have within yourself, and they are destroying you. You must look within yourself with your wisdom and throw away all your faults. Stand in the center, look with wisdom into your house, and throw away the quality of faultfinding.

"The faultfinding thoughts of your mind are biting you like mosquitoes and drinking your blood. Chase them away and you will be free. It is useless to be finding fault with others. Correct your own faults instead."

### 878.

When a tree blooms, the branches split open and the buds appear. They are not immediately visible. Then when the flowers open, the fragrance emerges and the qualities of the flowers are revealed. Their qualities identify their nature.

In the same way, from each of you, from the body itself, the bud of truth and wisdom must emerge. And from the budding wisdom, the flower of divine wisdom must bloom, breaking through from inside. Only then will it be revealed whether one is a demon, a beast, or a man.

Anyone who has a beautiful fragrance is an *insān,* a true man. Anyone who has a foul smell is a beast or a demon. Anyone who is attached to someone of his own blood, anyone who has the smell of blood, is of a lower birth.

The flowers of your qualities will reveal your true nature. If you have the fragrance of God, you will have the fragrance of an *insān kāmil,* a perfected man. There will be light in your face, beauty in your heart, and sweetness in your speech. If you look with wisdom, you will see that this is natural to man.

Reflect on this and conduct your life accordingly.

879.

Absolute faith in God is great.
Greater yet is your duty.
Greater yet are good conduct and modesty,
Sincerity, reserve, and fear of wrongdoing.
Greater yet are Allah's qualities,
His actions and His conduct.
Greater yet is for a perfected man
To act with Allah's qualities,
Surrendering to Him as His slave.

One who realizes this and acts accordingly will be a sun that gives light and peace to the whole world.

880.

If man spreads the net of desire on the ocean of illusion in his mind, what will he catch? He will catch only whatever happens to be there. His net will be filled with dirt and the things that will destroy him. There is nothing fragrant there. The bad things in the ocean of illusion will rot and decay in your mind, body, actions, and wisdom, giving them a terrible odor. But despite the stench, the mind and desire have a great liking for these things.

If, however, you hold the net of wisdom in the hands of absolute faith and spread it out on the sea of the divine knowledge called *'ilm,* you will receive the riches of God's benevolence. They will be fragrant and resplend with light as Allah's undiminishing wealth of *'ilm,* grace, faith, and wisdom in all three worlds. Their taste will never change, and they will never spoil. If you taste even one drop, your heart and body will turn to gold. This precious and indestructible wealth will be kept in Allah's treasury.

Man must think and take what is good and lasting.

881.

Today, there is an eclipse of the sun. When the light of the sun is obstructed by the moon, it is called a solar eclipse, is it not? This is an example we can see with our eyes. Although the sun is very bright, there is a darkness which can hide the light.

When the sun dawns, it brings daylight. How bright it is then! No amount of clouds can make it completely dark. However, we must understand from the example of the eclipse that there is a darkness which can occlude even the sun's brightness.

Like this, God has created within man a pure resplendence that is like the sun. But there are eclipses which can conceal that sun, too: the five elements (earth, fire, water, air, and ether), mind, desire, illusion, anger, hastiness, impatience, intoxicants, lust, theft, murder, falsehood, arrogance, the pride of the ego, doubt, selfishness, obsession, hatred, greed, fanaticism, envy, the sixty-four arts and sexual games, and the feeling of 'I' and 'mine'. The darkness of these qualities and actions will occlude even the beautiful light of grace that comes from God's qualities and His good thoughts.

But the sun perseveres and finally dispels the darkness. If, with certitude and faith in Allah, Allah's light, the analytical wisdom of the *Qutb (Ral.)*, and divine luminous wisdom, man succeeds in dispelling the worldly darkness that comes to conceal him, he will be a true man.

### 882.

Because a crab has ten legs, it cannot walk straight. If a man has a connection to the ten sins, he cannot walk straight.

The ten sins are arrogance, karma, *māyā,* earth, fire, water, air, ether, mind, and desire. He will cut everything with the claws of mind and desire and put it in his mouth. He will not be able to walk straight, nor will he allow the good things to grow.

### 883.

When flies bite a bull, it can chase them away with its long tail. But a horse has a short tail with long hairs; thus, although it twists its tail and shakes its body, the flies continue to drink its blood.

Like this, as long as man does not have the proper growth of wisdom, he cannot rid himself of the bloodsucking suffering he experiences in the world. When he tries to bring an end to his suffering through mind, desire, and worldly learning, he is like a horse trying to shake off flies with a tail that is too short.

You should use the growth of wisdom to chase away your sufferings.

### 884.

If a man looks at another man's eyes, relying on them to guide him when he walks, he will fall head over heels. When you walk, you must rely on your own eyes.

In the same way, as long as man continues to look at the faults of others, he will fall. He will fall without realizing his own faults. Only by looking at his own faults can he avoid further mistakes.

### 885.

Son, when a cobra moves into the path of a man, it raises its hood and stares at him. The man becomes very frightened by the hissing and the fierce look of the snake. If the snake moves a little more, the man becomes even more frightened. Some men shiver in terror, some actually fall unconscious, and there are those whose hearts stop beating.

It is also like this when a man is mesmerized by the fierce look and compelling words of someone who tricks him into saying and doing what he wants. Just as a snake can frighten a man, one man can mesmerize another by fierce acts and words.

Now when a snake looks at a man, if the man will stare back at it sharply, the snake will not do anything to him. In just that way, if a man will look back sharply at the one who is trying to mesmerize him, if he will look back with the faith, certitude, determination, and trust that God is with him, and if his heart keeps resonating with *Allāhu,* then he need not be frightened by anything.

### 886.

There was a man who roamed here and there, searching for a guru. Though he met many gurus, he was unable to find one who was suitable. None of them conformed to his ideal of what a guru should be like. He began to grumble, "What is this? What is happening to the world? I must find a good guru."

Then he met a chameleon and began to question it. "Have I come to the path of wisdom?"

The chameleon nodded its head.

"Have I become a great man in the world?"

The chameleon nodded its head.

"Have I completed my studies and reached the shore?"

The chameleon nodded its head.

"I am in heaven, am I not?"

The chameleon nodded its head.

"Have I rid myself of ignorance?"

The chameleon nodded its head.

"Am I living in a state of non-attachment?" (The man had a wife and a huge family.)

The chameleon nodded its head.

"Do I have all happiness, the wealth of wisdom, and everything in completeness?"

The chameleon nodded its head.

"O guru, will you give me further explanations and teach me?"

The chameleon nodded its head.

The man caught hold of the chameleon, put it in a cage, took it to his house, and cared for it. No matter what questions it was asked, the chameleon nodded its head.

Why? Because chameleons are always bobbing their heads.

But a man who is truly wise will cut through all your thoughts and tell you that everything you are doing is wrong. You, however, will reject the wise teacher who corrects you and look for one who will agree with you and nod his head like a chameleon.

No real teacher will accept you if you search with this attitude. If you don't like to throw away your thoughts, you will need a guru who is like a chameleon. If, however, you are willing to throw away what you already have, you might get a wise man as a teacher.

### 887.

A child was worrying in the sheikh's presence. "Where did you go?" asked the sheikh.

She said, "I was thinking of a place to escape."

"Good," the sheikh answered. "If you want to escape from this world, you will have to go to heaven. If you want to go to heaven, you will have to be in heaven while you are here in this world. But if you are in hell here, you will have to go to hell. Where else could you go?

"If you want to escape from all the difficulties and accidents in the world, you must become an ant and creep away. As long as you are like iron, *irumbu*, rather than like an ant, *erumbu*, you cannot go anywhere. When you are iron, a magnet can pull you. As long as a magnet can pull you, you will not be able to hide anywhere. Become smaller and smaller like an ant, and the world will leave you of its own accord."

888.

Some thirsty travelers went to a house and asked for water. The woman there gave them a sweet beverage in a pot. After they drank it, they were curious. "From which well did you draw this water?" they asked.

Jokingly, her husband pointed to a well by the house. "The water is there."

That night, the travelers came back with pickaxes and other equipment and tried to dig out and lift up the well. Seeing this, the owner of the well ran outside and exclaimed, "What are you doing?"

"We are trying to lift out the well so we can get the sweet drink you gave us before. We want to take this wonder to the people of our country."

The man of the house said, "What we gave you was sap from the palmyra plant. We played a joke on you. What fools you are, trying to lift out a well!"

Ashamed, the travelers picked up their tools and went on their way.

★

Like this, the states of inner patience, contentment, trust in God, and praise to God are contained within man as the *Katpaha Virudcham,* the tree of the plenitude of faith, the quality of God that gives you whatever you ask. Wisdom is the taste made by God to quench man's thirst, and it is within all human beings.

But without analyzing and tasting wisdom, man samples the things in the world and says they are tasty. "This water is good, that god is good, this devotion is good, that prayer is good, this race is good, that guru is good." In this manner, they taste all the divisions and differences.

Only on the day man tastes the pure water of God, who is within him as the most deep and wonderful well, will his thirst be quenched. Rather than trying to taste and take things that belong to others like the man who tried to take the other man's well, man must dig his own well and drink of its cooling water. In this way his thirst can be permanently quenched.

889.

Would you attempt to draw milk from a cow's backside? You

would only get urine, would you not? If you want milk, you must find the place from which milk will flow. If you use your wisdom before you try to draw milk, everything will be all right.

God has given you eyes, a nose, a mouth, and ears. He has given you a heart, and He has given you the wisdom to analyze and see that you do what is correct. If you act according to your wisdom, you will receive milk. If you do not analyze properly, if you reach for the backside, you will get urine. When you understand and act correctly, that in itself is milk.

890.

> Develop love within yourself.
> Through love, develop wisdom.
> Through wisdom, develop truth.
> Through truth, develop compassion.
> Through compassion, develop peace
> And equality toward all.
> As the completion of that peace
> Develop all the qualities of God.
> Through God's qualities, develop your actions.
> Through those actions, realize yourself.
> When you realize yourself
> You can see and know God.
> You can see Him within yourself.

891.

A child asked the sheikh, "Do you have any suggestion as to how we can attract more people to the Fellowship and to our meetings so that we can make the Fellowship grow?"

The sheikh replied, "After you make yourself grow, it will be easy to make the Fellowship grow.

"These are the things you must have to help you grow; these are the things you must have at your meetings:

First is patience.

Second is inner patience, or *sabūr.*

Third is contentment, or *shakūr.*

Fourth is to give all responsibility to God, *tawakkul-'alallāh.*

Fifth is to give all praise to God alone, *al-hamdu lillāh.*

Sixth is determination, determined faith in Allah.

Seventh is the absolute faith, the *īmān* by which you can further establish and strengthen your determination.

Eighth is compassion.

Ninth is the awareness that there is only one family.

Tenth is equality, seeing all lives as equal to your own.

Eleventh is the sharp point of intellect that gives you the awareness to treat all lives as your own.

Twelfth is to be as concerned about the hunger of others as you are about your own and to give your food away.

Thirteenth is not to kill any life, not with a weapon, a thought, the mind, or the eyes; not to kill because of race or religion or color or beliefs. You must have the purity of the light of wisdom which will cut away these evil qualities.

Fourteenth is the subtle wisdom to be aware that the pain and illness of every life are like the pain and illness of your own body and life.

Fifteenth is the eye to see all lives as one.

Sixteenth is to realize that God exists omnipresently in all lives, to have absolute faith and trust in Him, to imbibe the qualities of His path, and to put them into action.

Seventeenth is to realize that all lives have both good and evil qualities. If evil qualities come, you must be forbearant and patient. If good qualities come, you must try to elevate them by giving them more wisdom.

Eighteenth is to do duty without selfishness or attachment.

Nineteenth is to realize the faults you may have committed in the past and to try not to commit those faults in the future. Then, if anyone else committed a fault, realizing that it may be the same fault you committed in the past, you must forbear with patience and show love. You must realize that the other person is not at fault and that you committed the fault first. Realize that, in time, others can correct themselves in the way you corrected yourself. While existing in a state of awareness, try to correct them gradually. Teach them the wisdom of peacefulness, establishing and conducting yourself in the state of tranquil brotherhood.

Twentieth is to realize the ways of justice within God and man and to perceive unity.

Twenty-first is to realize that God has created all kingdoms and that He rules them all with divine justice. He rules all lives with pure and perfect justice. Realize what that justice is, take it into yourself, and act accordingly.

Twenty-second is to become the king of your body. Within your body are many worlds and millions of creations—all the creations of all the worlds are within you. All the creations visible on the outside are seen within as shadow forms, as energy forms, as cell forms, as demonic bloodsucking forms, or as beastly forms. You must become king of justice for that world, making God's justice into the justice of your rulership and bringing forth that justice to rule all the animals within you.

Twenty-third is to become human. If you are going to be a king, your justice must be consistent. Man's justice must be brought to men; you must do duty with justice. The king's justice must be brought into human justice, so that, as a man, you will be able to show that justice to all lives. Become human, dwell amidst human beings, and bring to your awareness the peace, tranquillity, and justice of true man.

Twenty-fourth is conscience. God's justice must be brought into your conscience, warning you at every moment. You must rule from within the compassion of your wisdom.

"These twenty-four qualities are the twenty-four letters of the *Kalimah,* the word of God. If you accept the *Kalimah* into your heart, strengthening it, you will know with absolute faith that no one is worthy of worship but Allah, the One of limitless grace and incomparable love, the One who gives the undiminishing wealth of grace. If you understand this state and surrender fully, you will pray, '*Lā ilāha illallāhu:* There is nothing other than You, O God. Only You are Allah.' If you spend every breath in Him, performing 43,242 prostrations to Him every day, you will grow. When you have progressed like this, you have reached the state where you can help the Fellowship grow.

"Now you must gently enter the beauty of God. You must gently enter His love. After you enter His love, you must nourish good conduct, respect, modesty, virtue, and fear of wrongdoing. I am asking you to grow within that culture of goodness. Each child must grow like this."

892.

There was a man who wanted to marry. He looked for a beautiful girl, and finally he found and married a girl who appeared to be quite beautiful. But when he was taking her around to parties, he discovered she had a slight hunchback. He was so embarrassed to be seen with her that he divorced her and found another woman. She too seemed beautiful, so he married her and took her home. He was very proud of her. But what did she do? As soon as night fell, she would sneeze, and she would continue to sneeze throughout the night. She sneezed so much that he could not sleep. He thought, "What is this? I gave up a hunch-backed wife for a sneezing wife!"

He divorced her, too, and looked again. He found another beautiful girl, married her, and took her home. But he found that she farted the whole night through. What a horrible smell! He had to leave her in the bedroom and sleep outside, for he could not bear the noise or the smell; the whole house was stinking.

He thought, "This seems to be my fate. I was looking for beauty and married the first girl, but I found she was hunchbacked; she looked like an old woman when she walked. The second one looked beautiful, too, but she sneezed the whole night through. And no one could stay with the third one because she farts like a fox." He was fed up by this time, and absolutely exhausted.

★

In the same way, whoever goes around searching for perfect beauty in this world will never have peace in his life. Somewhere or other there will always be a shortcoming. Looking throughout the whole world for beauty, he will always complain about one thing or another. Finally he will be driven to the state of wanting to commit suicide. If you desire external beauty, this is how it will end. You will suffer defeat just like the man in this story.

If, however, you look for good qualities, good conduct, good actions, good behavior, sincerity, modesty, reserve, fear of wrong-doing, and faith and trust in God, if you desire what has wisdom, this will preserve your exaltedness in this life and the next.

### 893.

A bull began to think, "I plow the whole day, and when I come home I am tied up. They give me only a little grass and a bit of water each day. I have no peace. I cannot even eat what I want. Is this going to be my life?" The bull was feeling quite sorry for himself.

A passerby saw the sorrow on the bull's face and told its owner,

"Why don't you untie this bull and let him loose for a little while? Let him walk around." So the bull was set free.

The bull was extremely happy. He looked around and saw what appeared to be a lot of green grass. But when he went close to it, he found that the blades of grass were hardly long enough to take into his mouth. He moved to another patch of green and then another, still searching for grass to eat. There is a saying, "The grass is always greener on the other side of the fence," and so the bull roamed, dissatisfied and hungry.

When the bull finally gave up and went home, there was no food there either. So he went to a neighbor's farm and began to eat the crops. The watchman caught the bull, beat him, and tied him up. When the owner came to take the bull home, he asked the bull, "Why did you do this?"

The bull answered, "The whole day long I tried to eat, but oh, my fate! I couldn't bear my hunger so I went there to steal something. This man caught me, tied me up, and beat me. Now I can hardly walk. This is my fate. Instead of eating your food and being content, I became greedy and earned this beating. This is the result of leaving my rightful place."

★

Like this, man's birth and death are in his hands. Poverty and wealth are also in his hands, as well as the truth and falsehood of his life. Instead of realizing it, man looks at the world and runs around, saying, "My life is better here. No, my life is better there." He wanders from place to place, and what happens in the end? He encounters the same fate as the bull. He runs here and there but nothing seems to satisfy him. In the end, he begins to steal land, women, and gold.

When he steals these things from the world, time beats him up, satan catches him, demons drink his blood, his arrogance eats him up, his anger burns him up, and hastiness and impatience crawl into him and begin to destroy him, atom by atom. Thus he dies in sorrow, having found no peace from the time of his birth until the time of his death.

If only you would realize this! Know the truth of God's creation, think with His wisdom, and accept what God has created as food for you with contentment and surrender to Allah. Praise Him, saying, *"Al-hamdu lillāh,"* and that will become the wealth of your life.

A farmer worked so hard that he had no time to bathe or relax. He had to work very hard to feed his children. He had only one loincloth to wear, and he never took it off. He never even had time to change his loincloth or to sleep.

The loincloth finally began to complain, "*Aiyō,* the sweat and the smell! I have never even seen water. He never bathes, and he doesn't even wash me. This place stinks. I have been on his backside for thirty or thirty-five years. What suffering I have undergone! When will I ever be free? He is not going to let me go easily, so I'll have to start biting him."

And so the loincloth made him itch and itch, and the farmer began to scratch and scratch. At last, the farmer thought, "If I bathe in the pond, the itching might stop." But even after he bathed, the loincloth continued to make him itch.

"You satan!" the man cried, searching frantically for another loincloth. Finally, he found one, pulled off the one he had worn for so long, and flung it on the ground by the pond.

The loincloth heaved a sigh of relief, "After thirty-five years, at last I am free!" But as soon as the farmer left, a man came by who had a skin disease on his backside. He spotted the loincloth on the ground, so he put it on in place of his own and bathed in it. The loincloth soon realized that this second backside was far worse than the first. It was wet and soggy and smelly. After the man had bathed, he too took the loincloth off and tossed it aside.

Then another man found it and put it on. His smell was even more foul, and he had sores all over his body. When he had finished bathing, he also took off the loincloth and threw it on the ground. The next man who came had bleeding piles. The one after him had a 'bad' disease. The next one had festering sores. And so on.

In this way, the loincloth came to see a thousand backsides a day, one after another. It thought, "*Aiyō,* at least when I was on the farmer I saw one backside, and he only smelled of sweat. Since he discarded me, I haven't had a moment's peace. Oh, the backsides I have smelled!" Gradually the cloth gave way, falling apart fiber by fiber.

If a loincloth prefers a better life, it can only end up on someone else's backside. It may go through most of its life on one backside, but if it decides it wants a better life, it can only go to a different backside. A loincloth cannot rise above its station in life or change its fate. Once a loincloth, always a loincloth.

★

The life of man is like that loincloth. He has blood ties and desire for land, women, and gold. He has mind and desire. He has all these things, but he seeks liberation, peace, and tranquillity. He thinks he has to go off alone and meditate in order to reach heaven, so, leaving his family and gold behind, he searches for peace in the jungle; but since he carries his mind and desire with him, when he meditates all the things within him come to use him as their loincloth. One thing wears him from one side, another wears him from another side. The qualities of the snake and the monkey come to wear him. Four hundred trillion, ten thousand qualities and demons wear him.

As a result, he experiences all kinds of foul smells and karma. Despite his meditation, he is forced to experience them all. In the very place he intends to rid himself of these sorrows, he experiences what the loincloth experienced when it tried to be free. He suffers while he meditates and he suffers while he prays. And then he says, "Father of my father, is this to be my fate?"

Finally, his body, wisdom, and strength waste away, and he is reduced to skin and bones. His fate is like that of the loincloth; he gives way and falls apart, little by little. Such is the fate of the man who sets out to achieve liberation without relinquishing his desires.

Man must think. He must realize which things inside him are killing and swallowing him and try to escape from them with wisdom. He must kill them and break out of their midst. If he can, he will achieve a good life of exaltedness and serenity. If he succeeds in killing the qualities which are trying to kill him, God's qualities will appear within him, and he will have the connection to God.

If man can realize this with wisdom, then no matter where he is he will be in meditation. Wherever he is, wherever he lives according to that truth, he will be in meditation and there will be peace.

895.

If a man tries to stop the flood when the banks of a lake break and the waters flow into the city, he will be swept away. It is not the fault of the lake; it is the fault of the man who thought he could save the city. First, he should have understood the force of the flood. He should have understood and reinforced the banks before they broke.

You must do good to protect the country. To do that you must have the necessary wisdom, ability, and understanding. Before the floods come, you have to build a dam. You must know the water level, the strength of the banks, and the rate at which the water rises.

One who understands will know how much rain will fall. According to that, he will make arrangements for the excess water to be released in the proper way, thus safeguarding the countryside. One who rushes in at the last minute to stop the flood, without making previous arrangements, will be the first to be destroyed.

Like that, those who forget Allah and lose their wisdom, yet still go around saying, "I will help, I will do," will be destroyed. But one who has Allah and wisdom within, one who has the perfect faith called *īmān* will be able to help himself and others.

896.

*Child:* Words about destruction are being spoken outside in the world, but while I am enjoying unity with my sheikh on the inside, I am not disturbed by it.

*Bawa Muhaiyaddeen:* That is correct. If you stay in your rightful state, whatever comes to destroy you will itself be destroyed. If you have Allah's representatives within you in the proper place, whatever comes to destroy you will be destroyed. One who has fear does not have Allah. One who has Allah does not have fear. Trust in God, *tawakkul-'alallāh.*

897.

When a flower blooms, its fragrance lasts for only three days to a week. But if a wise man extracts the essence of the flower's fragrance before the flower fades, the scent will last for many years.

This world is sometimes known as *poo-loham,* the flower world, and *nara-loham,* the man world. The place in which humans live is *poo-loham,* the flower garden of creation where the beauty of God's power is revealed. Among these creations there is a large flower called *qalb-poo,* the flower of the heart. A man of wisdom will extract the essence of truth from the flower of the heart before the flower fades. Then he will have it always. One without wisdom, however, will let the flower fade.

A wise man will extract the essence of Allah which he brought with him from the world of the souls. The fragrance of Allah's benevolent grace is in the *qalb,* the innermost heart. Distill what is in the *qalb,* discard the form, and take the essence, where man and Allah merge.

898.

*Child:* After everything ends, what prayers should we say to Allah when we come into His presence?

*Bawa Muhaiyaddeen:* When you are in His presence, do the prayer which must be done before Him. When everything else has been completed and you have come to His immediate presence, you will see only yourself. You will not see anything else. Your beauty will be God's light, your speech will be His speech, your actions will be His actions, His conduct will be your conduct, and His prayer will be your prayer. What else is there for us to do?

Only when you have come to that state, only when you have all His attributes within yourself, will you have reached His presence. Otherwise, you are not in front of Him—you are far away. If you are far from Him, do the things you were told to do earlier. When you are in His presence, do what He does.

899.

*Child:* Could Bawa Muhaiyaddeen say something about how to open the heart?

*Bawa Muhaiyaddeen:* In whatever room you live, you need a key to open the door. In the same way, no matter what religion, color, or race you belong to, no matter what philosophies or doctrines you follow, if you want to open the rooms of Allah you need the key of *īmān,* the key of absolute faith and determination. That key will open any lock.

You must believe in the truth that there is nothing other than Allah. He alone is the permanent truth, the One who has no beginning, no end, and no form. He exists everywhere. He is a power, One that does not diminish regardless of how much each creation takes from it. He is perfect completeness. Have perfect faith in Allah and turn the key of *īmān,* saying, *"Lā ilāha illallāhu.*

There is nothing other than You, O God. You are Allah." Then Allah's house will open to you. There is a room in which His resonance, resplendence, explanation, and light exist. *"Al-hamdu lillāh,"* you will say. "All praise belongs to God." It is in this state that you will be able to open the *qalb,* the innermost heart.

900.

*Child:* Does God always see a balance between a person's qualities and the difficulties in his life?

*Bawa Muhaiyaddeen:* God has given you everything. He has given you rain. He has given you high mountains and valleys. He has given you oceans and lands. He has given you everything—a body, a life, everything. You have to know that. He has given you the way to climb up, to climb down, to walk, to sit, everything. You must think. He has given you the balance.

You must understand the balance you hold in your hands. God does not need to examine the balance, because He has given you everything. When trying to climb a mountain, you will fall if you lose your balance. It is your responsibility. He will merely watch. He will look at you and say, "O man, why have you lost your balance like this?"

But of course, if we fall He will lift us up. He will comfort us and say, "All right, in the future realize that when you climb a mountain you need a stick to support yourself. Be careful." He will comfort us when we fall in our ignorance. He will come to save us and help us, and He will tell us, "Should you not have known this? You need to be cautious, do you not?"

But no matter how many times He comes to lift us up and help us, we continue to fall whenever we lose our balance. It is in our hands.

There is a bridge between heaven and hell, a very subtle bridge of wisdom, which is as narrow as the edge of a sword. To cross this bridge, first, we must surrender to God and leave the world behind. Then we must walk carefully on the edge of that sword: illusion is on one side and hell is on the other. As we walk, the storms of illusion and hell will try to knock us off the bridge, shoving us this way and that. This is why we must leave behind us the world of illusion, the world of *māyā.* We must walk across the bridge of wisdom with the balance of faith in God in order to reach *gnānam,* divine wisdom. If we lose our balance, we will surely fall.

414

## 901.

*Child:* Why are we always falling down? Bawa Muhaiyaddeen says it is our fault.

*Bawa Muhaiyaddeen:* I did not say it was your fault. If you are wondering why you are falling, you have only to look at it through your wisdom. There must be some weakness, whether it is in the leg, the hand, the body, or in wisdom or faith; there must be a lack of strength in one of those supporting parts. Because it has lost its strength, you have fallen down.

If you support yourself with the strong stick of faith in Allah, unwavering faith without the slightest doubt, you will not fall. As long as that stick retains its strength, you will not fall.

## 902.

*Child:* Is everyone born with an awareness of that strength?

*Bawa Muhaiyaddeen:* A tree is contained within a seed, although we cannot see it. You must have seen how the flowers, fruits, and leaves of massive trees grow from a tiny seed.

In the same way, the strength is within you, in your seed. God has given you everything. If you believe this with certitude, you will become aware of that strength.

## 903.

*Child:* But how does that awareness come?

*Bawa Muhaiyaddeen:* You have the awareness. Everything is within you. The flowers are there, the branches are there, the leaves are there, the raw fruit, the ripe fruit, the taste, everything. Look within.

## 904.

*Child:* So you have to discover it, right?

*Bawa Muhaiyaddeen:* It is because of your awareness that you scratch when you itch. You have the perception to know where you itch, and your intellect tells you to scratch. When you scratch in that place, you make it peaceful.

This is how you must find the treasure within you, using divine analytic wisdom. Then you can avert whatever difficulties or dangers come to you.

## 905.

*Child:* How can one progress from imagining another's sorrow and suffering to actually experiencing it as if it were his own?
*Bawa Muhaiyaddeen:* Only if adequate wisdom, the quality of comforting, and the duty that God does emerge within you will you have that experience. It is the transformation within you that makes you experience the suffering of others as your own.

## 906.

The rose flower has a fragrance which you can experience and enjoy. You and the nose experience it together.

Just as you inhale the fragrance from a flower and enjoy it with your nose, you must inhale the sorrow of others with the nose of your wisdom, experience it, and then comfort them. This is Allah's work. This is His duty.

## 907.

*Child:* Will Bawa Muhaiyaddeen speak about the five duties? He often talks about duty to God, duty to the sheikh, duty to the Fellowship, duty to the family, and duty to the world.
*Bawa Muhaiyaddeen:* There are hundreds of millions of duties, not just these five. The three thousand gracious attributes of Allah are His duties, the ninety-nine actions are His duties. You spoke of only five. What are our duties? There are hundreds of thousands of kinds of duties.

First of all, do service to God. God is the *Katpaha Virudcham,* the tree of the plenitude of faith which gives you everything you ask. Nourish that tree within you with the water of wisdom. That is duty to God.

Then do service to the sheikh. The true sheikh is the ripe fruit on that tree. Taste that fruit and preserve its nourishing sweetness within you. That is duty to the true sheikh.

Do service for the Fellowship. The Fellowship is a place of light that exists to dispel the darkness in the heart. Those who have attained wisdom in that place must do duty with a loving heart. The duty of wisdom is to know your own self, and when you realize yourself, you will realize your own state. As soon as you understand your own state, you will see the plenitude of God dwelling within you and you being within God. Then there will

416

be no duality. With the three thousand gracious qualities of God, you will show compassion to all lives. That is duty to the Fellowship and to the children of the Fellowship. It will become a precious gem for your life.

What does it mean to do duty to the family? Is there something called a family? The family and the world are really one. The whole world is your family. Do duty for the world. Be one who loves all lives, one who exists as the form of compassion, and be of service and help them. That is duty to the world family.

Therefore, with your good qualities, actions, and conduct, acquire God's qualities. To acquire His qualities and serve others, bringing love and peace to their hearts, is your duty and Allah's miracle. When you attain that state, all lives will bow to you.

## 908.

*Child:* Is it correct to see satan as a personification outside yourself? It is often spoken about as such. Or is satan just the qualities or illusions inside us?

*Bawa Muhaiyaddeen:* Satan is inside. It is better to recognize him inside. Evil qualities are satan. If you have the qualities and actions of God, then that is God. If you have the qualities of satan, if you have the vanity, the envy, and the jealousy of satan, if you lose faith and begin to doubt God, then that is satan.

Here is the difference between this world and the next, hell and heaven: if you have the qualities of God, it is heaven; if you have the qualities of satan, it is hell. If you repel evil qualities with wisdom and take Allah's qualities, actions, and conduct, that is your grace. It is the heaven where Adam *(A.S.)* once was, and you also will be there, where you once were.

## 909.

*Child:* How do we know whether a true human being exists within a person?

*Bawa Muhaiyaddeen:* When a flower falls on you, you take it in your hand and hold it to your nose, inhaling its fragrance. But when an insect falls on you, you shout in fear, "*Aiyō,* grandmother!" and run away. Is there not a difference between the two? With your wisdom, you know the difference between a biting insect and a fragrant flower.

If you look with wisdom, you will know that anyone who is

like a fragrant flower is a true human being, and anyone who bites like an insect is someone who merely looks like a man. If you have wisdom, you will understand the difference.

910.

All of everything is within the heart of each man. His world is within him, and all the creations of God are within him. Also, there is an agreement relating to the length of his time in the world. The day a man's world dies is the day of his destruction. The day on which he is awakened from his death is his Day of Reckoning. All of creation is brought back to life on that day. And the day on which judgment is given to all is his Day of Judgment. Each person has the Day of Reckoning and the Day of Judgment within him. Each person contains the eighteen thousand universes.

To wisdom, the outer world in which we live is only a tiny particle of the inner world. If one atom of the inner world were to be cut into a million pieces, this world would be only one millionth of a piece of that atom.

The world has a connection to earth, fire, water, air, and ether. It functions with these elements, and it rotates continually. But one day, when a disagreement occurs between any of these five elements, your world will end.

The world rotates around the one point of God's grace; that is its axis. *Qutbs* and *olis* exist in the world to protect the world of grace within man. The *qutbs* and *olis* will exist within true men to protect them and the kingdom of truth within them. When a man with trust and faith in God prays, they will be within him. But if he changes into an animal and loses his faith in God, they will not stay; they will return to the indestructible land, the kingdom of God. And when they do leave, this rotating world of particles will be destroyed. This is known only to the one who stays within that one point.

It will be good if you know your world, your Day of Reckoning, and your Day of Judgment. Then you can go to the realm where there is no destruction. If you overcome the world of death, you can go to the world where there is no death. If you overcome the Day of Reckoning, you can go where you will not be brought back. If you understand judgment, you can go to a place where there is no judgment—you can go to Allah.

911.

*Child:* Should we do our work knowing this? Believing your words to be the truth, should we work with a view toward the end? How should we finish our worldly duties? How should we prepare ourselves for the end?

*Bawa Muhaiyaddeen:* How can you take my words as the truth? You must take Allah's word as the truth. What has Allah said? Take that as the truth. You must not accept my words as truth merely because I said them. You must accept what Allah has said.

The correct way to think is, "Allah has said these words, the sheikh is teaching us the words of Allah, and therefore I believe them." Then you must ask the way. You must see that the sheikh's words coincide with the words of Allah and ask yourselves, "How must we change ourselves? How can we be saved from this?" That is how you must place your trust.

Then, if you ask him the way, he will tell you. He will say, "Death is in your hands. It can come to you before the blinking of an eye. Death can come at any moment, even while you sleep or while you eat. Death is constantly hanging over you. It has no time or season.

"Death is always in front of us. It can strike us before a word can leave our lips, before we can lift a morsel of food or a drop of water to our mouth. This is the truth. Death is real.

"Time, however, is not real. You must not live believing that time is real. But because death is a reality, you must spend every moment thinking of what you must do. Because death is hanging over you at every moment, you must be ready to die before it can attack you."

As soon as you have determination, certitude, and absolute faith, you will realize that everything here in this world is subject to death. You will say, "Everything created, everything that exists in a form, is bound to die. Evil desires are tormenting me. Desires are eating me. All the things subject to death are eating me, demanding me to bring them this and that! Therefore, I must kill them immediately."

If you can cut them away, the death in front of you and hanging over you will recede, and you will have eternal life. In the state of *hayāt,* eternal life, you will have no fear.

Until then, every breath holds death in front of you. Those who are deceiving you and eating you from the inside are spirits, desires, thoughts, illusions, attachments, blood ties, happiness, and love for the world. All these feelings arise from your base desires. Things subject to death continue to torture you. They must die. Cut them away with one blow. The day you cut them away from you is the day of eternal life.

912.

*Child:* I'd like to ask Bawa Muhaiyaddeen about a dream I had approximately a week ago.

There was a house with a piece of property next to it, and on the property were fifteen or twenty small wells or springs which were like holes in the ground. I looked into the house and saw a number of people who were very sick, very close to death. Then I looked into each of the wells. They were extremely poisonous, full of demons and viruses. Only one person in the house was able to walk around, and he and I went up to each of the wells. He said the Third *Kalimah* and blew into each well. Then, with a shovel, he cleaned away the debris.

Before this, the atmosphere all around had been very thick and heavy. When we were almost finished, we looked back at the area of the yard in which we had been working, and all the darkness had cleared. There was a lot of light and clarity, and the people in the house who had been sick were up and moving around.

*Bawa Muhaiyaddeen:* That is a good dream. The house is the house of Allah, the Fellowship. It is the house of God for all people, for all the children who live in the world. They are all afflicted by poisons and disease. They have the poisonous wells of religious and racial differences: my religion, your religion, my race, your race. They drink of these poisonous waters, trying to alleviate their thirst. In the places where they dwell, many diseases, ghosts, demons, evil thoughts, desires, satans, and devils have caught them and are eating them from within, making them very ill.

When we try to make their wisdom grow, what do they do? They turn the pure wisdom, the clear water which is being given to them, into poison, and then even divine knowledge is poisoned! They inject their karmic and poisonous qualities into pure wisdom. Instead of accepting the pure water, the pure wisdom, they inject their own religion, caste, fanaticism, bigotry, and biases into the water, making it poisonous. They drop the things of the world into pure wisdom, and they poison the things which belong to the hereafter, making poisonous even the wisdom of the ocean of knowledge.

They forget what will appease their thirst, what will ease their fatigue, what will give them life. As a result they drop religion, race, color, and the arrogance of the ego into the well, making poisonous even those things that could appease their thirst.

The twenty-four letters in the *Kalimah* plus the soul make twenty-five, which are represented by the twenty-five wells. Karma poisoned and sickened everyone, and they were unable to walk on the path to Allah. Everything was surrounded by darkness. If this is the state in which people exist, what can we do? What shall we do?

We must do the *Kalimah*, the Third *Kalimah*. It is our *qurbān*, the prayer of perfection which cuts away the animal qualities and the evils within. "*Subhānallāhi, walhamdu lillāhi, wa lā ilāha illallāhu, wallāhu akbar, wa lā hawla wa lā quwwata illā billāhi, wa huwal 'alīyul 'azīm:* Glory be to God; all praise belongs to Him; there is nothing other than You, O God. You are Allah who is most great; none has the majesty or the power to sustain except for God, who is the majesty and supreme glory."

The Third *Kalimah* is the *qurbān* for all the poisons. When this was recited in your dream, all the poisons, all the corpses inside the wells, and all the debris were swept away. The darkness became light, all the people rose up, their illnesses went away, and the water became tasty. Divine knowledge became radiant, filling everyone with life. This is the meaning of your dream.

Therefore, all of you—each child—must give up your differences and use the Third *Kalimah* to cut away all the evil qualities within. Only Allah exists in a state of equality. He is the religion. He is the philosophy. Trust only Him. You must have the determination and the faith to pray to Him alone. He is the only king for everything. He alone is worthy of worship.

The world, religious fanaticism, racial differences, desires, and colors must die. They are all poisonous and they must die. If you drink these poisons, you will be sickened for life, living in a deathlike state in which you cannot walk the path to the next world or to God. To remain in that state is hell. All who do not walk toward Allah are dead and in hell. Only those who do walk toward Allah are alive.

Accept only Allah. If we reach the state of one family, one God, and one prayer, we will no longer have the illnesses you saw in your dream.

## 913.

At one time, people were inquiring about my heritage: where I came from, which family I came from, and what my ancestry was. They asked me repeatedly and their whole purpose was to trace my lineage. No thought of Allah came to them. They were not people who had faith in Allah; they believed in lineage, ancestry, heritage, pedigree, and family connections. There was no realization of our original heritage, our real heritage. They were interested only in the ancestry which began in this world, and not about our ancestry in the world of the souls.

Allah gave me a kingdom in this world. When I was the leader of that kingdom, I ate and lived in peace and freedom, but I did not really look after the joys and sorrows of my people. My ministers were busy satisfying their own needs, and the people suffered because of it. I was protecting my family, but I was not truly helping the people.

It was no use talking to my family about this, so I asked Allah, "O Allah, who gave me this kingdom? I want to look after the needs of my people, alleviate their suffering, and make them peaceful. I want to do Your duties; I want to be able to see into the hearts of the people and, knowing their illnesses and needs, help them. I have no desire for this kingdom. Please take it away and give me permission to do duty in Your kingdom."

He granted my wish. Then I experienced all that they experienced, all their joys and sorrows. To release them from slavery, I became a slave to Allah. I am a slave doing the duty of a slave. Since I gave up my heritage, what can I tell people about my heritage?

Allah is the only One who is eternal; His ancestry is the only true ancestry. Our ancestors have gone away, one by one. They came and they left. There is no point in reciting their names. I talk only about my present heritage. My history is to know the One who created everything. Only God's history is complete and unchanging. He is the One who is indestructible, the One who will exist forever. All created beings have changing histories. What is the purpose of telling you stories of things that change and die so quickly? What is the purpose in holding on to the story of something that is going to expire, something that will slip out of our hands anyway?

There is only one God and one family of Adam *(A.S.)*. Only Allah is worthy of worship. He is the One of limitless grace and incomparable love. His family alone is the real family. Whoever joins that family, whoever is born into and lives in that family, receives the grace of all the universes.

But what is the use of telling this to these people? They will not understand. They look through the mirror of the mind and the desires of the world. Those who look for heritage will not understand Allah's plenitude, His wealth of divine knowledge, and the mercy and compassion of all the universes.

It would be a waste of time to read of my history and all my sufferings. Read of the heritage of Allah and the qualities His prophets brought. That is real heritage. Other things are just book knowledge, a waste of time.

For what is happening in the present moment, say, "*Al-hamdu lillāh,* all praise belongs to God." For what will happen in the future, place your trust in Allah.

There is only one history that will never perish, either in the world of the souls, this world, or the world of God; only one history will exist forever. The understanding of that history is our history, our story.

### 914.

A disciple asked, "Is there any human being who has seen the Rasūlullāh, the Prophet of Allah *(Sal.)*?"

The sheikh answered, "One who acts with all of the Rasūlullāh's *(Sal.)* words, qualities, actions, inner patience, contentment, and his quality of giving all responsibility and praise only to God has seen the Rasūlullāh *(Sal.)*. One who has nothing but Allah within him has seen the Rasūlullāh *(Sal.).*"

### 915.

*Child:* Saint Bistāmī *(Ral.)* said that if one of his followers were seen in hell, he would take the disciple's place, thereby lifting him out of hell. What does this mean?

*Bawa Muhaiyaddeen:* That is not quite correct. When someone is in hell, the one who tries to lift him must be at a higher level. Why? When a man lifts someone out of hell, he does not take his place in hell; he should not go down. He must remain in his own state while raising the other person; then the one who was in hell is elevated to his peaceful state.

Bistāmī *(Ral.)* really said, "One who holds out the hands of faith in Allah, with the resonance of *'Lā ilāha illallāhu:* There is nothing other than You, O God, only You are Allah,' to those who lie in the hell-fire of ignorance, lifting them to the pure place of *Īmān-Islām,* is a follower of the Rasūlullāh *(Sal.)*."

Moreover, Bistāmī *(Ral.)* and all those who were with him were followers of the Rasūlullāh *(Sal.)*. They were the children of Adam *(A.S.)*, of the lineage of Abraham *(A.S.)*, and followers of Muhammad *(Sal.)*. Bistāmī *(Ral.)* may have said that those who were with him followed his path, but he would not have called them his followers. He would have said, "I cannot claim the followers of the Rasūlullāh *(Sal.)* as my followers. I have no right."

This is the truth about that saying. You asked the question and we are giving you the explanation from the clarity of absolute faith, and telling you the ways in which faith can be strengthened.

### 916.

*Child:* The ultimate is for us to reach Allah's resplendence, but are heaven and hell created things or are they states we will come to in the next world?

*Bawa Muhaiyaddeen:* They are created. Here is an example.

A seed is encased by a skin which decays while a tiny point within the seed germinates and grows. In man, the part which is destroyed belongs to hell, and the part which arises as life joins the essence of grace. Both parts are connected to Allah.

Wrong and right are God's responsibility. In everything which has been created, everything which has appeared, the part belonging to the world will perish. The rest belongs to the next world, the world of purity. Everything with form, everything created, also contains that wealth of Allah's benevolent grace which is imperishable. The things which conceal this grace will perish. They are wrong, bad; life is right, good. The perishable is bad, the imperishable is good; creation is wrong or bad, the essence of grace is right or good.

If you understand this and take on the ninety-nine powers, or *wilāyats* of Allah, if you acquire His qualities and conduct, you will see what exists as ninety-nine within ninety-nine within ninety-nine. Out of the ninety-nine, if you take one particle, one *wilāyat,* and cut it into ten million pieces with the sword of faith, and then take one of these particles and cut it again into ten million pieces, and then if you look within one of these particles, you will find ninety-nine particles revolving round and round, one without touching the other. These are the wonders of His *wilāyats.* As you continue to cut, they go on and on. Become a slave to that power, and it will absorb you into its completeness.

### 917.

*Child:* One who is striving for heaven thinks that in heaven he will receive rivers of milk, honey, divine knowledge, intoxicating grace, and things like that. Will he?

*Bawa Muhaiyaddeen:* It may be like that. But first, the river of milk must flow in his *qalb,* his innermost heart, and the river of honey must flow from his faith. Then the undiminishing river of *'ilm,* or profound knowledge, must flow from the knowledge of His grace, and the imperishable fruit of grace should grow and ripen within his own *qalb.* He must build heaven within his *qalb* and live in Allah's kingdom here.

What he acquires here, the honey and the house he builds here, the service he does here, the wealth of Allah's grace he receives here, and everything he earns here, he will receive there. If he builds hell here, he will receive hell there. If he does good here, he will receive good there. If he does evil here, he will receive evil there.

His own good qualities will be of service to him on the Day of Reckoning. They will become houris, celestial virgins with the appearance of tiny children, and they will serve him in this world and the next. This service is called *qismat,* or perfect duty. If one uses his good qualities to do service for the people in the world, then the same good qualities will become the subtle beings which will serve him in the hereafter. Prayer will be a flowered swing in which celestial beings will rock him to and fro. The fullness of his qualities here will bear fruit there.

There is a river of Allah's *'ilm* and there is a river of honey. There is also a river of intoxicating nectar, but the intoxication is with Allah: one is intoxicated by Allah's *'ilm,* His words, and His truth. One's own good qualities become precious gems, and one's own actions become the beauty of his house in the hereafter.

Many more things have been described, but this is certain: if rivers do not flow in one's *qalb* here in this world, they will not be found in the hereafter. These are things I have seen.

Thus, a man will be in heaven if he will make Allah his wealth, saying with faith, certitude, and determination, "*Lā ilāha illallāh:* There is nothing other than You, O God. Only You are Allah." To take every breath in remembrance of Allah, praising only Him and placing all your trust in Him, is the treasure of a man's prayer. Wherever he may be, one who has this treasure is in heaven.

### 918.

*Child:* In the Qur'an, Allah says that He will purify some people after they die and take them to heaven. And yesterday, an Arab told me that Allah has affirmed that whoever says, "*Lā ilāha illallāhu*" will enter heaven, but He did not say when. Also, will you speak of the time between death and the Day of Reckoning?

*Bawa Muhaiyaddeen:* There are people who pray to Allah without the world being aware of it. Allah alone is worthy of worship, and Allah alone knows who worships Him. Those who have not accepted the world and whom the world has not accepted go straight to Allah. They have no world. They have only Allah.

Next, *lā ilāha illallāhu:* when one accepts this *Kalimah* and dies in Allah, he is in heaven. One who says the *Kalimah* and accepts it, becomes it. What Allah says is true. To look at Allah's words without doubt is truth.

Finally, if a person dies having placed all his trust in God, he will come to life the moment he is placed in the grave. That is his Day of Reckoning. The day of death and the Day of Reckoning are in each individual's own hands, under his control.

Death and life are one. They are one time. The body imagines a difference between them, but there is no difference if you have no time in you. The time between death and the Day of Reckoning passes before the closing and opening of an eyelid. All of this happens within you. It is there in every breath. The body and the base desires have differences and time, but when faith, wisdom, and understanding come, there is no time. There is only Allah.

### 919.

*Child:* In a *hadīth,* a traditional story, the Rasūlullāh, Prophet Muhammad *(Sal.)* said that those who dwell in heaven will see

Allah all the time, that He will be clearly visible.

*Bawa Muhaiyaddeen:* When the Rasūlullāh *(Sal.)* went on *Mi'rāj,* to commune with Allah, a veil separated the Rasūlullāh *(Sal.)* from Allah. Allah spoke to him from behind this veil. They discussed prayer and worship, and Allah told the Rasūlullāh *(Sal.)* to tell all He had spoken of to his followers.

When they had finished talking about prayer and about his followers, the Rasūlullāh *(Sal.)* said, "Allah, I want to see You. I must see You."

Allah said, "Remove the veil and look."

On the other side of the veil was a mirror, a brilliant mirror in which the eighteen thousand universes could be seen. When he looked into the mirror, the Rasūlullāh *(Sal.)* saw only himself; he saw his own form and his own beauty. He saw a sixteen-year-old youth with a beautiful and radiant face. Then Allah spoke to him.

How does one see Allah in that state? Allah's resplendent truth is the brilliant mirror in such a one's heart. When he looks into this mirror, he sees his own beauty and he knows himself. If he sees all of Allah's qualities and actions within himself, then he will see his own unchanging, eternal, sixteen-year-old beauty. If he holds nothing equal to Allah, he will see Allah's beauty, His plenitude, and the resplendence called *Nūr.*

Thus he sees both the power of *insān kāmil* and the power of Allah. Then the veil of his body is removed, and his heart becomes Allah. They become one. When he comes to that state, he is within God and God is within him.

When the Rasūlullāh *(Sal.)* returned from *Mi'rāj,* his followers asked him, "Did you see Allah?" Both 'Ā'ishah *(Ral.)* and Fātimah *(Ral.)* asked the Rasūlullāh *(Sal.)* if he had seen Allah, but the Prophet *(Sal.)* could only say, "If I speak of that mystery now you will not understand. You will see it later." Only to 'Umar ibnul-Khattāb *(Ral.)* did he reveal the secret.

One who does not see Allah within himself will never be able to see Allah on the outside. But one who has seen Allah's benevolence within himself will see Allah. What will he see? He will see himself. His own innermost heart will be the brilliant mirror, and when he looks into that mirror, he will see himself in its light.

920.

*Child:* In a *hadīth,* the Prophet *(Sal.)* said that one should trust

427

one's brother, but he should also tie up his camel. What does this mean?

*Bawa Muhaiyaddeen:* The words of the Rasūlullāh *(Sal.)* are always true. You must certainly trust your brother. That is good. But you must also catch and tie up the camel of blood ties and selfishness, the camel which grazes on Allah's truth and justice and your wisdom. The relationship of blood ties grazes on its neighbor's land; that is its selfishness. Our neighbors are also our brothers; therefore the camel of selfishness has to be tied. If it is not, the unity of brotherhood will be destroyed. You must love your brethren, but the camel, the beast that carries the burden of the world, must be tied up.

### 921.

*Child:* How does one surrender to the sheikh?

*Bawa Muhaiyaddeen:* That is a good question. Have you observed the rose? Where is its fragrance? The fragrance is mingled with the rose, in every petal. If you pluck the rose and smell it, the scent will be evident in every petal. Have you noticed that? The fragrance is in the rose, is it not? It is not something separate.

In the same way, if you are connected to the sheikh with faith, certitude, and determination in every petal of the flower of your heart, if your faith and love and life are mingled with him, then through that surrender and unity the fragrance of the sheikh's wisdom will mingle with your innermost heart, your *qalb.*

### 922.

*Child:* Since that occurs within the heart, is it necessary to be in the physical presence of the sheikh for it to happen?

*Bawa Muhaiyaddeen:* When the fragrance is in the rose, there is no separation. There is no way the fragrance can disconnect itself from the flower. It will waft through the air, but it will not separate from the petals. If the fragrance has not yet settled into the flower, then you can know it as separate. But once it has permeated it will never leave.

Like that, if the fragrance of the sheikh has settled into the flower of your *qalb,* your heart, then it is not necessary for you to be always in his physical presence. The fragrance and the flower will be one; there will be no separation. If the 'I' and the 'you' are not there, there will be no separation. You will be one. Give up the 'I' and become one with the sheikh.

923.

*Child:* Does spending time in the physical presence of the sheikh help the fragrance to settle into the flower?
*Bawa Muhaiyaddeen:* It is difficult to say. It is doubtful whether that is enough. Only if you fall into the fire will you know the heat of the the fire. If you put one end of a log into fire, it will get hot, but you will still be able to touch the other end. You can touch it or pour water on it, air can flow over it, and you can even put out the fire with it. But if the whole log has fallen into the fire, you cannot touch it.

In the same way, if you have fallen into the sheikh, satan cannot touch you, the mind cannot touch you, desire cannot touch you and attachments cannot touch you. They will not dare come close to you.

However, if even one part of you is outside the sheikh, satan can take hold of you, and the base desires, cravings, blood ties, and all those things can make contact with you. But if you fall entirely into the sheikh, he will burn whatever falls in, and you will no longer exist; only the sheikh will be present.

This should be your state when you are with the sheikh. Whether or not you are in his physical presence is not important; it is the state in which you conduct yourself that is important.

924.

*Child:* How can we make our bad qualities work for us? How can we make them into good things?
*Bawa Muhaiyaddeen:* Does one realize one's evil qualities? Once you do realize them, it is easy, is it not?

When you have the wisdom to recognize your qualities, you can give them two or three whacks with wisdom and say, "Go over there and keep quiet!" You must have that control. Once they become obedient to your control, show them love and tell them to do God's duties.

925.

*Child:* I have been here for some time. But I have fear. There is so much fear that I am unable to see unity between myself and the sheikh. The fear brings about a separation between the 'you' and the 'I' and between myself and the sheikh.

*Bawa Muhaiyaddeen:* It is not fear; it is lack of certitude. What you call fear is a lack of the certitude of faith. If you have faith and certitude, there is no fear.

There is the feeling of 'I' in you. You lack faith, certitude, and determination in what you want to achieve. This weakness is the fear you feel. The feeling of 'I' in you is between you and the sheikh, hindering unity. That is the cause. Lack of faith can keep you separate from good people, good things, and even from God.

### 926.

*Child:* How can we obtain wisdom from a sheikh?

*Bawa Muhaiyaddeen:* It is easy to obtain wisdom. First, acquire good qualities from the sheikh. After that, you must acquire his actions, conduct, and behavior. If you can obtain these from him, it will be easy to acquire wisdom. It is like digging a well and finding a free-flowing spring. Dig and find your spring of wisdom and you will have no further want. You can use it for all purposes: to bathe, to drink, and to give to others.

### 927.

*Child:* I wonder if you would give an explanation of the verse in the Qur'an which is called the *Sūratul-Kāfirūn*. Someone told me that you said it is good for concentration.

*Bawa Muhaiyaddeen:* It is good to recite the *Sūratul-Kāfirūn* in order to realize something and increase your awareness of it. This will strengthen your *qalb,* your innermost heart. It will make the *qalb* determined and unwavering, but only if it is already firm and strong.

No matter what you recite, you must have faith. If you recite with faith, it will strengthen you. Otherwise, it will not benefit you.

### 928.

Son, this is a world, and everyone in it is a traveler. There are many intersections in this city world, and policemen work to direct the traffic and help prevent accidents. The policemen look to see in what direction the people want to go and signal them to proceed when it is safe. You have seen this.

God has given me a job. There are four religions in the world; they form an intersection. At this intersection, God has placed His representatives, *qutbs,* and *olis* to direct the people safely on their journeys.

If you have chosen your path, the sheikh will signal you to proceed in that direction. If he sees in your heart and face that you have decided to journey to *māyā* and the world, he will point you in that direction. But if you do not already have a map, he will show you the path to the west, toward God. If you ask the way, he will show you the path to God. He will say, "I too came from there, and I am going back. Do you want to go? This is the path, this is the way to go."

The sheikh is a representative. He will stand at the intersection of the four religions and teach wisdom, the qualities of God, love, good conduct, the human rights of His kingdom, the explanations, God's ninety-nine powers, and His compassion toward all lives. The sheikh will tell you that there is one race and one God, and that He alone is worthy of worship. From the state of unity, the sheikh will speak of the one race, the one religion, and the one family. He will say, "This is where you must go. Here is the house of peace and equality. Here is the kingdom of our Father. Understand this. This is our own country." The sheikh will give you explanations. He will show you the path.

The sheikh is always a traffic policeman. Whether there is a prophet here or not, there is always a sheikh. He is here to prevent accidents.

If you go with faith to ask the way from the sheikh, he will explain. If you listen and follow his advice, you will reach your Father's place.

929.

Happiness and sadness need limits. When joy comes, do not enjoy it; simply say, "*Al-hamdu lillāh,* all praise belongs to God." Joy must have a limit. When sadness comes, do not suffer. Sadness must also have a limit.

Profit and loss need limits. We should not be happy or sad, and we should not give praise or blame because of profit or loss. They too must have limits.

Poverty and wealth need limits. Happiness does not come with wealth; a rich man does not live without sorrow. He may have money, but he also may have suffering because of his mind, wife, or children. Too much wealth can lead to misery. As a man's wealth expands, desire and craving may increase, while his qualities, compassion, and love for others decrease.

He may search for praise and status. The arrogance of the 'I' in him may swell, while faith in God dwindles. He may feel that he can do everything, that no one is greater than he. If these things happen, his qualities will change, and both the joy and sorrow in his actions will affect him. Then, even if he has money and status, he will have no peace. For he fails to realize that God's qualities, actions, and faith are his real profits; they are the limitless wealth that will bring him peace.

Praise and blame are within man. If he realizes that both praise and blame make him suffer, he will understand, "There is no one other than You, O Allah—*lā ilāha;* You are Allah—*illallāhu.*" He will discover peace and retain only that which is the wealth and equality in his life. Because his actions and conduct will be full of compassion, he will be able to give peace to everyone.

### 930.

Has a king ever lived in peace? He is afraid when he sleeps and afraid when he is awake. Throughout his life he is afraid. He does not have even two minutes of peace. His thought of wanting to conquer this kingdom and that kingdom makes him suffer day and night. When he wages war, many lives are murdered, and these deaths worry him. But even so, he will probably continue in order to satisfy his ego.

When a king rules his kingdom with the arrogance of ego, it becomes a fatal disease for him as well as for his subjects.

It makes no difference whether a man is a king or a beggar. Only if he has God's qualities, actions, patience, tolerance, and equality will he have peace.

### 931.

Hurricanes, volcanoes, floods, tornadoes, and earthquakes can occur within us as long as we hold onto the earth. The biggest world is the mind. As long as we hold it within ourselves, some thing or some thought becomes too much for us, and the volcano erupts. The volcano of anger, the arrogance of 'I', and the posses-

432

siveness of 'mine' are the fires which erupt from the mountains of earth within us. As soon as the volcano erupts, the mind goes haywire and we go crazy.

As the volcanoes erupt, we become obsessed with love, lust, land, fighting, gold, and the wilderness. We become obsessed with caste, religion, titles, fame, and learning. Erupting from within us, these obsessions make us crazy.

Therefore, we must feed them with the wisdom which will pacify them and keep them within certain limits. "Keep quiet for a while," we must tell them. "Stop!" Each must be kept within its proper limit, proper place, and proper balance. Only then can we acquire the peace we need. Peace is our greatest wealth, and we must strive to obtain it.

With wisdom, we must control the seven base desires: earth, fire, water, air, ether, mind, and desire. They wander around and bring us one thing or another. We must control them with wisdom. "Wait a little," we must tell them. They may try to rush you into doing what they want, but you must be constantly alert and stop them. In a few days, they will tire. They will realize that they are wasting their time, call you a madman, and stop worrying you.

Then you can tie them up with their own tiredness. When they are tied up, show them love and teach them wisdom and good qualities, little by little. Feed them with good faith. Bridle them with certitude; let wisdom ride upon them and take them around to show them what is right and what is wrong, gradually taming them. Then the seven base desires will calm down and obey you, and both of you will have peace.

### 932.

In every thought and every moment, we must mingle with God. Every intention and every thought must mingle with God. We must perform each action with God's actions.

God is always watching us. Whenever we do something evil, we must immediately realize that He is observing us and can hear what we say. He can smell the scent of what we do. When we speak, we must realize that He knows every word. He knows what we taste.

All our thoughts must be thought with the faith that He knows and that He is watching. God is justice. He is hidden within us. He knows the right and the wrong in everything we do. We must realize this with wisdom and trust Him with perfect certitude.

Just as the ant finds food that even the eye cannot see, we too must taste the sublime nectar of Allah, which is unknown to mind and desire. That is the wisdom of *gnānam*. Our earlier thoughts should be erased from our minds, and we must speak every word with the fear of wrongdoing, remembering that God is always in front of us.

The weapons and tricks of magic, mesmerism, miracles, and occult powers must be as far beneath us as the slippers we walk on. True surrender occurs only when we act with God's qualities and actions.

### 933.

If we see separations among people, we will also see a separation between ourselves and God. When we act with separation toward other people, God's qualities are separate from us. When we separate from good qualities and good conduct, we separate from God. When we find ourselves separate from other social classes and religions, we are separate from the compassion of God. Whenever we see separation, it is a signal that we are separate from God.

Through the qualities of God, we must find equality and unity in our lives. The qualities are our peace, the undiminishing and eternal wealth of our lives, the treasure that will never perish. If we see this wealth, we will not see separations between races, religions, or colors. For everyone, there is one God, one race, and one prayer. This is the state that gives peace to the human race.

### 934.

When the world praises you, hell laughs in glee. When the world opposes you, hell cries in sorrow, "O my God, we are losing one of our people!"

### 935.

What does it matter whether the wealth and property of a miser stay with him or leave him? Since he will not help the poor and hungry or share his wealth with them, it is of no consequence whether he lives or dies.

## 936.

What does it matter if the poisonous *etti* tree flowers and bears fruit? Its fruits and flowers are beautiful, but they are of no use to anyone. If a tree does not give fruit that can satisfy hunger and thirst, of what benefit can it be?

## 937.

Even a precious stone in the mouth of a poisonous snake can be valuable to a man at some time or other. But honey on the anus of the dog of desire can never be of benefit.

A good thought in the midst of bad qualities can sometimes be of use, but desire can never be useful.

## 938.

A friend without love
Charity without compassion
Devotion without truth
Prayer without faith
Learning without wisdom
Progress in life without proper
conduct
Friendship from one without beauty
in his heart and face
Life without correct behavior
Human beings without unified lives

None of these are of any use. There is nothing to be gained from relationships with people who have such qualities.

## 939.

The faith of a man without determination
The prayer and life of a man without certitude
The heart of a man without strength of faith
Entreaties to God without true devotion
The verdict of a man without justice
The intellect of a man without conscience

None of these will result in good, either in this world or in the next.

940.

The life of a man without patience
The qualities of a man without *sabūr*, or
    inner patience
The devotion of a man without *shakūr*, or
    contentment
The learning of a man without *tawakkul*, or
    surrender to God
The thoughts and intentions of a man
    without *al-hamdu lillāh*, the quality of
    giving all responsibility and praise to God
None of these will result in clarity.

941.

Everything lives in expectation of food. Weeds and grass need water, birds hope for fruit, and fish hope for insects and algae. Everything alive is hoping for something to eat. Is there anything that does not expect food? Seeds depend on the earth, and men look forward to the produce which grows from the seeds. The eyes await light, the ears await sound, the body cannot exist without the breath, the nose awaits smell, and the tongue awaits taste. Mind and desire hope for sexual arts. Everything is connected to something else. Tell me, if you can, of even one thing that does not depend on something else. Even the backside of a man who wants to reach heaven expects a loincloth.

Similarly, everything a man does, even his meditation and learning, is done in expectation of something. His eyes expect countless scenes and visions; mind and desire expect an infinite variety of things. Everything one does in life is done in expectation of something else, in order to live.

Each of us must accept this. Everything is a slave to everything else, everything has a relationship to everything else. Each helps the other; all lives depend on others. This is life. All lives are like this. Each man expects knowledge, a job, titles, wealth, a good life; he expects to find a wife, and the wife expects to have children; a woman expects a husband, and a husband expects a house and land. Throughout our lives, our bodies expect things.

A wise man must think, "I have come to this world. Why did

I come here? What did I bring with me? What did I come to do? Who came along with me? Where am I going? Who is my help? All that I have here seems to depend on something else. Each of my limbs depends on one another; they are connected to one another. What did I bring? I brought only my soul. Who has a connection to my soul? Allah. Then I must live connected to only Allah. I need only His help."

Analyze with wisdom and establish the connection to Allah. We must give up the connection to temporary things and allow our souls to be connected to the permanent wealth and grace of Allah.

When that exalted state and wisdom come, you will say, "Al-hamdu lillāh, all praise is to God." Then no matter what happens you will be content. Whether or not you receive what you want, you will place your trust in God for what is to come.

Let whatever happens, happen. Al-hamdu lillāh. The proper way to conduct your life is to give all responsibility to the one God. There is no point in crying or howling. This is life. Each child must consider this. You must have inner patience, contentment, and trust in God. You must say, "Al-hamdu lillāh, all praise belongs only to God." Before every action give all responsibility to God. There is only One who will help; give Him all the responsibility and conduct your life accordingly. If you do something carelessly, you must ask for Allah's forgiveness. If something good happens, say, "Al-hamdu lillāh." And if something bad happens, you must still say, "Al-hamdu lillāh." You must be content and say to God, "This is Your responsibility," praise Him, and place your trust in Him for whatever is to happen. Then Allah will be with you, doing your work, and you can follow Him.

### 942.

Scratch only the place that itches: do not scratch everywhere. And when you do scratch, scratch only while it is itching or you will develop a sore.

With wisdom, analyze the sadness and the wrong thoughts that enter your mind and then throw them away. Do not let the mind be continually upset about this. Worry is endless. Throw those thoughts away and try not to commit the same faults again. Try to do what is good.

## 943.

If the roof of your house leaks, how do you stop it? You cannot patch it with salt or sugar, because they dissolve. Neither can any of your ideas, your words, or your speeches repair a leak. You must find out why the roof leaks and what is needed to mend it properly. You must find the broken tile and replace it with a new one.

Similarly, if there is a leak in the body, which is the house of your birth and your mind, you must understand how to patch it.

A leak in your life must be repaired with patience, inner patience, contentment, trust, good qualities, and faith and certitude in Allah. If you repair the leak with good qualities, and if patience and faith hold fast, there will not be any more leaks, and life will become peaceful.

## 944.

Trust in Allah
And the path will open.
Do not trust in yourself;
It will block the path of your life.

## 945.

Anger is the guru of sin. When you are impatient, a heaviness follows due to the accumulation of gas. If the gas escapes, your anger will go away, but if it stays in your stomach, it will be very uncomfortable. And if it moves to your chest, it will constrict your breathing. This is what anger does.

When anger comes, it displays its pomp and magnitude, destroying a man's good qualities so that he loses respect in the eyes of others. If he does not control his anger, it will lead him to wrongdoing and even murder.

A wise man must control his anger by first killing the elephant of arrogance with the spear of wisdom, and then, with contentment, sitting on the throne of *sabūr*, or inner patience. That will make him great among men.

## 946.

*Child:* I had a thought today. I heard the sheikh speak about snakes. All my life I have had an affinity for reptiles, and I raise snakes and lizards. I therefore have trouble understanding the evil or satanic aspect of snakes, and the polarity of good and evil, in terms of certain symbols. I used to have a little zoo.

*Bawa Muhaiyaddeen:* The animals on the outside are replicas of the animals inside, which are poisonous shadows that harm others. Snakes have enough poison to kill many people. An iguana can kill thousands of lives in an instant, merely by sticking its tongue into an anthill and pulling it back into its mouth. This is why these and all other creatures who kill lives are considered dangerous.

In a similar manner, the snakes and iguanas inside are murdering everything and everyone, and the elephant of arrogance is trampling all the gardens. The animals within you will one day turn around and kill you. You can associate with animals on the outside by learning the appropriate ways to control them, but it is hazardous to associate with the human animal. An animal disguised as a man is extremely dangerous. Be very careful when you deal with the selfish human animal which eats up everything in the world.

947.

When a buffalo bathes, it loves to anoint itself with mud. Mud is fragrant to a buffalo: it uses the mud like sandalwood paste. After an elephant bathes, it loosens the mud at the bottom of the river with its feet, sucks it up with its trunk, and squirts the mud onto its head and body. When it leaves the river, it is even dirtier than before it bathed. After a man bathes, he powders his body and applies various scents. All three apply external things hoping to beautify themselves.

But when an *insān kāmil,* a perfected man, bathes, he not only washes away all the dirt on his body, but also his bad qualities, which correspond to the seventeen *purānas,* or Hindu scriptures: arrogance, karma, *māyā,* the three sons of *māyā* known as *tārahan, singhan,* and *sūran,* obsession, hatred, miserliness, attachment, fanaticism, envy, intoxicants, lust, theft, murder, and falsehood. He washes away worldly dirt, mind, desire, and attachment, and applies the sandalwood paste of Allah and His beauty, qualities, fragrance, and duty.

This is the eternal fragrance. It is the difference between a perfected man, a man, a buffalo, and an elephant.

Son, in an orchard there are millions of fruits with different colors, fragrances, and tastes. If you try to taste every fruit, thinking they are all yours, you will be wasting your time, and your time on earth is limited. Use wisdom to find out which fruit is the most delicious to you.

There is a fruit called Allah. Its flavor is infinite. In one drop, there are seventy thousand flavors. If that unchanging sweetness just touches your tongue, it will give you undiminishing strength. For man it is the most exalted fruit.

Everything else is hell, physical and mental visions which will sicken you. These may be acceptable to other beings, but they are not suitable for a true man, so do not waste your time biting into them. Within the limits of your time here, take only what is meant for you, eat it, and you will realize the benefit.

Do not waste this opportunity; you do not know what is going to happen to you in the next moment. Think about it, and take what is due to you now.

Son, in the orchard of the world there are millions of differences: my religion, my race, my God; your religion, your race, your God; I am different, you are different. If you spend your allotment of time going from one thing to another, exclaiming, "This is a miracle, that is a tremendous force, this is huge," and so on, you will be wasting your life. God created things and adorned the world, and man copies them and decorates the world with toys. Find the One who created everything, find the One who is the fruit of divine wisdom and absorb His taste. That will truly benefit you.

## 949.

In a temple, church, or mosque, the one who is in charge is usually paid a salary to perform rituals, or *pūjās*. However, if he performs *pūjās* just because he receives a salary, there will be no devotion; his eyes will be focused on his income, and he will not be aware of the greatness of the deity to whom the *pūjā* is made. He will concern himself with the offerings of fruits and coconuts and cakes and incense, and not with the deity, the devotion, or the ceremony.

He will never have the fear of God. All his thoughts will revolve around his salary, and this will burn his devotion to ashes, separating him from God and the qualities of God, and leading him to hell. Such a man cannot reach the completeness of full attainment.

This is the opinion of one who is wise, and you, my children, must think about it and act correctly.

950.

If someone visits a fish market, what is his intention? He is going there to buy fresh or dried fish, meat, crabs, or the intestines or head of a goat. A fish market has a foul and bloody stench. He will never be able to buy attar in a fish market. He will never be able to buy God. He will never be able to buy the truth. Would he go to a fish market to buy grace? Would he go there to buy *gnānam,* divine wisdom? Never!

Dog and cats and rats live in the fish market. Snarling and snapping at each other, they pick through all the bowels, feathers, fins, and heads that are thrown away. "This is mine, that is yours," they squabble, fighting each other for some discarded thing. Finally, every one of them is bleeding, having been dragged around and bitten.

This is the scene in a fish market. By day and by night, there are dogs and cats hanging around. Even in the dark, the rats and cats and dogs come, running here and there to sniff out and snap up any head or remnant of bowel that has been tossed out. That is the work of the dogs and cats and rats. They cannot find God there. There is only the foul odor of fish and blood and blood ties.

If you want to find God, you must go in search of a *gnāna sheikh,* and through him you must obtain the grace and the qualities of God. Obtain the resplendence of his divine wisdom and merge within it, so that you may escape from this market of hell. He can cut away your connections to this market and help you to avoid the stench of the bowels. He can cut away your ignorance, your attachment to your wife and children, your blood ties, your attachment to your property, house, and livestock, and your attachment to land, gold, and women. He can cut away the stench of all these attachments.

The wise person will give up the market; he will give up the fish market and the meat market, and he will also escape from the barking and biting of dogs. He will go to the sheikh and learn to put his trust in God and to develop the devotion to God.

Casting off his attachment to land, gold, and women, he will surrender to God and obtain His fragrance, His qualities, His grace, His treasure, and His kingdom. But that is rare. Such people are very, very rare.

Those people who go to the sheikh with their fish market ideas, those who go like the dogs and cats and rats in the fish market will never obtain the treasure the sheikh has. They will only pick up the things he has discarded: land, gold, women, blood ties, selfishness, and jealousy. The sheikh has taken these from the world and then thrown them out. He has thrown away gold and wealth. He has discarded the separations of the 'you and I'. He has discarded the separation of 'your religion, my religion', 'your race, my race'. He has discarded praise, honors, titles, jealousy, treachery, deceit, anger, and lust.

All the countless evil qualities found in the world have been thrown into the street. They will fight over these things just like dogs and cats and rats, shouting, "This is mine! And that is mine too!" It will be like a battlefield, and they will be separated from the sheikh, from God, from God's *rahmat,* or infinite benevolence, from His kingdom, from His undiminishing wealth, and from the treasures of the world of the souls, this world, and the next.

The sheikh discards the treasures of ignorance, and whoever picks up what he has discarded has caused himself to be discarded from the service of God, from the service of the people, and from the service of the sheikh. He will never obtain the *rahmat* of God.

### 951.

When a honeybee searches for honey, it sits on flower after flower, trying to detect their nectar. Its whole intention is to obtain honey. It does not search for feces; its only love is for the honey, the fragrance, and the pollen. It does not need feces. It flies for long distances to find flowers. It sits on a flower and draws the honey, then carries the honey in its mouth and the pollen on its feet, returns to its hive and deposits them there. Little by little, it makes large quantities of honey. It does not search for anything else. If there is any other scent, whether it is the odor of feces or even the sweet fragrance of attar, it will not be attracted by them. It goes directly to a flower to take its honey.

In the same way, one who is truly searching for God, one who is searching for God's grace and truth and qualities, flies to a sheikh as a honeybee flies to a flower. What does he need from that flower? He needs the wisdom and honey which is God's grace. To obtain the honey of grace and God's qualities and actions, he must sit by the side of the sheikh and extract them from the sheikh, just as a bee extracts honey from a flower. That is his honey.

The disciples must sit on the *qalb,* the innermost heart, of the sheikh and imbibe the honey. Around him there may be land, gold, women, treasures, feces, urine, gold, silver, or platinum. There may be silk and velvet. There may be wealth and happiness, house and property, families and tribes. There may be thrones and palaces and many treasures. All these and more may surround the sheikh, but the true disciple will never sit upon any of them because they do not have the fragrance he is seeking. They do not have that honey.

If he sits only on the heart of the sheikh, then he can obtain the honey of grace, the honey of *gnānam,* the honey of God's light, the honey of the resplendence called *Nūr,* the honey of the kingdom of God's grace, the honey of God's mystery. That disciple, that devotee, the one who does service to the sheikh, service to God, and service to all mankind, will sit on the heart of the sheikh and drink of his honey. He will not sit on the world.

On the other hand, those who prefer the gold, silver, wealth, women, land, races, religions, colors, gems, houses, properties, health, and happiness that surround the sheikh will never gather any honey, for those things all belong to the earth. What they think is gold is not really gold; it is earth. The precious stone is not a precious stone; it is hell. They will never find honey from any of these things. Anyone who places his faith in these things will perish with them. If it is something that belongs to the earth, he will go to the earth. If it belongs to hell, he will go to hell. If it belongs to *māyā,* to illusion, he will go to *māyā.* He will never be able to extract honey.

This is what a person with a great deal of experience in the world has said. This is what the Sufi sheikh has said.

### 952.

A Sufi *gnāni* called his disciple and told him, "O disciple, come here. Hold your finger on your temple and try to research and analyze what the world is like. Research that."

Then he said, "Secondly, hold your finger on the tip of your nose and try to make an analysis of yourself. Reflect on yourself.

Think about how you were formed as an egg, as a fetus. What did you do when you were a fetus? What did you do after you were born? What did you do when you were drinking milk from your mother's breast? What did you do when you were a toddler? What did you do when you were at school? What did you do when you were playing? Think about all this. What did you do after you got married? What did you do when you ate your food? From whom did you try and grab your food? What lies did you tell? What did you steal? Whom did you beat? Whom did you bite? After you got married, what did you do? You gave birth to your children. What happened after that? What happened to your children? Now you are getting old, do you see what is happening to you? What will you do next? You are past your youth. You are getting old. Where are you about to go, and what will you take with you? What are you going to do about this? What are the faults you found in this world? Have you found the faults in the world? Have you understood your faults? Have you understood the right and wrong in yourself? Have you understood your falsehood and your theft? Have you understood your trust in God and your devotion? Have you understood your relation to God, or have you understood your relation to earth, your relation to *māyā,* and your relation to women? Have you understood all this? And through these relationships, what faults have you committed? What good have you done? Think about it. You have come here, and now where will you go? You came as an egg, you lived in the world, and now where will you go? Where did you live earlier, before you were even an egg? Think of all this for a while. Think. Analyze yourself and make a judgment on yourself. Do not backbite about the world. Do not find fault with the world.

"Third, hold your finger on your mouth and keep your mouth closed. Then you can obtain peace. Think of yourself and then find some ultimate judgment on yourself. Close your mouth and and then pass judgment on yourself.

"Fourth, hold your hand against your chest, over your heart, and try to develop a state of peacefulness. Try to develop judgment and justice. Only then can you obtain peace and tranquillity."

This is what a Sufi *gnāni* said to his disciple. Reflect on it.

### 953.

A Sufi *gnāni* gathered his disciples together and showed them a lake. The lake was turbid and muddy with all the world's dust, dirt, filth, and insects, which had been carried there by the wind, by rain, and by flood. "Come along, my disciples," he said. "There is water here. Drink it."

Most of the disciples complained that it was either dirty, or muddy, or turbid and therefore unfit to drink. The sheikh was watching as each of them spoke his mind. There was one disciple, however, who had wisdom. Dipping his two hands into the water, he pushed the dirt on the surface to either side. The dirt, dust, and insects separated off, and then he scooped the clean water in his cupped hands and drank. Then, as all the others watched, he rose and bowed in obeisance to the sheikh. The sheikh embraced him, saying, "You are a wise disciple."

This is what the world is. Where there is a sheikh there will also be the difficulties of the world. All the dirt that comes with the rains will fall into that lake, and there will be filth, insects, and foul odor. The floodwaters will pour into it. All the happiness and sorrow of the world will come. Ghosts and demons will come, as well as hell, *maya,* and karma. Everything will collect in that lake. But anyone who is doing service to God, service to the sheikh, and service to people must not be discouraged by these things. With his two hands of *iman,* of faith, certitude, and determination, he should push the dirt aside and drink of the true water, the water of grace, the water of *rahmat,* or infinite benevolence. Then he should come and perform his service to the sheikh.

The sheikh will embrace him because the disciple has not seen differences. Such a disciple does not look at the world for the filth and evils of the world. Pushing them all aside, he takes only the pure water. He is the one who will do the triple service to the sheikh. He is the true devotee, the one who will merge with God and thus give peace to the people. He is the one who will show compassion and love to the people. He is the truly wise person, the true disciple. This is what the *gnana sheikh* said.

Anyone who is not in this state, anyone who does not push aside the filth and drink only of the truth of the sheikh, will gather all the dirt, atoms, and filth of the world. He keeps on digging and digging in the lake, muddying the water. Instead of trying to clear the water so that he can drink it, he is stirring up the mud. He is the one who disturbs the lake. Unable to quench his troubles and to rid himself of his birth and his karma, he will thoroughly disturb the water and then he will hand it over to the vultures. Anyone who continually digs up the lake will never correct himself. It is very difficult for anyone who is in this state to become peaceful. This is what the Sufi sheikh said.

You and I must reflect on this. Water is common to all. The wise man is also common to all. The water will quench everybody's thirst and remove everybody's dirt and stench. Its peacefulness will give peace and tranquillity to all. Even when dirt collects in the water, the water will push it down to the bottom or beat it against the shore. The wise person will always remove the surface dirt and drink the pure water. He is the one who will merge with God and the sheikh. He will get rid of his karma and obtain the station of *gnānam* and paradise. This is what the *gnāna sheikh* says. You and I must think about it.

954.

Consider the apple tree. It is a relatively small tree that bears many, many fruits. One tree might bear hundreds of thousands of fruits. The leaves and the blossoms do not weigh much on the tree. Even the tiny fruits do not weigh much, but as the fruits grow bigger and bigger and their color changes, the weight steadily increases. Some apples can weigh a pound. There are some huge apples that can weigh even one and a half pounds, and when hundreds and thousands of these fruits grow on a tree, its branches sag toward the ground. But however much the tree is pulled down by the weight, it does not blame anyone. Neither does it eat its own apples. Even if the ripe fruits fall to the ground, animals will come and eat them, or the earth will swallow them up— but the tree does not eat them. The owner of the tree will pluck the apples, pack them up, and send them off to the market in trucks. When people buy and eat them, their hunger and fatigue are soothed. But the apple tree has no desire for the many fruits it bears. It will never eat its own fruit.

Like that, a wise person, one who does service to God, one who lives with the sheikh and does service for him, one who surrenders to the sheikh and learns his wisdom, one who longs for the *gnānam* of the sheikh, who joins the sheikh and who wishes to reach the station of God, will be like an apple tree. He will have no love for things of the world. Whatever treasures, gold, ripe fruits, or fragrance he may obtain, he will simply bend and bend some more as his burden continually increases, without an iota of complaint or resentment. In the way that these things came to him, he will give them to others. He will do his duty for others without a trace of selfishness, blood ties, or attachment. What collects around him are the things that belong to karma, to the dog of desire, and things that come from charity, and he will give them away in the form of charity. Because he does not heap these burdens on himself, he prevents the karma from attaching itself to him. He also prevents the arrogance from attaching itself to him and the illusion of *māyā* from descending on him. He is the wise person, the intelligent person, the true devotee.

If he were to collect arrogance, karma, and *māyā,* he would become subject to many births. Evil would connect itself to him. Once arrogance, illusion, and satan's qualities of anger, lust, miserliness, bigotry, passion, and envy are attached to him, then the other five evils of intoxicants, sex, theft, murder, and lies will also attach themselves. Thus, he would become a victim of karmic rebirths. Whoever can push these evils aside and escape from them can become victorious over karma.

This is what the *gnāna sheikh* says. You children must think about it. You and I, let us think about this.

### 955.

The Sufi sheikh says: Consider an apple seed. It is a very tiny seed which must be planted at the proper time, after you have plowed the land. Within that seed is a tiny point. When the point begins to grow, a seedling appears, and it will develop two leaves. One is *lā ilāha:* There is nothing other than You, O God. The other is *illallāhu:* Only You are Allah. Later those two leaves drop off, and more stems sprout. Eventually, it becomes a tree with many branches. Later, the tree begins to flower. The flowers are innumerable. Later still, young fruits emerge from the flowers. The fruits mature, developing color and fragrance. As the tree grows, the original apple seed has disappeared, but the apples are within the tree. They come from the flowers and from the baby fruits. The original seed is lost, but new seeds form in each new fruit, perhaps five or six in each fruit. They will produce new trees and new fruits, with the identical color and fragrance. The original apple taste comes back, the original apple fragrance, and all the apple qualities. They were all in the tiny point in the original seed. They are not separate from that original seed, are they? No.

Man comes from the seed of God's grace. That light of grace falls on the fertilized ovum. Then the elements of earth, fire, water, air, and ether surround the fetus as the flesh grows, and he finally comes out crying the name of God. By the time he grows into a man, his original seed has been destroyed, but the qualities of the seeds he obtained from the grace of the kingdom of God remain as His qualities, actions, and the purity of the soul. The seeds of that purity, and of light, justice, and the laws of justice, must grow within him, and he must display the original taste and qualities of the kingdom of God. He must display the grace and beauty and love of God. These are the five and six seeds, the five outer *furūd* and the six inner *furūd,* or obligatory duties. He must understand them, return to his original state, and display the qualities, fragrance, duty, light, purity, patience, grace, and beauty of God, the qualities of embracing all lives. All these fruits will develop within him, and when you cut one open, there will be the five and six duties, the lights that will dazzle from within. That is the state he must obtain. To destroy the original seed which contains the world and arrogance, karma, and *māyā* is the true victory; then he will reach peace. We must reflect over this.

Man who has been born into the world and grows in it must think about this. This seed of ours must go, and the new seed must develop. This is what is called *gnānam,* or divine wisdom. It is called pure *gnānam.* This is what the *gnāna sheikh* says. Therefore, you and I and all those who have faith in God must think about it.

### 956.

At one time, there was a Sufi *gnāni* called Hasanul-Basrī *(Ral.)* and a woman saint called Rābi'atul-'Adawiyyah *(Ral.).* Both were exalted individuals, deeply devoted to God. Rābi'atul-'Adawiyyah *(Ral.)* was redeemed by God from the slavery of the world. Hasanul-Basrī *(Ral.)* saw her frequently and learned much wisdom from her.

One day the great, rich, and wise people in that country assembled before Rābi'ah *(Ral.).* "Rābi'atul-'Adawiyyah," they said. "We have come with the intention of asking you to get married."

"I am grateful for all the trouble you are taking," she replied. "But if I am to marry, I must marry a very wise man."

"Hasanul-Basrī is a man of wisdom. Would it please you to marry him?" they asked.

Rābi'ah *(Ral.)* replied, "If I am to marry it must be to a person who can give me the answers to four important questions. My entire life is dedicated to finding these answers."

The elders told Hasanul-Basrī *(Ral.)* of Rābi'ah's *(Ral.)* conditions and asked him if he could answer her questions. *"In shā'allāh,"* he replied, "if God wills it. That is God's work." So they brought him to Rābi'ah's *(Ral.)* home.

Rābi'atul-'Adawiyyah *(Ral.)* spoke to Hasanul-Basrī *(Ral.)*. "These respected gentlemen think I should marry you, but before I agree I have four questions for you. If you can give the correct answer to each, then I am willing to accede to their request."

"Tell me what the questions are," he said.

"First, if I were to die today, would I die in the state of a *kāfir,* a disbeliever, or in the state of a *mu'min,* a true believer? Are you able to answer that question?"

Hasanul-Basrī *(Ral.)* replied, *"In shā'allāh.* Allah alone knows the answer to that question."

"That is true. Here is my second question. As soon as one is placed in the grave, there is an inquiry into good and evil. If I died today, would the two angels, Munkar and Nakīr *(A.S.),* write good things about me or evil things about me? Can you give me an answer to that?"

Again Hasanul-Basrī *(Ral.)* replied, *"In shā'allāh.* Only God knows that."

Then she asked the third question, "On the Day of Qiyāmah, on the Day of Reckoning, I will be awakened and given the scroll that was written in my grave. Will it be given to me in my right hand or my left hand? Can you give me the answer to that?"

Once again Hasanul-Basrī *(Ral.)* said, *"In shā'allāh.* I do not know. Allah alone knows the answer to that."

Rābi'ah *(Ral.)* then asked the final question. "One day God is going to bring me to judgment. After He makes His inquiry, will He give me hell or will He give me heaven? Can you tell me the answer to that?"

Still again Hasanul-Basrī *(Ral.)* had to reply, *"In shā'allāh.* For that, too, it is God alone who knows."

Rābi'ah *(Ral.)* said, "O Hasanul-Basrī, you spoke the truth. You cannot answer these four questions. Only Allah can answer them.

I have been constantly working and studying so that I might understand the answers to these four questions. This is what I am still striving for. If I marry you and you do not know the answers, and if I have to continually serve you, then my true work will be neglected and I will never find these answers.

"So you see, Hasanul-Basrī, if you had known the answers to these four questions, I would have accepted you in marriage, but you are unable to answer them. You do not know for yourself. If I marry you at this time, imagine what my state will be. Therefore, Hasanul-Basrī, marry someone who is free to marry you. My work is to find out the answers to these questions."

### 957.

After some time had gone by, Hasanul-Basrī *(Ral.)* went in search of Rābiʿatul-ʿAdawiyyah *(Ral.)*. When he found her, he said, "I have a lot of love for you. My heart yearns for you. My heart intends you. Please marry me."

Rābiʿah *(Ral.)* said, "Hasanul-Basrī, your request is reasonable, but I have already attached myself to someone else. I love someone else, and I have become His property. Having placed my trust in Allah, I have become His property. I cannot have attachment and love for two. I can love only one. My heart does not have room for two, only for one. I belong to Him. If you want to marry me, you must ask Him for permission. If He gives His permission, then I can marry you."

We must try to understand what God's service is, what true service is. Think about this, and reflect upon how we can merge with God. Then we can find our own freedom.

### 958.

The Sufi sheikh said: There was an emperor by the name of Ibrāhīm ibn Adham *(Ral.)*. His wealth was all in gold, gems, and silver. His cups were made of gold and studded with gems. His slippers were studded with gems. The ornaments and clothes he wore were made of gold. His sword was made of gold and studded with gems. His crown was gold and studded with the nine types of precious gems. His palace, his doorways, everything was made of gold. Even his bed was made of gold. He had inherited this property from his father, his grandfather, and his great-grandfather. And whenever Ibrāhīm ibn Adham *(Ral.)* journeyed, he traveled with a retinue of forty people. Even their clothes and swords were made of gold and gems.

One day, when Ibrāhīm ibn Adham *(Ral.)* was sleeping on his golden bed in his golden palace, he heard footsteps on his roof. "Who are you? Who is on my rooftop?" he called out.

He heard a reply. "I am the one who is walking on your roof."

Again Ibrāhīm ibn Adham *(Ral.)* asked, "Who is walking on my roof?"

A man's voice replied, "My camel came here to find some grass to graze, and I came in search of my camel."

Angrily, Ibrāhīm ibn Adham *(Ral.)* said, "You madman, you crazy man! How do you expect to find grass on top of my roof? How do you expect a camel to walk on my roof?"

The man replied, "Is that so? You do not think that a camel would graze on your roof; yet you are seated on a golden bed with velvet coverlets and golden pillars all around you, and you keep calling for God. How can God come there? God has no house. God has no bed. He has no mattress. He has no crown. How can He come to you there? If God can come to you there, then isn't it possible for a camel to be on your rooftop? If you can realize who the fool is, that might be helpful."

"What he says is true," Ibrāhīm ibn Adham *(Ral.)* admitted to himself.

The man said, "I will think about the camel on top of your roof, and you had better think about whether God will come to you in your golden bed." Saying this, he went away.

Ibrāhīm ibn Adham *(Ral.)* thought about this over and over again. "This is not good," he realized. He called his minister. "Open the palace gates and all the doors and invite everybody to visit me. Anyone may enter freely as long as he wears good clothes when he comes. Beat the drums and make this announcement."

When the announcement was made, hordes of people came to enter the palace. Everyone was dressed in garments of velvet and silk. Among them came an old man. His clothes were tattered and torn and ragged. He ran in through the gates. The guards gave chase, but when they looked into his face, they saw it was resplending with light, and they could not bring themselves to stop him. Soon, he was inside the palace.

Ibrāhīm ibn Adham *(Ral.)* saw him and asked, "What is the

451

trouble with you? Why are you dressed so filthily in my palace?"

The old man said, "I have only come to a rest house."

"How dare you call this a rest house, you crazy man! This is not a rest house!"

"What else is it if it is not a rest house?" the man said.

"This is not a rest house, this is the palace of Ibrāhīm ibn Adham, don't you know that? This is the palace of a king."

"Is that so?" responded the old man. "When I look at it, I see only a rest house. I do not see it as a palace. How did it come into your possession?"

"This was my father's and I inherited it from him."

"Where did he go? And who gave it to him? Your grandfather? How did he get it? He got it from his father. And so on, for perhaps ten generations." Then he looked around and asked, "Where are all of them now, this father, grandfather, and great-grandfather?" Ibrāhīm ibn Adham *(Ral.)* said that they had all died and gone away.

"So for them, in their respective times, this was a rest house, wasn't it? Each one came, stayed here for a little while, and left. And when you die, you will also leave it. It really is a rest house, isn't it? I have come here for a while, and soon I will go. You will stay here for a while, and then you will go away. They came and went; now you have come and you too will go. This is not a palace. Ibrāhīm ibn Adham, think about this. This is only a rest house." And then the man went away.

By this time, Ibrāhīm ibn Adham's *(Ral.)* brains had become all topsy-turvy, so he called his ministers and said, "O ministers, let's go to the jungle and go hunting. Get the horses ready. Gather all the hunters together and let's go."

While they were hunting, the king took off on his own to chase a deer. As he was aiming his bow and arrow at the deer, the deer opened its mouth and spoke, saying, "Ibrāhīm ibn Adham, you are hunting me. You are trying to kill me. Why aren't you looking at the one who is hunting you and trying to kill you? 'Izrā'īl *(A.S.)*, the Angel of Death, is right there. He has come to hunt you. You had better try to escape. You are stalking me, trying to kill me, but you are not trying to escape from the Angel of Death, who is stalking you." The deer said this as it ran away.

Ibrāhīm ibn Adham *(Ral.)* thought, "What the deer said is true. One day the Angel of Death will hunt me down and kill me."

He turned his horse around and rode through the jungle, where he found a shepherd tending his flock. "Come here," he called to him. He took off his golden robes and put on the shepherd's clothes; then he gave away his crown, his clothes, all his valuable ornaments, his horse and bridle, saying, "You take these, and I'll take your clothes and go on my way."

The one who had come searching for the camel on the roof was Khidr Nabī, the Eternal Prophet *(A.S.)*. It was also Khidr Nabī *(A.S.)* who had come to the palace as an old man. So Ibrāhīm ibn Adham *(Ral.)* went to the Eternal Prophet and learned much wisdom from him.

Eventually he decided to visit the *Ka'bah* in Mecca. As he walked, he would stop and prostrate himself before God after each step or two. He would also stop and pray in mosques all along the way. Thus it took him fourteen years to get to Mecca.

About that same time, Rābi'atul-'Adawiyyah *(Ral.)* also had the intention to see God, to go to Mecca and meet God. It was her intention to go to the *Ka'bah*. When Ibrāhīm ibn Adham *(Ral.)* got to Mecca, he was unable to find the *Ka'bah,* because the *Ka'bah* had gone in search of Rābi'ah *(Ral.)*. He was thoroughly disappointed. He hit his head and beat on his chest. "Where is the *Ka'bah*? For fourteen years I have been praying and journeying toward it, and now I can't find it." He questioned the people he saw.

Someone said, "The *Ka'bah* has gone in search of a woman. The *Ka'bah* has gone to Rābi'atul-'Adawiyyah."

"Who is she?" Ibrāhīm ibn Adham *(Ral.)* demanded. "How can she do such harm? How can she make such a mistake? For fourteen years I have been looking forward to seeing the *Ka'bah!*"

The people advised him to wait for a while, to be patient. "It will come back," they assured him.

"Why are you talking about patience? I have been praying for all these years, and now a woman has taken the *Ka'bah* away with her." Then he asked, "Where can I find this woman?"

Angrily, he ran to where they directed him. Rābi'ah *(Ral.)* was seated.

"Are you Rābi'ah?"

"Yes," she replied.

"Why did you cause this harm? Why did you commit this fault?"

Rābi'ah *(Ral.)* said, "I committed no fault. Why are you saying this? I did not commit a fault."

Ibrāhīm ibn Adham *(Ral.)* said, "For fourteen years I have been journeying toward the *Ka'bah,* praying all the way. Now I find that you have drawn the *Ka'bah* to yourself. Think how many people must be suffering and grieving over what you have done. Think how many people might have the same craving I have. How can you commit such a crime?"

Rābi'atul-'Adawiyyah *(Ral.)* replied, "I did not commit crimes nor did I invite the *Ka'bah* to come to me. That may be the work of God. My intention was not to see the stone that you are trying to visit. I came to the *Ka'bah* to meet Allah, not to see or kiss the stone you speak of. If you have any questions about it, you had better ask God, because it is His work."

Immediately, God's voice came to Rābi'ah *(Ral.),* "Rābi'ah, hold your tongue. When Moses expressed the desire to see Me, and I showed him just an atom of My light, Mount Sinai split into forty pieces. One atom of My light split that mountain into forty pieces. I did not show My entire *rahmat,* My entire benevolence. I didn't show My entire self. I displayed only an atom of My *rahmat,* an atom of My light. It is difficult to see Me; to see even an atom of My light is too powerful for you. If you see My light, you will simply vanish into it."

And God also said, "You must do your duty. Continue to do your duty."

When she heard this, Rābi'ah *(Ral.)* prostrated herself before God and gave thanks to Him. Then, turning to Ibrāhīm ibn Adham *(Ral.),* she said, "For fourteen years you have been walking toward the *Ka'bah.* But the distance between the *Ka'bah* and where you started walking is only as far as your voice could travel. God knows even your intentions, so if you had called, He would have heard your voice.

"If you had truly prayed even once, the *Ka'bah* would have come to you. If you had surrendered to God, if you had given up everything else and surrendered to God, praying to Him even once, then the *Ka'bah* would have come in search of you. But you kept that idol, you kept an image of the *Ka'bah* as you prayed. By your attachment to this idol, the stone, you kept a veil between yourself and Allah. You were looking toward the earth, you were looking at the world, at the mosques, and praying as you walked.

But you did not pray to God directly. You have wasted fourteen years of your life. For fourteen years you have walked and prayed, but it was all in vain. Not even once did you pray to God correctly. Even now, if you can truly pray to God just once, hell will become *harām,* or prohibited, to you."

★

This comes from the history of the Sufis. This is what a Sufi *gnāni* explained.

Let us all think of what worship and prayer to Allah means. Allah's intention, worship, and prayer are like this. If we do not understand this, what point is there for you or I to worship Him? What use is there for you or I to study or to pray to Him? Let us reflect on what Rābi'atul-'Adawiyyah *(Ral.)* said.

959.

One who does not have truth within himself
Should not speak about truth.
He will not realize its value,
And his speaking about truth
Will diminish the splendor of God.

960.

One who does not judge himself
Should not set out to judge others.
If he does so,
It will be contrary to the justice of God
And will cause harm
Both to himself and to the one he judges.

961.

One who does not have faith in God
Should not set out to create faith in others.
It will be like setting fire to an orchard full of trees which are already bearing good fruit.

962.

One who does not have absolute faith or *īmān,*
Accepting God and His kingdom within himself,
Should not exhort others to have faith.

The result will be like the faith of a man caught in the jaws of a crocodile.

### 963.

If you pray without facing the *Ka'bah*,
The intention of your prayers will be misdirected.

### 964.

Always pray behind an *imām* or the Qur'an.
If you pray without following either of these,
Your prayers will be futile.

### 965.

Face Allah when you pray.
Keeping Him directly in front of you,
Direct your prayer to Him.
Such a prayer will attain fulfillment.
A prayer that does not have a connection between you and Allah will be like oil poured into fire.

### 966.

Perform ablutions
To clear the house of your *qalb*, your inner heart,
Then spread the prayer mat of *īmān*,
Absolute faith and certitude in God, in that *qalb*.
Keeping Allah in front of you
Face the *Ka'bah*,
Look toward Him and pray.
That will be an exalted prayer
And will give fulfillment.
Otherwise, your plight will be like that of a man who, having accidentally fallen into a pit filled with a thousand snakes, is being bitten all over his body. The poisonous thoughts of your mind, into which you have fallen, will sting you over and over again.

### 967.

Realize at every moment, with your *īmān*, that Allah is in front of your very eyes. If you think that Allah is not there, and if you do something that is *harām,* impermissible, that will become the fire in hell that will burn you.

Realize with your wisdom and faith that Allah is listening to your every word and knows your every breath. Speak only what is good and do only what is good. If you pray to God without that faith, hell will follow you, and tomorrow you will be a log of firewood in hell.

Think about this, and whenever you look at something or speak, realize that God is seeing you and hearing you.

### 968.

Do not look at everything and say indiscriminately, regarding good and bad, "The Qur'an says this, the Qur'an says that." The Qur'an is a seal, a light of Allah. There are two pairs of opposites, *halāl* and *harām,* what is permissible and what is impermissible, and *dhāt* and *sifāt,* the essence and what is created. The Qur'an shows both. To avoid what is *harām* and take what is *halāl,* to discard the evils in the *sifāt* and take the *dhāt*—that is the Qur'an. Try to understand this and act accordingly.

If, instead, you carry around the Qur'an and quote from it without understanding it, that will become the fire of hell that will torment you later.

### 969.

Do not think that everything you have learned is wisdom and *'ilm,* divine knowledge, and do not think that everything you have understood from the Qur'an is *'ilm* and wisdom. The Rasūlullāh *(Sal.)* said, "Search for *'ilm* in the universe of *'ilm.* Go there. Find someone who has *'ilm* and study from him." If you search for and learn *'ilm* from one of wisdom, you will understand prayer, worship, *īmān,* Islam, *'ibādat* or service to God, the *sirr, sifāt,* and *dhāt* or the secret, manifestation, and essence, *khair* and *sharr* or good and evil, *halāl* and *harām* or permissible and impermissible, and *insān* and *hayawān* or man and beast. You will understand the enlightened ones, the prophets, *qutbs,* angels, archangels, and Allah.

If you do not study that *'ilm,* then what you have studied and what you have received is not *'ilm.* All the wisdom and *'ilm* you have learned and what you have received is not that treasure. It will be like the fish that lives in the salty ocean and cannot live anywhere else. That study and learning may be a treasure for this world, but it will not be valuable in the hereafter.

970.

One who has understood and attained *īmān,* absolute faith, will know that all of everything is Islam. He will see the seed of Islam in everything and will see the *qudrat* of Allah, His power, in every creation. Therefore, he will not discriminate against any other being, or discard him.

*Īmān-Islām,* perfect certitude and purity of faith in Allah, will not cause pain to any heart, any *qalb.* One who has the heart of *Īmān-Islām* will not hurt any other heart. One who has acquired the wealth of *īmān* will have the *sabūr,* inner patience, which will comfort all lives. *Shakūr,* contentment, will be his life. *Al-hamdu lillāh,* the praise of Allah, will be his worship. And *tawakkul-'alallāh,* surrendering to Allah, will be his state.

At each *waqt,* each moment, he will say, *"Al-hamdu lillāh,"* and for the next moment, he will say, *"Tawakkul-'alallāh."* This will be the life of one who is *Īmān-Islām.* He will not think of anything other than Islam and will not hold anything as equal to Allah. His only treasure for the *dunyā,* this world, and *ākhirah,* the hereafter, will be Allah and the Rasūl *(Sal.).* The plenitude of the wealth of the *dunyā* is the Rasūlullāh *(Sal.).* And the wealth of *ākhirah* is the *rahmatul-'ālamīn,* the grace of all the universes. That is Allah's wealth. This will be his treasure, and he will share it with all lives. This is *Īmān-Islām.*

One who is in this state will not try to capture for himself either the world or the lives in the world. He will seek and take only Allah and His treasures as his permissible wealth. This is the wealth that belongs to *Īmān-Islām.* Allah's three thousand divine attributes, His ninety-nine *wilāyats,* His miracles, actions, and powers are the wealth of *Īmān-Islām,* the wealth for the three worlds of *awwal, dunyā,* and *ākhirah.* His qualities, His conduct, His duties, and His grace are the law for this wealth, and God has placed His qualities as the law in the Qur'an. To capture other lives and other countries is not the law in the heart of one who is *Īmān-Islām.*

The Rasūlullāh *(Sal.),* from the time he appeared to the time he departed, did not keep anything in his hands other than Allah. He did not keep the *'ilm* or knowledge of the world. The only wealth he had in his hands was the qualities of Allah and the *'ilm* of those qualities. Therefore, that will be the wealth of one who has understood *Īmān-Islām*.

Allah alone has the *daulat,* the wealth, to know everything. Whether one has *īmān* or not, whether he is a *mu'min,* a true believer, or not, whether he is Muslim, one of purity, or not, only Allah can give that judgment.

971.

Do not wave your religion and the Qur'an as<br>a banner<br>And wage war to capture countries and land.

Whoever does this is not following the words and actions of the Rasūl *(Sal.)* and Allah.

Allah sent down the Qur'an, this *Īmān-Islām,* saying that the war to be waged is within ourselves for the sake of His grace and for the wealth of the hereafter. If we can continuously fight against our own desires and the demonic forces within, saving our own kingdom from being destroyed by the inner illusory forces and saving the kingdom of the hereafter, we will receive Allah's treasure, His *daulat.*

The Qur'an was sent down to each life. Whoever wages this war within himself and safeguards and protects his own kingdom and the treasures of God and His wealth is a *mu'min* called *Īmān-Islām,* one with perfect certitude and faith in Allah. Only one who has fought and won this war can be called this.

But those who place the Qur'an and their religion in front of them and set out to capture the world and its wealth of hell are acting opposite to the words and qualities of Allah. They should realize that Allah has kept a day tomorrow called Judgment Day. Allah knows.

972.

*Bawa Muhaiyaddeen:* To understand *īmān,* we need wisdom and *'ilm.*

*Question:* We go on saying, "Wisdom, wisdom," but how can we understand wisdom?

*Bawa Muhaiyaddeen:* If a child is naughty, what do you do? You spank him. Like that, if the mind is naughty, you must spank it with wisdom and control it. That is wisdom. That is what we must seek. Please realize this.

## 973.

Islam is honey, a honey of light. It is very delicate. If even one drop touches you, everything within you will be turned to light and will become tasty. That is Islam.

But what the world calls Islam and what we keep and practice as Islam is bitter and dark. That is not Islam. We must reflect on this and attempt to scoop up the honey of light that is true Islam. That light is within the Qur'an.

> Take what is good,
> Leave the darkness
> And come into the light.
> Then you will understand.
> Leave the *sifāt*, the manifested creation,
> And come to the *dhāt*, the essence.
> Then your wisdom will understand.
> Leave the *sharr*, the evil,
> And come to the *khair*, goodness.
> Leave what is *harām*, impermissible,
> And come to what is *halāl*, permissible.
> Leave the *nafs*, the desires,
> And come to the place of firm certitude of *īmān*.
> Give up anger
> And come to the house of *sabūr*, inner patience.
> Give up vengeance and treachery
> And come to the house of *shakūr*, contentment.
> Give up the hell of the world
> And come to the house of the grace of Allah.
> Give up the learning of the world
> And come to the learning
> Of Allah's three thousand divine attributes
> And His ninety-nine *wilāyats* and their actions.

Only then will you discover even one tiny atom of His grace.

We must realize this according to the meanings of the Sufis. *Bismillāhir-Rahmānir-Rahīm.* May all praise and praisings be to Allah alone. *Āmīn.*

### 974.

The battle sword of the Qur'an and Islam is *sabūr* and *al-hamdu lillāh*. If, with the hand of *īmān*, absolute faith in God, you pick up that sword and cut away all the evil qualities from your own heart, that is Islam. This is the victorious sword that Prophet Muhammad *(Sal.)* carried in his hand. To wage war within yourself against your own evil qualities and to cut them away, using *īmān* and the *Kalimah* is Islam. The qualities of *sabūr, shakūr, tawakkul,* and *al-hamdu lillāh,* inner patience, contentment, surrendering to the will of God, and giving all praise to God are the victory sword of *īmān,* and this is the only sword that Islam should use.

We who have faith in God, who is the One of limitless grace and incomparable love, should never use the precious Qur'an for selfishness or for whatever the mind wants. We should not quote the Qur'an and Islam to justify our bad actions. It should be brought forth only for true justice.

All those who have Islam and the Qur'an not just in their hands but also in their hearts should reflect on this. This is what we who are in the pure state of *Īmān-Islām* should reflect on. The war we must fight is within ourselves against our own evil qualities. To see unity among all lives, embracing all lives as our brothers and sisters, is Islam. Dividing one person from another is not Islam. We must think about this.

*As-salāmu 'alaikum wa rahmatullāhi wa barakātuhu,* may the peace, the beneficence, and the blessings of God be upon you. *Āmīn.*

### 975.

*Bismillāhir-Rahmānir-Rahīm,* in the name of God, Most Merciful, Most Compassionate. May all praise and praisings be to Allah alone. May we give all responsibility to God, the One of limitless grace and incomparable love, the One who gives us of His undiminishing wealth of grace. *As-salāmu 'alaikum wa rahmatullāhi wa barakātuhu,* may the peace, the beneficence, and the blessings of God be upon you.

For all three worlds, the world of *awwal,* the time of creation, *dunyā,* the world in which we live, and *ākhirah,* the hereafter, God has given us the most precious treasure. He created what is known as Adam *(A.S.)*, then He made the world, and He gave explanations of the hereafter. We, the children of Adam *(A.S.)*, must realize this.

We were all born as one family. Whether we live in the east, west, north, or south, the human generation is one race. And what is called God or Allah is one. The one God sent down His teachings to all the prophets. Out of all the prophets that came, twenty-five were specially selected, and out of these, eight were the chosen ones, having the greatest clarity: Adam, Noah, Abraham, Ishmael, Moses, David, Jesus, and Muhammad, may the peace of God be upon them all. Through these eight prophets God proved His secret to the people. Finally, all the teachings and commandments that were sent down from the beginning to the time of Muhammad, the Rasūl *(Sal.)*, were gathered together in what is called the Qur'an.

We must look at the Qur'an in two different ways. There are the opposites of *khair* and *sharr* or good and evil, *dhāt* and *sifāt* God's grace or essence and the manifested creation, and *halāl* and *harām* or permissible and impermissible. One section exists as the laws and justice of God, and the other exists as the section of darkness.

In this state, we who are the children of Adam *(A.S.)* must realize that we must discard all that is evil and accept and act upon only what is good. That is the law of righteousness. We must simply discard what is evil; we need not denounce or attack anything.

What is called Islam was brought as perfect purity by the Qur'an. It is brotherly unity. Islam is to bring together as one family all the children of the one mother who have divided into four separate sections. The Qur'an teaches us to see what is good as good, while discarding what is evil. It is the law of justice. It shows us patience, inner patience, contentment, surrendering all to the will of God, and giving all praise to God. We, the children of Adam *(A.S.)*, must understand this.

The Qur'an and its explanations are very deep in meaning. Therefore, we who are the children of Adam *(A.S.)* should not hold up the Qur'an as a banner for the slightest reason. We should not quote from the Qur'an and use it for waging wars, for our fights and quarrels, for our anger toward others, or to gain things of this world. The world is *sharr*, evil, and has to be discarded.

The opposite, *khair,* which is goodness, must be accepted and put into action. The Qur'an should only be used for what is good. It shows brotherhood and unity, not divisiveness and discrimination. It soothes those who are weeping in sorrow. It gives solace to those who are suffering and makes them smile. It comforts those who are ill and protects them. It explains the wealth of God to those who are poor. It gives peace to those who are mentally ill. It gives wisdom to those without wisdom. It creates faith in those without faith and makes them bow in reverence to God. What is called the Qur'an is, in reality, something that has great value and very deep meaning.

The true meaning of Islam and the Qur'an is quite different from what people accept today, in the midst of so much fighting and strife. People quote Islam and wave the Qur'an as a banner for their wars. This is not correct. The Qur'an discards what is evil and shows only goodness, unity, and tolerance. *Tawakkul-'alallāh,* giving all responsibility to God, and giving all praise to God, saying, *"Al-hamdu lillāh,"* with every breath is the Qur'an and Islam.

No matter how large the ocean is, it cannot quench our thirst, can it? The ocean cannot quench the thirst of any life. But if there is a pond, however small it may be, it can comfort many lives, appeasing thirst and dispelling fatigue. Like that, the Qur'an comforts so many lives, dispelling fatigue and hunger and clearing away the dirt. This is the meaning of the Qur'an and Islam. When you quote from the Qur'an, those words must only demonstrate peace and equality. When you say "Islam," you must show patience, equality, and peace. When you show what is good, that goodness points to Islam, but when you show what is evil, that evil is something that has been discarded from the Qur'an .

The treasures, kingdoms, and titles of this world are all *sharr* and have been discarded from the Qur'an. Fighting and waging war for these worldly things, seeking vengeance, committing treacherous acts, telling lies for worldly gain, eating *harām* or impermissible foods, lying out of jealousy for the sake of titles and positions—all these cannot be called Islam. And you cannot quote the Qur'an, saying that these actions appear there, because these actions are totally contrary to the Qur'an.

The Qur'an shows the brotherhood where we live as one family and eat off the same plate in unity. The Qur'an shows the brotherhood where we live in harmony, the way it is in the church or the mosque, where the beggar and the king are equal. It shows the brotherhood where we embrace each other, whether in the place of prayer or in the home. If two people have a fight, the next time they meet, they will look each other in the face and embrace and beg forgiveness from each other. The Qur'an and Islam tell us to ask forgiveness from God for our own faults, to dispel our anger, and to embrace each other in the next moment.

These are the explanations of the laws of the Qur'an from the beginning of creation to the hereafter. Lying, vengeance, treachery, jealousy, and murder should never be done in the name of Islam. Islam is brotherly unity, tolerance, and peacefulness. It is to purify each heart with the water of the *Kalimah* which the Rasūl *(Sal.)* brought, washing away the darkness and creating peace.

But there are some people who hold up the Qur'an with anger, jealousy, and selfishness, using the Qur'an and Islam for their own self-gain and pride. The Qur'an should never be mentioned with these qualities, but should be mentioned only where there is righteousness. Anger, treachery, deceit, discrimination, divisiveness, and all that is impermissible have been thrown out of the Qur'an. All these sections belonging to the world have been eliminated from the Qur'an, and they must be eliminated from man, too. Man must take what is *khair* and eliminate what is *sharr*. In this way, the Qur'an must be used to show what is good and to eliminate what is evil, and this is Islam. Just bringing to the lips the words Qur'an and Islam for the slightest reason is not correct. The word Islam means unity, brotherhood, and harmony. It does not see differences among people; it only sees peace and harmony among all lives. This is Islam. This is the Qur'an. Every one of the children of Adam *(A.S.)* must realize this.

The words of the Qur'an are the divine words of Allah. If we take even one atom from the Qur'an, we will find countless meanings, beyond our understanding. If we split that one atom with our wisdom and then divide it into ten million pieces and take one of those pieces and examine it, we will find ninety-nine, ninety-nine particles revolving round and round without one touching another. These are His *wilāyats,* His powers, revolving around each other inside that tiny particle. If we take one of those particles and divide it into five million pieces and then take one of those particles and examine it, there too we will find ninety-nine, ninety-nine particles revolving one around the other without touching one another. If we take that particle and divide it into two and a half million pieces and then take one particle and examine it, we will find ninety-nine particles revolving around each other without touching. If we take one of those pieces and cut it into a million particles and take one of those and examine it, we will find ninety-nine, ninety-nine particles revolving one around the other without touching. If we take one of those particles and divide it into five hundred thousand pieces, each of those particles will show ninety-nine, ninety-nine revolving one around the other. If we take one of those particles and cut it into one thousand pieces, again we will see ninety-nine, ninety-nine particles revolving round and round without one touching the other. If we take a particle from that and cut it into one hundred pieces and examine it from the station of wisdom within wisdom, again we will see ninety-nine, ninety-nine particles revolving one around the other without touching. As we keep examining these, we find it going deeper and deeper within, while the power is becoming greater and greater.

These ninety-nine are the *Asmā'ul-Husnā,* the divine names of Allah. God has three thousand divine attributes and ninety-nine *wilāyats* or powers. Everything is in the form of atoms, and every particle contains the *qudrat,* the power of Allah. Everything moves through His power. We who are Islam must realize this. This is the Qur'an. This is His *wilāyats.*

One who calls himself Islam will never harm anyone, take revenge, or be treacherous toward anyone. We must realize this. Islam must realize this. The name "Islam" has very deep meaning and is of inestimable value, and it should never be held up for falsehood, robbery, or murder. Islam is brotherly unity that can appease the thirst of the entire world. This is the Islam which was brought by Prophet Muhammad *(Sal.).* All of everything, all the universes, and all of creation is contained within the Qur'an. But failing to understand this, we hold up and quote the Qur'an and Islam for the slightest reasons.

We who are in the world must realize that the Qur'an is the divine law of righteousness, which was given to show brotherly unity, to make lives peaceful, to forgive in the presence of faults, to teach patience and compassion and to comfort all lives. We must have *sabūr, shakūr, tawakkul,* and *al-hamdu lillāh.* This is the Qur'an and Islam. All my brothers and sisters who have *īmān,* perfect faith in God, must realize this. *Āmīn. Āmīn.*

# GLOSSARY

Unless otherwise indicated:
(A) Indicates an Arabic word
(T) Indicates a Tamil word

*ahādīth* (A) The plural of *hadīth*. Traditional stories spoken by the prophets. See also: *hadīth*.

*Ahmad* (A) The beauty of Allah's qualities contained within the innermost heart, the *qalb*. That heart shining with the light of Allah's qualities is *Ahmad*. When the beauty of the light of the heart is reflected in the beauty of the face, that beauty is Muhammad *(Sal.)*. (In Tamil, *muham* means face; in Arabic it is *muhayyan.*)

This is not merely a name that has been given. It is a name that comes from within the ocean of divine knowledge, the *bahrul-'ilm.*

Allah is the One who is worthy of the praise of the *qalb*, the innermost heart. Lit.: Most praiseworthy.

*aiyō* (T) An exclamatory expression, "Oh no!"

*ākhirah* (A) The hereafter; the next world; the kingdom of God.

*al-hamdu lillāh* (A) "All praise is to You!" Allah is the glory and greatness that deserves all praise. "You are the One responsible for the appearance of all creations. Whatever appears, whatever disappears, whatever receives benefit or loss—all is Yours. I have surrendered everything into Your hands. I remain with hands outstretched, empty and helpless. Whatever happens in the present and whatever is going to happen is all Yours." Lit.: All praise belongs to Allah!

*alif, lām, mīm, hā', dāl* (A) Five letters of the Arabic alphabet. In the transformed man of wisdom, these letters are represented as: *alif*—Allah; *lām*—the *Nūr*, the light of wisdom; *mīm*—Muhammad *(Sal.)*. *Hā'* and *dāl* correspond to the body of five elements (earth, fire, water, air, and ether), and to the *sirr* and the *sifāt*, the secret and the manifestations of creations.

*Allāh Muhammad* (A) Whatever is manifested from Allah and then returns and remains as Allah Himself. When the *Nūr Muhammad* merges with Allah that is His complete state; the completeness is His beauty.

*Allāhu akbar* (A) God is great.

*Allāhu ta'ālā Nāyan* (A & T) God Almighty; God is the highest. *Allāhu* (A) the beautiful, undiminishing One; *ta'ālā* (A) the One who exists in all lives in a state of humility and exaltedness; *Nāyan* (T) the Ruler who protects and sustains.

*Āmīn* (A) So be it. May He make this complete.

*anāthi* (T) The beginningless beginning; the state in which God meditated upon Himself alone; the period of pre-creation when Allah was alone and unmanifested, unaware of Himself even though everything was within Him; the state before *āthi;* the state of unmanifestation.

*'arsh* (A) The throne of God; the plenitude from which God rules; the station located on the crown of the head which is the throne that can bear the weight of Allah. Allah is so heavy that we cannot carry the load with our hands or legs. The *'arsh* is the only part of man that can support Allah.

*'arshul-mu'min* (A) The throne of the true believer; the throne of one who has steadfast *īmān* (absolute faith, certitude, and determination); the throne of an *insān,* a true man who has that perfect certitude of *īmān.*

Allah resides within the heart which praises Him and within the tongue which praises Him, the tongue which speaks only virtuous thoughts, the tongue which speaks the truth and praises the truth.

*(A.S.)* (A) The abbreviated form of *'alaihis-salām*—Peace be upon him!

*Asmā'ul-Husnā* (A) The ninety-nine beautiful names of Allah; the plenitude of the ninety-nine duties of God; the manifestations of His essence, the *sifāt* of His *dhāt.* His qualities are the manifestations which emerge from Him. When God performs His duty, these manifestations of His essence are brought into action; His qualities become His *wilāyats* or duties.

*'asr* (A) The third of the five-times prayer in Islam; also means era, time, and afternoon.

*as-salāmu 'alaikum* (A) May the peace and peacefulness of Allah be upon us. This is the greeting of love. *As-salāmu 'alaikum, wa 'alaikumus-salām.* One heart embraces the other with love and greets it with respect and honor. Both hearts are one. In reply, *wa 'alaikumus-salām* means: May the peace and peacefulness of Allah be upon you also.

*as-salāmu 'alaikum wa rahmatullāhi wa barakātuhu* (A) May the peace, the beneficence, and the blessings of God be upon you.

*āthi* (T) The time when the *Qutb (Ral.)* (the wisdom which explains the truth of God) and the *Nūr* (the plenitude of the light of Allah) manifested within Allah; the period after *anāthi,* the beginning of light; the time of the dawning of the light; the world of grace where the unmanifested began to manifest.

*attar* (Persian) A fragrant essential oil.

*auliyā'* (A) The plural of *walī.* The favorites of God. Those who are near to God, referring to holy men of Islam.

*awwal* (A) The creation of all forms; the stage at which the soul became surrounded by form and each creation took shape; the stage at which the souls of the six kinds of lives (earth-life, fire-life, water-life, air-life, ether-life, and light-life) were placed in their respective forms. Allah created these forms and then placed that 'trust property' which is life within those forms.

*āyat* (A) A verse in the Qur'an or in a *hadīth,* a traditional story.

*Badr* (A) The first battle of Badr was fought in the month of *Ramadān,* A.H. 2 (March 2, A.D. 624) between the followers of Muhammad *(Sal.)* and the Quraish. This victory at Badr consolidated the power of Muhammad *(Sal.)* and is regarded by Muslim historians as one of the most important events of history. The second battle of Badr was a bloodless victory, and took place in the month of *Dhul-Qa'dah,* A.H. 4 (April, A.D. 626).

   The inner meaning of these battles is the fight between truth and falsehood. The goal is not to conquer lands but to use faith to conquer the hearts of the people.

*bahrul-'ilm* (A) The ocean of divine knowledge.

*Bismillāhir-Rahmānir-Rahīm* (A) In the name of God, Most Merciful, Most Compassionate. *Bismillāh:* Allah is the first and the last, the One with the beginning and without beginning. He is the One who is the cause for creation and for the absence of creation, the cause for the beginning and for the beginningless; *ar-Rahmān:* He is the King, the Nourisher, the One who gives food. He is the Compassionate One. He is the One who protects the creations. He is the Beneficent One; *ar-Rahīm:* He is the One who redeems, the One who protects from evil, who preserves and who confers eternal bliss; the Savior. On the Day of Judgment and on the Day of Inquiry and on all days from the day of the beginning, He protects and brings His creations back unto Himself.

*daulat* (A) This has two meanings. One is the wealth of the world, or *dunyā*. The other is the wealth of the grace of Allah. The wealth of Allah is the wealth of the divine knowledge known as *'ilm* and the wealth of perfect *īmān*, that is absolute faith, certitude, and determination.

*dēvas* (T) Celestial beings.

*dhāhuth* (Persian) A throne.

*dhāt* (A) The essence of God; His treasury; His wealth of purity; His grace.

*dhikr* (A) The remembrance of God. It is a common name given to certain words in praise of God. Of the many *dhikrs*, the most exalted *dhikr* is to say, "*Lā ilāha illallāhu*—There is nothing other than You. Only You are Allah." All the others relate to His *wilāyats* or His actions, but this *dhikr* points to Him and to Him alone. See also: *Kalimah; lā ilāha illallāhu.*

*dhul-fiqār* (A) Double-bladed sword of *īmān* and wisdom; ruler or lord of the neck or vertebrae.

*dīn* (A) The light of perfect purity; the resplendence of perfectly pure *īmān*, absolute faith, certitude, and determination. Lit.: certitude of faith or belief.

*dunyā* (A) The earth world in which we live; the world of physical existence; the darkness which separated from Allah at the time when the light of the *Nūr Muhammad* manifested from within Allah.

*fard* (A) An obligatory duty.

*fikr* (A) Concentration on God.

*firdaus* (A) The eighth heaven. If we can cut away the seven base desires known as the *nafs ammārah,* what remains will be Allah's qualities, actions, and conduct, His gracious attributes, and His duties. If man can make these his own and store them within his heart, then that is *firdaus.* That is Allah's house, the limitless heaven. That will be the eighth heaven, Allah's house of infinite magnitude and perfect purity.

*furūd* (A) The plural of *fard.* The five *furūd* refer to the five pillars of Islam: *īmān* or absolute faith, prayer, charity, fasting, and *hajj,* or holy pilgrimage.

*gnāna sheikh* (T & A) Teacher; a gnostic with divine wisdom.

*gnānam* (T) Divine luminous wisdom. If man can throw away all the worldly treasures and take within him only the treasure called Allah and His qualities and actions, His conduct and behavior, if he makes Allah the only treasure and completeness for him—that is the state of *gnānam.*

*gnāni* (T) One who has gained divine luminous wisdom.

*hadīth* (A) In Islam, a traditional story spoken by the prophets. These are the words or commands of Allah which were received by Prophet Muhammad *(Sal.)* and the other prophets, and were then conveyed and demonstrated to the people. Also, *hadīth qudsī:* the words of Allah that were given directly to the prophets without Gabriel *(A.S.)* as an intermediary. Sometimes a story about the prophets.

*hajj* (A) A pilgrimage; the fifth *fard* or obligatory duty in Islam. This duty must be done wearing the *kafan,* the shroud of one who has died to the world. Before you undertake the *hajj,* you must share your wealth amongst those who are poor. If you have a wife and children, then you must divide your wealth among them also. Even the inner desires must be surrendered. All of the self must die for the *hajj.*

*halāl* (A) That which is permissible or lawful according to the commands of God and conforms to the word of God. This relates both to food and to divine knowledge, or *'ilm.*

*harām* (A) That which is forbidden by truth and forbidden by the warnings or commands of God. To those who are on the straight path, *harām* means all the evil things, the actions, the food, and the dangers that can obstruct the path.

*hayāt* (A) The plenitude of man's eternal life; the splendor of the completeness of life; the *rūh* or the soul of the splendor of man's life.

*hayawan* (A) Beast.

*'ibādat* (A) Worship and service to the one God.

*'ilm* (A) Allah's divine knowledge.

*imām* (A) One who leads the congregation in the five-times prayer of Islam.

*īmān* (A) Absolute, complete and unshakable faith, certitude, and determination that God alone exists; the complete acceptance of the heart that God is one.

*Īmān-Islām* (A) The state of the spotlessly pure heart which contains Allah's Holy Qur'an, His divine radiance, His divine wisdom, His truth, His prophets, His angels, and His laws.

When the resplendence of Allah is seen as the completeness within this pure heart of man, that is *Īmān-Islām*. When the complete unshakable faith of this pure heart is directed toward the One who is completeness and is made to merge with that One; when that heart trusts only in Him and worships only Him, accepting Him as the only perfection and the only One worthy of worship—that is *Īmān-Islām*.

*indira jālam* (T) The magic tricks of *māyā* which extend into space; the tricks of magic performed in space, e.g., beckoning the sun, moon, stars, or bending the sky into a bow.

*insān* (A) True man; a true human being; the true form of man; the form of Allah's qualities, actions, conduct, behavior, and virtues. One who has the completeness of this form and has filled himself with these qualities is an *insān*.

*insān kāmil* (A) A perfected, God-realized being. One who has made Allah his only wealth, cutting away all the wealth of the world and the wealth sought by the mind. One who has acquired God's qualities, performs his actions accordingly, and contains himself within those qualities.

*'ishā'* (A) The fifth of the five-times prayer of Islam which is said after darkness has fallen.

*Islam* (A) Spotless purity; the state of absolute purity; to accept the commands of God, His qualities, and His actions, and to establish that state within oneself and to worship Him alone.

Islam is to cut away the desire called *'ishq,* to accept Him and know Him without the slightest doubt, and then to worship Him. To strengthen one's *īmān* or absolute faith, certitude, and determination; to accept "*Lā ilāha illallāhu:* There is nothing other than You, only You are Allah" with absolute certitude, and to affirm this *Kalimah*—that is the state of Islam.

*jihād* (A) Holy war. The greater *jihād* or religious war is waged by the believer against his evil desires and bad qualities. The external *jihād,* prescribed by the *sharī'at* for the repulsion of oppressors, must be conducted under a truly righteous *imām* within rigid restrictions and may be continued only to the limit of what is needed to repel the aggressors.

*jinn* (A) A genie; a fairy; a being created from fire.

*Ka'bah* (A) The cube-like building in the center of the mosque in Mecca. On the path of *sharī'at,* one of the five obligations or *furūd* is the pilgrimage to the *Ka'bah,* known as *hajj.*

Another meaning: the innermost heart, or *qalb,* which is the original source of prayer; the place where a true man or *insān* meets Allah face to face. Whoever brings his heart to that state of perfection and prays to God from that heart will be praying from the *Ka'bah.*

*Kalimah* (A) *Lā ilāha illallāhu:* There is nothing other than You, O God. Only You are Allah.

The recitation or remembrance of God which cuts away the influence of the five elements (earth, fire, water, air, and ether), washes away all the karma that has accumulated from the very beginning until now, dispels the darkness, beautifies the heart, and causes it to resplend.

The *Kalimah* washes the body and the heart of man and makes them pure, makes his wisdom emerge, and impels that wisdom to know the self and God. See also: *dhikr; lā ilāha illallāhu.*

*kalu balla* (Sinhalese) The black dog of worldly desire. The dog of desire which lies in front of the station of the innermost heart or *qalb.* If you chase that dog away and look within, you will find the heart of God, the *qalbullāh.* If the divine knowledge known as *'ilm* and the perfect certitude of faith known as *īmān* are present, then God can be seen within that heart. But first that dog must be chased away. As long as that dog is there, Allah will never be revealed, nor will the angels or the heavenly beings, for the dog will be barking all the time.

*kāmil sheikh* (A) A perfected teacher of wisdom.

*karma* (T) The inherited qualities formed at the time of conception; the qualities of the essences of the five elements; the qualities of the mind and desire.

*Katpaha Virudcham* (T) The wish-fulfilling tree. See also: *Sidratul-Muntahā.*

*khair* (A) That which is right or good; that which is acceptable to wisdom and to Allah, as opposed to *sharr,* that which is evil or bad.

*kursī* (A) The gnostic eye; the eye of light; the center of the forehead where the light of Allah's *Nūr,* His resplendence, was impressed on Adam's *(A.S.)* forehead. Lit.: The seat of the resplendence of Allah.

*lā ilāha illallāhu* (A) There are two aspects. *Lā ilāha* is the manifestation of creation, *sifāt. Illallāhu* is the essence, or *dhāt.* All that has appeared, all creation, belongs to *lā ilāha.* The One who created all that, His name is *illallāhu.*

"There is nothing other than You, O God. Only You are Allah." To accept this with certitude, to strengthen one's *īmān* or absolute faith, and to affirm this *Kalimah* is the state of Islam. See also: *dhikr; Kalimah.*

*lām* (A) The Arabic letter which correlates to the English consonant 'l'. In the transformed man of wisdom, *lām* represents the *Nūr,* the resplendence of Allah. See also: *alif.*

*maghrib* (A) The fourth *waqt,* or time, of the five-times prayer in Islam. Lit.: The time of sunset, or the west.

*mahēndira jālam* (T) The tricks and magic created by the forces or energies of the mind.

*mantra* (T) An incantation or formula; the recitation of a magic word or set of words; sounds imbued with force or energy through constant repetition, but limited to the five elements. (The *Kalimah* is not a mantra.)

*māyā* (T) Illusion; the unreality of the visible world; the glitters seen in the darkness of illusion; the 105 million glitters seen in the darkness of the mind which result in 105 million rebirths. *Māyā* is an energy or *shakthi* which takes on various shapes, causes man to forfeit his wisdom, and confuses and hypnotizes him into a state of torpor. *Māyā* can take many, many millions of hypnotic forms. If man tries to grasp one of these forms with his intellect, though he sees the form he will never catch it, for it will elude him by taking on yet another form.

*māyā jālam* (T) The tricks of *māyā;* the tricks and magics performed in the realm of illusion.

*mīm* (A) The Arabic letter which correlates to the English consonant 'm'. In the transformed man of wisdom, *mīm* represents Muhammad *(Sal.).* The shape of *mīm* is like a sperm and from this comes the *nuqtah* or dot which is the form of the world. See also: *alif.*

*Mi'rāj* (A) The night journey of Prophet Muhammad *(Sal.)*

through the heavens, said to have taken place in the twelfth year of the Prophet's *(Sal.)* mission in the month of *Rabī'ul-Awwal*. During this event the divine order for five-times prayer was given. Lit.: An ascent.

*mubārakāt* (A) The supreme, imperishable treasure of all three worlds: the beginning, or *awwal;* this world, or *dunyā;* and the hereafter, or *ākhirah*. That wealth and the One who gives that wealth is Allah and nothing else.

*muham* (T) Face or countenance. In combining Tamil with Arabic, Bawa Muhaiyaddeen *(Ral.)* defines Muhammad *(Sal.)* as *muham* and *aham,* the face and the heart, the beauty of Allah's countenance, or the beauty of the heart as reflected in the face. See also: *ahmad*.

*Muhammad (Sal.)* (A) The common meaning for Muhammad *(Sal.)* is the last of the line of prophets, the Rasūlullāh *(Sal.),* the Messenger of God who was born in Mecca in A.D. 570 and died in A.D. 632.

However, the original Muhammad *(Sal.)* is a resplendence. When the darkness of satan is discarded from Allah, that which remains is Allah Himself, His beauty. The resplendence of this beauty is Muhammad *(Sal.)*.

*mu'min* (A) A true believer; one of true *īmān,* or absolute faith, certitude, and determination.

*munivar* (T) One who performs *siddhis,* or elemental miracles. Also a sage.

*nabī* (A) A prophet. One who has received direct inspiration by means of an angel, or by the inspiration of the heart, or by seeing the things of God in a dream.

*Nabī Mustafar-Rasūl (Sal.)* (A) *Nabī*—prophet; *Mustafā*—the chosen one; *ar-Rasūl*—the Messenger. A name used for Prophet Muhammad *(Sal.)*.

*nafs* or *nafs ammārah* (A) The seven kinds of base desires. That is, desires meant to satisfy one's own pleasure and comforts. All thoughts are contained within the *ammārah. Ammārah* is like the mother while the *nafs* are like the children. Lit.: Person, spirit; inclination or desire which goads or incites toward evil.

*Nūr* (A) The resplendence of Allah; the plenitude of the light of Allah; the completeness of Allah's qualities. When the plenitude of all these becomes one and resplends as one, that is the *Nūr*—that is Allah's qualities and Allah's beauty.

*Nūr Muhammad* (A) The beauty of the qualities and actions of the *wilāyats* or powers of Allah; the beauty of the face or countenance. See also: *Muhammad (Sal.); Nūr.*

*olis* (T) Those who have realized the state of *īmān* (faith, certitude, and determination); those who have disappeared within the resplendence of Allah, shining and radiating without the least trace of fault or blemish.

*pūjā* (T) Ritual devotion; offering flowers, fruits, milk, and honey and various things to the idols of chosen deities.

*purānas* (T) Stories, usually referring to the Hindu scriptures. Bawa Muhaiyaddeen *(Ral.)* speaks of the seventeen *purānas* within man as the qualities of arrogance, karma, and *māyā;* the three sons of *māyā: tārahan, singhan,* and *sūran;* obsession, anger, miserliness, attachment, fanaticism, envy, intoxicants, lust, theft, murder, and falsehood.

*qalam* (A) The pen with which God is said to have pre-recorded the actions of men. The Prophet *(Sal.)* said the first thing which God created was the pen *(qalam)* and that it wrote down the quantity of every individual thing to be created, all that was and all that will be, to all eternity. Lit.: A reed pen.

*qalb* (A) The heart within the heart of man; the innermost heart. Bawa Muhaiyaddeen *(Ral.)* explains that there are two states for the *qalb.* One state is made up of four chambers which represent Hinduism, Fire Worship, Christianity, and Islam. Inside these four chambers there is a flower, the flower of the *qalb,* which is the divine qualities of God. That is the second state, the flower of grace or *rahmat.* God's fragrance only exists within this inner *qalb.*

*qalbullāh* (A) The heart of Allah.

*qismat* (A) Perfect duty; God's duty of preordaining; performing good actions and acts of service. Lit.: Fate or destiny; to apportion to each what is due.

*Qiyāmah* (A) The standing forth; the Day of Reckoning.

*qudrat* (A) The power of God's grace and the qualities which control all other forces.

*Qur'an* (A) The original Qur'an is a wealth entrusted to man by Allah in the time of *arwāh,* the world of souls, when He placed within the form of man His actions, His duties, and

476

His limitless qualities.

The Qur'an, the book, provides the explanation of all these actions, duties, and limitless qualities. These revelations or *wahys* came from Allah to Prophet Muhammad *(Sal.)* through the Angel Gabriel *(A.S.)*.

qurbān (A) Externally, it is a ritual method for the slaughter of animals to purify them and make them permissible, or *halāl,* to eat. Inwardly, it is to purify oneself by cutting away the animal qualities within one's heart, thus making one's life *halāl* to be sacrificed in the devotion and service of God.

Qutb *(Ral.)* (A) Divine analytic wisdom, the wisdom which explains; that which measures the length and breadth of the seven oceans of the *nafs* or base desires; that which awakens all the truths which have been destroyed and buried in the ocean of *māyā;* that which awakens true *īmān* (absolute faith, certitude, and determination); that which explains to the *hayāt,* to life, the state of purity as it existed in *awwal,* the beginning of creation; the grace of the *dhāt,* the essence of God, which awakens the *hayāt* of purity and transforms it into the divine vibration.

Qutb *(Ral.)* is also a name which has been given to Allah. He can be addressed as *Yā Qutb* or *Yā Quddus,* the Holy One. *Quddus* is His *wilāyat,* His power or miracle, while *Qutb (Ral.)* is His action. *Wilāyat* is the power of that action. Lit.: Axis; axle; pole; pivot. Also, a title used for the great holy men of Islam.

Qutbiyyat (A) The wisdom of the *Qutb (Ral.);* the sixth level of consciousness; divine analytic wisdom; the wisdom which explains the truth of God.

Rabbil-'ālamīn (A) Lord of all the universes, Allah.

Rahīm (A) The One who redeems; the One who sustains; the One who protects from evil, who preserves and who confers eternal bliss; the savior. On the Day of Judgment and on the Day of Inquiry and on all days from the day of the beginning, He protects and brings His creations back unto Himself.

Rahmān (A) The Merciful; the Compassionate, Most Gracious; Beneficent, Kind, and Understanding; the Cherisher, Nourisher, Protector. One of the ninety-nine names of God. He is the One who has endless compassion for all lives. He is compassionate and helpful to all lives.

*rahmat* (A) God's grace; His benevolence; His wealth. All the good things that we receive from God are called His *rahmat.* That is the wealth of God's plenitude.

Everything that is within God is *rahmat,* and if He were to give that grace, it would be an undiminishing, limitless wealth.

*rahmatul-'ālamīn* (A) The mercy and compassion for all the universes. The One who gives everything to all His creations.

*(Ral.)* (A) The abbreviated form of *Radiyallāhu 'anhu* or *Radiyallāhu 'anhā.* May Allah be pleased with him/her.

*rasūl* (A) Apostle or messenger; one who has wisdom, faith in God, and good qualities; one who behaves with respect and dignity toward his fellow men; one who has completely accepted only God and has rejected everything else; one who has accepted God's divine words, His qualities and actions, and puts them into practice.

Those who from time immemorial have been giving the divine laws of God to the people; those who have such a connection with God are called a prophet, or a *rasūl. Yā Rasūl* is a name given to Prophet Muhammad *(Sal.).*

*Rasūlullāh (Sal.)* (A) The Messenger of Allah; Prophet Muhammad *(Sal.).*

*sabūr* (A) Inner patience; to go within patience, to accept it, to think and reflect within it. *Sabūr* is that patience deep within patience which comforts, soothes, and alleviates mental suffering.

*Yā Sabūr*—one of the ninety-nine names of Allah. God, who in a state of limitless patience is always forgiving the faults of His created beings and continuing to protect them.

*saivam* (T) Inner purity; in common usage it means a vegetarian.

*sajdah* (A) Prostration in prayer.

*(Sal.)* See: *Sallallāhu 'alaihi wa sallam.*

*Sallallāhu 'alaihi wa sallam* (A) God bless him and grant him peace. A supplication traditionally spoken after mentioning the name of Prophet Muhammad *(Sal.).* Frequently abbreviated *(Sal.).*

*sayyid* (A) A descendant of Prophet Muhammad *(Sal.).*

*shakūr* (A) Contentment; the state within the inner patience known as *sabūr;* that which is stored within the treasure chest of patience.

This is the plural form in Arabic of the word *shukr* which means gratitude and thankfulness leading to contentment. In these texts only the plural is used to avoid confusion.

*Yā Shakūr*—One of the ninety-nine beautiful names of Allah. To have *shakūr* with the help of the One who is *Yā Shakūr* is true *shakūr*.

*sharī'at, tarīqat, haqīqat, ma'rifat* (A) The four steps of spiritual ascendence:

*sharī'at*—the realization of good and evil and conducting of one's life according to good.

*tarīqat*—the unswerving and complete acceptance of the good and the carrying out of every action accordingly.

*haqīqat*—the realization of Divinity and the beginning of communication with God.

*ma'rifat*—the state of merging with God.

*sharr* (A) That which is wrong, bad, or evil, as opposed to *khair* or that which is good.

*sheikh* (A) Teacher of wisdom.

*siddhar* (T) One who performs *siddhis*, or elemental miracles.

*siddhi* (T) Magic; miracle; supernatural abilities commonly called miracles and obtained by controlling the elements.

*Sidratul-Muntahā* (A) A tree in the seventh heaven, having its roots in the sixth. Lit.: The lote-tree of the extremity.

*sifāt* (A) The manifestation of creation; attributes, all that has come to appearance as form.

*singhan* (T) See: *tārahan*.

*sirr* (A) The secret of Allah.

*Subhānallāhi Kalimah* (A) The Third *Kalimah: Subhānallāhi wal-hamdu lillāhi wa lā ilāha illallāhu wallāhu akbar wa lā hawla wa lā quwwata illā billāhi wa huwal-'alīyul-'azīm:* Glory be to God, and all praise is to God. And there is nothing other than You, O God; only You are Allah. And Allah is most great, and none has the majesty or the power to sustain except for God, and He is the majesty, the supreme in glory.

A prayer revealed and explained to Prophet Muhammad *(Sal.)* to be said as a part of the *qurbān,* for the purpose of removing the beastly qualities of animals about to be slaughtered for food and to kill the beastly qualities within man that cause him to want to hurt other lives.

*subhat* (Persian) A term used in Persia and Turkey for what is known in other locales as *fajr,* the first of the five-times prayers which are obligatory to all Muslims.

*Ṣūfiyyat* (A) The fifth level of spiritual ascendence; the state of one who has transcended the four religions and has merged with God.

In the station of *Ṣūfiyyat,* one speaks without talking, sees without looking, hears without listening, relishes fragrances without smelling, and learns without studying. That knowing cannot be learnt, and that understanding cannot be acquired by mere study. These and many other such states come with acquiring the qualities of God and losing oneself within those qualities. Although one still exists within the body, he has built within himself the palace of divine luminous wisdom. One who has perfected this state is a Sufi.

*sūran* (T) See: *tārahan.*

*sūrat* (A) A chapter of the Qur'an (spelled with the Arabic letter *sīn*). Lit.: A row or series.

*sūrat* (A) Form or shape, such as the form of man (spelled with the Arabic letter *ṣād*).

*swami* (T) A word of respectful address; a spiritual preceptor.

*tantra* (T) A trick; a cunning trick performed with a selfish motive of self-praise or self-gain.

*tārahan, singhan,* and *sūran* (T) The three sons of *māyā* or illusion. *Tārahan* is the trench or the pathway for the sexual act, the birth canal or vagina. *Singhan* is the arrogance present at the moment when the semen is ejaculated. It is the quality of the lion. *Sūran* is the illusory images of the mind enjoyed at the moment of ejaculation. It is all the qualities and energies of the mind.

*tasbīḥ* (A) The glorification of God.

*tawakkul-'alallāh* or *tawakkul* (A) Absolute trust and surrender; handing over to God the entire responsibility for everything.

*Tiru Marai* (T) The original Qur'an; the inner Qur'an inscribed within the heart. All the secrets and the essence, the *sirr* and the *dhāt* from the three worlds of *awwal, dunyā,* and *ākhirah* (the beginning of creation, the physical world, and the here-after) have been buried and concealed within the Qur'an by Allah. There He has concealed the explanations of the *dhāt,* the essence of grace, and of the manifestations of creation known as *ṣifāt.* There He has concealed the *alif, lām,* and *mīm;* these three are the *dhāt.* That is why it is called the *Tiru Qur'ān. Tiru* means triple in Tamil.

All of everything is contained within that Qur'an. All of Allah's wealth is contained there; all His *wilāyats* or powers are present in their fullness in the Qur'an, the *Tiru Qur'ān.*

*toluhai* (T) The performance of prayer where one remembers only God to the exclusion of everything else.

*Uhud* (A) The battle fought by the followers of Prophet Muhammad *(Sal.)* and the victory that was gained over the Muslims by the Quraish, A.H. 3. Uhud is a hill about three miles from Medina where the battle was fought. The Prophet *(Sal.)* had a tooth knocked out. The inner meaning is the battle between good and evil.

*vīna* (T) A stringed instrument of India.

*wilāyats* (A) God's power; that which has been revealed and manifested through God's actions; the miraculous names and actions of God. See also: *Asmā'ul-Husnā.*

*Zabūr, Jabrāt, Injīl, Furqān* (A) The four religions or the four steps of spiritual ascendance. The inner form of man, the *sūratul-insān,* is made up of the four religions. The four religions constitute his body.

First is the religion in which man appeared, the religion in which forms are created. That is *Zabūr,* Hinduism. In the body, Hinduism relates to the area below the waist.

Second is *Jabrāt, Hanal,* Fire Worship, which relates to hunger, disease, and old age. That is the area of the stomach.

Third is *Injīl,* or Christianity. That is the region of the heart which is filled with thoughts, emotions, spirits, vapors, many tens of millions of forms, the five elements, mind and desire, and four hundred trillion, ten thousand types of spiritual worship.

Fourth is *Furqān,* the religion sent down to Moses *(A.S.)* and Muhammad *(Sal.).* It corresponds to the head. It is made up of the seven causes (two eyes, two ears, two nostrils, and one mouth), and it gives explanations through these.

*zuhr* (A) The second of the five-times prayer of Islam, the early afternoon prayer which is said after the sun begins to decline at midday.

# INDEX

*Bis* denotes that the reference can be found twice on a designated page *(e.g., 50 bis)*. *Passim* denotes that the references are scattered throughout the pages indicated *(e.g., 102-107 passim)*. Numbers in bold denote major references *(e.g., 83)*.

beauty *(continued)*
  of Rasūlullāh's *(Sal.)* face, 427
  of women, 78, 194
bee, 95, 442-443
beggar and king are equal, 464
being, human; *see* human being
belief in God; *see* God, belief in
believer, true, 16, 60, **61,** 72, 88-89,
  222 *bis,* 225, 328, 459
  prerequisites for becoming, **237**
  throne of, 12, 13, 369
  *see also* human being, true;
    perfected man; sheikh
betel nut, 297
Bible, 226, 368-369
bigotry, 85, 99, 144; *see also*
  discrimination, racial and
  religious; prejudice
bile, 32
billboards of hell, 27, 272
bird of wisdom, 122, 124-127
birth(s), 33, 39, 79, 113,152, 238
  cut away, 49, 78, 321
  karma of, 44, 45, 60, 119, 120
  know your, 32, 65
  place of, 170, 374
  re—
    freedom from 106, **216**
    into God, 45, 105, 302, 321
    karmic, 44, 447
    into light form, **195,** 302
    within the mind, 266, 302
  seed of, 69, 108, 448
  unique—of man, 80, 216
  and walking, time of, 355-356
  and world, 77 *bis*
birthright of man, 38, 59, 80, 350
*Bismillāhir-Rahmānir-Rahīm,* 42,
  319, 322, 348, 356
Bistāmi, Saint *(Ral.),* 423-424

black magic, 304, 311
blame; *see* praise, and blame
blind man, **142-144**
  and deaf man, 343
blood, 310, 319, 399 *bis*
blood ties, 34, 46, 47, 51, 142-143,
  220, 377, 395-396, 428; *see also*
  attachments; relatives
body, 48, 77 *bis,* 81, 91, 106, 107
  *bis,* 215, 315, 321, 407, 438
  beauty of, 89, 113-114, **235**
  cage of, 76, 79, 80 *bis,* 107 *bis,*
    118, 216, 293
  destruction of, 188, 310, 319 *bis*
  of earth, 115, **319-320,** 326
  elements of, 45, 69, 84, 129, **195,**
    315
  flower within, 314
  happiness of, 238-239
  holes in; *see* body, openings in
  horoscope of, 69 *bis,* 95
  inner, 195, 391; *see also* light,
    form; soul
  karma in, 281
  light, 95-96, 220-221, 316
  male and female, 147
  openings in, 15, 59, 383, 392
  rebirth of, 195, 302 *bis*
  smell of, 317, 319 *bis*-320
  time limit of, 326
  transform, 45, 315
  truth and, 109, 122
  unity within, 316
book
  how to read this, 6-9, 18-20
  inner, 18, 73-74, 106, **209-211,**
    215-216
  learning, 300, 342, 345
  *see also* heart, innermost
bookkeepers, 209-210

bow and arrow, 256, 294
bragging, **94-95**
*bramachāri,* true, 171, 241-243
brass, 120, 284
break heart of stone, **121-122**
breath, 112, 147-148, 305
bride, 30
  and high-caste man and
    shoemaker, 296-297
bridge, 69, 414
brotherhood, Qur'an shows, 463-464
buffalo, 52, 79, 349-350, 439
bull, 115, 309, 345, 401, 408-409
burdens, 141-142, 218-219, 380-
  381 *passim*
business, 80
call to prayer; *see* prayer(s), call to
camel, 263-264, 354, 451
  tie up—, 427-428
cancer, 49, 311, 312, 339; *see also*
  disease; illness
cap, do not wear God as a, 88
capacity, know the—of others, 29
cat, 67, 294, 308, 338, 345, 350,
  379, 441-442
celibacy, 171; *see also bramachāri*
cells, 258, 319, 353
cemetery, 19, 388
center within man, 398
certificates, 387-388
certitude; *see* faith, certitude, and
  determination
chaff, winnow, 116, 325-326
chameleon, 119, 300-301, 402-403
changes, man 105-106, 116-117
charity, 225, 226, 234, 292 *bis,* 303,
  372-373, 447
chieftain; *see* God, the Chieftain
children, 283, 355
  do not teach neighbors', 79

children *(continued)*
  feed—milk of grace, 225
  sheikh's, 379
  three kinds of, 220-221
  *see also* baby
China, "Go even unto," 5, 386
Christianity, 127; *see also* religions,
  four
clarity, 7, 65, 71-72, 77, 179, 294,
  309, 378, 426
clothing, 238, 392
clouds, like karma, 72
cobra, 131-132, 261-263, 268-269,
  316, 402
  five-headed—of the senses, 34,
    304-305, 336; *see also* senses,
    five
  and frog, story about, 335-336
  ruby in mouth of, 150-151
  *see also* snake(s)
comfort, 51, 252, 323, 373, 379,
  414, 416
Commandments, Ten, 42
communists, 239
company of good people, 191-193
  *passim*
comparison, have nothing in—to
  Allah, 11
compassion, 174, 215, 224, 225,
  232, 271, 272, 292 *bis,* 300, 376
completeness; *see* faith, absolute;
  life, completeness of
conceit, 46, 51
conception; *see* birth, seed of
conduct, good, 60, 70, 72, 79, 291,
  300, 369
connection(s) to God; *see* God,
  connection to
conquer, don't try to—God's
  kingdom, 223, 364

faith *(īmān) (continued)*
    lack of, 53, 250-251, 300, 430, 455
    perfect, 36, 60, 73, 209, 219, 412, 466
    prayer mat of, 456
    prepare your heart with, 267
    in sheikh, 260, 378
    stick of, 415
    take your—to God, 85
    taproot of, 66, 325, 394
    tree of, 34, 89, 394-395
        known as *Katpaha Virudcham,* 128, 331, 395, 404, 416
    true—will be the switch, 341
    without wisdom, **295-296**
    *see also Īmān-Islām*
falcon, 100
falling down, 402, 415
false, it's all, 64, 221; *see also* deception
falsehood, 48, 118, 124; *see also* lies
fame, 6
family, 30, 225, 417
    one, 170, 421, 423, 462
    *see also* Adam *(A.S.),* family of; mankind, family of
fanaticism, 61, 332
    religious, 51; *see also* discrimination, racial and religious
*fard; see* duty(ies), five obligatory
farm, 93, 115-116, 309
fascinations, overcome, 32, 44, 60
fasting, true, **226-228;** *see also* food; hunger
fate, 300, 411
Father, God the; *see* God, the Father
father raises children; *see* sheikh, advises his children

Fātimah *(Ral.),* 427
fault(s), 50, 93-94, 108, 127, 300, 357, 387, 406, 411-412
    correct your own, 224, 282, **331-332, 398-399**
    finding, 77, 87, 96, 135, 401-402, 444
    recognize one's own, 228, 314
fear, 36, 280 *bis,* 287 *bis,* 412, 429-430, 432
feather, king looks through, 167-168
Fellowship of Bawa Muhaiyaddeen *(Ral.),* **405-407, 416-417,** 420
female; *see* woman
fetus, 444, 448
fight(ing), 80, 125-126, 129, 331, 345, 389; *see also* war(s)
*fikr; see* contemplation
filter, 321
*firdaus; see* heaven
fire, 42, **173-174,** 292, 300, 317, 429, 455
    of elements, 59, 118; *see also* elements
    of God's truth, 147
    of hell; *see* hell, fire of; hell, fuel of
    of karma, 142
    of Zoroastrianism, 126
fish, 96-97, 239-240, 318, 373, 390-391
    market, 441-442
flashlight, 341
flattery, 335, 336; *see also* praise
flavor; *see* taste, flavor
flesh, do not eat, 152
flood, 411-412
flower(s), 310, 333, 399, 417-418
    husband and wife as—and the fragrance of, 50

flower(s) *(continued)*
  of innermost heart, 59, 100,
    106-107, 260, **412-413**
  rose, 314, 416, 428 *bis*
  sheikh as, 442-443
  snake as—garland, 131-132
followers of Rasūlullāh *(Sal.)*, 181
food, 56, 129, 263
  created seventy thousand years
    earlier for each being, 226
  of crows, 135-137
  do not crave, 267, 365
  each creation seeks, 254-255, 436
  eating—of evil qualities, 376,
    382
  forbidden *(harām)*, 221, 259, 352,
    363, 382, 456-457, 460
  of God, 81, **226-227,** 232, 234,
    243-**244,** 259, 270 *bis,* 365,
    382, 409 *bis*
  hoarding, 305
  permissible *(halāl)*, 61, 221, 232,
    259, 305, 352, 363, 382, 457,
    460
  *see also* chaff, winnow; fasting;
    fruit; hunger; nourishment;
    seed; tree; vegetarian
fool(ing), **129-130,** 204, 378, 394
forbearance, 119-120, 244
forbidden; *see* food, forbidden
  *(harām)*
forces, 101-104 *passim,* 127, 171,
  213, 350, 390, 459; *see also*
  elements; energies; evil(s),
  forces
forest, 91
forgiveness, 224, 464-465
  of God; *see* God, forgiveness of
form(s)
  dark, 349-350

form(s) *(continued)*
  original, 169, 337
  fortress, 396-397
  fox, 99, 153, 165-169 *passim,* 244-
    245, 345, 347-350, 361
  fragrance, 358, 439, **447-448**
  of flowers, 260, 399, 416, 417,
    428 *bis*
  snake had, 131-132
  of God; *see* God, fragrance of
  *see also* evil, odors
free will, 359-360
freedom, 44, 124-125, 256, 361-
  363 *passim*
  in all three worlds, 41, 43
  of unity with God, 366, 367
friends, 271
  with evil qualities, 30, 361; *see
    also* evil qualities
friendship, 29-30, 83, 270 *bis*
frog, 190-191, 335
fruit(s), 4, 34, 92, 225, 269-270,
  300, 314, 384, 440, **447-448**
  of God; *see* God, fruit of
  grows from a seed, 240, **394-395**
  of *Kalimah,* 261; *see also*
    *Kalimah(s)*
  poisonous, 294, 295, 435
  *see also* chaff, winnow; food;
    seed; tree
fun, making—of, 303 *bis*
funerals, in *hadīth,* 267-268
*Furqān; see* religions, four
*furūd; see* duty(ies), five obligatory
Gabriel *(A.S.),* 233
gambling, **175-176**
games, 74
garbage truck, 218
Garuda, 262-263
gas, 340, 438

gateways of *'arsh* and *kursī,* 59
gem, 115, 132, 299-300
glasses for the eye of the heart, 260
*gnānam; see* wisdom, divine
*gnāni; see* man, of wisdom
goat(s), 139-140, 232, 320, 327,
    347, 380-381
  and brass pot, 295-296
  *see also* animals
God, 33, 46, 196, 229-230, 284,
    389-390, 433-434
  accept, 11, 17, 128, 273, 355-
    356, 398, 421-422
  actions of, 48, 69, 70, 217, 222;
    *see also* God, qualities of, and
    actions of
  alone exists, 287-288
  attributes of, three thousand
    divine, 11, 458, 460, 465; *see
    also* God, names of; God,
    qualities of, three thousand
  beauty of, 40, 57, 81, 94, 98, 99,
    113, 149, 305, 358
    manifest, 282
    radiant, 72
    will never perish 89-90, 114
    *see also* beauty
  believe in, 91, 94 *bis,* 101; *see also*
    believer, true
  belongs equally to all, 223, 353
  benevolence of, 217, 229-230,
    236, 313, 337, 356, 361, 400
    shown to Moses *(A.S.),* **454**
    *see also* God, grace of,
      benevolence of
  beyond everything, 18
  burden of, **129-130**
  the Causal One, 360
  certitude in, 374, 398-399
    lack of, 239

God, certitude in *(continued)*
    *see also* faith, certitude, and
      determination; faith,
      certitude of
  the Chieftain, 31, 74, 255
  children of, 207, 220-221; *see
    also* Adam *(A.S.)*
  commandments of, 18
  compassion of, 31, 69, 80, 120,
    146, 215; *see also* compassion;
    God, qualities of,
    compassionate
  conduct of, 70
  connection to, 15, **144-145,** 148,
    195, 207, 371, 374
    cut off satan to have, 11-14, 119
    establish 135, 170-171, 341,
      411, 437
    in heart, 279; *see also* heart,
      God within
    lack of, 209; *see also* God,
      separation from
    through prayer, 15; *see also*
      God, prayer to
    through sheikh, 372; *see also*
      God, qualities of, sheikh
      teaches; sheikh
  controls everything, 101-104
    *passim*
  creation(s) of, 23, 30, 112, 126,
    225, 353, 365, 398
    all—are within the body, 146,
      378 *bis,* 407; *see also* body
    are filled with miracles, 76,
      187; *see also* God, miracles
      of; miracles
    explanation of, **258-259**
    friend to, 61
    heaven and hell, 424-425; *see
      also* heaven(s); hell

God, grace of *(continued)*
  radiance of, 45
  resonance of, 211; *see also* God,
    resonance of
  splendor of, 36; *see also* God,
    splendor of
  wealth of, 58, 92, 105, 223, 225,
    281, 304, 333, 382; *see also*
    God, wealth of
  words of, 59; *see also* God,
    word of
  *see also* grace
  gratitude toward, 117
  grow, 344, 346
  happiness of, 46
  in heart; *see* heart, God within
  history of, 5, 381, **422-423;** *see
    also* God, story of
  house of, 208, **214-215**
  and the hungry tiger, story of,
    **393-394**
  intentions of; *see* God, will of
  and Islam, **217-219, 388-390,
    461;** *see also* Islam
  journey to, **334-335,** 431; *see also*
    God, path to
  judgment of, 38 41, 87, 197, 230,
    459; *see also* judgment; Day
    of Judgment
  justice of, 46, 70, 125 *bis,* 161,
    215, 337, 455
  bring—into your conscience,
    374, 407
  laws of, 46, 462
  within you, 40, 197, 259, 284,
    364
  *see also* justice
  keep—in front of you, 109, 398,
    434, 456 *bis*
  the King, 396-397

God *(continued)*
  kingdom of, 41, 66 *bis,* 91, 206,
    366, 448
  belongs equally to all, 135,
    138, 223
  crown of, 47; *see also* God,
    crown of
  don't try to capture, 223, 364
  make—your, 205, 388, **422-423**
  within man, 4, 68, 94, **352-
    353,** 364; *see also* God,
    within, man
  must be ruled by a true man,
    **168-169**
  reach, 36, 45, 47, 74, 96, 98 *bis,*
    294; *see also* God, reach
  what is in—?, **102**
  *see also* kingdom
  know, 34, 39, 59, 101-105,
    118-119, 221, 367, 381, 405
  knows
  all His creations, 1, 211, 433
  no time, 85
  language of, 332
  law of, 458, 462
  light of, 144, 195, 213, **247-248,**
    336-337, 362
  become, 4, 121, 346, 382-383
  *Nūr,* 10, 11, 109, 112, 148, 229,
    **258-259, 314**
  resplendence of, 128, 368,
    395, 427; *see also*
    Muhammad *(Sal.), Nūr*
  within, 259, 340, 366, 390;
    *see also* God, within, man
  *see also* God, resplendence of;
    light
  lights of *(olis),* 386-387, 418, 431
  Lord of all the universes *(Rabbil-
    'ālamīn),* 221, 223

God *(continued)*

  love of, 33, 46, 70, 86, 217, 273,
      407
    can be destroyed, 50, 51
    establish state of, 206
    taste of, 272
    from us, 377, 395
    *see also* love
  within man, 209, **229,** 325, 346,
      366 *passim,* 371, 374, 386,
      **427;** *see also* God, kingdom
      of, within man; God, power
      of, within man
  man forgets, 161, 356, 412
  meditate on, 253, 306
  meet—directly, 121
  merge with, 9, 85, 108, **246-248,**
      346, 350, 367, 390, 413, 450
  messenger of; *see* Muhammad
      *(Sal.),* the Rasūlullāh *(Sal.)*
  mingled within everything, 16,
      71-72, 194-195, 218, 229,
      250; *see also* God, within,
      everything
  miracles of, 34; *see also* miracles
  mystery of, 8, 58, **250-251,** 368,
      427
  names of, 16, 73, 458, 460, 465;
      *see also* God, attributes of;
      God, power of, ninety-nine
  nourishment of, 152, 305, 365
  obeisance to, a *hadīth,* 221
  offerings to, 101-105
  the One, 5, 7, 16-17, 23, 58, 59,
      85, 345
    eternal without form, **101,**
        **146,** 344, 422-423
    with many names, **16**
  open realms of, 229, 337; *see also*
      heart, open; space, open

God *(continued)*

  path to, 39, 85, 280, 373
    accidents on the, 385
    go on the, 279, **283,** 324, **374**
    sheikh shows you the, **431**
    *see also* God, journey to
  patience of, 70; *see also* patience
  peace of, 41, 61, 99 *bis,* 316, 360,
      432
    gives, 230, 331, 398
    *see also* peace
  perfection of, 47, 48, 176, 318;
      *see also* perfection
  the Power, 146, 148, 195, 218, 413
    controls everything, **101-105,**
        194, 212, **359-360**
    within everything; *see* God,
        mingled within everything
    story of guru in the east and
        sheikh in the west, **246-248**
  power(s) of, 121, 212, 334, 353,
      366, 375, 412, 458
    within man, 312, 395; *see also*
        God, within, man
    ninety-nine, 109, 208, 314,
        395, **425-426,** 460,
        **464-465**
    the learning of, 386
  praise to, 25-26, 42, 70, 72, 328,
      340, 353, 375, 376
    *al-hamdu lillāh,* 52, 59, 108, 217,
        274, 321, 414, 431, 437
    meaning of, 43
    and *tawakkul-'alallāh,* 56, 66,
        140, 194, 458; *see also*
        God, trust in
    *see also sabūr, shakūr, tawakkul,*
        *al-hamdu lillāh*
  pray(ers) to, 11, 29, 34, 52, 124,
      **208-209,** 279, 256, 352

God, pray(ers) to *(continued)*
    correct way to, **5,** 211, **310–311,**
        375 *bis*
    in His presence, **246–248,** 383,
        413
    and the story of Ibrāhīm ibn
        Adham *(Ral.),* **450–455**
    and surrender, 234, 329, 353;
        *see also* God, surrender to
    true, 102, **125–127,** 147, 229,
        243, 293, 329, 371
    *see also* God, worship of;
        *Kalimah(s);* prayer(s)
    prize of, 305 *bis*
    protection of, 247–248, 316, 332,
        346–347; *see also* protection
    qualities of, 33, 85, 105, 193, 253,
        304, 313, 376, **391,** 417, 448
    acquire, 39, 56, 115, **191,** 235,
        273, 320, 324, 330, 354,
        361 *bis*
    act with, 32, 66, 108, 110, 144,
        147, 345, 400, 434
    and actions of, 34, 45, 106,
        129, 265, 284, 360–361,
        397, 400, 432 *bis*
    see, 110; *see also* God, see
    thread needle of wisdom
        with, 392
    *see also* God, actions of
    are His kingdom, 66 *bis; see also*
        God, kingdom of
    as clothing for life of man, 238
    beauty of, 36, 149, 324; *see also*
        God, beauty of
    build eternal house with,
        **357–358**
    compassionate, 259, 319; *see also*
        God, compassion of
    develop, 405

God, qualities of *(continued)*
    grow fruit of, 99; *see also* God,
        fruit of
    honey of, **174–175**
    a king must rule with, 205–
        206, 432
    make your qualities, 70, **197,**
        352, 405
    nurture, 106–107, 225
    offer to Him 102, **104**
    one who has, 265, 273, 361
    protection of, **316**
    reborn in, 45, 86
    receive, 120
    represented by chaste wife, 65
    revealed, 44, 427
    seek; *see* God, search for,
        qualities of
    separation from; *see* God,
        separation from
    sheikh teaches, **220, 339–340,**
        **441–443**
    sow the seed of, 81, 100, 115,
        116 *bis*
    take on, 47, 60, 66, 295, 317,
        397–398, **405–407**
    three thousand, 23, 109, 206,
        208, 264, 357, 386, 395,
        416–417; *see also* God,
        attributes of, three
        thousand divine
    treasure of, 8, 108, 116, 273–274;
        *see also* God, treasure(s) of
    understand, 294; *see also* God,
        understand
    war between—and satan's
        qualities, **14;** *see also* satan;
        war(s), holy
    wealth of, 8, 304, 432; *see also*
        God, wealth of

God, qualities of *(continued)*
   *see also* qualities
   reach, 45, 108, 120, 135, 144,
     235, 294
     how to, **130-131,** 187-188,
       **446-447**
   realms of, open, 229, 337; *see also*
     heart, open; space, open
   remembrance of; *see Kalimah(s)*
   representative(s) of, 70, 97, 209,
     221, **255,** 302, 359, 412
   resonance of, 218, **247-248,** 361;
     *see also* God, sound of
   resplendence of, 61, 69, 111,
     **247-248,** 314, 368; *see also*
     God, light of
   responsibility of, 1, 23
   responsibility to
     give all, 9, 52, 222, 243, 321,
       331, 351, 461
     is Islam, 389, 463; *see also*
       Islam
     and reach Him, 111, 374; *see*
       *also* God, reach
     then act accordingly, 194
     for what happens next, 140,
       350, 359, 382, **437**
     for your learning, 372, **373**
     *see also* God, surrender to;
       God, trust in; *sabūr, shakūr,*
       *tawakkul, al-hamdu lillāh*
   return to, 148, 367, 381
   the Ruler, 58, 146, 210, 223,
     284, 360, 386
   search for, 123-124, 257, 279,
     313, **442-443**
     do not wander and, 66, 377-378
     and the green dove of the
       mind, **127-128**
     qualities of, 34, 108, 223, 260

God, search for *(continued)*
   and reach Him, 23, **130-131;**
     *see also* God, reach
   and the sparrow of subtle
     wisdom, **125-127**
   *see also* God, journey to; God,
     path to; God, seek
   secret of, 4, 254, 462; *see also* God,
     creation(s) of, secret of *(sirr)*
   see, 37, 58, 108, 110, 115, 127,
     329, 367
     and family of Adam *(A.S.),* 64,
       70
     a *hadīth,* **426-427;** *see also*
       *hadīth*
     only, **3-4,** 46
     within, 90 *bis,* **102, 396,** 405;
       *see also* God, within man
   seed of, **394-395, 448;** *see also*
     God, qualities of, sow the
     seed of
   separation from, 70-71, 172, 434,
     440-441; *see also* God,
     connection to; God, qualities
     of, separation from
   service to, 11, 33, 41, 115, 209, 222,
     416, 442, 446, 450; *see also*
     God, duty to; God, slave of
   slave of, 11, 41, 222, 236, 259, 400
     Bawa Muhaiyaddeen *(Ral.)*
       becomes, **422-423**
     a *hadīth,* **328-329;** *see also hadīth*
     *see also* God, devotee(s) of
   and socialism, **206-207**
   son to, 51
   sound of, 35, 375; *see also* God,
     resonance of
   speak to, 3-6 *passim,* **313-314,** 397
   speaks to Rābi'atul-'Adawiyyah
     *(Ral.),* **454**

gold, 46, 58, 60, 65, 110, 120, 316-317, 400
golden pot of Karuppan, 160-161
*Golden Words of a Sufi Sheikh,* how to read, 6-9, 18-20
good(ness), 23, 60 *bis,* 129, 196, 225 *bis,* 407, 460, 463
   conduct, 70, 72, 79, 92, 291, 300, 369
   for country, 122, 125 *bis*
   and evil, 35, 37, 64, 116, 124 *bis,* 195, 376, 382; *see also* evil, qualities; evil, *sharr;* right and wrong
   of God; *see* God, goodness of
   qualities; *see* qualities, good
grace, 33, 37, 59 *bis,* 67, 118, 237, 424
   attainment of, 31, 118, 176, **362**
   benevolent, 98, 217, 223 *bis,* 236, 340, 362, 397
   rain of, 277-278, 307
   of divine knowledge; *see* knowledge, divine, grace of
   food and water of, 365
   of God; *see* God, grace of
   honey of, **174-175,** 220
   light of, 51, 401, 448
   treasure of, 111, 217, 366
   water of, 311
   wealth of, 92, 119, 340
   wisdom of, 37, 68
   world of, 129, 366, 418
grafting, 312
grass is always greener, 408-409
gratitude, 83, 117, **142-144,** 238, 338-339, 355
   men without—are dangerous, 153
grave, 19, 210, 303, 449
greed, 89, 98, 271, 393
group, one, 353

guru, 68, 235-236, 269, 377, 402-403
   story of
      goat, brass pot and, 295-296
      wife, disciple and, 184-186
   *see also* sheikh
*hā',* 69, 217; *see also alif; lām; mīm*
*hadīth,* 17, 221-222, 232-233, 267-268, 285-286, 328-329, 389-390, 426-428
   of Arab and Rasūl *(Sal.),* 179-182
   "Go even unto China," 5, 224, 386-387
   "O Muhammad! I would not have," 42-43
   *see also* Muhammad *(Sal.)*
hair, 113, 305
*hajj,* 227
*halāl; see* food, permissible *(halāl)*
hand(s)
   left and right, 449
   of Rasūlullāh *(Sal.),* held only Allah, 458-459
happiness, 46, 98, 101, 116, 254, 273-274, 306, 330-331, 338
   of the body, 122, 238-239
   and sadness, 47, 209, **367**
   unhappiness, 281
   *see also* sorrow, suffering
*haqīqat; see* prayer, four steps to; religions, four
*harām; see* food, forbidden *(harām)*
harm to others, 54, 73, 84, 189, 225, 294, 302, 387, 393-394; *see also* hurt
harvest, 47, 116, 309
Hasanul-Basrī *(Ral.),* **448-450**
hastiness, 49, **50** *bis,* 51, 354
hatred, religious; *see* bigotry; discrimination, racial and religious

hurt *(continued)*
  do not—a slave of God, 328-329
  *see also* harm to others
husband; *see* marriage
hypocrisy, 50, 56, 67, 123, 235-236,
    271, 294
'I', 60, 87, 88, 128, 170
  arrogance of, 253, 271, 272, 336,
    432-433
  "can do," 397
  control the, 35
  dispel the, 46
  will die when wisdom matures,
    307
  "will help," 412
  and you', 110, 113, 122, 172,
    253, 428-430
    sheikh speaks of, **182-183**
    *see also* 'mine and yours'
  *see also* arrogance; egoism; 'mine
    and yours'; pride
*'ibādat; see* worship
Ibrāhīm ibn Adham *(Ral.)*, **450-455**
ice, story of man's creation is like,
    384-385
ideas, preconceived, 308; *see also*
    thoughts
idols; *see* gods, false
ignorance, 52 *bis,* 117, 120, 121,
    309, 330, 345, 393
  dispel, 32, 61, 72, 92, 97-98, 114,
    300, 380
  known as *māyā,* 156
  pond of, 176-178, 310
  understand—with wisdom, 240,
    326, 394
  *see also* illusion
iguana, 119
*illallāhu,* 47, 60; *see also* God
illness; *see* disease

illusion(s), 108, 335-336
  arrogance, karma and, 57, 58, 75,
    129
  caves of, 348
  love shown by, 338-339
  magnetic current of, 379
  *māyā,* 69, 76, 156, **194-195,** 220,
    315, 320, 385, 447
    overcome, 32, 33
    shadow lives of, 213
    three sons of, 176, 312, 341,
      352
    winds of, 78
  ocean of, 68, **96-97,** 300, 305,
    307, 318, 347, 400
  pond of, 176-178
  woman of, 78, 383
  *see also* ignorance
*'ilm; see* knowledge, divine
*imām,* 456
  make sheikh your, 375
  Rasūlullāh *(Sal.)* as, 385
*īmān; see* faith
*Īmān-Islām,* 210, 225, 228, 321,
    364, 368, 424
  prerequisite to, **42-43, 237, 250**
  wealth of, **458-459**
  *see also* faith; Islam; purity; *saivam*
impatience, 36, 50, 67, 108, 438;
    *see also* patience
impermissible; *see* forbidden
impurity, 219, 362
independence, **41**
*Injīl,* 127; *see also* religions, four
injustice of man, 139-140
ink cannot write His mystery, 8
inner battle; *see* war, holy
inner patience; *see* patience, inner;
    *sabūr, shakūr, tawakkul, al-hamdu
    lillāh*

light, 17, 121, 208-209, 382-383, 460
  of absolute faith, 368-369
  body, 95, 220; *see also* light, form;
    soul
  and darkness, 92, 121, **195-197**
  form, 169, 195, 302, 316; *see also*
    light, body; soul
  of *gnānam*, 300
  of God; *see* God, light of
  of grace; *see* God, grace of
  of *Nūr; see* God, light of, *Nūr*
  original, 148
  of soul; *see* light, body; light,
    form; soul
  of a true sheikh, 341-342
  of wisdom; *see* wisdom, light of
limits, 60, 326, 431, 433
lion, 114, 149, 236, 345
  fox and four buffaloes, 349-350
  story of man who helped, **162-166**
lives; *see* life (lives)
lizard, 243-244, 438-439
lock and key, 396
loincloth, story of, 410-411
lotus, 66, 115, 310
love, 33, 47, 50, 51, 113, 117, 177-
    178, 211
  of all lives, 46, 62, 303
  of God; *see* God, love of
  sensual; *see* lust
  shown by illusion, 338-339
  of a true sheikh, 337
  and truth, 60, 254
  your neighbor as yourself, 75
luck and horseracing, 175
lust, 31, 32, 37, 69, 118, 133
  control of, 35, 97, 291
  intoxication of, 49, 60, 198
  is greater than the ocean, 68
lying; *see* lies

*maghrib; see* prayer, five times of
magic, black, 304, 311
magnetic energies; *see* energies,
    magnetic
magnifying glass, 390
makeup, gold needs no, 317
male and female, **147-149**
  *see also* marriage; woman
man, 48, 144, 195, 212, 251, 264,
    298, 328
  animal qualities of; *see* animal(s),
    man with the qualities of
  arrogance of, 119, 133, 148, 160-
    161, 324, 397-398
  and astrology, 279-280
  blind, **142-144,** 343
  body of; *see* body
  burdens—bears, 141-142, 218-
    219, 381
  carries time, 144
  changes, 105-106, 116-117
  connection of—to God, 144-
    145, 148, 170-171, 195, 209,
    255, 341, 381
    breaking, 11, 119, 372
    *see also* God, connection to
  creation of, 10, 98, 145, 323-324,
    **384-385,** 397; *see also* God,
    creation(s) of
  cruelty of, 134-135, 139
  duty of; *see* duty(ies)
  enemies within, 13, 75, 119,
    330-331
  energies within, 147, 266-267;
    *see also* energies
  evil qualities of; *see* evil, qualities,
    within man
  exalted, 10, 138-139, 224 *passim,*
    254, 324
  forgets God, 161

man *(continued)*
-God, 170, 203
God within; *see* God, within man
good, 129, 172-173, 196
gratitude of, 142-143, 162-166
hard-hearted, 54
heart of; *see* heart
idols within, 104; *see also* gods, false
know; *see* self, know your
life of; *see* life
mesmerized, 402
nature of, 309, 319
original
   state of, 117, 179, 385, 392, 448
   treasure of; *see* God, treasure(s) of
perfect; *see* perfected man
potentialities of, 48, 359-360, 392
reflect properly, 38, 49, 374-375
rich—and woodcutter, 157-160
rightful station of, 390-391
satan's qualities and; *see* satan
in search of a perfect wife, 407-408
seed known as, 346
seventy-three groups of, 88-89,
   210, 276
smell of, 262
son of; *see* Adam *(A.S.)*, children of
suffering of; *see* suffering
a Sufi's fear of, 189
three worlds within; *see* world(s),
   all three; world(s), next
true; *see* human being, true
truth within, 124, 267, 318-319,
   366, 455; *see also* truth
ungrateful, 163-166; *see* also
   gratitude
will fall down, 401-402, 415
of wisdom, **25-26,** 61, 127-144,
   265, 299, 307, 315, 369, 403,
   412-413, 438

man, of wisdom *(continued)*
become, 91, 97, 106
find, 105, 125-127, 204-205
follow, 55, 86
love of, 337
*see also* human being, true;
   perfected man; sheikh;
   wisdom
*see also* life; people, other; self
mankind, 19, 135, 196, 230, 285
family of, 70 *bis,* 88-89, 225, 276;
   *see also* Adam *(A.S.)*, family
   of; family
Mansūr al-Hallāj *(Ral.),* 249-250
mantras, 146, 149-152, 235, 246-247
map, this book is a, 19
*ma'rifat; see* prayer, four steps to;
   religions, four
marketplace of world, 170-171, 350
marks, seven diacritical, 11-12
marriage, 50, 65, 82, 241-243, 322
   *bis,* 323, 448-450
maturity, 20, 33, 44, 55, 120, 149-
   152, **184-186**
*māyā; see* illusion, *māyā*
Mecca, 453
medicine, 79, 257, 312, 315, 319, 337
meditation, 101, 235-236, 252 *bis,*
   253, 351, 376
house of, 357-358
in jungle, 66, 251-252, 411
true 241-243, 246-248, 306,
   383 *bis*
*see also* prayer(s)
memorizing the Qur'an, 226
mental illness, 268, 387, 463
messenger
Allah's; *see* Muhammad *(Sal.),*
   the Rasūlullāh *(Sal.)*
become—to God, 11

milk, 112-113, 117, 309, 380-381, 404-405, 425
of compassionate love, 174
*mīm*, 69, 217-218, 373; *see also alif; lām*
mind, 32-36 *passim*, 82, 83, 109, 115, 144, 298-300 *passim*, 395
agitation of, 38 *bis*, 57 *bis*, 58, 129-131 *passim*, **432-433**
animals of; *see* animals, inner; animals, man with the qualities of; mind, monkey of
baby of, 286-287
banana, 354
cat of, 67, 294, 308 *bis*
cobra of, 335-336
control—with wisdom, 62-68 *passim*, 73, 75, 91, 100, 111, 112, 459-460
and *Asmā'ul-Husnā*, 73
and *Kalimahs*, 121 *bis*
correct, 47, 67, 76, 80, 96, 111 *bis*, 331-332; *see also* self, correct
creation of, 62
darkness of, 36, 44, 45, 118, 121
death of, 105
and desire, 37, 99 *bis*, 120-121, 130-131, 272, 311-317 *passim*, 331, **346,** 352, 361, 411; *see also* desire(s)
destroy, 29-38 *passim*, 123 *bis*
discard, 57, 107, 122, 280, 374, 380-381, 401 *bis*
donkey of, 334-335
doubt in, 280 *bis*
forms within, 252, 259
horse of the, 175-176, 305, 351
like writing on water, 299, 355
and mantras, 235

mind *(continued)*
miracles of, 310 *bis*
and mirror, 63
monkey of, 52, **62-63,** 94, 100, 123 *bis*, 313
control, 75, 89, 112, 235-236, **432-433**
*see also* animal(s), inner; animal(s), man with the qualities of
mountain of, 299-300
ocean of, 68, 305, 347
parrot of, 127-130, 235
peace of, 32, 33, 61, 79, 81, 110, 306
poisonous thoughts of, 456
rock, hard, 300
rule, 40, 45, 60, 78, 125 *bis*, 151-152
sheikh transforms, 284, 371-372
speed of, 175-176
thoughts of, 64-65, 279-280, 302-**303,** 437
tree of, 130-131
world of, 266-267, 281-282, 329, 355
*see also* animal(s); desire; peace; thoughts
'mine and yours', 35, 46, 47 *bis*, 110, 170, 335; *see also* 'I, and you'; separations, 'I'
minister(s)
and king seeking wisdom, 154-157
thirty-second, 370-371
who advise, 301
miracles, 101-104 *passim*, 120 *bis*, **186-190,** 246-248, 259, 353, 434
of God, 34

miracles *(continued)*
true, 76, 96-97
worldly, 75, 105, 120 *bis,* 123,
**188**, 310
mirage, 310, 342, 362
*Mi'rāj,* 427
mirror, 63, 278, 293, 299, **368,** 427
miser, 98, 434
mistakes, avoid further, 402
mocking others, 81
modesty, 111, 238
money, 84, 95, 237, 259, 260, 304,
377
story about accumulating, 157-160
*see also* God, wealth of; wealth
monkey, 293, 299, 345
king, 168-169
mind; *see* animals, inner; animals,
man with the qualities of;
mind, monkey of
moon, 72, 147-148; *see also* sun
Moses *(A.S.),* 42, 454
Mount Sinai, 454
mountain, 120, 309, 313-314, 414
mouth(s), 37, 84, 272, 340, 383; *see
also* tongue
*mubārakāt; see* wealth of all three
worlds
Muhammad *(Sal.),* 3-4, 395, 462
beauty in the face is, 217-219,
222 *bis,* 235
except for you, God would not
have created anything, 42-43
followers of, 181, 424
*mīm* represents, 217, 373
mouth of, 286
*Muttu,* 307
*Nūr,* 3-4, 10, 218, 259; *see also*
God, light of, *Nūr*
pearl of, 307

Muhammad *(Sal.) (continued)*
Rasūlullāh *(Sal.),* 222-227, 385-
386, 423-428 *passim,* 458-459
on *Mi'rāj,* 427
story of
Arab and satan go to, 179-181
Arabs tending goats meet,
232-233
deer, hunter and, 230-232
man sent to kill, 389-390
saw the beauty of his face, **427**
Uwais al-Qarani *(Ral.)* and,
274-277
sheikh is light of, 373
sword of, 13
was chased, 273
*see also hadīth; rasūls*
*mu'min; see* believer, true; perfected
man
*munivar,* 241
Munkar and Nakīr *(A.S.),* 209, 449
murder; *see* kill(ing)
music, 34, 77, 330-331
Muslim, 459
*Muttu Muhammad; see* Muhammad
*(Sal.), Muttu*
mystery of God; *see* God, mystery of
*nafs ammārah; see* desire(s), base
Nakīr and Munkar *(A.S.),* 209, 449
names of God; *see* God, names of
nation, progress of; *see* country,
progress of—(nation)
needle, for mending, 392
neighbor(s), 75, 81, 302 *bis,* 428
net, 96, 318, 400
next world; *see* world, next
ninety-nine divine powers
*(wilāyats); see* God, power of
nomads, 263-264
non-duality, 366, 416; *see also* duality

praise
and blame, 74, 106, 115, 124, 328,
431-432
to God; *see* God, praise to
of the world, 106, 300, 335-336,
434
pray(ers), 17, 74-75, 85, 101, 125-
126, 224 *bis,* 228-229, 382
call to, 385
five times of, 15, 42, 209, 227
four steps to, 2, 6; *see also*
religions, four
to God; *see* God, prayer to
within the heart, 354; *see also* heart
house of, 208-209
intention of, 456 *bis*
mat, 25, 293, 456
for others versus oneself, 329
perfected, 112
within prayer, 71
without praying, **3**
ritual, 146, 440-441
of *Sūfiyyat,* 3, 15, 102
treasure of man's, 425-426
true, 105, 147, 310, 330, 354, 398;
*see also* God, prayer to, true
way to, 118, 130-131, 192, 307, 411
*see also Kalimah(s);* worship
preaching, 53, 54, **63, 92,** 340, 363
prejudice, 46; *see also* bigotry;
discrimination, racial and
religious
pride, 31, 48, 49, 75, 78, 91, 118,
161, 464
self, 88, 95, 272, **335-336, 372,**
397, 398
*see also* arrogance; egoism; 'I';
'mine and yours'
prison, 367
prizes, 305

problems, don't try to correct
others', 331-332
profit and loss, 37, 109
prohibited; *see* food, forbidden
*(harām)*
prophet(s), 13-16 *passim,* 112, 224,
226, 395
brought Allah's words, 7, 17, 285
eight chosen, 462
eternal, 453
Moses *(A.S.),* 42, 454
*see also* Muhammad *(Sal.)*
protection, 292
of God; *see* God, protection of
of sheikh, **379;** *see also* sheikh
*pūjā(s),* 101, 105, 440
punishment, 221, 240
*purānas,* 294, 333, 341, 352
story of Vasistar and Arunthathy,
**241-243**
purity, 285, 353, 358, 458
Islam is; *see* Islam, is perfect purity
of soul; *see* soul, purity of
*see also* impurity
*qalb; see* heart, innermost, *qalb*
*qismat* (perfect duty), 425
*Qiyāmah; see* Day of Reckoning
qualities, 37, 113, 115, 294, 304, 414
and actions, 30, 45, 327
animal; *see* animal(s), qualities
as idols within man, 104-105
bad; *see* evil, qualities, bad
of the elements; *see* elements
four virtuous, 111, 125, 191, 238
of God; *see* God, qualities of
good, 36, 42, 87, 92, 215, 300, 397
acquire, 32, 108
sheikh teaches, 430
will serve you on Day of
Reckoning, 425

qualities *(continued)*
  of the heart; *see* heart, qualities of
  know—of others, 29 *bis*, 30, 327
  male and female, **147-148**
  of satan; *see* satan, qualities of
  sinful, 172, 327
  worldly, 264
  *see also* karma
*qudrat; see* God, power of
Qur'an, 226, 426, 456
  Inner *(Tiru)*, 8, **17-18,** 237, 328, 366, **368-369**
  is a light of Allah, 457
  and Islam, **459-466**
  laws of, 222, 458, 462, 464-465
  seven levels of wisdom within, **11-12**
  sounds of, **12,** 18
  *Sūratul-Kāfirūn,* 430
  twenty-eight letters of, 211
  verses (6,666) of the, 16-17, 42, 219, 395
*qurbān,* 421
Qutb(s), 128, 340, 385, 418, 431
  analytic wisdom of, 375, 401
  within God, 203, 258
  *kursī* is station of, 59
  *see also* Qutbiyyat; wisdom, divine analytic
Qutbiyyat, 259, 394
  divine analytic wisdom of, 61, 63, 114, **214**
  divine wisdom of, 100, 106 *bis,* 120-121
  explaining wisdom of, 11, 179, 213-214 *passim,* 293, 352-353
  *see also* Qutb(s); wisdom, divine analytic
Rābi'atul-'Adawiyyah *(Ral.),* 448-450, 453-455

race, 80, 82, 144, 312
  the children of Adam *(A.S.)* belong to one, 17, 223, 344-345, 350, 385
  *see also* bigotry; discrimination, racial and religious
racehorse; *see* horse
racial discrimination; *see* discrimination, racial and religious
*rahmat; see* grace, benevolent
rain, 29, 99, 224, 277-278, 300, 307, 333
rare, things which are, 265
*rasūl(s),* 26, 224; *see also* Muhammad, the Rasūlullāh *(Sal.)*
Rasūlullāh *(Sal.); see* Muhammad, the Rasūlullāh *(Sal.)*
rat, 67, 134-135, 236, 308, 345, 375, 441-442
ray(s), 145, 258, **384,** 390
realization of self; *see* self, realization
realms, open God's, 229, 337; *see also* heart, open; space, open
rebirth(s); *see* birth, rebirth
Reckoning, Day of; *see* Day of Reckoning
reflect, 51, 110
relationships, 436-437
relatives, 304; *see also* blood ties
religion(s), 16, 40, 51, 144, 170-171, 332, 343, 420-421, 459
  four, 2, 6, 125-127, 190, 349-350, 430-431
  Islam; *see* Islam
  one, 345
  selfishness of, 312
  study all—with wisdom, 70
  true, 170-171, 222, 421
  *see also* Islam; prayer(s), four steps to

514

remembrance; *see dhikr*

representatives of God; *see* God, representatives of

resentment, 67

resonance of God; *see* God, resonance of

respect, 55, 111 *bis*

resplendence of God; *see* God, resplendence of

responsibility; *see* God, responsibility to, give all

rest house, 367, 451-452

restaurants, 362-363

revelation(s), 17 *bis; see also* sound

revolution within you, 363

rice, 325

ridicule, 80, 86, 303, 378

right and wrong, 77 *bis,* 210, 216, 397, 424

  analyze, **61,** 301, 324, 351, 387

  conscience cautions as to, 55

  God knows—within us, 433-434

  *see also* evil, *sharr;* good(ness) and evil; *khair* (good)

righteousness, law of, 462, 465

rivers in heaven, 425

rock

  of the heart, 54, 121, 309

  of mind, 299-300

roof

  leaky, 438

  story about the camel on, 451

roots, 302; *see also* taproot

rose; *see* flower(s), rose

*rūh; see* soul

ruining others, 87

rule yourself, 40, 367

ruler(s); *see* God, the Ruler

*sabūr; see* patience

*sabūr, shakūr, tawakkul, al-hamdu lillāh* (inner patience, contentment, surrender to the will of God and praise to God), 99, 191, 209, 214, 352, 354, 405

  conduct your life with, 66, 140, 354, 436, 458

  in a *hadīth,* 267

  preface to Islam, 42, 461, 466

  prerequisites for a true believer, 16, 51-52, **237**

  *see also* contentment; God, praise to; God, responsibility of; God, surrender to; God, trust in; patience

sadness; *see* sorrow

Saint Bistāmī *(Ral.),* 423-424

Saint Mansūr al-Hallāj *(Ral.),* 249-250

*saivam,* definition of, 152, 320-321

salt, 314-315

sandalwood tree, 318-319

satan, 88-89, 136, 212, 234, 250-251, 363, 429

  cut off connection to, 11-14

  distracts away from goodness, 283

  qualities of, 3, 10-14, 70-71, 196, 197 *bis,* 352-353, 385, 417, 447

  and Saturn, 178-179

  snake deceived by, 131-132

  story of Rasūlullāh *(Sal.),*—and Arab, 179-181

  *see also* hell

Saturn, 178

scenes of creation, 282, 365; *see also* visions

school, 95-96, 326; *see also* study; teach(ing)

science, 18, **187-190,** 333

scolding others, 81

scorpion, poisonous love of a, 337
scratch only the place that itches,
    437
scriptures, divine—found in heart,
    17
sea; *see* ocean
season(s), 29, 375, 384
secrets, inner and outer, 48, 60, 238,
    359; *see also* God, creations of,
    secrets of; God, secret of
seed(s), 211, 318, 343-344
    benefit from, 47, 81, 100, 115 *bis,*
        356, 393-394
    growth of, 29, 108, 346, 415,
        424, **447-448**
    original, **447-448**
    of *Qutbiyyat,* 120
    *see also* chaff, winnow; food; fruit;
        tree
self
    analyze, 387, 415, **443-444,** 449-
        450
    control, 30, 36, 50 *bis*
    correct, 76, 234, 278, 300, 331-332,
        369; *see also* mind, correct
    deception, 351-352, 394; *see also*
        deception
    destruction, 87, 116, 272
    don't use Qur'an and Islam
        for—gain, 464
    judge your, 38, **198,** 364, **444**
    know, your, 29, 31, 48, 60, 96, **115,**
        126-127, 253, 255, 339, 427
    look at, 304
    lose, 9, 120
    open, 229
    pride; *see* pride, self
    realization, 58, 59, 74 *bis,* 124 *bis,*
        178, 405
    teach, 77

self *(continued)*
    *see also* human being, true; life;
        perfected man; sheikh
selfishness, 31, 33, 118, 271, 312,
    330, 356, 428
senses, five, 34, 39, 59, 83, 127,
    304-305, 308, 315, 336; *see also*
    sound; vision(s)
separation(s), **40,** 90, 344, 345,
    428 *bis,* 430
    from God and human beings,
        cause of, 17, 70, 172, 349-350,
        434
    between man and woman, 322
    *see also* 'mine and yours'
serenity, 46, 48, 100; *see also* peace
service; *see* duty(ies); God, duty of;
    God, duty to; God, service to;
    sheikh, service to
seventy-three groups of man, 88-89,
    210, 276
seventy-two groups of man, 210
sexual
    arts and games, 330, 334
    frenzy, 37
shadow forms, 353; *see also*
    animals, inner
*shakthis; see* energies
*shakūr; see* contentment
*sharī'at; see* prayer, four steps to
sharing, 111, 309
*sharr; see* evil, *sharr*
shaving, 113, 305, 378
sheikh
    advises his children, 55-56,
        220-221, 282-284, 443-444
    as light, **341**
    as traffic policeman, 431
    corrects student with wisdom,
        **337, 371-372,** 391

wisdom, 29-49 *passim*, 34-40
  *passim*, 64 *bis*, 67-75 *passim*, 83
  *bis*, 114-118 *passim*
  analytic, 208, 253, 314, 354 *bis*,
    375
  analyze with, 38, 282, 324 *bis*,
    329 *bis*, 356-357, 404-405,
    429, 437 *bis*
  anger poisons, **49,** 67-68, 119
  and banana tree, 323-324
  bird of, 122, 124-127
  bridge of, 414
  craziness for, **257-258**
  dam of, 93-94
  dig with, **18-20,** 362
  divine, 62, 69, 100, 123, 214 *bis*,
    362
    definition of, 148
    fruit of, 440
    *gnānam*, 124, 131, 240, 434, 448
    king who sought, **154-157**
    *see also* knowledge, divine;
      wisdom, seven levels of
  divine analytic, 35, 63, 73, 77, 84,
    102, 208, 214, 254, 315, 396,
    415
    analyze with, 43, 59, 86, 105-
      107 *passim*, 152, 256, 293-
      295
    *see also* Qutb(s); Qutbiyyat;
      wisdom, seven levels of
  divine luminous, 106, 214, 298,
    315 *bis*, 396
    *see also* wisdom, seven levels of
  ears of, 59
  enemies of, 49, 67-68, 272, 331,
    **432-433**
  eye of, 32, 33, 37, **49,** 59, 116, 253
  false, 92, 94
  and Fellowship growth, **405-407**

wisdom *(continued)*
  of grace; *see* grace, wisdom of
  growth of, 5, 240, **326,** 401, 420
  and ignorance, 240, 326, 394
  insanity for, 257-258
  karma obscures, 72
  lack of, 43, 53, 117, 298, 317 *bis*,
    **330** *bis*
  liberation of, 123
  life of, 391
  light of, 40 *bis*, 57, **72,** 144, 308
    *bis*, 340
  magnifying glass of, 390
  man of; *see* human being, true;
    man of wisdom; perfected
    man; sheikh
  maturity of, 20, 55, **184-186**
  milk of, 113, 379-381, 404-405
  and the mind, 64-67 *passim*, 72,
    75, 78-79, 89, 115, 118, 280
    *bis*, 299-300, 459-460
  mirror of, 63
  needle of, 392 *bis*
  net of, 400
  nose of, 315, 340, 416
  obsession for, 257-258
  oceans of *māyā* must be crossed
    with, 97
  open your, 31, 60, 115, 211
  perfect, 228
  polish your, 48
  of *qalb*, 115-116
  of Qutbiyyat; *see* Qutbiyyat
  seek, 36, 61, 105, 330-331
  seven levels of, 68, 72, 83, 114,
    147, 152, 315, 321
    explanation of, **11-12, 213-**
      **215**
    know God with, 2, 90 *bis*,
      315 *bis*, 334

wisdom, seven levels of *(continued)*
    as the seven diacritical marks,
      **11-12**
  of sheikh; *see* sheikh
  six levels of, 152, 213-214
  sparrow of, 125-127
  speak, 29, 70
  and strychnine tree, 295
  study, 38, 70-72, 95-96
  subtle, 214 *bis; see also* wisdom,
    divine
  sword of, 13
  taste of, 193
  victory of, 121
  wealth of, 10, 248
  within wisdom, 88, 102, 105,
    211, 340
  *see also* human being, true; man
    of wisdom; perfected man;
    *Qutbiyyat;* sheikh
wise man; *see* man of wisdom;
  perfected man
wishfulfilling tree; *see* tree, of
  divine knowledge
wit, sharp, 271
witchcraft, 134
witness for both sides, 301
woman, 111, **147-149**, 322-323
  desire for, 45, 78
  *see also* marriage
wonder at self, not world 304
woodcutter, story about, 157-160
words; *see* speech
world(s), 74-84 *passim*, 89-90, 161,
  223, 316, 350, 396 *bis*, 409, 460
  all three, 30, 109, 113, 120, 238
    *bis*, 374, 381, 435, 461
    poverty in, 43 *bis*
    protect, 94
    stealing in, 226-227

world(s) *(continued)*
  understand, 69, 265-267
  wealth of, 35, 220, 226-229
    *passim*, 236-238 *passim*,
    337, 340, 358, 392 *bis*, 398-
    400, **425-426**, 458; *see also*
    God, wealth of
  *see also* world, next
  as prayer mat, 25, 293
  children, three kinds in the,
    220-221
  correcting the, 76, 77 *bis*, 234
  of creation, 208, 215-216,
    364-365, 419, 440
  creation of, 461-462
  cut attachment to, 156, 287, 382
  desire the, 282, 386 *bis*
  divisions in, 19
  do not believe in, 64, 94
  do not preach to, 363-364
  escape from, 403
  and family are one, 417 *bis*
  a good man in the, 125 *bis*, 259
  of grace, 129, **418;** *see also* God,
    grace of; grace
  has not changed since the
    beginning, 116
  and hell, 374, 434
  of illusion, 324-325, 414
  inner, 113, 151-152, **212-213,**
    327, **418,** 432
  is a dot, 48 *bis*, 278
  is mute, 282
  is prison, 367
  is rest house, 367
  justice of God in the, 46
  leader of the, **204**
  let go of, 156, 380
  marketplace of, 170
  the mind is the, **281-282**

# BOOKS BY
# M. R. BAWA MUHAIYADDEEN (RAL.)

# ABOUT THE
## BAWA MUHAIYADDEEN FELLOWSHIP

Muhammad Raheem Bawa Muhaiyaddeen *(Ral.)*, a Sufi mystic from Sri Lanka, was a man of extraordinary wisdom and compassion. For over seventy years he shared his knowledge and experience with people of every race and religion and from all walks of life.

The central branch of The Bawa Muhaiyaddeen Fellowship is in Philadelphia, Pennsylvania, which was the home of M. R. Bawa Muhaiyaddeen *(Ral.)* when he lived in the United States before his passing in December, 1986. The Fellowship continues to serve as a meeting house, as a reservoir of people and materials for everyone who is interested in his teachings.

The Mosque of Shaikh Muhammad Raheem Bawa Muhaiyaddeen is located on the same property; here the five daily prayers and Friday congregational prayers are observed. An hour west of the Fellowship is the *Mazār*, the resting place of M. R. Bawa Muhaiyaddeen *(Ral.)* which is open daily between sunrise and sunset.

If you would like to visit the Fellowship, or to obtain a schedule of current events, branch locations and meetings, please contact:

The Bawa Muhaiyaddeen Fellowship
5820 Overbrook Avenue
Philadelphia, Pennsylvania 19131

Phone: **1-215-879-6300**
or **1-215-879-8604** (voice mail)
Fax: **1-215-879-879-6307**

E-mail: **info@bmf.org**
Website: **www.bmf.org**